CONTENTS

5. ACCOMMODATION 77

6. POST OFFICE SERVICES 99

7. TELEPHONE 111

15. LEISURE 283

16. SPORTS 307

17. SHOPPING 321

18. ODDS & ENDS 339

19. THE PEOPLE 359

20. MOVING HOUSE OR LEAVING BENELUX 365

APPENDICES   371

INDEX   389

ORDER FORMS   397

IMPORTANT NOTE

All countries have their idiosyncrasies and most encompass a variety of ethnic groups, languages, religions and customs, not to mention continuously changing rules, regulations (particularly regarding business, visas, and work and residence permits), laws and costs. Note that a change of government can have far-reaching effects on many important aspects of life in many countries. **I cannot recommend too strongly that you always check with an official and reliable source (not always the same) before making any major decisions or taking an irreversible course of action. However, don't believe everything you're told or read – even, dare I say it, herein!**

Useful addresses and references to other sources of information are included in all chapters and in **Appendices A** and **B**, to help you verify details. Important points have been emphasised in **bold** print, some of which it would be expensive, or even dangerous, to disregard. **Ignore them at your peril or cost!** Unless specifically stated, the reference to any company, organisation or product in this book doesn't constitute an endorsement or recommendation.

AUTHOR'S NOTES

- 'Holland' has been used in the title (and throughout the book) instead of 'The Netherlands', because this is the name that most English-speaking foreigners use for the country. It doesn't refer to the two provinces, Noord-Holland and Zuid-Holland, which also use this name. Note also that the Belgian province of Luxembourg is not to be confused with the Duchy of Luxembourg, to which the word 'Luxembourg' normally refers.

- Frequent references are made in this book to the European Union (EU), which comprises Austria, Belgium, Denmark, Finland, France, Germany, Greece, Ireland, Italy, Luxembourg, the Netherlands, Portugal, Spain, Sweden and the United Kingdom, and the European Economic Area (EEA), which includes the EU countries plus Iceland, Liechtenstein and Norway.

- All times are shown using am (ante meridiem) for before noon and pm (post meridiem) for afternoon. All times are local, so check the time difference when making international telephone calls (see **Time Difference** on page 355).

- Costs and prices are shown in euros (€), which became the official currency of Belgium, the Netherlands and Luxembourg (Benelux) on 1st January 2002. They should be taken as estimates only, although they were mostly correct at the time of publication.

- His/he/him also means her/she/her (please forgive me ladies). This is done to make life easier for both the reader and (in particular) the author, and isn't intended to be sexist.

- All spelling is (or should be) British English.

- Warnings and important points are shown in **bold** type.

- The following symbols are used in this book: ☎ (telephone), ▤ (fax), ✉ (e-mail), 💻 (Internet).

- Lists of **Useful Addresses** and **Further Reading** are contained in **Appendices A** and **B** respectively.

- A list of useful websites can be found in **Appendix C**.

- For those unfamiliar with the metric system of weights and measures, imperial conversion tables are included in **Appendix D**.

- A map of the Benelux region is contained in **Appendix E**.

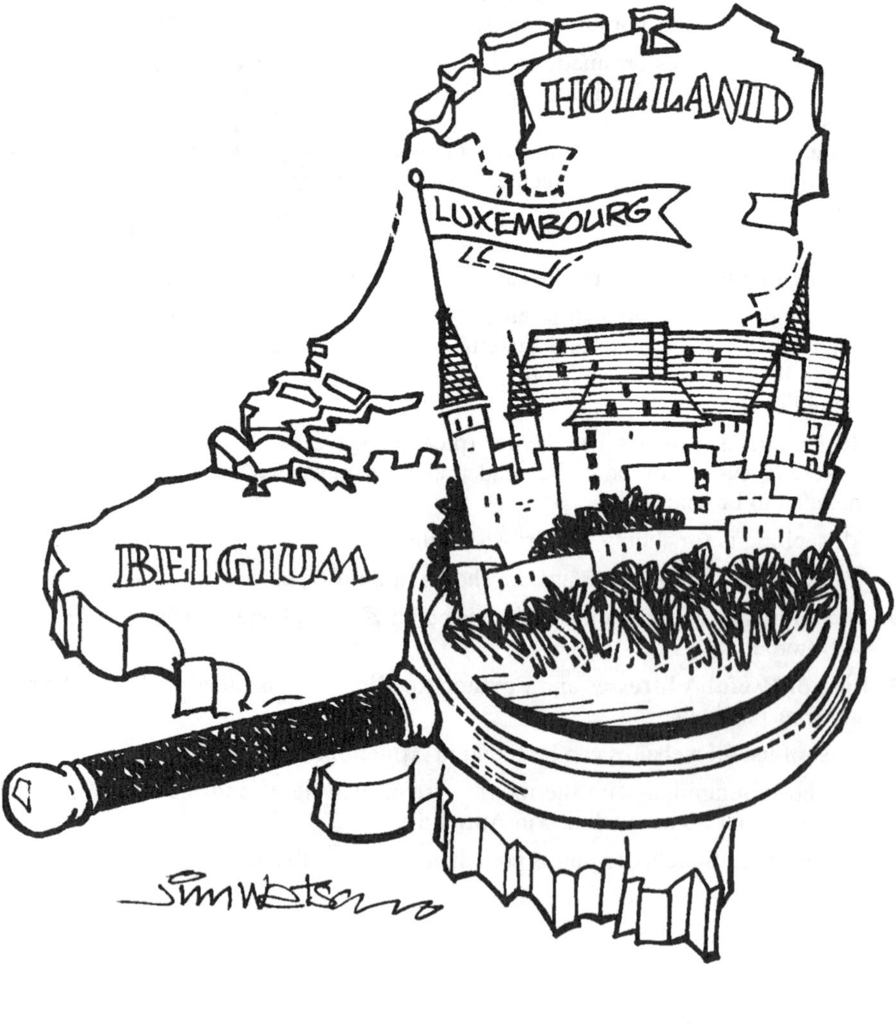
HOLLAND
LUXEMBOURG
BELGIUM
Jim Watson

INTRODUCTION

Whether you're already living or working in Belgium, Holland or Luxembourg or just thinking about it – this is **THE BOOK** for you. Forget about all those glossy guide books, excellent as they are for tourists; this amazing book was written especially with you in mind and is worth its weight in visas. *Living and Working in Holland, Belgium & Luxembourg* is designed to meet the needs of anyone wishing to know the essentials of life in these countries, including immigrants, transferees, temporary workers, businessmen, students, retirees, long-stay tourists, holiday homeowners and even extra terrestrials. However long your intended stay, you'll find the information contained in this book invaluable.

Basic information isn't difficult to find about most countries and a multitude of books is published on every conceivable subject. However, reliable and up-to-date information in English specifically intended for foreigners living and working in Benelux isn't so easy to find, least of all in one volume. Our aim in publishing this book was to help fill this void and provide the comprehensive practical information necessary for a relatively trouble-free life. You may have travelled abroad on holiday, but living and working in a foreign country for an extended period is a different matter altogether – adjusting to a different environment, culture and language, and making a home abroad can be a traumatic and stressful experience.

You need to adapt to new customs and traditions and discover the local way of doing things, for example, finding a home, paying bills and obtaining insurance. For most foreigners, overcoming the everyday obstacles of life has previously been a case of pot luck. **But no more!** With a copy of *Living and Working in Holland, Belgium & Luxembourg* to hand you'll have a wealth of information at your fingertips. Information derived from a variety of sources, both official and unofficial, not least the hard won personal experiences of the author and her researchers, their families, friends, colleagues and acquaintances. *Living and Working in Holland, Belgium & Luxembourg* is a comprehensive handbook on a wide range of everyday subjects and represents the most up-to-date source of general information available to anyone planning to live or work abroad. It isn't, however, simply a monologue of dry facts and figures, but a practical and entertaining look at the life in a foreign country.

Adapting to living in a new country is a continuous process, and although this book will help reduce your 'beginner's phase' and minimise the frustrations, it doesn't contain all the answers (most of us don't even know the right questions to ask!). What it will do is help you make informed decisions and calculated judgements, instead of uneducated guesses and costly mistakes. **Most importantly, it will help save you time, trouble and money, and repay your investment many times over.**

Although you may find some of the information a bit daunting, don't be discouraged. Most problems occur only once and fade into insignificance after a short time (as you face the next half a dozen!). The majority of people living in Benelux would agree that, all things considered, they love living there. A period spent in Benelux is a wonderful way to enrich your life, broaden your horizons and hopefully please your bank manager. I trust this book will help you avoid the pitfalls of life in Benelux and smooth your way to a happy and rewarding future in your new home.

Good luck!

David Hampshire (editor)
November 2001

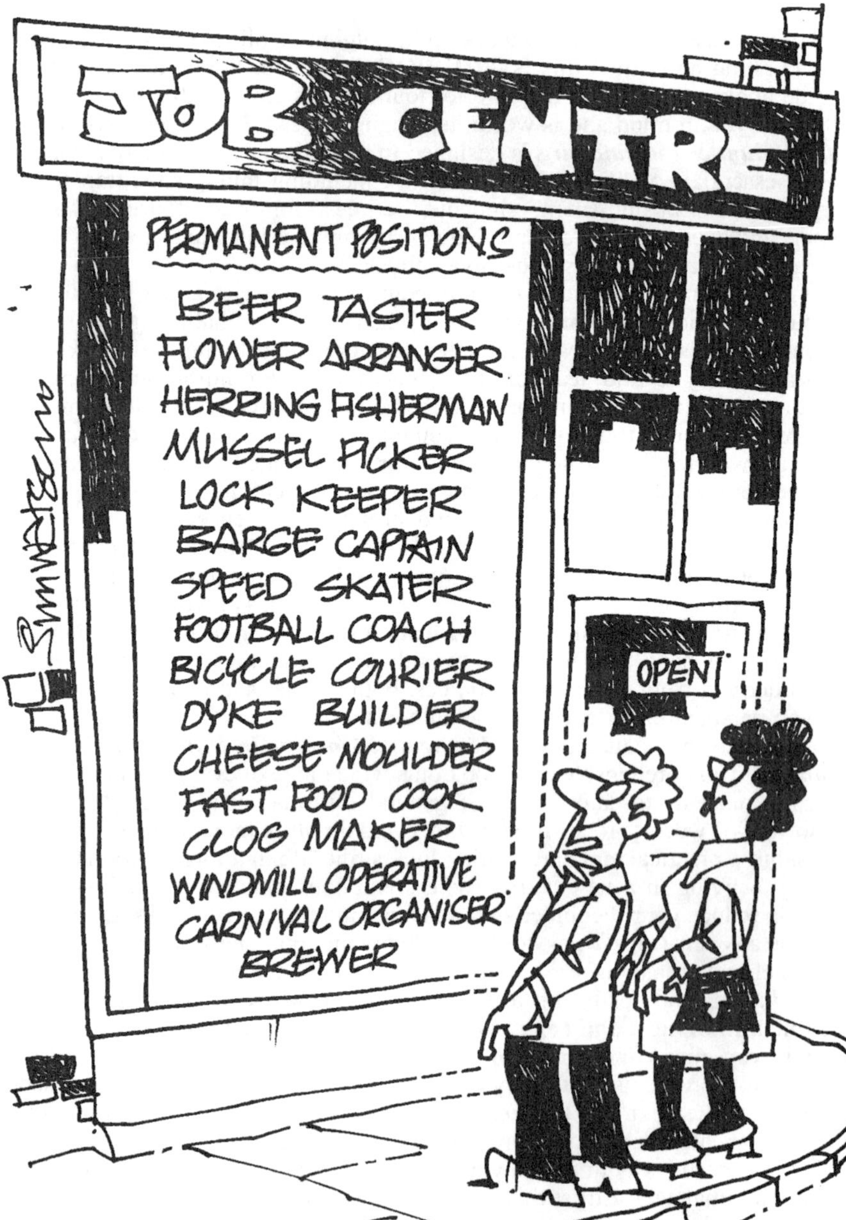
JOB CENTRE
PERMANENT POSITIONS
BEER TASTER
FLOWER ARRANGER
HERRING FISHERMAN
MUSSEL PICKER
LOCK KEEPER
BARGE CAPTAIN
SPEED SKATER
FOOTBALL COACH
BICYCLE COURIER
DYKE BUILDER
CHEESE MOULDER
FAST FOOD COOK
CLOG MAKER
WINDMILL OPERATIVE
CARNIVAL ORGANISER
BREWER
OPEN

1.

FINDING A JOB

Finding a job in Belgium, Holland or Luxembourg may not be quite as difficult as the statistics would lead you to believe, but it does take a certain amount of experience, a number of qualifications, a lot of perseverance and more than a little luck. If you're a national of a European Union (EU) country, you already have the right to work in the Benelux under the EU's freedom of movement provisions. Once you've found a job, you simply register with the appropriate authorities where you will be living and a residence permit is automatically granted (see **Chapter 3**). Non-EU nationals without automatic rights to work in Benelux will find it rather more difficult because any potential employer must seek the approval of the local labour or employment office in order to hire a non-EU foreigner.

Foreigners are found in large numbers throughout the Benelux countries, and the numbers are probably much higher than official statistics suggest, as those working for the various international organisations (particularly those in and around Brussels and The Hague) often aren't considered as residents. Luxembourg must hold the record for Europe with 25 per cent of its population and over 50 per cent of its workforce made up of foreigners. Belgium and Holland report around 9 per cent foreigners in the general population. As in much of Europe, illegal immigration is considered a major problem, particularly the use of Belgian and Dutch ports as staging posts for the smuggling of illegal immigrants into the UK is widespread. Like other European countries, the Benelux nations have tightened their immigration laws in recent years, both to protect local citizens' rights in a period of high unemployment and to discourage trafficking in economic refugees.

Foreigners from the EU are generally accepted in Benelux, although there's some lingering resentment toward Germans, particularly in Holland, dating from World War II. The Benelux region has a long-standing reputation for welcoming legitimate refugees and has taken in several thousand in recent years from Afghanistan, Iraq and the former Yugoslavia, especially from Kosovo. The UN High Commissioner on Refugees has publicly acknowledged Belgium and Luxembourg as having among the best refugee integration programmes in Europe – which isn't to say that there aren't pockets of racism and occasional incidents of intolerance towards foreigners.

Employment Prospects

Being attracted to Benelux by its cuisine, orderliness and lifestyle may be laudable, but doesn't rate highly as an employment qualification. You should have a positive and credible reason for living and working in Belgium, Holland or Luxembourg. Simply being fed up with your boss or the weather won't be enough. Bosses in Benelux have their own sometimes fearsome reputations and even the locals complain incessantly about the weather, which tends to be cool, damp and dreary for much of the year. It's extremely difficult to find work outside the largest cities and towns if you don't speak at least one of the official languages fairly fluently. Jobs of any sort can be very hard to find in rural areas and you need to be aware of the wide range of job categories for which you will need a formal qualification or certificate. If you want a good job, you must usually be extremely well-qualified and probably at least bi-lingual. In small countries like those of Benelux, it can be surprising how tight-knit local communities are and it's a great advantage to have friends or contacts who can help with your job hunt.

Unemployment

In the late '90s, Belgium had an unemployment rate of over 13 per cent (an even higher rate in the French-speaking Walloon region was offset by a lower rate in Flemish areas). Luxembourg, at the other end of the spectrum, has for a long time had the lowest unemployment rate in Europe, at around 3 per cent, although even this rate is considered high in such a small country with a large foreign population and little room for growth in any but the most highly skilled employment categories. Holland took action in the early '90s to liberalise and expand their employment base by reducing social charges and some social benefits. As a result of these sometimes painful measures, unemployment hovered around 6 per cent throughout the decade and Holland is often held out as an example to the other nations of Europe. Working hours, however, have been cut drastically to the point where 'part-time' employment is almost the norm.

Economy

The economies of Belgium, Holland and Luxembourg have been formally linked since the creation of the Benelux Customs Union in the late 1940s. In many ways, the Benelux Customs Union anticipated the current European Common Market and, by 1960, the three countries (now commonly referred to as Benelux) enjoyed full freedom of movement for labour, capital and services within their own 'harmonised' region long before Brussels came to be associated with European bureaucrats and cross-border regulations.

Belgium: Like so many aspects of Belgian life, when you talk about the economy, you need to distinguish between the Flemish part of the country in the north and the Walloon (or French-speaking) part in the south. Before the Second World War, the Walloon region was dominant in terms of wealth and industrial power, as a major coal mining and steel-producing region for Europe. As the coal mines were exhausted and the ageing steel factories proved inefficient and unprofitable to run, economic power shifted to the Flemish region, which has since become highly industrialised, primarily in light manufacturing and chemical industries. There's an intense rivalry between the two regions – possibly the result of the role reversal. Today, the Belgians are known for their sales skills and administrative talents. (Perhaps that's why Brussels has become synonymous with the EU!) The port city of Antwerp has one of the largest and busiest ports in the world and is also noted for petroleum refineries and petrochemicals, as well as for its diamond industry. The Belgian government is trying to promote the service and electronics sectors as alternatives to the dying steel and coal industries in the south, but Belgium's reputation as a land of intensive regulation and bureaucracy tends to discourage many would-be entrepreneurs.

Holland: For centuries, Holland has been known as a land of traders. Import and export are still the mainstay of the Dutch economy, probably because of its lack of natural resources and the need to import many basic industrial items. Over the last couple of decades, the resourceful Dutch have built up a strong service sector to overcome the issue of natural resources and it's estimated that the service sector generates 66 per cent of GNP as well as providing 70 per cent of employment. Amsterdam is the centre for many service related businesses, and there are vast office and industrial estates in many of the surrounding suburbs. The port city of Rotterdam is host to much of the more traditional 'heavy' industry, including natural gas production.

Luxembourg: Iron and steel has been the major industry in tiny Luxembourg for many decades and is the source of the general wealth and prosperity of the country. Recently, Luxembourg has found a new niche as headquarters for much of Europe's banking, financial and insurance industry. With some of Europe's most 'relaxed' laws concerning reporting of interest and investment earnings, Luxembourg is attractive to residents of neighbouring countries, especially Germany and France, for investments and insurance policies they prefer not to report to their own tax authorities. Luxembourg also boasts an upmarket tourist industry, possibly aimed at taking care of all those foreign investors.

Industrial Relations

As you might expect, the Benelux region is among the most highly unionised areas of Europe, with extensive legislation regulating the relationship between employers, employees, the government and the trade unions. In Belgium, about 65 per cent of all workers are union members, in Luxembourg, the figure is around 50 to 55 per cent, while Holland averages 'only' about 30 per cent union membership (still higher than most of the major European countries). Union membership isn't compulsory in most industries, but all companies over a certain size must establish a Works Council, which is consulted regularly before management takes major decisions, and the relationship between management and workers is generally one of co-operation. There have been very few days lost to strikes in recent years anywhere in the Benelux countries.

Work Attitudes

Across the three nations of Benelux, it's fair to say that the people are hard-working. Each nation, however, manifests this characteristic in a different way.

Belgium: Once again, the workforce in the Flemish provinces tends to resemble the Dutch, while the workforce in the Walloon areas adopts a more French attitude. In both regions, work and private lives are strictly separated, and it's considered very bad form to be seen taking *ad hoc* tea or coffee breaks or to chat at length on the telephone or with colleagues on personal matters when you're supposed to be working. The Flemish pride themselves on being highly organised, although Flemish businesses tend to have a simpler and less formal organisational structure and you're more likely to see upper management on the shop floor than in the French part of the country. The Walloons tend to prefer a management style based on Gallic formality, with less direct interaction between workers at different levels. Oddly, both the Dutch and the French regard their Belgian counterparts as distinctly disorganised and often rather inefficient despite the existence of a bureaucracy and regulations covering every possible circumstance.

Holland: The Dutch are widely regarded as the hard-headed business people of Europe. They're known for their negotiation skills and also for their fair-mindedness, if perhaps also for a certain lack of humour involving business dealings. You will find them to be big fans of the consensual approach to management, which translates into lots of meetings. Few Dutch people are shy about expressing their opinions in public and business meetings tend to last until each participant has had his say.

Luxembourg: Luxembourgers, while probably the most internationally aware and oriented nation in Europe, are also among the most conservative. Even the national motto, *Mir wëlle bleiven wat mir sin* (We'll remain as we are) suggests a certain smug satisfaction with the way things are and always have been in Luxembourg. Hard workers, Luxembourgers tend to be business-like and rather formal during working hours.

BENELUX AND THE EU

Belgium, Luxembourg and Holland were among the six founding members of the European Community (now known as the European Union, or EU) in 1957 along with France, Germany and Italy. Brussels is home to many of the councils and organisations which now make up the European Union, to the extent that the word 'Brussels' has become a synonym (or, maybe more correctly, a euphemism) for the bureaucracy and directives of the EU (as in 'Brussels has banned bananas that are too straight' or 'the latest directive from Brussels' – which is always useful for local politicians wanting to avoid responsibility for an unpopular new law!). Luxembourg is also home to a number of EU agencies, including the Court of Justice and the European Investment Bank.

Nationals of all EU states have the right to work in Benelux without a work permit, provided they have a valid passport or national identity card and comply with the country's laws and regulations on employment. EU nationals are entitled to the same treatment as Belgian, Dutch or Luxembourg citizens in matters of pay, working conditions, access to housing, vocational training, social security and trade union rights; families and immediate dependants are entitled to join them and enjoy the same rights.

There are still barriers to full freedom of movement and the right to work within the EU: for example, some jobs require job applicants to have specific skills or vocational qualifications. The EU has developesd a general system for the recognition of professional qualifications and specific guidelines for mutual recognition of a number of specific qualifications (see below). There are restrictions on employment in the civil service, where the right to work may be limited on grounds of public policy, national security or public health.

The European Commission in Brussels employs around 12,000 staff, including a large number of translators and interpreters. The various EU organisations in Luxembourg also account for several thousand jobs, open only to citizens of EU countries. You can apply for many of these jobs in your home country; qualifying examinations (particularly for translator positions) are advertised regularly in international publications and newspapers. Working for the EU has many advantages, including a full or partial exemption from local taxes, exemption from the national social security system (they have their own lucrative internal system of social benefits) and status as an 'international civil servant' (see **International Civil Service** on page 26).

QUALIFICATIONS

The three Benelux countries adhere to the EU's general system of recognition of diplomas and qualifications, which means that if your occupation is regulated in Belgium, Holland or Luxembourg, you will have to have your home country qualification or experience formally recognised in order to practise your profession in Benelux. Certain professions (mostly in medicine) have been 'harmonised' across the EU, so you may find your qualifications are automatically accepted. For other professions, you must prove that your training and experience covered a similar subject matter and duration as that of the locally required qualification. You may also be required to demonstrate your fluency in one or more of the local languages. If you're lacking in any significant respect, you may be given the opportunity to qualify by passing an examination or performing further supervised practice. To determine what the qualification criteria are for your profession, contact the regulatory board or professional society for your profession in your home country. They will put you in contact with the appropriate agency in your destination country if they don't have specific information about reciprocity. In the UK, general information can be obtained on regulated professions from the DTI, Bay 212, Kingsgate House, 66–74 Victoria Street, London SW1E 6SW (☎ 020-7215 4648).

It's also possible, particularly if you practise a trade that is regulated in the country to which you plan to go, to obtain a Certificate of Experience, documenting three to six years' practical experience. This can be particularly useful if you've been self-employed in a trade. In the UK, you can apply for a Certificate of Experience by contacting the Association of British Chambers of Commerce (☎ 01203-695688).

Under normal circumstances, any university degree or academic diploma should be recognised in Benelux, but if you anticipate any difficulties you should contact one of the National Academic Recognition Information Centres (NARICs). These are available in all EU member states; a list can be found on the Internet (⌨ www.namss. org.uk/naric.htm).

Belgium: Belgium may be the European champion in terms of the number of occupations that are regulated and require some form of licence or certification. Many trades (e.g. photographer, used car dealer, plumber, electrician, bricklayer) require you to register your qualifications with the appropriate Chamber of Crafts and Trades (*Chambre des Métiers et Négoces/Kamer van Ambachten en Neringen*), particularly if you're planning to be self-employed.

Holland: Holland also has a large number of professions and independent trades requiring registration or licensing. Once you're in Holland, you can enquire at the Dutch job centre (*Arbeidsbureau*) or contact a local Chamber of Commerce (*Kamer van Koophandel*) for specific information about your profession. You can obtain a booklet (in English!) entitled *To Work in the European Union: The Recognition of My Qualifications* from either COLO (*Centraal Orgaan van de Landilijke Opleidings-organen*, Bredewater 8, 2715 CA Zoetermeer, ☎ 079-352 3000, ⌨ www.colo.nl) through IRAS (*Informatiecentrum Richtlijn Algemeen Stelsel*, postbus 29777, 2502 LT The Hague, ☎ 070-426 0390, ⌨ www.nuffic.nl/do/index-en.html). COLO's website has an English-language section including addresses of centres throughout Holland.

Luxembourg: With 50 per cent of the work force foreign born and no national university system, Luxembourg is familiar with foreign qualifications, especially academic degrees and diplomas.

GOVERNMENT EMPLOYMENT SERVICE

There's a European Employment Service (EURES) network, members of which include all EU countries plus Norway and Iceland. The member states exchange information regularly on job vacancies, and local EURES offices have access to a considerable amount of information about applying for jobs and living and working conditions. The international department of your home country employment service can put you in touch with one of their Euro-advisers, who will give you advice on finding work in Benelux. Euro-advisors can also forward your details to the national employment service of the country you're interested in. The EU website (🖥 http://europa.eu.int) contains information about EURES and EURES-related agencies in many European countries, as well as factsheets concerning specific countries.

Belgium: Belgian government employment services are available by region and by language. The main employment service for the Brussels region is the ORBEM/BGDA (*Office régional Bruxellois de l'Emploi/Brusselse Gewestelijke Diest voor Arbeidsbemiddeling*) and there are sub-regional employment offices, SSE/STD (*Services subrégionaux de l'Emploi/Subregionale Tewerkstellings diensten*), throughout Flanders and Wallonia. The ORBEM/BGDA lists office hours, addresses and phone numbers, as well as job postings on its website (🖥 www.orbem. be or www.bgda.be).

Holland: The central governmental employment service in Holland is called the *Arbeidsvoorziening* and maintains job centres (*gewestelijke arbeidsbureaux*) in most cities and towns throughout the country. Addresses and phone numbers for local offices are listed in the phone book. The *Arbeidsvoorziening* also has an innovative website (🖥 www.werk.com or http://werk.net) which combines job postings with job-hunting advice and an online forum for job-hunters – in Dutch.

Luxembourg: Until fairly recently, the government employment service, ADEM (*Administration de l'Emploi*), was the only legally authorised recruitment agency in Luxembourg. Old habits die hard and ADEM offices are still an excellent place to start a job search, as most employers still list the majority of their job vacancies with them. Besides job postings, ADEM offers language training for foreigners (free of charge under certain circumstances if you're looking for work). Even non-EU citizens can register with the national employment office to look for work in the Duchy.

RECRUITMENT AGENCIES

The Benelux countries are well served by private recruitment agencies, many of which operate on a European or worldwide basis. Some executive level management and information technology jobs are listed with headhunters in London or New York, particularly where broad international experience or English-language fluency is required. There's also a variety of small to medium-size recruitment agencies in the US and UK specialising in international placements. Agents place advertisements in daily and weekly newspapers and trade magazines but don't mention the client's name (not least to prevent applicants from approaching the company directly, thus depriving the agency of its fee).

Many of the standard European and international employment agencies, such as Adia, Manpower, PA Consulting Group and Michael Page, have offices in Brussels, Amsterdam, Luxembourg city and other cities in the Benelux region. Locally owned and operated agencies often post clerical and administrative jobs in their shop windows. Most legitimate recruitment services charge the employer a fee based on the annual salary paid to the successful candidate. Fees can run to as much as 40 or 50 per cent of a year's salary, which the headhunter may have to refund if you don't survive the initial probationary period (anything from one to six months). Be extremely wary of recruiters who demand a fee up front from the job applicant or expect you to reimburse them for postage, telephone costs or other charges incurred during the course of the job hunt.

INTERNATIONAL CIVIL SERVICE

The Benelux region offers some unique opportunities for employment in what is sometimes called the 'international civil service' sector. Brussels is home to not only the European Commission (central administrative body of the EU) but also to a number of other international and multinational organisations and agencies. Working for these government and quasi-government agencies often entitles you to a sort of semi-diplomatic status, a variety of tax and social benefits and often a 'comfortable' salary.

Foremost among these opportunities is the European Union, often referred to simply as 'Brussels' on account of its overwhelming presence there. The EU and its various agencies, directorates, organisations and support functions employ more than 12,000 people in the area around Brussels and around 2,000 more in Luxembourg. Only EU nationals can apply, and for most jobs you're expected to have fluency in at least one or two languages other than your mother tongue. If you speak one of the more 'unusual' languages of the EU (e.g. Finnish, Greek or Danish), your chance of being hired will greatly improve and you may find yourself eligible for special training programmes as well.

A few departments and agencies within the EU are gearing up for the addition of new member states, and a working knowledge of Polish, Hungarian or Czech could also come in handy. The EU agencies try to maintain a balance among employees from the various member countries, and British nationals are traditionally underrepresented in many job categories; this is one place where British nationality can be a distinct advantage in looking for a job! The European Commission has Press and Information Offices in the UK, where you can obtain information about jobs and careers in Brussels and elsewhere. It's also possible to be posted to Brussels via the British Civil Service; the programme is called European Fast Stream and details are available through Recruitment and Assessment Services, Innovation Court, New Street, Basingstoke, RG21 7DP (☎ 01256-846466). The EU website (🖳 http://europa.eu.int) includes links to many of the agencies and other departments within the EU, an increasing number of which are posting job vacancies on their websites.

NATO is another international organisation located in Belgium, employing around 3,000 people at its headquarters, and a few thousand more at Supreme Headquarters

Allied Powers in Europe (SHAPE) located at Le Casteau, near Mons in France. Employment is limited to nationals of the member countries (although this includes quite a few more than the 15 members of the EU, including the USA). Apply through the delegation of your home country. The British delegation is at Autosnelweg Brussel-Zaventem 1, 1110 Brussels (☎ 02-726 4774). NATO has a website (🖳 www. nato.int), which includes links to lists of civilian job vacancies within the organisation.

The United Nations maintains a number of agencies in The Hague in Holland, including the International World Court of Justice. Job postings can be found either on the UN website (🖳 www.un.org) or through the links at 🖳 www.unsystem.org to 'other international organisations'. There are also a number of non-government organisations (NGOs) located in various cities throughout the Benelux region, some of which enjoy some or all of the advantages of the so-called International Civil Service. Jobs for these and other international agencies are regularly posted in international publications such as *The Economist* or the *Guardian Weekly*, as well as on the organisations' websites.

The Hague is also the home of many foreign delegations, embassies and consulates. Although upper level employment is restricted to the diplomatic corps of the various countries, most government delegations hire clerical and linguistic staff from the local labour force. However, if you're a non-EU national, you may need an unrestricted work permit before they will consider you for employment; for this you will usually need to have lived in the country for at least five years and have obtained a permanent residence permit.

TEMPORARY AND CASUAL WORK

Temporary and casual work includes the following:

- Office work – well paid if you're qualified, this is generally the easiest work to find on account of the large number of temporary secretarial and office staff agencies.
- Work in the building trade – this can be found by applying directly at building sites and through industrial recruitment agencies such as Manpower.
- Jobs in shops and stores over Christmas and during sale periods.
- Gardening jobs in private gardens, public parks and garden centres, particularly in spring and summer.
- Peddling ice cream, cold drinks and fast food, e.g. in tourist areas or at trade shows and fairs.
- Work as a security guard (long hours for low pay).
- Nursing and auxiliary nursing in hospitals, clinics and nursing homes. (Temps are often employed through nursing agencies to replace permanent staff at short notice.)
- Newspaper, magazine and leaflet distribution.
- Courier work (own transport required – motorcycle, car or van).

- Driving jobs, including coach and truck drivers, and ferrying cars for manufacturers and car hire companies.

- Miscellaneous jobs such as office cleaners, babysitters and labourers – these can be obtained through a number of agencies specialising in temporary work.

You can find temporary agencies, such as Adia, Adecco and Manpower, in most larger cities. Be particularly careful about jobs that may require permits or other forms of qualification. In Holland, for example, you will need a permit to work even temporarily as a street vendor or at a market stall. The building trades are strictly regulated in Belgium and some trades may not be open to foreign nationals even on a temporary or casual basis, or you may require specific (and difficult to obtain) licences or permits. It's sometimes possible to find seasonal employment, usually in agricultural regions, e.g. harvesting tulip bulbs in Holland, or tourist areas during the summer holiday season.

VOLUNTARY WORK

Many of the organisations that arrange training and work experience programmes, such as AIESEC, also host volunteer programmes for students and young people. For those willing to pay their own way, the Earthwatch Institute offers a variety of volunteer opportunities, mostly in support of various types of environmental and cultural research projects. Contact Earthwatch Institute Headquarters, 680 Mount Auburn Street or PO Box 9104, Watertown, MA 02471, USA (☎ 617-926-8200, ✉ info@earthwatch.org) or, in the UK, Earthwatch Europe, 57 Woodstock Road, Oxford OX2 6HJ, UK (☎ 01865-311600, ✉ info@uk.earthwatch.org).

The Belgian-based Association of Voluntary Service Organisations maintains a directory of volunteer opportunities throughout the world, and the group Action Without Borders maintains a directory website (🖥 www.idealist.org), which lists volunteer and paid job postings for voluntary organisations around the world.

Volunteer work is also a good way for a trailing spouse to maintain her (or less frequently, his) career involvement during a tour of duty abroad. Often, non-EU national spouses find they cannot easily obtain a work permit after their arrival in a Benelux country; or they may have difficulty finding employment in their usual profession due to qualification or language impediments. Many expatriate clubs and associations offer opportunities for volunteer work which, although unpaid, can help you avoid an awkward gap in your CV on return to your home country.

JOB HUNTING

If you're primarily looking for a job amongst the large multinational companies or international agencies and organisations located in Benelux, you can use a CV or resume in English similar to the one you'd use in your home country. Job hunting among the smaller, local companies calls for a CV prepared according to local customs and style. Be careful how you present your talents and experience, whether you're using a CV or the shorter American style resume. Beneluxers are a modest and rather conservative people and may see your claims for major accomplishments in prior jobs as bragging. Even if you did single-handedly save millions of euro for your last employer by working through your lunch break or cutting the distance between your desk and the coffee machine, it's safer to supply only a brief explanation of your assigned duties in each job you've held. Your cover letter should generally be in the same language as the job posting you're responding to, unless the employer has specifically requested applications in English. The following are general comments about the differences in style between the three countries but, if in doubt, have a local native speaker (preferably someone who knows the company or industry you're interested in) check your application before you submit it.

Belgium: Although some employers prefer to see a one-page summary CV first (more like an American resume), a CV for Belgium normally includes quite a lot of detail and can run to three pages or more. Employers will expect to see exact dates of employment, as well as the dates of birth of each of your children. Include results for any examinations listed and don't forget to mention how many people you supervised in each position you've held. Belgian employers like to see mention of extracurricular activities; any civic or social club affiliations should be mentioned, especially if you've held an office or other responsible position. You should include a summary of your professional goals at the end of the CV. You don't need to include copies of diplomas or other certificates mentioned in the document with your application, but you should bring copies of these (if you have them) to any interviews in case you're asked for them. Your covering letter should be typed, preferably on letterhead paper and in the proper language (Flemish for companies in the Flemish provinces, French for companies in Walloon, or English for an international employer). If you're applying for a job in Brussels, use French or English if you aren't sure what language to use. Belgian employers don't always reply to applications, especially unsolicited ones, so if you haven't received a response within four weeks, you can assume you've been rejected.

Holland: The Dutch expect a straightforward, factual CV, which should be short – no more than a page or two. Like the Belgians, Dutch employers place great importance on extracurricular, civic and social activities, so be sure to list them. It isn't necessary to include copies of diplomas or certificates, although you should bring copies with you to interviews. It's customary in Holland to provide a summary or profile of the type of position you're seeking at the beginning of the CV or resume, just after your personal identification information. The Dutch are starting to use the American style resume, with more 'subjective' information about the candidate (i.e. you can boast a little bit about your accomplishments, but don't go overboard), mostly for executive positions or candidates with extensive experience. Covering letters should be typed except for jobs in a few specific sectors such as medicine, where a handwritten covering letter is still the norm. (This is where a local contact who is familiar with these peculiarities comes in handy.) Keep your covering letter formal and direct, explain your interest in the job or company you're applying for, and end by asking for an interview. (The Dutch are known for their directness.) Employers generally respond fairly quickly to job applicants, even when the application was unsolicited, so feel free to call if you haven't had a response within two weeks.

Luxembourg: With so many foreigners in the workforce, most employers in Luxembourg are familiar with a wide variety of CV styles. CVs for Luxembourg should include a good photograph and exam results where applicable. Be sure to include your language skills, with an evaluation of your written, reading and speaking level for each language claimed. Employers in Luxembourg place great value on extracurricular activities in school and on social and civic responsibilities, so be sure to include these either in your CV or in your covering letter. Covering letters in Luxembourg should be hand written in French or English. Like the French, the Luxembourgers place great faith in graphology and they use it to determine if you're a good 'fit' for both the position and the organisation.

Newspapers & Magazines

National and local newspapers and magazines in Belgium, Holland and Luxembourg carry job ads, often concentrated in the Saturday editions. In Belgium, around 65 per cent of jobs advertised in newspapers are aimed at Flemish speakers. The major daily newspapers are *Le Soir*, *De Standaard*, *He laatste Nieuws* and *De Gazet van Antwerpen*. In Holland, the Saturday newspapers also carry job listings: *NRC Handelsblad* (management posts), *De Volkskrant* (especially training and healthcare fields), *De Telegraff* (sales personnel) and the *Algemeen Daghblad*. In Luxembourg, job ads appear daily but are clustered on Wednesday and Saturday in the bilingual *Luxemburger Wort/La voix du Luxembourg*.

Within each country, there are specialised industry publications that carry employment advertising, such as the *Ingenieursinformatie* in Holland (for engineers). Industry publications from the UK, Germany and other countries may carry ads for positions in Benelux and other areas, particularly those requiring specialised skills.

International newspapers and magazines that sometimes carry advertising for executive positions in Benelux include the *Financial Times* (Wednesday and Thursday for the UK edition, Friday for the international edition), the *Frankfurter Allgemeine Zeitung* (in the huge Saturday jobs section), the *Wall Street Journal* (for business managers), the *Economist* (economic professions, university teaching and administrative positions as well as executive posts in international organisations and many EU postings), the *International Herald Tribune*, and occasionally even the London Sunday newspapers.

Internet

Most of the newspapers and publications mentioned above are available on the Internet and the appointments advertisements are available for searching or browsing. Some employment agencies and 'headhunters' maintain websites where they post positions available or solicit CVs from potential candidates. There's also a growing range of international recruitment websites you can visit; if you register, you will be notified of jobs meeting your requirements. Sites to visit if you're looking for work in Benelux include:

- 🖥 www.overseasjobs.com

- 🖥 www.monster.be (for Belgium), www.monster.ne (for Holland). There isn't a www.monster.lu yet, but you can sometimes find jobs in Luxembourg on the Belgian site or listed on www.monster.fr (France) or www.monster.de (Germany).

- 🖥 www.luxjob.lu – a whole site for job listings in Luxembourg!

⌨ www.stepstone.com – a European focused job site with separate areas for jobs in each country.

Many of the international organisations located in Benelux and the agencies of the European Union list current job openings on their websites. These website postings often give much more detailed information about available jobs than advertisements in the press and it may be possible to apply for these jobs using the agency website. Don't forget also to check the websites of the national employment agencies.

Recruitment Agencies & Employment Offices

Apply to international recruitment agencies acting for Benelux companies or offices recruiting executives and key personnel as well as to recruitment agencies in Belgium, Holland or Luxembourg. Also contact the government employment services (see page 25) in the country where you wish to work, or use your own government's EURES-affiliated employment service.

Current Employer

One frequently overlooked source of overseas jobs is your current employer. This will apply mainly if you work for an international company or at least an organisation with one or more offices in Benelux. It's far easier for your current employer to justify the transfer of someone to the Brussels office or the factory in Utrecht who's already familiar with the company's policies and procedures than to hire a foreigner in Benelux. This can be particularly useful if you need a work permit. Make sure your personnel department knows of your interest in working overseas, especially if you already speak and read one or more foreign languages. Mention your interest to any Benelux contacts you have within your own company who might be willing to mention your name to fill a local vacancy.

Unsolicited Job Applications

Apply directly to British, American and other international companies with offices or subsidiaries in Benelux. Send written inquiries to Benelux companies and follow up by phone when you're in the country and available for an interview. If you have friends in the area, it may help to have them introduce you or present your CV to their employer, as personal contacts and references are considered important.

WORKING WOMEN

Although there are EU and national laws requiring equal pay and equal opportunities for women in the work force, you will find few women in management or other positions of authority anywhere in the Benelux region. This is no doubt partly due to the rather traditional and conservative culture in all three countries; women have been rather slow to enter the workforce, preferring to attend to home and child care responsibilities, although the number of working women has been rising over the last decade or so. Another factor is the difficulty in finding affordable, reliable child care, and the reluctance of many families to leave child care responsibilities to 'outsiders'. While roughly 50 per cent of Benelux women now work (compared with only 30 to 35 per cent 25 years ago), they're far more likely to hold part-time jobs than men. Unemployment figures are considerably higher among women than men.

Women's salaries are still 20 per cent lower on average than men's, even in jobs considered comparable. Opportunities for promotion and career development are often unavailable to those on part-time status or where it's assumed that a woman will be taking advantage of generous maternity leaves and allowances.

It's illegal for employers to discriminate against women in recruiting or promoting staff, but in practice it can be virtually impossible to prove why a particular candidate didn't receive a desirable job or promotion. Foreign women with business or management credentials may have better luck with multinational, British or American based companies if they aspire to management level positions. Many British and American women's organisations maintain job banks for their members or can direct you to networking groups for career women.

SALARY

Benelux has long been a prosperous region in Europe, and salaries are generally above average, although not as high as those in Germany and France. All three countries have a minimum wage and both Holland and Luxembourg permit a lower starting salary for workers under 23 or 18 years of age. Annual salary increases are often controlled by an industry collective agreement and pegged to local cost of living increases. In Belgium, your salary may depend on your age and, while salary levels rarely appear in job advertisements, the desired age range will give you an idea of what an employer is willing to pay.

Taxes throughout the Benelux region are higher than what you may be used to in your home country, particularly if you're coming from the UK or the US (see page 258), so remember to take this into account when considering your salary. The Belgians have the highest income tax rates, followed by the Dutch. Although Luxembourg has a reputation as something of a tax haven, this is largely based on indirect taxes rather than income tax.

If you have friends or acquaintances living in Benelux or who have lived there, ask them what an average or good salary is for your trade or profession. For many employees, particularly executives and senior managers, their remuneration is much more than the money they receive in their monthly pay packets. Some companies provide benefits such as a company car, private school fees, interest-free home or other loans, and membership of local clubs or sporting organisations. These additional benefits are usually taxable, however, and this should be taken into account when calculating your net take-home pay or comparing competing job offers.

SELF-EMPLOYMENT

If you're an EU national or a permanent resident, you can be self-employed or work as a sole trader in the Benelux countries, provided you meet the qualification requirements of your profession (see page 24) and register your business with the appropriate authorities. It's illegal to simply hang out a sign and start a business without the proper registration. While the national governments are keen to encourage the establishment and growth of small to medium-size enterprises (SMEs), you should be prepared for a veritable deluge of paperwork and red tape (*chasse-papier* in French, or *rompslomp* in Dutch), no matter where you go in Benelux; this is, after all, the heartland of the 'harmonised' EU. SMEs (PME, for *petites et moyennes enterprises*, or KMO for *kleine en middelgrote ondernemingen*), although defined slightly differently by the three governments, make up a large percentage of local businesses in Benelux and employ a significant proportion of the local populations. All three governments make tax, investment and financial incentives available to start-up businesses, especially those which will create new jobs for local residents. These incentives are generally available to foreigners willing to establish themselves in the local community as well as to native entrepreneurs.

Belgium: To set up a business of your own in Belgium, you must establish yourself under one of the available legal business structures, which include a partnership (*société en commandité par actions* or SCA/*commanditaire vennootschap op aandelen* or CVA) and various forms of limited liability company, the most common of which is the SPRL/BVBA (*société privée à responsabilité limitée/besloten vennootschap met beperkte aansprakelijkheid*) or private limited liability company. Requirements for establishing a business structure include the filing of the company statutes, a statement of ownership interests and posting of the required capital in a company bank account. It's also possible to establish a branch (*succursale/bijhuis*) of a foreign company in Belgium. But whether you start a new company or open a branch of an existing one, the business or branch must be registered with the Commercial Court (*Greffe du Tribunal de Commerce/Griffie van de Handelsrechtbank*) and with the Register of Commerce (*Registre de Commerce/Handelsregister*). You must also obtain a VAT number from the VAT administration before you can charge for your goods or services. An SME (PME/KMO) is defined as a business employing fewer than 50 people and with a turnover of less than €4 million per year. Above these limits, the accounting, reporting and auditing requirements are considerably stricter than for smaller companies.

Faced with all this bureaucracy, you will be happy to know that help is available from a number of sources, including the British Chamber of Commerce of Belgium and Luxembourg, rue d'Egmont 15, 1050 Brussels (☎ 02-540 9030), and the American Chamber of Commerce in Belgium, avenue des Arts 50 bte 5, 1040 Brussels (☎ 02-513 6770/6779, ⌨ www.amcham.be). The Brussels Chamber of Commerce (avenue Louise 50, 1050 Brussels, ☎ 02-648 5002, ⌨ www.ccib.irisnet.be) will help you with the business set-up procedures and review and evaluate your business proposal for a small fee, as will the National Federation of SMEs of Belgium (*Fédération des PME/Verbond van KMO*, rue de Stalle 90, 1080 Brussels, ☎ 02-376 8557). There's also an English-speaking self-help group called Focus, which publishes a booklet called *Getting Started – Legally*. Focus is located at Rue Lesbroussart 23, 1050 Brussels (☎ 02-646 6530) and is affiliated to the Focus organisation in London, as well as to WICE (the Women's Institute of Continuing Education, although it's now co-educational) in Paris.

Holland: The process of setting up a business in Holland is similar to that described above for Belgium. There are three different types of partnership structure and you should be aware that under Dutch law partners are personally liable for the acts and financial obligations of the partnership. The most popular kind of limited liability company is the BV (*Besloten Vennootschap met Beperkte Aansprakelijkeid*). Once established, it's relatively easy to change the corporate structure to that of a public corporation (NV or *Naamloze Vennootschap*) and back again as conditions warrant. In Holland, a small business is one that meets two of the following criteria: fewer than 50 employees, turnover of less than €3.6 million and assets not exceeding €1.8 million. As a 'small' company, you can file a simpler set of financial reports at the end of the year and your accounts aren't subject to an external audit.

Luxembourg: In Luxembourg, you must obtain permission from the Ministry of Small and Medium-size Businesses (*Ministère des Classes Moyennes*) to start up your own business. To obtain permission, you must submit documentation relating to the incorporation of the business or the setting up of a company or partnership, a resume of your professional qualifications and a certificate of solvency to show not only that you can make a living from your business, but that you've already done so in another country. You will be expected to have a qualification and experience in an appropriate area, and your business must be registered with the Commercial Court (*Registre de Commerce et des Sociétés*) and with the local VAT office. You will be required to use the services of a notary to draw up your company statutes (*actes de constitution*) and there are various stamp duties and registration fees to pay. A small business is one with fewer than 50 employees and annual turnover of less than LF160 million. There are six different types of business structure in Luxembourg, the most popular of which is the SARL (*société à responsabilité limitée*), roughly equivalent to the BV or SPRL described above. You must re-apply for your business permit if the nature of your business changes.

TRAINEES & WORK EXPERIENCE

AIESEC is a student-run, non-profit organisation which offers paid internships in business and technical fields in around 90 countries and territories, including Benelux. You can contact the AIESEC chapter at your university for details of qualifications and application procedures. In the UK contact AIESEC UK, 29–31 Cowper Street, London, EC2A 4AT (☎ 020-7336 7939). AIESEC has a website (🖳 www.aiesec.org) containing detailed contact information by country.

Transitions Abroad magazine is a good resource for information on all kinds of educational and exchange programmes. The online version (🖳 www.transitions abroad.com) includes country-by-country listings of programmes for study, work, internships, volunteering, language study, etc. – all in searchable form.

The European Union and EURES have a number of programmes for young people interested in training and work experience abroad. Contact your country's national employment services agency or the national trade association for the industry in which you wish to train, who may be able to put you in contact with a suitable Benelux employer.

AU PAIRS

Working as an au pair is an opportunity for young people between the ages of 17 and 27 years to live, work, travel and study in a family setting. Within Europe the term 'au pair' is strictly defined in both national law and a series of European Commission directives and should not be confused with the designation 'nanny,' which indicates a trained (often qualified) child care professional (also considerably more expensive to hire than an au pair!). The au pair system is designed to give young people an opportunity to live abroad, learn a new language or improve their foreign language skills and experience a foreign culture while living in a family environment. In the Benelux countries, many of the families seeking au pairs are well-to-do expatriate executive or diplomatic families rather than 'typical' nationals. The Dutch, for example, have been slow to warm to the idea of taking foreign strangers into their homes to care for their children and Dutch law did not formally recognize au pairs until the mid-1980s. While this may limit the possibilities for living *en famille* with genuine Belgians, Dutch or Luxembourgers, it does improve your chances of accompanying your host family on their exotic foreign holidays or participating in the diplomatic lifestyle.

Au pairs are usually contracted to work for a period of between six and 12 (sometimes 18) months, often coinciding with the local school year. An au pair is generally placed in a family with small children, where her (or less frequently, his) duties will include child minding and light housework during the day, combined with occasional evening babysitting. Light housework may include such things as simple meal preparation for children, laundry and ironing, vacuum cleaning, making beds, dusting and taking children to and from school and other activities. As an au pair, you should not be expected to care for mentally or physically handicapped children.

Work-related responsibilities must not exceed five hours a day, and an au pair is entitled to at least one full day off each week (including at least one Sunday a month in Belgium). The host family must also make reasonable allowances for the au pair to attend language or other classes, pursue cultural interests and observe their own religious celebrations or practices. In exchange for these duties, an au pair is provided with room and board and must be given her own bedroom (to allow some time away from the children!) and a monthly stipend that is considered 'pocket money' rather than salary. The host family is responsible for enrolling their au pair for the national social insurances according to local laws and must arrange for adequate health insurance (sometimes through an extension to their own family coverage) to cover the au pair in the event of accident or illness.

Your experience as an au pair will depend entirely on your relationship with your family. If you're fortunate enough to work for a warm and friendly host family, you will have a wonderful experience, lots of free time and possibly some memorable holidays. Many au pairs grow to love their children and families and form lifelong friendships. On the other hand, abuses of the au pair system are common in all countries and you may be treated like a servant rather than a member of the family. Many families engage an au pair simply because it costs less than employing a nanny. If you have any problems or complaints about your host family or the duties you have been assigned, you should refer them to the agency that found you your position (if applicable). The laws regarding au pair situations in Benelux (and throughout Europe) are strictly enforced and, if you can't turn to your placement agency for help or in the case of serious abuse of the system, you should go directly to the local employment office. **There are many families to choose from and you shouldn't feel that you need to remain with a family that treats you badly or disregards the laws.** You're usually required to give notice if you wish to go home before the end of your agreement, although this won't apply if the family has broken the contract.

If you're an EU national, you only need a valid passport and you aren't required to arrange a position before arriving in a Benelux country, although you must register with the local authorities once you've accepted a position. At a minimum, you must have a residence permit, and all Benelux countries require that a copy of your au pair contract or agreement be registered with the local employment office. Applicants from non-EU countries must apply for and receive the appropriate work permits and residence documents in their home countries before entering Benelux (see **Work Permits** on page 65).

An au pair position can be arranged privately with a family or through an agency, although using an agency is normally the best way to ensure that everyone involved is sticking to the rules. There are many au pair agencies in the UK that place English-speaking au pairs with families throughout Europe. There are also au pair agencies in Belgium, Holland and Luxembourg. The better agencies are members of one or more of the international au pair organisations, which promote a standard code of conduct that includes the vetting of host families and periodic checks on your welfare during your stay. Some agencies will put you in touch with other au pairs they've placed nearby and may even run occasional social events or activities to encourage you to get out and around on your own. You should also feel free to contact the agency if you encounter problems (either personal or with your family) during your contract period.

On your initial contact, the agency will send you an application form (questionnaire) that requests details of your background, skills, and interests so that it can place you with a compatible family. They should also require character (moral) and child care references, a medical certificate and school references. Au pairs must normally have had a high school education, school leaving certificate or equivalent and should have a working knowledge of one or more of the official languages of the host country (usually French for those interested in going to Belgium or Luxembourg). You will be required to register for at least ten hours a week of language training once you're placed. (All three countries in Benelux require proof of registration for language classes before you leave home!) Agency registration fees vary, although there are maximum fees in some countries, e.g. around £50 in Britain, and often these cannot be charged until you've been placed.

The best approach is to contact a number of agencies to compare their fees, terms and services. Some au pair agencies have Internet sites, e.g. the International Au Pair Association (🖥 www.iapa.org) and the Universal Au Pair Association (🖥 www.uapa. org), as do the organisations that administer the various codes of conduct across the industry. Many international job posting boards on the Internet also list au pair opportunities (see page 30).

WORKING ILLEGALLY

Perhaps it has something to do with the number of European Union agencies headquartered in the region, but you will find that working illegally isn't nearly as common in Benelux as it is in some other areas of Europe. To start with, the Belgians, Luxembourgers and Dutch are generally rather law abiding folk with a heavily regulated work environment that makes life extremely difficult if you lack the proper documentation. Although no one denies the existence of illegal workers and 'under the table' jobs, in Benelux most opportunities for this type of employment involve low-paid, menial work that can be not only dirty but often downright dangerous.

All three national governments have cracked down on the use of illegal workers, as immigration officials are under increasing pressure to stem the tide of unwanted foreigners looking for economic opportunities in Europe. The port cities of Antwerp in Belgium and Rotterdam in Holland are well known as staging areas for illegal refugees hoping to enter the UK and, while waiting for their opportunity, many foreigners resort to selling drugs or prostitution or whatever they can do to earn money quickly.

Unscrupulous employers use illegal labour in order to pay low wages and avoid paying mandatory social insurances, especially for workers unable to obtain residence visas and work permits. If you're caught working illegally, you can be fined or jailed; if you're deported, you can be banned from re-entering Europe for up to five years, even as a tourist. Employers caught hiring illegal workers are also subject to fines and penalties, and there's no telling what your employer might do to avoid getting caught.

LANGUAGE

English is a popular foreign language and is widely understood throughout the Benelux region. However, with the exception of some large multinational companies and international organisations which have declared English to be their official internal working language, you will need to know one or more of the local languages. French, German and Dutch are the main languages used in Benelux, but they aren't interchangeable in all areas. Knowing and using the proper local language can help considerably, not only in your job search but also in getting settled into your new community. Most areas offer a variety of language classes for foreigners (see **Language** on page 160).

Belgium: Of the three countries that make up Benelux, Belgium's linguistic history and situation is probably the most complex. Belgium has three official languages: French, Flemish (*Vlaams*) and German. Flemish is virtually identical to Dutch, with the exception of a few local terms and expressions, although certain areas in Flemish-speaking Belgium have local dialects that can sometimes be incomprehensible to speakers of standard Dutch. Nevertheless, the terms Flemish and Dutch are often used interchangeably for the language of Flanders. The French spoken in Belgium is standard but with its own distinctive accent (at least according to the French!) and a few specialised words, notably the use of *septante* and *nonante* for 70 and 90 instead of *soixante-dix* and *quatre-vingt-dix*. (Oddly, the Belgians do use *quatre-vingt* for the number 80 rather than *octante*, which is used in Switzerland and some other francophone areas of the world.) Almost 60 per cent of the Belgian population speak Flemish/Dutch as their first language, 40 per cent are francophones and there is a small German speaking region (with less than 2 per cent of the population) in the eastern part of the country along the German border.

Belgium is officially divided into linguistic regions, with Flemish the official language of the five northern and north-eastern provinces (Antwerp, East Flanders, Flemish Brabant, Limburg and West Flanders). French is the official language of the five Walloon provinces in the south (Hainaut, Liège, Luxembourg, Namur and

Walloon Brabant). The city of Brussels and its surrounding area are legally designated as a bilingual region, although individual towns may insist on asserting one language over the other, depending on the results of the latest local elections. Even the small German population is recognised as a distinct linguistic region under Belgian law. Within each region, the majority of residents speak the designated language and most road signs, government services and public schooling are available only in the official regional language. Driving across Belgium can be particularly confusing, as most cities and towns have both a French and a Flemish name, which often bear little resemblance to each other, e.g. the city of Mons, in French, is Bergen in Flemish. (See also **Chapter 11**.)

English is widely spoken in and around Brussels and Antwerp, and you're likely to find more English speakers in the Flemish areas of Belgium than in Walloon. Except for the highest level diplomatic appointments (where you will only need to be fluent in Diplomatese), you will be expected to have some knowledge of the appropriate regional language no matter what sort of job you're applying for. Having both French and Flemish can be a major advantage in the job hunt as no more than 20 per cent of Belgians are bilingual in the two major national languages, and they're more likely to live in Flanders than in Walloon. French is probably the 'preferred' language for the Brussels area on account of the concentration of international organisations (which are often heavily subsidised by the French government to encourage and insist upon 'la francophonie'!) and the preponderance of French-speaking residents who work in those organisations. On the other hand, there are far more jobs available (owing to the concentration of industry and commerce) in the Flemish part of the country.

Holland: Compared with the intricacies of Belgium and Luxembourg, Holland is reasonably straightforward from a linguistic point of view: the official language is Dutch (*Nederlands*). The official version of the Dutch language ('high Dutch') is sometimes referred to as ABN (*Algemeen Beschaafd Nederlands*) or 'standard civilised Dutch.' There are some differences in vocabulary, pronunciation and popular expressions between ABN and the varieties of Dutch spoken in Belgium.

Like their neighbours in Benelux, the Dutch are accomplished linguists and you will have no trouble finding people who understand and speak excellent English. It isn't uncommon for a native of Holland to speak two, three or even more foreign languages fluently, usually English, German and French. Although it's possible to get by in a large multinational company speaking only English, you will have a much easier time, both at work and after hours, if you have a good working knowledge of Dutch. Dutch can be a difficult language to learn, in part because of the unique pronunciation of certain letters and sounds – ask a native speaker some time to teach you to say 'Van Gogh' properly! The other difficulty is finding someone with whom you can practise speaking, as so many Dutch are fluent in English and more than happy to speak it with you.

Luxembourg: The national language of Luxembourg is (depending on who you talk to) Lëtzebuergesch, Letzeburgisch or Luxembourgeois. This local 'language' is often described as a dialect of German, although it's also related to Dutch and has adopted many words from French. For the most part, Lëtzebuergesch is a spoken language used by the 'true' Luxembourger among family and close friends (perhaps as a means of identifying each other in a country where half the population are foreigners). If you already know German, you will probably be able to pick it up fairly quickly, although there are some local variations that are largely incomprehensible to all but natives. French and German (the standard varieties) are widely spoken and used throughout Luxembourg, French being the language of choice for most government and administrative functions and German the language of the media. English is also widely spoken and understood in businesses and shops.

While it may be possible to work for a multinational company knowing only English, it's highly recommended to know some French or German (or better still, both) before you start looking for work in Luxembourg. The government employment service claims that bilingualism is a 'minimum' requirement, with a third language strongly recommended for anyone seeking employment in the Duchy. Because of its use in administrative matters, French is considered the more 'formal' and businesslike of the national languages. If in doubt which language to use in any given situation, French is normally the safer choice, especially in professional situations or any dealings with government agencies or officials. German is often associated in popular usage with the lower classes and less skilled workers.

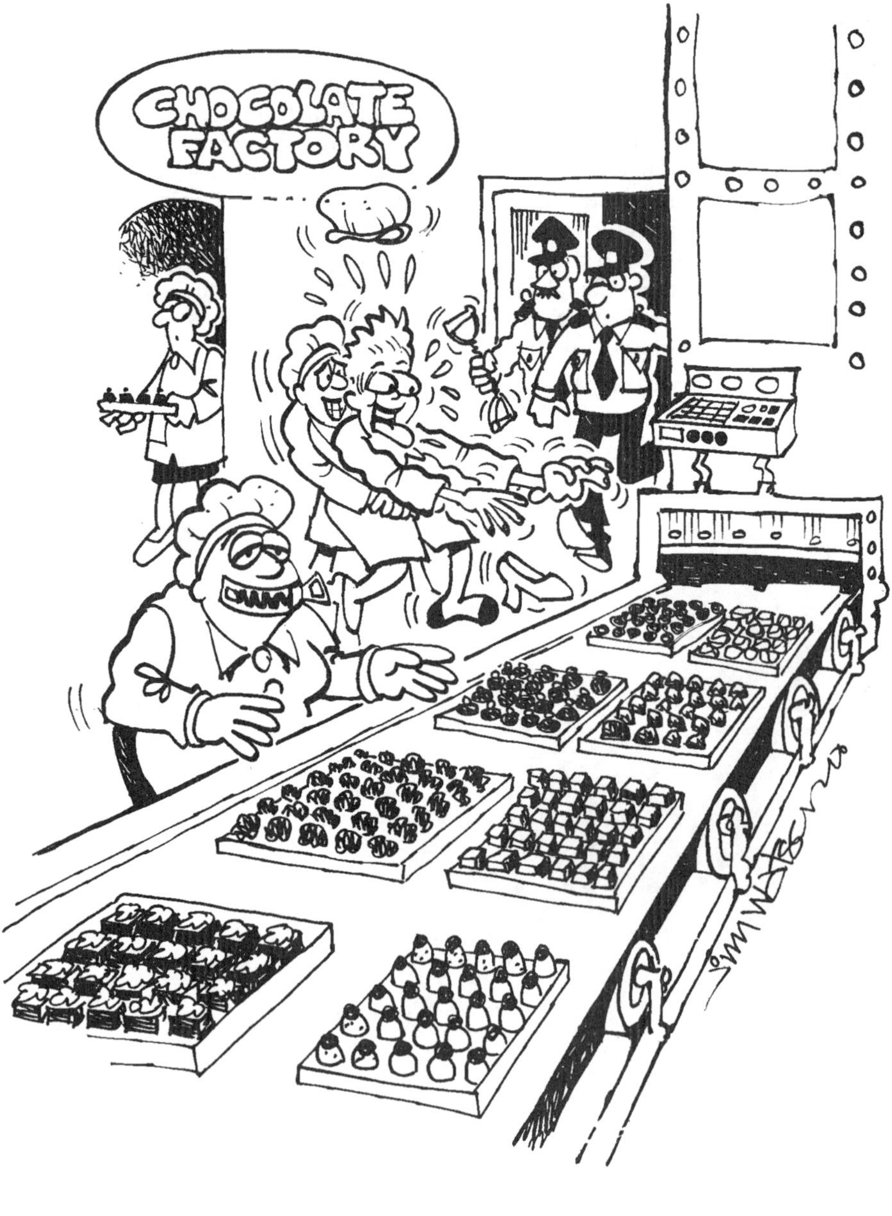
CHOCOLATE FACTORY

2.

WORKING CONDITIONS

W orking conditions in Belgium, Holland and Luxembourg vary according to national labour laws, collective agreements (*conventions collectives*) and individual employment contracts. Foreigners are subject to the same working conditions and rules as local citizens, although there are different rules for the various categories of employees, e.g. directors, managers, white collar and blue collar workers. In general, part-time employees receive the same rights and benefits as full-time employees on a pro rata basis.

Employees in Benelux enjoy excellent working conditions and social security benefits (at a price!) and extensive rights under labour law and the various controlling agreements. Labour laws provide guidelines as to basic conditions of employment, including working hours, overtime payments, holidays, trial and notice periods, dismissal, health and safety regulations and trade union rights. Workers have the right to form and join unions, which negotiate collective agreements with individual employers or industries within a region according to broad guidelines set by national federations of unions and employers (see page 56). Larger companies are required to have a works council, which meets regularly with management to discuss business and social issues.

TERMS OF EMPLOYMENT

Negotiating an appropriate salary is only one aspect of your working conditions. When negotiating your terms of employment for a job in Belgium, Holland or Luxembourg, the checklists on the following pages will prove useful. The points listed under General Positions (below) apply to most jobs, while those listed under Executive Positions usually apply to executive and top managerial appointments only.

General Positions

Salary

- Is the total salary (including expenses) paid in euros or will it be paid in another country (in a different currency) with expenses for living in Belgium, Holland or Luxembourg?
- Is the total adequate, taking into account the cost of living in Belgium, Holland or Luxembourg? Is the salary index-linked?
- When and how often is the salary reviewed?
- Does the salary include a 13th month's salary, a vacation bonus and annual or end-of-contract bonuses?
- Is overtime paid or time off given in lieu of extra hours worked?

Relocation Expenses

- Are removal expenses or a relocation allowance paid?
- Does the allowance include travelling expenses for all family members?
- Is there a limit and is it adequate?

- Are you required to repay relocation expenses (or a percentage) if you resign before a certain period has elapsed?
- Are you required to pay for your relocation in advance? This can run into many thousands of euros for normal house contents.
- If your contract is terminated by your employer before a certain period has elapsed, under what conditions will your repatriation expenses be paid or reimbursed?
- If employment is for a short period, will your relocation costs be paid by the employer when you leave Belgium, Holland or Luxembourg?
- If you aren't shipping household goods and furniture to Belgium, Holland or Luxembourg, is there an allowance for buying furnishings locally?
- Do relocation expenses include the legal and estate agency fees incurred when moving home?
- Does the employer use the services of a relocation consultant?

Accommodation

- Will the employer pay for a hotel (or pay a lodging allowance) until you find permanent accommodation?
- Is subsidised or free (temporary or permanent) accommodation provided? If so, is it furnished or unfurnished?
- Must you pay for utilities such as electricity, gas and water?
- If accommodation isn't provided by the employer, is assistance provided to find accommodation? What does it consist of?
- What will accommodation cost?
- Are your expenses paid while looking for accommodation?

Working Hours

- What are the weekly working hours?
- Does the employer operate a flexi-time system? If so, what are the fixed working hours? How early must you start? Can you carry forward extra hours worked and take time off at a later date or carry forward a deficit and make it up later?
- Are you required to clock in and out of work?
- Are you paid for overtime or can you take time off in lieu?
- Are you required to work additional hours each week to compensate for extra official company holidays?

Leave

- What is the annual leave entitlement? Does it increase with age?
- What are the paid public holidays? Is Monday or Friday a free day when a public holiday falls on a Tuesday or Thursday respectively?

- Is free air travel to your home country or elsewhere provided for you and your family, and if so, how often?

Insurance

- Is extra insurance cover provided besides obligatory insurance?
- Is free life insurance provided?
- Is health insurance provided for you *and* your family? What does it include?
- For how long will your salary be paid if you're ill or have an accident?

Company Pension

- What percentage of your salary must you pay?
- Are you able to pay a lump sum into the pension fund in order to receive a full or higher pension?
- Is the pension transferable to another employer or to another location with the same employer?

Employer

- What are the employer's prospects?
- Is his profitability and growth rate favourable?
- Does he have a good reputation as an employer?
- Does he have a high staff turnover? If so, why?
- Are free or subsidised language lessons provided for you and your spouse?
- Is a travelling allowance paid from your local residence to your place of work?
- Is free or subsidised parking provided at your place of work?
- Is a free or subsidised company restaurant provided? If not, is a lunch allowance paid?
- Will the employer provide or pay for any professional training or education required, if necessary abroad? Will he pay for a part of the total cost of non-essential education, e.g. a computer or language course?

Miscellaneous

- Are free work clothes or overalls provided? Does the employer pay for the cleaning of work clothes (workshop or office)?
- Does the employer provide any fringe benefits, such as subsidised in-house banking services, low interest loans, free petrol or mileage allowance, employee shop or product discounts, sports and social facilities, and subsidised tickets, e.g. for local theatres or sports events?
- Do you have a written list of your job responsibilities?

- Have your employment conditions been confirmed in writing? (For a list of the possible contents of your employment conditions, see page 46.)
- If a dispute arises over your salary or working conditions, under the law of which country will your employment contract be interpreted?

Executive Positions

- Is private schooling for your children paid for or subsidised? Will the employer pay for a boarding school in the Benelux region or abroad?
- Is the salary index-linked or protected against devaluation and cost of living increases? This is particularly important if you're paid in a foreign currency that fluctuates wildly or could be devalued against the euro. Are you paid an overseas allowance for working in Belgium, Holland or Luxembourg?
- Is there a non-contributory pension fund besides the compulsory government scheme? Is it transferable and, if so, what are the conditions?
- Are the costs incurred by a move to Belgium, Holland or Luxembourg reimbursed (e.g. the cost of selling your home, employing an agent to let it for you or storing household effects)?
- Will the employer pay for domestic help or a contribution towards the cost of a servant or cook?

  Is a car provided? With a chauffeur?
- Are you entitled to any miscellaneous benefits, such as membership of a club or company credit cards?
- Is there an entertainment allowance?
- Is there a clothing allowance? For example, if you arrive in Amsterdam in the winter from the tropics, you will probably need to buy new winter clothes.
- Is compensation paid if you're made redundant or fired? Redundancy or severance payments are compulsory for nearly all employees in Benelux (subject to length of service), but executives often receive a generous 'golden handshake' if they're made redundant, e.g. after a takeover.

EMPLOYMENT CONTRACTS

Throughout Benelux, an employment contract exists as soon as you undertake a job for which you expect to be paid, although employees nearly always have a written employment contract to document the existence of a formal work relationship. Especially as a foreigner, you should ask for a written contract if one is not automatically offered to you. You may be required to submit a copy of your employment contract to local officials when applying for your residence permit, especially if you're in a 'protected' category, such as an au pair.

There are three different kinds of employment contracts and it's important that you understand which applies to you. A limited time contract is one that ends after a set period of time, such as six months or a year; contracts for specific work end when the work you've been hired to do is completed; indeterminate contracts are those for 'permanent' jobs, which can only be terminated according to the terms of the contract regarding notice periods and severance pay. In most cases, if you don't have a written contract by the first day you start a job, you're assumed to be a permanent employee and subject to the privileges and obligations of all other permanent employees, depending upon the level of the job and the salary you're being paid. Limited term contracts are often subject to restrictions, particularly concerning how often and under what circumstances they can be renewed or when the job must be converted to a permanent (i.e. indeterminate contract) position.

All employment contracts are subject to the national labour laws, and references may be made to other regulations such as collective agreements. Anything in contracts contrary to statutory provisions and unfavourable to an employee may be challenged in a labour court, but in principle you're allowed to strike an agreement with your employer that waives some or all of your rights under the law or collective agreement. As with all contracts, you should know exactly what an employment contract contains before signing it. The legally binding version of an employment contract is normally the one written in one of the local languages (e.g. French or Flemish in Belgium, Dutch in Holland, and French in Luxembourg), but you can and should ask for at least an informal translation into your own language if you're unsure of any of the terms or provisions.

EMPLOYMENT CONDITIONS

Employment conditions contain an employer's general rules and regulations regarding working conditions and benefits that are applicable to all employees, unless stated otherwise in your employment contract. Employment conditions may include the following:

- validity and applicability;
- salary and benefits;
- 13th month salary and bonuses;
- working hours and overtime;
- flexi-time;
- travel and relocation expenses;
- social security;
- health insurance;
- company pension fund;
- unemployment insurance;
- salary insurance;
- annual holidays;
- public holidays;
- compassionate and special leave;
- paid expenses;

- probationary and notice periods;
- education and training;
- pregnancy and confinement;
- part-time job restrictions;
- changing jobs and confidentiality;
- acceptance of gifts;
- retirement;
- dismissal;
- union membership and workers' councils.

All the above points are explained in this chapter or a reference is given to the chapter where the subject is covered in more detail.

Validity & Applicability

Employment conditions usually contain a paragraph stating the date from which they take effect and to whom they apply.

Salary & Benefits

Your starting salary is stated in your employment contract and details of salary reviews, planned increases and cost of living rises may also be included. Salaries in job contracts are normally stated in gross terms, prior to all deductions and withholdings for benefits, taxes and social security. Salaries are generally paid monthly, although they may be quoted in contracts on an hourly, monthly or annual basis, depending on the type of job you're being offered. If a bonus is paid, such as a 13th month's salary or the so-called 'holiday bonus' in the summer (see page 48), this should be stated in your employment contract. Be aware, however, that if you're quoted an annual salary in your contract, you should divide this by 13, 13.5 or even 14 to arrive at your monthly gross pay; the exact figure depends on how the regular 'bonuses' are calculated (see below). General points such as the payment of your salary into a bank or post office account and the date of salary payments are usually included in employment conditions. Many employers in Benelux will only pay salary or wages directly into a bank account – no handing round of paycheques or pay packets on pay day! You will receive a pay slip (usually filling most of an A4 page) that itemises your salary, bonuses and any premiums or special rates and shows tax and other deductions, including any amounts paid in by your employer for your benefit.

Salaries are generally reviewed once a year, in accordance with the prevailing industry or regional labour agreement. Pay increases are carefully monitored and negotiated on an industry-wide basis, although there's usually some provision for small 'merit-based' increments for employees performing exceptionally well.

13th Month's Salary & Bonuses

Many employers pay a 13th month 'bonus' to their employees; a few even add a half of a 14th month's pay to that, usually payable at the end of the year. This year-end or Christmas bonus (*prime de fin d'année/jaarpremie*) should be incorporated into your contract if you've been quoted an annual salary. In your first and last year of employment, the 13th month bonus (and any summer holiday bonus) is paid pro rata if you don't work a full calendar year. Some employers offer a variable profit sharing or productivity bonus (*participation aux benefices/aandeel in de winst* or *prime de productivité/produktiviteitspremie*), depending on the performance of the company, branch or department.

In Belgium, you're entitled to a holiday (vacation) bonus of 85 per cent of a month's salary, normally paid during the summer or whenever you take your main annual holiday. This should be included in your employment contract and the amount of the bonus included in the annual salary figure you've been quoted. (You may need to divide your annual salary by 13.85 to find your gross monthly salary.) Holiday bonuses are less common (not to mention less generous) in Holland and Luxembourg, normally amounting to half a month's salary when they're given. Some managerial or executive jobs include a full month's 'holiday bonus'. Any such bonuses should be specified in your terms of employment, including when they are to be paid and any pro rata payment for starting or leaving during a year. You may not be eligible for your holiday bonus until you become eligible for holiday time (see page 52).

Some employers operate a separate profit-sharing or performance-related bonus system, whereby they pay an annual sum (usually at the end of the year or the end of the fiscal year if the company doesn't operate on a calendar year system). The amount of the bonus depends on the company's overall performance, the attainment of specific goals during the year, and may be calculated as a percentage of each employee's annual or monthly salary over the period. Your eligibility for this type of bonus may or may not be part of your employment contract. (It certainly makes a nice surprise at the end of the year if you get one!)

Working Hours & Overtime

Working hours in the Benelux countries vary according to your employer, your position, the industry in which you're employed and the regional or industry collective agreements that apply to your employer. The standard working week (i.e. the hours you're expected to work on a regular basis) can be no longer than 40 hours in Luxembourg and Holland and no more than 39 hours in Belgium. After that, workers must be paid overtime, at rates that vary according to the requirements and conditions of the extra hours worked. Of course, none of these restrictions applies to you if you're a top executive (*direction/directie*) or manager (*cadres/kaderleden*) or if you own your own company (in which case, you love your work so much that you don't even notice the hours ticking by).

Belgium: Although legally the standard working week in Belgium is 39 hours, most collective agreements call for shorter working weeks of between 35 and 38 hours. Some labour organisations are calling for a standard 35-hour week, in the hope that this will inspire more hiring, especially in industries threatened with workforce reductions. Under Belgian law, overtime rates must be paid for all work in excess of eight hours per day or 39 hours per week, and every employee must be given at least one 24-hour rest period each week. Work time is normally limited to 11 hours per day and 50 hours per week, although these limits can be exceeded if the collective agreement allows it and the employer has obtained the permission of the works council.

Holland: Employment contracts in Holland average around 37.5 hours a week for a full-time job, although the legal maximum for a standard working week is 40 hours. Many Dutch work shorter hours, as the government has tried to encourage part-time employment with full benefits as a way to head off unemployment. Working hours are flexible, in large part to permit overlapping of part-time schedules.

Luxembourg: The working week in Luxembourg is legally limited to 40 hours, with the payment of premiums for all overtime or work at 'unusual hours'. There's a legal maximum working day of ten hours, after which all work must be paid at overtime rates. Overtime must be approved in advance by the Ministry of Employment. The government of Luxembourg has granted permission for Sunday work to a few industries that operate continuous processing lines, as well as to a few of the tourist industries. Sunday work, however, must be entirely voluntary and is always paid at double the normal salary rates.

Flexi-Time

Some Benelux companies operate flexi-time working hours. A flexi-time system requires all employees to be present between certain hours, known as the block time, for example, from 8.30 to 11.30am and from 1.30 to 4pm. Employees may make up their required working hours by starting earlier than the required block time, reducing their lunch break or working later. Most business premises are open from around 7am until 6 or 7pm. Smaller companies may allow employees to work as late as they wish, provided they don't exceed the maximum permitted daily working hours (see above). Because flexi-time rules are often quite complicated, they may be contained in a separate set of regulations.

Travel & Relocation Expenses

Travel and relocation expenses in Belgium, Holland and Luxembourg depend on your agreement with your employer and are usually included in your employment contract or conditions. If you're hired from outside the region, your air ticket and other travel costs are often booked and paid for by your employer or his representative. In addition, you can usually claim any extra travel costs, e.g. the cost of transport to and from airports. If you travel to your new location by car, you can usually claim a mileage rate (actually a kilometre rate) or the equivalent air fare cost. Most employers pay your relocation costs up to a specified amount, although you may be required to sign a special contract which stipulates that if you resign before a certain period elapses (e.g. three to five years), you must repay a percentage of your removal costs, depending on your length of service.

An employer may pay a fixed relocation allowance based on your salary, position and the size of your family, or he may pay the total cost of removal. The allowance should be sufficient to move the contents of an average house (castles aren't usually catered for, except for upper level executives) and you must normally pay any excess costs yourself. If you don't want to ship your furniture to your new location, it may be possible to purchase furniture locally up to the limit of your allowance. For international relocations, it's common to receive an extra month's salary to cover incidentals, such as electrical equipment you will need to replace. Check with your employer. When they're liable for the total cost, companies may ask you to obtain two or three removal estimates.

Generally, you're required to organise and pay for the removal in advance. Your employer usually reimburses the equivalent amount after you've paid the bill, although it may be possible to get him to pay the bill directly or make a cash advance. If you change jobs within the Benelux region, your new employer may pay your relocation expenses when it's necessary for you to move house. Don't forget to ask, as they may not offer to pay (it may depend on how desperate they are to employ you).

Social Security

All Benelux employees, foreign nationals working in Benelux and the self-employed must enrol in the national social security system. There are a few exceptions, primarily for international civil servants (who have their own private insurance to replace the national social security plans, for which they aren't eligible). It may also be possible to remain in your home country's social security program while living in Benelux, if your employer acknowledges that you're on a temporary assignment and will be returning home within a year or two. Social security includes old age benefits (pension and disability), medical treatment, long-term care, unemployment and work accident insurance. There are special rules for people working in one country while living in another (as is often the case in Luxembourg), which allow you to choose between the system where you work and the system where you live. This choice may be influenced by your 'tax residence' status or the kind of benefits you're most likely to qualify for (see **Chapters 13** and **14**).

Contributions are usually calculated as a percentage of your gross income and are deducted at source by your employer. Most of the various 'contributions' (which are anything but voluntary) are at least partially paid by the employer and there are a few social charges that the employer pays entirely. Social security costs are high in all three countries (to cover the comprehensive and generous benefits available) and can easily total 30 to 40 per cent of your gross pay, including the portion paid by your employer. For details, see **Social Security** on page 228.

Health Insurance

Health insurance is mandatory for all workers in Belgium, Holland and Luxembourg and is considered a part of the social security system. All three countries are served by a combination of a national health service programme and private health insurers, although the interaction of these sectors works somewhat differently from one country to another. In Belgium and Luxembourg, the national health plan is mandatory and most people also carry private health coverage (often made available by employers) to reimburse them for the portion of fees not covered under the national plan. The Dutch national health care programme is mandatory for all workers up to a certain income level but only covers certain types of health care treatment, usually with a co-payment or deductible element. There is a second, optional level of health insurance available to deal with those services the basic system doesn't cover – mainly hospitalisation and major illnesses or serious injuries. Those who earn more than the threshold amount must carry private health insurance. For further information, see page 237.

Company Pension Fund

If you're working for a large international company, you may have the option to continue participation in the company pension plan while you're working in Benelux. Although the national social security systems include old age pensions, most Beneluxers provide for themselves through either a company or a private savings or insurance plan. For further information about private pension plans in Belgium, Holland or (especially) Luxembourg, see **Supplementary Pensions** on page 241.

Unemployment Insurance

Unemployment insurance is compulsory for all employees and is included in the various social security programmes. If you've been drawing unemployment benefit in another EU country, it's possible to receive your payments for up to three months while living in Benelux and looking for work there. For details see **Social Security** on page 228.

Salary Insurance

Employers in Benelux are required to pay you while you're off sick for at least 60 days, although in most employment contracts the period is six months. After that, salary insurance for sickness or accidents is included in your social security cover (see page 228).

Annual Holidays

Under the labour laws of each of the Benelux countries, all employees receive a holiday allowance equal to 20 working days (i.e. four weeks) per year, but the various collective agreements and local and industry practices mean that 25 working days (i.e. five weeks) is standard with most employers. Part-time employees receive a pro rata holiday allowance based on their normal working week. For example, if you normally work three days per week, your annual holiday allowance will be 15 days (five weeks at three days per week). Employers aren't allowed to count public holidays as annual holidays so, if a public holiday falls during your vacation period, you're entitled to an extra day off.

Some collective agreements provide for longer annual holidays or grant extra days to employees based on their age or length of service. In some industries, the collective agreement may also call for a summer shut-down when all or most employees are expected to take the largest block of their vacation time. Some businesses also close between Christmas and New Year, again requiring employees to use part of their holiday allowance unless they're needed to perform maintenance or other tasks during this time. Dates for company or plant shut-downs are normally posted well in advance on employee notice boards.

Be sure to ask about the process for requesting your desired holiday dates in advance, particularly if the bulk of your holiday time is already committed to business closure periods. There's often a formal process (including a special form) for submitting holiday requests, sometimes quite early in the year. Employees may be given priority for holiday leave based on seniority, age or family obligations (e.g. school schedules and spouses' vacation times).

You aren't normally permitted to take any holiday time at all while you're still in your probationary period and often you must complete at least six months or a year before you can begin to take the holidays you have accrued. In many companies, you accrue vacation time over a calendar year but may take the time you've accrued only in the next calendar year.

Public Holidays

Public holidays vary, as you might expect, from country to country, with Belgians and Luxemburgers entitled to up to ten paid holidays per year, while the Dutch must make do with seven to nine. The following is a list of the public holidays observed in the Benelux countries, where B indicates Belgium, NL Holland and L Luxembourg:

1st January	New Year's Day (B, NL, L)
February or March	Carnival (L)
March or April	Good Friday (NL)
March or April	Easter Monday (B, NL, L)
30th April	Queen's Birthday (NL)
1st May	Labour Day/May Day (B, L)
5th May	Liberation Day (NL)
May or June	Ascension (B, NL, L)
May or June	Whit Monday (B, NL, L)
23rd June	Luxembourgeois National Day (L)
21st July	Belgian National Day (B)
15th August	Assumption (B, L)
2nd September	Luxembourg City Fete (L city only)
1st November	All Saints' Day (B, L)
15th November	King's Day (B – government offices and banks)
25th December	Christmas Day (B, NL, L)
26th December	St. Stephen's Day/2nd day of Christmas (NL, L)

In Luxembourg, holidays falling on a Sunday are usually observed on the following Monday, but this is limited to two holidays each year. Belgian workers are entitled to an additional day off when holidays fall on a Sunday or other day not normally worked. The Dutch may simply drop holidays when they fall on a Saturday or Sunday, although this varies by company and industry.

Compassionate & Special Leave

Workers in most of the Benelux region have the right to time off with pay for a variety of family and personal events, including marriage (their own or that of a child), divorce, and the birth or death of a family member. Many companies also permit leave of absence with or without pay for professional or general education (see page 159), tending to sick family members and sabbaticals. The terms of such leave are normally included in your employment contract, terms of employment or collective agreements. Often you will need to submit proof of the event in order to claim your leave (or payment for the days you missed work). For example, you may be asked to submit a copy of a birth, death or marriage certificate in order to justify absences related to those events and to verify the relationship of the person involved.

Paid Expenses

Expenses paid by an employer are normally listed in your employment conditions. These often include travel costs from your home to your place of work, usually based on the cost of a monthly commuting pass for public transport or a kilometre allowance if you drive to work. Companies without an employee restaurant or canteen may pay a lunch allowance or provide luncheon vouchers. Expenses paid for travel on company business or for training and education are normally detailed in your employment conditions or listed in a separate document.

Probationary & Notice Periods

For most jobs there's a formal probationary period, lasting from a few days to a few months. During this trial period, an employment contract can be terminated by either side (meaning the new employee can quit or be sacked) with a minimum period of notice (seven days in Belgium) or (most often) no notice at all. The duration of the probationary period can be as short as seven days or as long as six months to a year depending on the level of the job, the salary and the classification of the employee. Generally, blue-collar jobs and trade workers have shorter probationary periods, lasting from one to four weeks, while white collar workers may be on probation for one to six months. High level executives and those earning particularly high salaries may have probationary periods of up to a year. Probationary periods can't be extended or renewed.

Once your trial period is over, you're subject to the local laws and customs concerning notice periods. Your notice period depends on your employer, profession and length of service and is usually stated in your employment contract and employment conditions. Termination of an employment contract must be made in writing and generally must be sent by registered letter, irrespective of which side is initiating the termination. An employee who wants to quit must normally give notice to the employer at least a month in advance. A severance payment is usually due on the termination of an 'indeterminate' employment contract, irrespective of who initiated the termination or the grounds for termination.

Belgium: Probationary periods can range from as little as seven days for manual workers to as long as a year for upper level executives or those earning a high salary. Even during the trial period, both employer and employee must give seven days' notice to terminate the contract with no financial penalty. After the probationary period, the employer and employee are free to agree on the appropriate notice period. If either side objects, the labour court uses a basic rule of 'three months for each commenced period of five years', which can be applied to both the notice period and the amount of severance pay, depending on the facts and circumstances of the particular case.

Holland: Probationary periods are optional in Holland and should be part of your employment contract. Either side can terminate the employment contract without notice during the trial period. After successful completion of a probationary period, customary notice to leave a job is one week for each year of service, up to a maximum of 13 weeks. Severance pay should be part of the original employment contract, but in the case of disputes the labour court will take all the facts and circumstances of the individual case into account, including the age of the employee, length of service and the likelihood of finding another job. Most defined term contracts don't include a severance benefit.

Luxembourg: Probationary periods are normally specified in collective agreements but may also be included in individual contracts. After completing their trial period, employees are required to give one to three months' notice to quit a job (depending on their length of service). Severance pay may be as little as one to three months' salary for industrial workers, or as much as one month's salary for each five years of service in other fields. There's normally a maximum severance of 12 months' salary for those with 30 or more years' service.

Education & Training

Employers in Benelux are often required either by law or under collective agreements to set aside a portion of their gross payroll or turnover for employee education and training. Works councils are often charged with reviewing the company training plan (including the part designated to provide special training for work council delegates!)

It's in your own interest to investigate courses of study, seminars and lectures that you feel will be of benefit to you and your employer. Most employers give reasonable consideration to a request to attend a course during working hours, provided you don't make it a full-time occupation. If you decide to pursue a formal degree or certification programme requiring several months' or years' study, your employer may agree to pay for the programme (including books, examinations and other costs) if you sign an agreement to reimburse him should you leave the company within a certain number of years after obtaining the qualification.

In Belgium, employees can take up to 240 hours of leave per year for professional training or 160 hours for general education. This leave is granted with pay, provided the employer approves both the timing and the course of study, and the employer is reimbursed up to certain limits by the employment ministry.

Pregnancy & Confinement

Women in the workforce are entitled to excellent employment benefits with regard to pregnancy and confinement, mostly administered under national social security plans. Paid maternity leave is guaranteed for all working women, irrespective of their length of service either with their current employer or in total. Belgium and Luxembourg offer a birth allowance and all three countries provide some form of family allowance, generally up to the age of 16, or under some circumstances up to the age of 25 for students ,e.g. in Holland.

Maternity leave is generally 16 weeks (15 weeks in Belgium), six weeks taken before the expected birth date and the rest after. You must notify your employer at least 21 days before you plan to start your maternity leave, although this can be waived or altered if there are medical reasons for doing so. Maternity benefits equal 100 per cent of your salary in Luxembourg and Holland. True to form, Belgium's system is more complex, paying 82 per cent of salary for the first 30 days and only 75 per cent thereafter. The difference can be covered by private health insurance.

Either parent has the right to unpaid 'child-rearing' leave of up to a year, after which they have the right to return to the same or a similar job at the same rate of pay and seniority as when they left. In practice, many people find it difficult to resume their career after a lengthy absence.

Part-time Job Restrictions

Restrictions on part-time employment are usually detailed in your employment conditions or contract. Most companies in Benelux don't allow full-time employees to work part time (i.e. moonlight) for another employer, particularly one in the same line of business. You may, however, be permitted to take a part-time teaching job or similar part-time employment (or you can write a book!). If you hold two or more part-time jobs, you may be required to notify each of your employers about your other jobs so that you don't exceed the legal limits for daily or weekly work time (and so that the authorities can ensure that you're paying the proper taxes and social charges!).

Changing Jobs & Confidentiality

Companies in a high-tech or highly confidential business may have restrictions on employees moving to a competitor in the Benelux region or within Europe. You should be aware of these restrictions, as they're enforceable under national and EU law, although it's a complex subject and disputes must often be resolved by a court of law. The laws regarding industrial secrets and employer confidentiality are strict but, like most labour law throughout Benelux, include considerable protection for the employee. If you breach this confidentiality, you will be dismissed and may be unable to find further employment in the region.

Acceptance of Gifts

Employees are normally forbidden to accept gifts of more than a certain value from customers or suppliers. Many suppliers give bottles of wine or small gifts at Christmas that don't breach this rule. (If you do accept a bribe, make sure that it's a big one and that you have a secret bank account and a secure get-away route!)

Retirement

Your employment conditions may be valid only until the official retirement age (in which case this will be noted in your employment contract). Retirement age varies from 60 to 65, depending on the industry and the country, but mandatory retirement based solely on age is not permitted. If you wish to continue working after you've reached retirement age, you may be required to negotiate a new employment contract (and you should also consider seeking psychiatric help!).

Dismissal

The rules governing dismissal and severance pay are complicated and generally depend on an employee's length of service, the reason for the dismissal (e.g. misconduct, redundancy) and whether the employee is subject to any special conditions, such as being on maternity leave or a member of a works council. After completing the probationary period of an indeterminate employment contract, an employee must be given the appropriate notice of termination, usually by registered letter specifying the grounds for the termination, the length of the notice period, official last day of employment and the amount of severance pay if this wasn't included in the original employment contract.

The notice period required from the employer is usually the same as that required when an employee quits (see **Probationary & Notice Periods** on page 53), except in Luxembourg, where a longer notice period for employer initiated terminations is sometimes required. In cases of termination for 'serious cause', the notice period can be waived or, as in Belgium, reduced to as little as three days. In any case, your employer can simply continues to pay your salary during the notice period without your needing to show up for work (if you can persuade him to do so!). Severance pay is normally based on the number of years' service but may be increased by the labour courts according to your circumstances (e.g. age, family situation, and the likelihood of your finding further employment). Usually, an employer will have to make some sort of severance payment even where he's sacking someone for serious cause, and in most cases the employer must notify the local or regional labour office before terminating any permanent employee. There's usually no severance payment at the end of a limited contract unless the contract is terminated early.

Union Membership & Workers' Councils

Nearly all workers in the Benelux countries are free to join, participate in or even form their own trade unions. There are no 'closed shops' and employers may not discriminate against workers for belonging to or not belonging to a trade union. Union membership is among the highest in Europe, although the Benelux region loses very little time to strikes and other industrial action, and labour relations are generally cordial.

Belgium: Roughly 60 per cent of Belgian workers (including the unemployed) belong to a union. Unions in Belgium are independent but are often linked to the major political parties. Every two years, unions and employers, through their respective federations, negotiate a nationwide agreement that sets the framework for local, plant and branch level contract talks. This national agreement normally sets a limit or range for pay increases, cost of living adjustments and terms for programmes of job creation or security. There are only a few categories of workers which aren't legally entitled to strike, but strikes are rare in Belgium and labour relations are generally good.

Employers with more than 100 staff must establish a works council (*conseil d'entreprise/ondernemingsraad*), which meets at least monthly with management to discuss work-related issues as well as the general business conditions of the enterprise. Workers are entitled to receive detailed information about the company, and the works council can (and often does) appoint its own auditor to review the accounts. There's no legal requirement for worker representation on the corporate board.

Holland: Union membership in Holland is relatively low for the region, accounting for only around 30 per cent of the workforce, but union agreements cover nearly three-quarters of all workers. There are three major federations of unions, which serve on the Social and Economic Council, an official advisory board to the Dutch government, along with the major employer organisations. Strikes are prohibited only for civil servants (who are nevertheless permitted to belong to unions), but strike action is rare.

Any company with more than 35 employees must have a works council (*ondernemingsraad*) and management must meeting with the entire workforce at least twice a year to discuss issues of concern to the enterprise and its employees.

Luxembourg: Around 60 per cent of the workforce in Luxembourg are union members. The unions are independently organised but belong to federations, which may be linked to the major political parties. The right to strike is extended to all categories of employees except government workers who provide 'essential services'. Legally, a strike can be called only after a lengthy conciliation process, and the National Conciliation Office must certify that all efforts at conciliation have failed before workers can take to the picket lines. As in the rest of Benelux, strike action is extremely rare.

All employers with at least 15 employees must have a works council, which represents the employees in collective bargaining situations and meets on a regular basis with management. Companies with more than 150 employees must establish a works council consisting of equal numbers of workers and managers. In companies with more than 1,000 employees, the workers must have an employee representative on the board of directors.

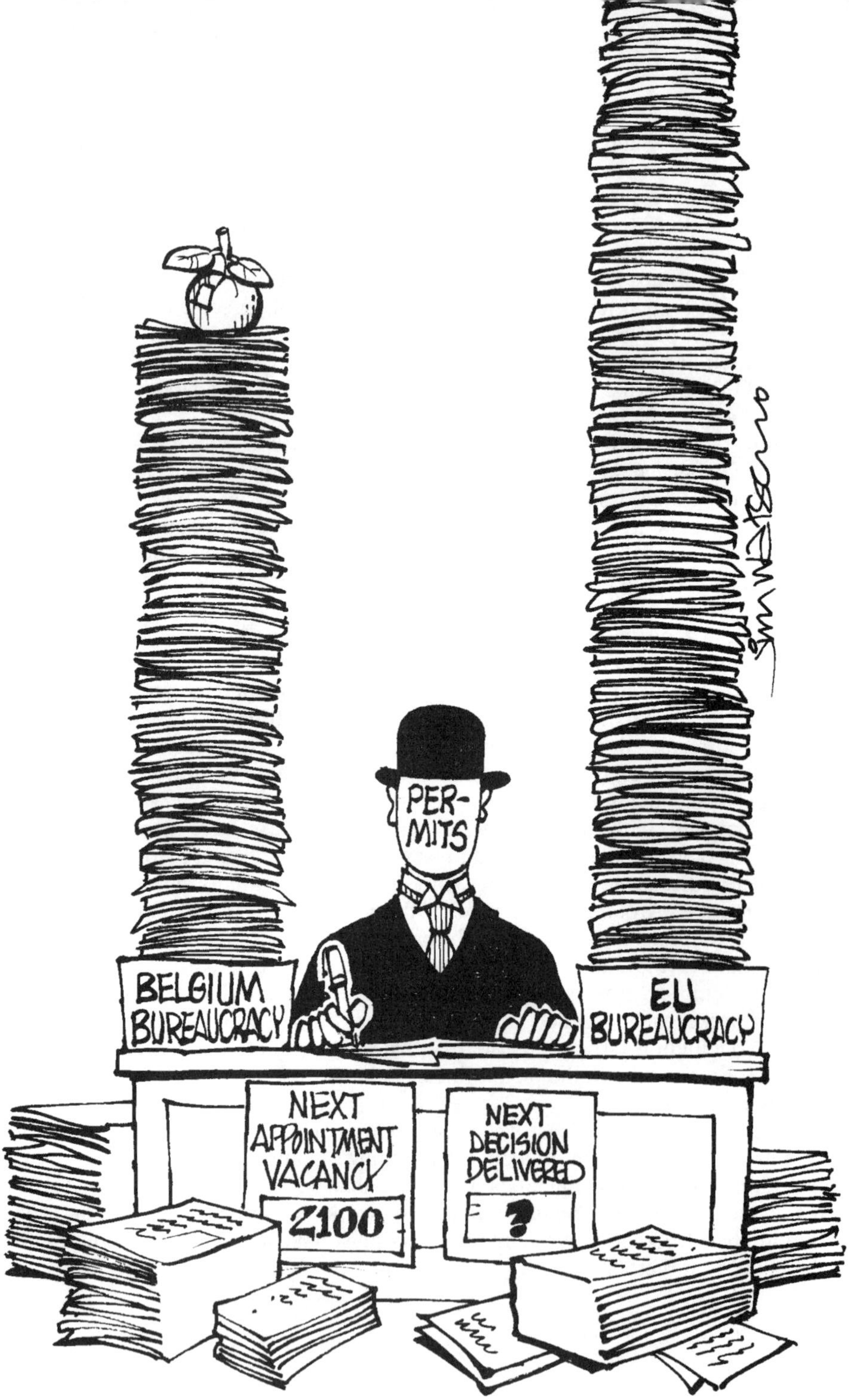
PER-
MITS
BELGIUM
BUREAUCRACY
EU
BUREAUCRACY
NEXT
APPOINTMENT
VACANCY
2100
NEXT
DECISION
DELIVERED
?

3.

PERMITS & VISAS

Bureaucracy anywhere can be confusing and apparently without rhyme or reason, and the Benelux countries are no exception – in fact, as the seat of the European Union, some might say they're the undisputed champions of the art form. If you plan to stay in Belgium, Holland or Luxembourg longer than three months, you must follow the regulations for obtaining a residence permit and, if necessary, a work permit.

EU nationals don't require a visa or a work permit to enter any of the Benelux countries to look for work. However, you should be aware of the regulations regarding registering with the local authorities as a resident foreigner and the requirements for carrying official identification at all times.

Immigration is a sensitive issue throughout Europe, particularly so in the Benelux region. Although the three nations have excellent reputations for their acceptance and treatment of refugees and asylum seekers, there are still serious social and cultural problems related to immigration, not the least of which is the popularity of Belgium and Holland as staging areas for those attempting to enter the UK illegally. Immigration and customs officials in all three countries have wide-ranging powers and plenty of experience in dealing with drug smugglers, illegal immigrants, human traffickers and much worse! Immigration is a complex and ever-changing subject and the information in this chapter is intended only as a general guide. You shouldn't base any decisions or actions on the information contained herein without confirming it with an official and reliable source, such as a consulate or embassy.

APOSTILLES

One of the first bits of bureaucracy you're likely to run into is the need to have foreign documents 'legalised'. Certain countries have traditionally required the relevant embassy or consulate to verify the validity of all foreign documents, such as birth certificates, marriage and death certificates and certain types of commercial papers, before they can be accepted locally. In 1961, the Hague Convention established the *apostille* as the official means of validating foreign documents, and in Benelux you will find that local officials will often expect you to obtain an *apostille* when submitting any form of official paperwork originating outside the Benelux countries (in addition to a translation of the document!).

An *apostille* is a numbered and dated certificate, sometimes referred to as a 'stamp' owing to its size and shape, which is attached to an official copy of the document by the issuing government. If you need to have a document, e.g. your birth certificate, legalised, you should send it to the appropriate government agency in the country where it was issued, requesting an *apostille*. **You must specify that you require an *apostille***, as there are other methods of legalising documents but only an *apostille* meets the requirements of the Hague Convention and is acceptable within Belgium or Holland. Luxembourg doesn't generally require you to obtain *apostilles* – perhaps because they're more used to dealing with foreigners and foreign documents. Some governments will legalise documents free, some require only a postage paid return envelope, while others charge a fee (although under the Convention this fee is supposed to be 'reasonable').

For documents originating in the UK, there's a charge of £12. Documents should be sent via registered mail to: The Legalisation Office, 20 Victoria Street, London,

SW1H 0NZ. In Ireland, documents should be sent to the Department of Foreign Affairs, Consular Section, 80 St. Stephen's Green, Dublin 2 with the fee of IR£10. Both Australia and the United States require you to have documents legalised by the state that issued the document, rather than by a national agency. Contact your local embassy or consulate for details of fees and for the addresses of the appropriate government agencies. Further information about *apostilles* is available from expatriate organisations in Belgium and Holland, and from embassy websites.

VISAS

Whether or not you need a visa to enter Belgium, Holland or Luxembourg depends on a variety of factors: your nationality, the length of your intended stay, the reason for your visit or stay and what other documents you've applied for or received. Nationals of the 15 European Union countries don't need a visa to enter any of the Benelux countries, whether for a short or long stay. You are, however, subject to various registration requirements, particularly if you're staying longer than 90 days (see **Residence Permits** on page 63). Nationals of other countries may or may not be subject to visa requirements (welcome to the wonderful world of bureaucracy!). The embassy or consulate of the country you're going to is usually the best source of information, but the regulations are complicated and subject to change, and consular officials aren't always entirely *au fait* with the latest interpretations or nuances. Don't be surprised if you receive confusing or even contradictory information from different officials, or if you're asked to provide documents or information in addition to the general requirements listed here.

All three countries are signatories of the Schengen agreement (signed in Schengen, Luxembourg), which permits free movement within the EU member countries, currently Austria, Belgium, France, Germany, Greece, Italy, Luxembourg, Holland, Portugal and Spain. Each member nation retains the right to refuse to allow you to enter, even with a valid visa, for any number of reasons including 'just cause' (which can sometimes be interpreted as 'just 'cause we don't like the look of you'). However, unless you're obviously carrying drugs or other contraband or act as though you may be smuggling in refugees or illegal immigrants, you probably won't even have to slow down as you cross the various Schengen borders.

For visits of up to 90 days within any six month period, tourists from North and South America, most non-EU European countries and many Pacific Rim countries don't require a visa. If you're going to any of the Benelux countries to conduct business or engage in a remunerated activity, even for a short period, you should check with the consulate to see whether some form of business visa or professional card (see page 66) is required. If you're a non-EU resident staying in Benelux longer than 90 days, you must have a visa stamped in your passport before you enter the country and should apply in person to your local consulate or embassy long before leaving home.

Short-stay Visa: For those who require a visa for stays of up to 90 days, the most common type of visa issued is the Schengen visa, which allows you freedom of movement within the ten nations of the Schengen agreement. You must apply for the visa of the country that is your primary destination during your stay, i.e. either where you will be staying the longest or, in some cases, the country where you will enter the

Schengen zone. Requirements for a Schengen visa vary slightly from country to country, but generally include: a passport valid at least three months past your intended departure date, an application form and one or more current photographs, proof of the purpose of your stay, confirmed lodging, sufficient funds to cover the costs of your stay and a return airline ticket. Processing the application can take a month or more, so plan accordingly.

Long-stay or Resident Visa: Nationals of Iceland, Liechtenstein, Monaco, Norway and Switzerland don't require a long-stay visa for stays of over 90 days unless they're planning to work or start a business. Citizens of all other non-EU countries must apply for a long-stay visa at the appropriate consulate or embassy in their country of residence and must have the visa stamped in their passport before travelling. Visas cannot be obtained or changed once you're in a Benelux country.

To apply for a long-stay visa, you will need a passport that's valid for at least three months beyond the first anniversary of your intended arrival date plus some or all of the following documents:

- a legalised birth certificate (i.e. with *apostille* – see above) and translation for each member of your family;
- legalised (*apostille*) copies of marriage or divorce certificates with translations, as applicable;
- a medical certificate from an approved doctor (the consulate or embassy will give you a list);
- the completed application form(s);
- passport-type photos (one to six or more, depending on the circumstances);
- a work permit (if you're planning to work) or evidence that your employer has applied for a work permit for you;
- evidence of eligibility to practise your trade in the country (if you're self-employed, a journalist or in some other regulated profession) or a professional card (see page 66), which serves as a work permit for some self-employed trades;
- a police report (sometimes called a 'certificate of good conduct');
- proof of financial resources (if you aren't going to take up employment);
- proof of health insurance;
- if a student, evidence of admission from an approved educational establishment;
- if an au pair, a copy of your agreement with a host family.

If you require a visa to enter the country and attempt to do so without one, you will be refused entry. Note that all three Benelux countries generally require you to have a work permit or evidence that your employer has applied for one on your behalf before you can even apply for a long-stay visa or residence permit (see below). If you're in doubt as to whether you require a visa, enquire at the appropriate consulate before making any travel plans. Long-stay visa applications often take at least three months to be approved and can take much longer.

Belgium: Of the three Benelux countries, Belgium probably takes the prize for having the most complex and detailed visa requirements. There are several different sorts of residence visas (which is the Belgian term for all long-stay visas), depending on whether you're coming to Belgium for employment, to retire or to join your spouse or other family members. It's possible to obtain a residence visa if you're going to Belgium to marry or live in a stable relationship with a Belgian citizen or someone already legally residing in Belgium, but there are additional documents you must submit with your visa application, including evidence that the person already in Belgium is able to support a foreign spouse or partner.

If you're going to Belgium for employment and aren't from the EU, your prospective employer must apply for a work permit first; once that has been issued, you can apply for your residence visa. **The Belgian embassy advises that the visa process can take up to a year**, so don't buy your travel tickets until your visa has been approved. A good place to check current information on visa requirements is official websites (🖳 www.belgium-emb.org or www.diplobel.org).

Holland: To apply for an MVV (*Machtiging voor Voorlopig Verblijf* or provisional residence permit), you must have a letter of intention from your employer verifying that he has applied for your work permit. If you're going to Holland for any other reason, you must provide proof that you have adequate funds to support yourself or that the partner or family member you're joining is able and willing to support you. Once the Ministry of Justice and Foreign Affairs is convinced that you meet the requirements for a long-stay visa, your local Dutch consulate or embassy will be authorised to issue your MVV. This is actually a temporary residence permit, which gives you the right to apply for a full residence permit when you arrive in Holland (see below). Waiting time for MVVs varies from three months to a year, although if you (or your employer) are using a Dutch-based relocation company, the paperwork can sometimes be expedited.

Luxembourg: A long-stay visa is known as a provisional residence permit (*autorisation de séjour provisoire*), which you must apply for at an embassy or consulate in your home country (or country of residence). The embassies and consulates of Belgium and Holland, as well as some other Schengen countries, are usually able to issue long-stay visas for Luxembourg if there's no Luxembourg diplomatic mission in your area.

RESIDENCE PERMITS & IDENTITY CARDS

All three Benelux countries maintain registers of foreigners living within their borders, and in most cases it's wise to register with the local commune or police and obtain a foreigner identity card even if you aren't required to have one.

Belgium: All foreign nationals coming to Belgium for a stay of more than 90 days must obtain a residence permit. An EU national is granted a temporary residence permit valid for three to five months, which can be renewed for a further three months once you've found a job and been registered with the Belgian Social Security system. You may then apply for an identity card and to be officially registered in the foreign population register. To obtain a temporary residence permit, simply register at the town hall of the commune where you're staying within three days of your arrival in Belgium.

Non EU-nationals must register with their local commune within eight days of their arrival in Belgium, even if they're living in temporary accommodation. You will need your residence visa to qualify for a temporary residence permit. Within two weeks of moving to a permanent residence, you must apply for a foreigner identity card and to be officially registered in the foreign population register.

To apply for your identity card, whether you're an EU national or not, you and family members over the age of 21 must go to the town hall in person to register. Children under the age of 12 will be issued with a 'name card', while children between the ages of 12 and 15 can apply for a child's card or an adult identity card. To apply for an identity card, each applicant needs three passport-size photos, a medical certificate, a police certificate (*certificat de bonne vie*), plus a work permit and visa if you're a non-EU national. The charge for the application varies from commune to commune, but is usually around €7.50. In some communes you may have to be fingerprinted.

All residents of Belgium over the age of 12 are required to carry their identity cards with them at all times. Although random ID checks are no longer permitted under Belgian law, a police officer can ask to see your identity card if he has 'reasonable cause' to suspect you of having committed a crime. If you can't produce your card, you can be held under 'administrative arrest' for up to 12 hours until your identity and your right to be in Belgium can be officially established. Children under the age of 12 must have their name cards with them (usually carried in a plastic envelope worn around their necks) any time they aren't with their parents. While you're waiting for your identity card to be issued, it's sensible to carry your passport with you at all times. Foreigner identity cards are renewable every year, and you must apply for a new card within eight days of moving home, even within the same commune.

Holland: All foreigners resident in Holland must register with the Aliens Police (*vreemdelingenpolitie*) within three days of their arrival, including EU nationals. The Aliens Police will register your presence and issue you with one or more forms that are required to apply for a residence permit and other formalities of Dutch life. Non-EU nationals must then apply to their local town hall for a residence permit. It's sensible for EU nationals to obtain a residence permit, even if it isn't mandatory, as this can simplify the process of applying for other services that require you to establish your legal status in the country.

To apply for a residence permit you will need some or all of the following documents: a passport (preferably valid for the duration of your stay or at least one month beyond the expiry date of the residence permit), two passport-size photos, birth and marriage certificates for all family members living with you (with *apostille*, if necessary), evidence of health insurance, proof of employment, rental agreement or other proof of your place of residence, and proof that you've registered with the Aliens Police. Residence permits (*D-document*) are issued for one year at a time, and you should apply to renew your permit at least four weeks before it expires. The Aliens Police generally send you a renewal application around six weeks before the expiry date, but it's up to you to contact them if you don't receive a form. To renew a residence permit, you must produce a passport that's valid for at least one month beyond the end of the renewal period. After five years of annual residence permits, you will be eligible to apply for a five-year permission to remain (*Vergunning tot verstiging*).

Luxembourg: In Luxembourg, all foreigners (including EU nationals) must register with the communal administration within three days of their arrival. If you're planning to stay in Luxembourg for more than a year, you must apply for a foreigners' identity card. When you register with your commune, you will be given an application form for an identity card along with a list of the documents required. These generally include: a passport containing your long-stay visa (provisional residence permit), a work permit or proof of adequate support, three passport-size photos, medical certificate, certificate of change of address from your previous place of residence, police report and a tax stamp.

Tax stamps must be obtianed from an office of the *Administration des Enregistrements et Domaines*, a department of the Ministry of Finance generally referred to simply as *l'Enregistrement*. There isn't an office in every town, but your town hall will advise you where the nearest office is. EU nationals are entitled to a free tax stamp. Citizens of the Americas, Singapore and Hong Kong are charged around €10. Nationals of all other countries pay around €30.

It can take up to a year for your identity card to be issued, and the local police may call on you to ask some routine questions or verify information, such as your salary. As in Belgium, everyone over the age of 15 must carry an identity card or passport at all times to prove their legal status or residence in the country. If you move house within Luxembourg, you must apply to have your identity card updated, and it's your responsibility to make sure you renew your card well in advance of its expiry date.

WORK PERMITS

EU nationals don't require work permits to find employment in Belgium, Holland or Luxembourg, or anywhere within the European Union for that matter. Non-EU nationals must have a work permit, usually applied for by their potential employer, in order to be legally entitled to work in the country. All three Benelux countries generally require you to have a work permit or evidence that your employer has applied for one on your behalf *before* you can apply for a residence permit or long-stay visa.

Belgium: There are three types of work permit in Belgium:

● **C permits** are valid for only one year, allowing the holder to work for multiple employers. They're usually issued to migrant agricultural or domestic workers and generally aren't renewable.

● **B permits** are valid for one employer and run for one year, after which they can be renewed (by the same employer, usually for the same job or job classification). If you change employers, your new employer must apply for a new B permit. You may find that you have to return to your home country and re-apply for a residence visa before you can start your new job! Once you've renewed a B permit four or more times, i.e. have lived and worked in Belgium for five years on the same permit, you can receive an unlimited A permit.

● **A permits** allow you to work for any employer in Belgium for an unlimited period of time. They're issued only to the following categories of applicant: the spouse of an A permit holder; the non-EU spouse of a Belgian national; the non-EU spouse of an EU national legally resident in Belgium; any foreigner with five years' uninterrupted (legal) residency in Belgium.

The B permit is the standard form of work permit for most foreigners. Applying for a B permit is the responsibility of the employer wishing to hire a non-EU foreigner. You must give your potential employer a certificate of health and three passport-size photos, which he then submits along with a copy of the proposed employment contract to the Ministry of Labour. Before issuing the work permit, the Ministry of Labour must determine that there's no Belgian or other EU national who can fill the position and they may send the employer candidates for the job from their lists of Belgians drawing unemployment benefit. (In the case of managerial positions, the permit is usually granted with little or no question.) It can take up to 12 weeks for a B permit to be granted.

Self-employed professionals from outside the EU must apply for a professional card (*carte professionelle/beroepskaart*) in order to work in Belgium. A professional card can be issued for a period of five years. You will need a passport, medical certificate and a police certificate (*certificat de bonne vie et moeurs/bewijs van goed gedrag en zeden*) in addition to proof of your qualifications in your profession. Be sure to check with a Belgian embassy or consulate in your home country, as some professions require evidence that you're already established in your field. For example, to qualify for a professional card as a journalist, you must produce press credentials and be eligible for a Belgian national press card; to qualify as a freelance writer, you will need to submit copies of published works and evidence of your income from freelancing over the past few years.

Holland: In Holland, the employer must submit an application for a work permit at least six weeks before you're due to start work and must prove that he has tried for at least five weeks to find a qualified Dutch or EU national for the position. It's almost impossible for a non-EU national to obtain a work permit for unskilled labour or non-executive jobs. The work permit is issued to the employer rather than to the employee and, when the work permit is granted, the Ministry of Labour notifies the Dutch embassy or consulate where the employee has submitted his visa application to confirm that the visa can be issued. The first work permit is issued for a period of one year. At least five weeks before the permit expires, the employer must apply to renew the permit, which is then valid for three and a half years. Once you've worked in Holland for three years continuously on the same work permit (i.e. for the same employer), you no longer require a work permit and are free to change jobs or employers.

It's essential that you register with the Aliens Police when you arrive in Holland (see **Residence Permits & Identity Cards** on page 63), as it's the Aliens Police who notify social security that you've taken up residence and are thus eligible to receive your SoFi number (see page 228). When you register, you will be given a form, which you must take to your local tax office, with your passport and a copy of your work permit (if you're required to have one). It generally takes about two months for the tax office to issue your SoFi number, and you cannot be paid until you have it.

Luxembourg: In Luxembourg, it's recommended that application for your work permit be submitted 'several months' before you start work. The Ministry of Labour requires proof that an employer has tried to find an EU national for the position and may submit candidates of its own from the local unemployment rolls. Under most circumstances, it's difficult to obtain a work permits for non-EU nationals for anything less than a managerial post.

Work permit rules don't apply to self-employed people, but you must obtain permission from the Ministry of Small and Medium-size Businesses (*Minstère des Classes moyennes*) in order to operate any sort of business or trade in the Duchy (see page 34). To obtain permission, you must submit documentation relating to the incorporation of the business or the setting up of a company or partnership, a resume of your professional qualifications and a certificate of solvency to show not only that you can make a living from your business, but that you've already done so in another country. You must re-apply for your business permit if the nature of your business changes.

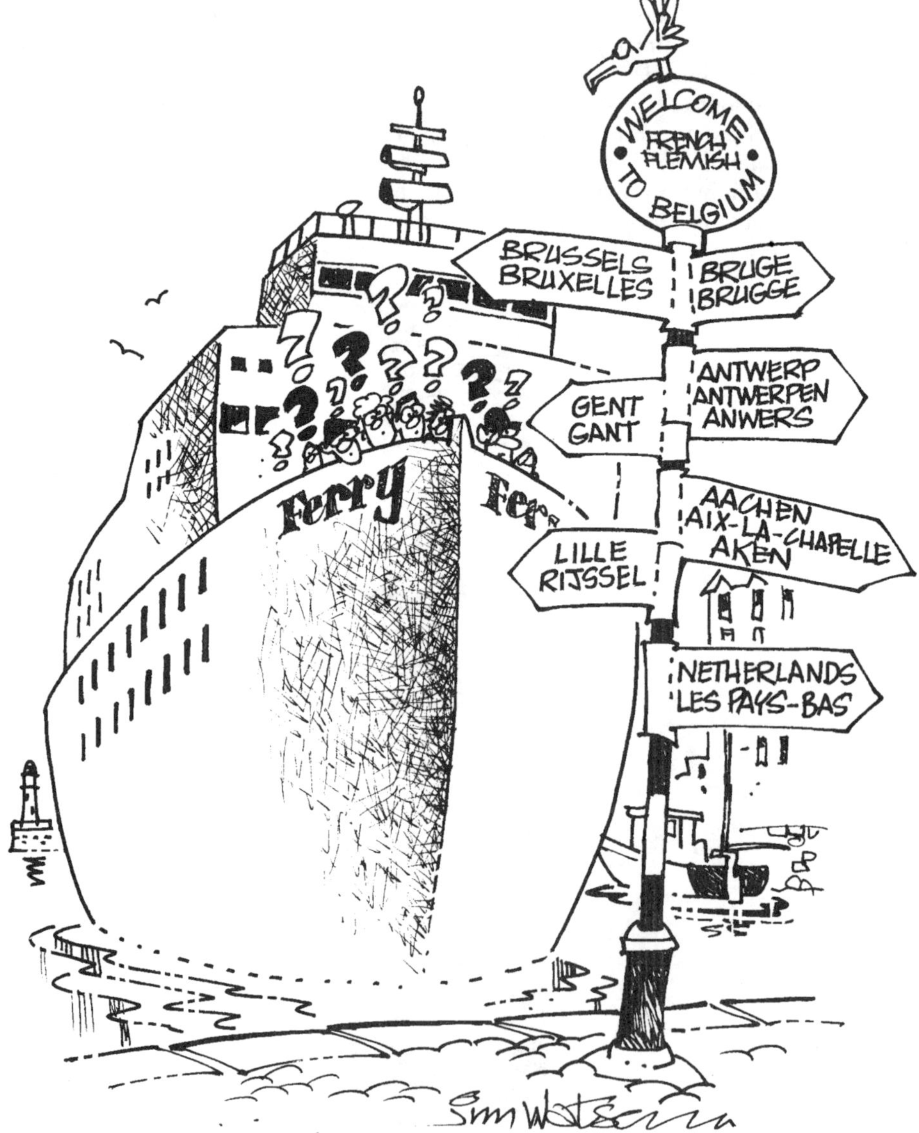
WELCOME
FRENCH
FLEMISH
TO BELGIUM
BRUSSELS
BRUXELLES
BRUGE
BRUGGE
ANTWERP
ANTWERPEN
ANWERS
GENT
GANT
AACHEN
AIX-LA-CHAPELLE
AKEN
LILLE
RIJSSEL
NETHERLANDS
LES PAYS-BAS
Ferry
Fer

4.

ARRIVAL

On arrival in Belgium, Holland or Luxembourg, your first task will be to negotiate immigration and customs. Fortunately, this presents few problems for most people, particularly citizens of member countries of the European Union (EU), Iceland, Liechtenstein and Norway (collectively known as the European Economic Area or EEA). Non-EEA nationals coming to Benelux for any purpose other than a short visit usually require a visa (see **Chapter 3**).

IMMIGRATION

All three Benelux nations are signatories to the Schengen agreement (named after a Luxembourg village on the Moselle River where the agreement was signed), which came into effect on 1st January 1995 and introduced an open-border policy between member countries. Other Schengen signatories are Austria, France, Germany, Greece, Iceland, Italy, Portugal, Spain and Sweden. Under the agreement, immigration checks and passport controls take place when you first arrive in a member country, after which you may travel freely between countries in the Schengen Zone. Therefore, when you arrive in any of the Benelux countries from another Schengen country, there are usually no immigration checks or passport controls such as those you will encounter when you arrive from outside the EU.

If you're a non-EU national arriving by sea or air from outside the EU, you must go through immigration for non-EU citizens. If you have a long-stay or residence visa, it will be cancelled (i.e. stamped with your date of entry) by an immigration official so that you can prove your date of entry when you register with local authorities. Be sure to ask for your passport or visa to be stamped on entry if you're planning to take up residence, as it can be difficult later on to prove that you entered the country legally if it isn't!

CUSTOMS

The Single European Act, which came into effect on 1st January 1993, created a single trading market and changed the rules regarding customs (*douane* – same word in French and Dutch) for EU nationals. The shipment of personal (household) effects to Belgium, Holland or Luxembourg from another EU country is no longer subject to customs formalities, although it's sensible to have an inventory of the items you're bringing with you. Those arriving in Benelux from outside the EU (including EU citizens) are still subject to customs checks and limitations on what may be imported duty-free, as outlined below.

Visitors

Visitors' belongings aren't subject to VAT when they're visiting Benelux for up to 90 days. This applies to the importation of private cars, camping vehicles (including trailers and caravans), motorcycles, aircraft, boats and personal effects. Goods may be imported without formality provided their nature and quantity doesn't imply any commercial aim. All goods, including vehicles and personal effects, imported duty-free mustn't be sold or given away in the Benelux region and must be re-exported before the end of the 90-day period.

If you enter any of the Benelux countries by road, you may drive through the border without stopping – in fact you may find it difficult to determine exactly where the border is, as many border posts have been dismantled and even the signs have been removed. However, any goods or animals that you're carrying must fall within the exemptions and mustn't be the subject of any prohibition or restriction. Note that customs officials can stop anyone for a spot check, e.g. searching for drugs or illegal immigrants, anywhere in the country and not just at the borders.

Non-EU Residents

If you're a non-EU resident planning to take up permanent or temporary residence in Belgium, Holland or Luxembourg, you're permitted to import your furniture and personal effects, including vehicles, motor homes, pleasure boats and aircraft, provided that you've owned and used them for at least six months prior to your move. If you've owned an item for less than six months and it was purchased within the EU, you may still import it duty-free provided you produce a value added tax (VAT) receipt; if it was purchased outside the EU, VAT must be paid on import.

If you're using an international mover or removal company to ship your household goods, they will be able to provide you with the forms you need to declare your goods for import. In addition, the removal agency will arrange for a customs broker to handle most of the formalities when your shipment arrives. If you're shipping your possessions yourself, you will need to contact the local customs office before your shipment arrives for information and forms for claiming an exemption from VAT. In most cases, you will be required to show that you've registered with the local authorities and have properly applied for a residence permit and identity card. You also need to provide a detailed list of the items you're importing for your personal use, including dates of purchase and current values or prices paid. Your shipments of personal goods must arrive within six months (in Belgium) or a year (Holland and Luxembourg) of your arrival to be exempt from tax. In Holland, you must apply in advance to the customs office that has jurisdiction over the town where you will be living. The Customs Directorate (*Directie Douane*) in Rotterdam publishes a booklet entitled *Moving to Holland* explaining the procedure. Contact Tax and Customs Administration, Customs Directorate, Postbus 50964, 3007 BG Rotterdam (☎ 010-290 4901).

Used cars and other vehicles can normally be imported without payment of VAT, provided you can produce proof that you've owned the car (i.e. it has been registered it in your name) for at least a year. Once you've imported your belongings into the country on a tax-exempt basis, you may not sell or give away any of the items within a year after import.

Not all items can be exempted from incoming taxes, even if they're part of your shipment of possessions. Alcohol and tobacco products may be subject to duty. Jewellery, precious antiques and works of art may be subject to special regulations or restrictions, and you should keep copies of all documents of purchase, sale or appraisal of such items to show to customs officials. There are specific regulations concerning the import of weapons (particularly firearms) and ammunition, which must be properly licensed and registered with local police. Certain kinds of plants and animals may require prior approval and health certificates.

Detailed information regarding customs regulations is available from customs offices and through embassies and consulates of Benelux countries abroad.

RESIDENCE PERMITS

All foreigners residing in Belgium, Holland or Luxembourg for longer than 90 days must register with appropriate local authorities (see **Residence Permits and Identity Cards** on page 63) within a few days of their arrival. In Belgium and Luxembourg, you must register at the local town hall or communal administration office and apply for a residence permit/foreigner's national identity card. (This applies to EU and non-EU nationals alike.) On arrival in Holland, all foreigners must register with the local Aliens Police, unless they're staying in a hotel. Non-EU nationals must then apply at the town hall for a residence permit (which is also recommended for EU nationals, although it isn't required). If you're going to be working in Holland, you will also need to apply for a SoFi (social security) number at the tax office so that you can get paid (see page 228).

EMBASSY REGISTRATION

Nationals of some countries are required to register with their local embassy or consulate as soon as possible after arrival in Benelux (or in any foreign country). Even where this isn't mandatory, embassies usually like to keep a record of their nationals who are resident in the country (it helps to justify their existence). Note that embassies and consulates can often be a good source of information and, if you have a problem with local bureaucracy, they can be contacted for help and advice.

FINDING HELP

One of the main difficulties facing new arrivals in any country is how and where to obtain help with day-to-day problems, e.g. finding a home, schooling, insurance and so on. This book was written in response to this need. However, in addition to the comprehensive information provided herein, you will also require detailed local information. How successful you are in finding help depends on your employer, the town or area where you live, your nationality, your language proficiency and your sex (women are better served than men through numerous women's clubs). There's a wealth of information available in local languages, although it isn't usually designed for foreigners and their particular needs. The offerings in English and other foreign languages usually aren't as extensive, although in the Benelux region you should have little or no trouble finding English guides and other material (particularly in 'international' cities such as Brussels, The Hague and Amsterdam). You may find that your friends and colleagues can help, as they're often able to proffer advice based on their own experiences and mistakes. But be careful: although they mean well, you're likely to receive as much false and conflicting information as accurate and helpful advice. (It won't necessarily be wrong, but may be invalid for your circumstances.)

Your community is usually an excellent source of reliable information, but you will probably need to speak one of the local languages to benefit from it. Some companies may have a department or staff whose job is to help new arrivals settle in, or they may contract this task out to a relocation company. Unfortunately, many employers in Belgium, Holland and Luxembourg seem totally unaware of (or uninterested in) the problems and difficulties faced by their foreign employees.

If a woman lives in or near a major town, she's able to turn to many English-language women's clubs and organisations for help. The single foreign male (who, of course, cannot possibly have any problems) must usually fend for himself, although there are men's expatriate clubs in some areas and mixed social clubs throughout the region. Among the best sources of information and help for women are the American Women's Clubs (AWC) located in Brussels, Antwerp, Rotterdam, The Hague, Amsterdam and Luxembourg city. AWC clubs provide comprehensive information in English about both local matters and topics of more general interest. Many provide data sheets, booklets, publications and orientation programmes for newcomers in the area. They also provide tips for local expatriates on their websites. Membership of the clubs is sometimes limited to Americans or those with active links to the US (e.g. through study, work or a spouse who works for a US company or the US government), but most publications and orientation programmes are available to others for a small fee. AWC clubs are part of the Federation of American Women's Clubs Overseas (FAWCO), which can be contacted through their website (💻 www. fawco.org).

In addition to the above, there are many social clubs and other organisations for foreigners in Benelux with members who can help you find your way around. They may be difficult to locate, as small clubs run by volunteers often operate out of the president's house and they rarely bother to advertise or take out a telephone directory listing. The Brussels area and The Hague, in particular, host a wide range of expatriate clubs and associations related to the diplomatic presence in those two cities. Many embassies and consulates provide information about clubs for their own nationals, and many businesses (particularly large multinational companies) produce booklets and leaflets containing useful information about local clubs and activities. There are even online expatriate clubs that offer a chance to meet and exchange information with other expatriates in the area and around the world. The Expatica website (💻 www.expatica.com) covers expatriate life in Belgium and Holland with a series of articles and interviews on some of the more unusual and 'challenging' aspects of living in a foreign country (as well as standard information).

CHECKLISTS

Before Arrival

The following list contains a summary of the tasks that should (if possible) be completed before your arrival in Belgium, Holland or Luxembourg:

- Obtain a visa, if necessary, for you and all your family members (see **Chapter 3**). Obviously this must be done before your arrival in Benelux.

- Find temporary or permanent accommodation and buy a car if you will need one. If you purchase a car in Benelux, you must register it and arrange insurance (see **Chapter 11**).

- If possible, visit your destination country before moving to compare communities and schools, and arrange for schooling for your children (see **Chapter 9**).

- Arrange shipment of your personal effects.

- Arrange health insurance for yourself and your family. This is essential if you aren't already covered by a private insurance policy and won't be covered automatically through your employer.

- Open a bank account and transfer funds. (You can open an account with some Benelux banks from abroad, even via the Internet.) It's best to obtain some local currency (euros from 1st January 2002) before your arrival, as this will save you having to spend time changing money on arrival.

- Collect and update personal records including medical, dental, school, insurance (e.g. car insurance), professional and employment (including job and bank references).

- Obtain an international driving licence, if necessary.

- Obtain an international credit or charge card, which will prove invaluable during your first few months in your new location.

Don't forget to bring all your family's official documents including birth certificates, driving licences, marriage certificate, divorce papers or death certificate (if a widow or widower), educational diplomas, professional certificates and job references, school records and student ID cards, employment references, medical and dental records, bank account and credit card details, insurance policies, and receipts for any valuables. You also need the documents necessary to obtain a residence permit (see page 63) plus certified copies, official translations and numerous passport-size photographs (students should take at least a dozen). Have the documents legalised, if necessary or make sure you know where to send documents for an *apostille* (see page 60) and how much the service costs.

After Arrival

The following list contains a summary of tasks to be completed after arrival in a Benelux country (if not done before):

- If you don't own a car, you may wish to rent one for a week or two until you buy one locally.

- Open a post office (see page 107) or bank account (see page 252) and give the details to your employer in order to get paid.

- Register at your local town hall (and with the Aliens Police if you're in Holland) within the first few days of arrival (see page 72).

- In Holland, make sure to apply for your social security (SoFi) number at the local tax office. You can't be paid until you have this and it takes about two months to obtain (see page 228).

- Register with your local embassy or consulate (see page 72).

- Arrange schooling for your children (see **Chapter 9**).

- Arrange whatever insurance is necessary (see **Chapter 13**) including:
  - health insurance for yourself and your family, if not taken care of by your employer (see page 234);
  - home contents insurance (see page 241);
  - car insurance (see page 195);
  - third party liability insurance (see page 242).

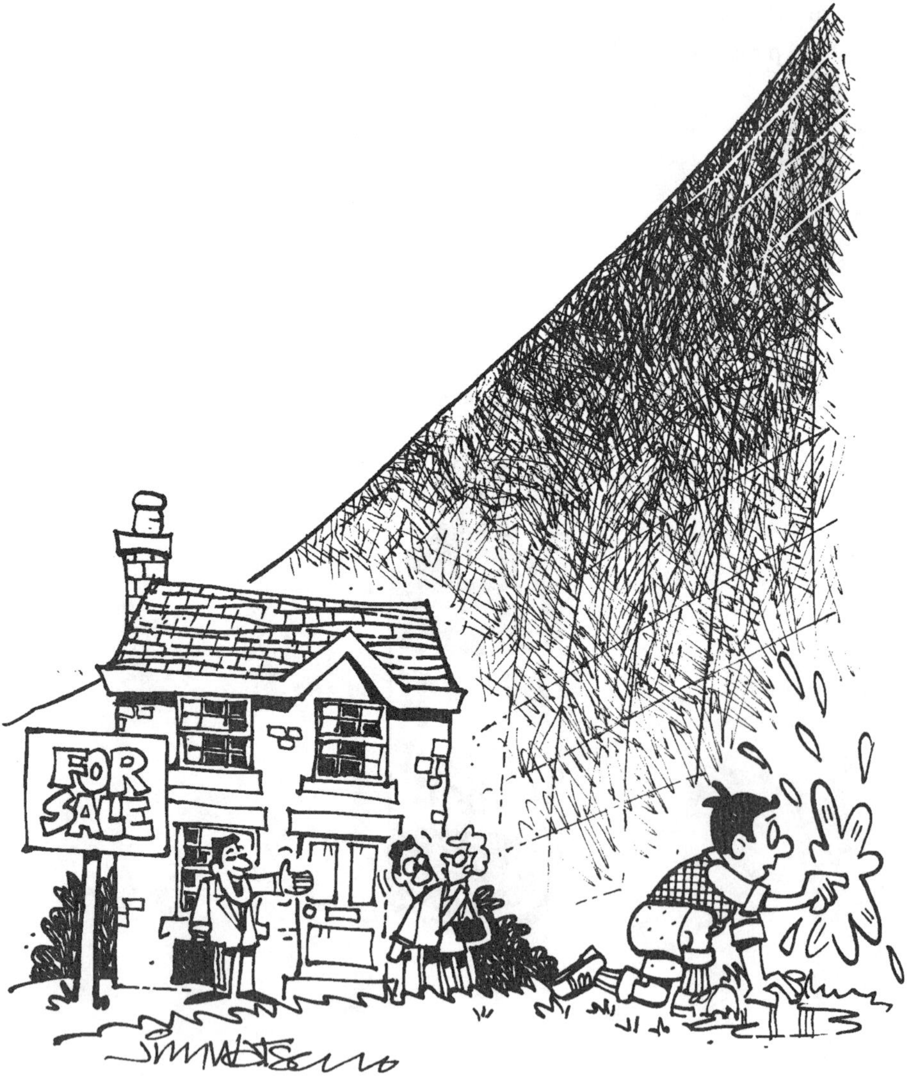
FOR SALE

5.

ACCOMMODATION

Finding suitable accommodation can be a problem in some parts of the Benelux region, depending on your requirements and your financial resources. The housing situation throughout the region varies greatly – from a relatively free and open housing market in much of Belgium to chronic shortages and strict regulation in Holland. Housing is available in most of Belgium, although the constant flow of bureaucrats and diplomats to and from Brussels makes the rental market tight in and around the capital. On the other hand, it can be extremely difficult to find housing in Holland, particularly in the Randstad (the ring of cities that runs from Amsterdam to Rotterdam and includes The Hague, Haarlem and Utrecht). The Dutch government controls virtually all low to medium price housing through its housing permit system, which excludes most new arrivals for at least their first two years in the country. Some large international companies setting up headquarters in Holland have bought large blocks of housing to assure adequate accommodation for their transferees, and this has affected the amount of private sector housing available for foreigners without corporate connections. Housing costs in Luxembourg reflect the general level of prosperity the Duchy has enjoyed, and rentals can be difficult to find, particularly in Luxembourg city. Many of the Duchy's workers (over half, in fact) commute each day from neighbouring Belgium, France or Germany, where housing costs are generally lower.

Across the region, home ownership is popular and on the increase. About two-thirds of Belgians own their own homes, despite the fact that there's little or no tax advantage in doing so. In Holland, all mortgage interest is deductible from income tax, and nearly 70 per cent of Dutch people own their own homes. Around three-quarters of Luxembourgers own their own homes, often building their dream home on a purchased plot of land.

TEMPORARY ACCOMMODATION

On arrival in Belgium, Holland or Luxembourg you may find it necessary to stay in temporary accommodation for a few weeks or months (perhaps while waiting for your furniture to arrive or your chosen apartment to become vacant). Some employers provide rooms, self-contained apartments or holiday homes for transferred employees and their families as part of the moving and relocation costs, but usually only for a short period.

Many hotels and bed-and-breakfast establishments cater for long-term guests and offer reduced weekly or monthly rates. In most large cities (e.g. Brussels, Amsterdam and The Hague), serviced apartments or 'apartment hotels' are available. These comprise fully self-contained furnished apartments with their own bathrooms and kitchens, and they're usually cheaper than a hotel and more convenient, especially for families. In rural areas, you can often find self-catering holiday accommodation available by the week or month, although this can be prohibitively expensive or impossible to arrange at short notice during the summer holiday season.

RELOCATION CONSULTANTS

If you're lucky enough to have your move paid for by your employer, he may arrange for a relocation consultant to handle the details. Relocation consultants generally work directly with large corporate clients who transfer their employees around the world on a regular basis and need to make transition periods as smooth (and short) as possible. Fees can run to several hundred (or even thousand!) euros per day. If you have special needs or requirements and enough money to pay for their services, you might wish to consider contacting a relocation consultant yourself – but don't be surprised to find that many of the larger agencies work exclusively with corporations. Most companies that make frequent use of relocation consultants offer employees a set package of services.

The main service provided by relocation consultants is finding accommodation (for rent or for purchase), arranging viewing and assisting with negotiations, especially where you and your family aren't fluent in the local language. Other services include handling the details of your move, arranging for temporary housing if needed, advising on local schools, health, transport and recreational facilities, and assisting you and your family with the various legalities, including immigration requirements. Some consultants offer or can refer you to seminars on living and working in Benelux, multi-cultural living and even language training. If you're interested in finding this kind of help for your relocation, it often pays to contact the local British or American expatriate clubs. Their members can recommend agencies or individuals, very often club members, who provide relocation services and know the area well. In other cases, local expatriate groups organise 'welcome' programmes for newcomers. These may include presentations by local relocation consultants, removal companies and other service providers.

BENELUX HOMES

Housing styles vary considerably between the Benelux countries, but homes are generally sturdily built and equipped with modern appliances. Recently built homes may have central heating, though older ones are more likely to have individual room heaters. Don't expect to find air-conditioning in Benelux homes – besides being expensive to run, it's rarely needed. In some older buildings in Amsterdam and other cities near water (e.g. Rotterdam and Utrecht), there can be serious problems with water damage and even rats.

Most accommodation is sold or rented unfurnished, and furnished apartments or houses are rarely available other than for short-term stays of a few weeks or months. 'Unfurnished' generally means that there are no lighting fixtures (just wires hanging from holes in the ceiling), no kitchen appliances or cupboards (sometimes you even have to provide your own kitchen sink!) and often no carpets or curtains. Built-in cupboards are rare, and storage can be a problem if you're planning to bring the contents of a large home with you.

Belgium: Around three-quarters of Belgians live in either detached homes or terraced properties. Semi-detached houses are rare. Apartments are common in the cities and, to a lesser extent, in the surrounding suburban areas. There's no shortage of housing, either for rent or to purchase, and housing prices and rents are generally reasonable. The main exception is the Brussels area, where demand exceeds supply, especially in desirable expatriate neighbourhoods.

Homes in Belgium are surprisingly large (at least when compared to Britain – Americans will no doubt find them small) and tend to be rather formally furnished and decorated. Gardens and yards are carefully and lovingly maintained, which may account for the rather 'inflated' terminology used in real estate adverts, whether for sale or rental property. In Belgium, a property described as a 'villa' means simply a house with a garden, while a 'flat' is a studio (i.e. single-room) apartment. The term '*appartement*' refers to a flat with multiple rooms (i.e. the bedroom is separate from the living room).

Holland: The situation couldn't be more different in Holland, which suffers from a chronic housing shortage, particularly when it comes to reasonably priced homes to rent or purchase. Public housing associations control an average of some 45 per cent of the Dutch housing market (as much as 70 per cent in certain desirable areas of large cities such as Amsterdam and The Hague). In order to rent or purchase housing in the 'public' domain, you need to be eligible for a housing permit from the local town hall or city housing department, proving your legal residence and family status, income level and justification for needing or wanting to live in that particular area or neighbourhood. Foreigners aren't eligible even to apply for a housing permit until they've lived in Holland for at least two years. Even then, the waiting list in Amsterdam and other major cities is up to eight years, especially for desirable neighbourhoods. As a newcomer, you will be limited to buying or renting on the private market, where prices are at the top of most ranges and increasing (although more slowly than during the boom years of the early '90s).

A distinctive feature of Dutch housing is its shape – narrow and tall, with tiny, twisting (and often, treacherous) staircases, small rooms and large, removable windows. Many old houses have a beam protruding from the front with a pulley attached to it for hoisting furniture and other large items up to the appropriate level and in through the window! At one time, the tax on houses was based on the width of the building, so it became customary to build on the narrowest piece of property and work upwards to create more living space or extra rooms. The practice didn't leave much space for niceties such as wide staircases, let alone lifts. By the time the tax rules were changed, the tall-and-narrow style had become 'traditional' in most Dutch cities.

Most Dutch homes have large front windows (even those in apartment blocks) and the Dutch don't generally bother with curtains. Perhaps they trust their neighbours not to stare into their windows when they shouldn't, or maybe the Dutch never do anything in their front rooms that couldn't or shouldn't be shared with the public at large. In any event, when you're out after dark or taking an early morning stroll before the sun comes up, you will be able to check out what all your neighbours are up to at that hour – at least in the front rooms of their houses. (Standing and staring at the scene, or even waving from the pavement as you stroll by, isn't, however, considered appropriate behaviour and may win you a reputation as a peeping Tom or worse.)

Luxembourg: Houses in Luxembourg reflect the general level of prosperity in the country. Luxemburgers enjoy all forms of modern appliances, luxurious appointments and other signs of the good life. Buildings tend to be constructed in the German style, whether apartments or detached houses, with high ceilings and large windows which open in two directions. Turning a window handle one way allows you to open the window (or door) casement style, usually swinging into the room; of you turn it the other way, the window (or door) tips into the room, allowing in air at the top without letting small children or animals fall out (or escape).

BUYING PROPERTY

You should give careful consideration to whether you're better off buying or renting property in Benelux. If you're staying for only a short time, e.g. less than five years, you're probably better off renting. Owning your own home isn't considered such an important an investment as it is in some other countries. Although property prices 'boomed' in the late '80s and early '90s, increases have slowed and high transfer (conveyance) costs discourage home ownership as an investment. The tax benefits of home ownership vary greatly.

Belgium: While property in Belgium is cheap by UK standards, the various fees, charges and deposits associated with buying a house and securing a mortgage are likely to discourage all but the most determined buyers. There's no mortgage relief on income tax and, if you resell the property within five years, you will be hit with capital gains tax. The good news is that mortgages are fairly easy to secure, but don't forget that total transfer fees will add 15 to 20 per cent to the price of a house, and there's VAT at 21 per cent to reckon with if you buy a new home.

Houses for sale are advertised in newspapers and through estate agencies, or you can use the 'sign hunting' method, i.e. looking for 'For Sale' (*à vendre/te koop*) signs on available properties. Listed prices are understood to be negotiable, and you normally make an offer that is somewhat below what you're prepared to pay and 'barter' with the vendor according to how keen you are to buy and how eager he is to sell. Having an estate agent to assist you with the process is usually sensible, even if you end up paying more than you would if you bought privately. Once a price is agreed, the buyer and the vendor sign a sales agreement (*compromis de vente/verkoopsovereenkomst*), which is usually secured with a non-refundable deposit equal to 10 per cent of the purchase price. At this point, the buyer has four months in which to obtain the balance of the money (in most cases by securing a mortgage) before the sale is concluded. In order to 'buy time', it's sometimes possible to purchase an option on the property for a period, during which the vendor may not sell it to anyone else; if you back out of the deal, you forfeit the option payment, so you should negotiate as small a sum as the vendor will accept.

The actual transfer or conveyance of the property must be done by a notary (*notaire/notaris*), who charges a fixed fee of 1 to 4 per cent of the purchase price. Generally, you must have a property surveyed, which will cost around €100, but your biggest expense will be the registration of the sale – a massive 12.5 per cent of the purchase price. It's possible to buy a property at auction, in which case you may save money, but the notary fees are doubled and you have only one month in which to secure a mortgage and complete the transaction.

Holland: House prices in Holland are high, at least for foreigners who aren't eligible for housing permits (as with rented accommodation – see page 83 – foreigners aren't eligible until they've lived in Holland for at least two years). Although housing prices have risen dramatically over the last decade, particularly in the unregulated private sector, uncertainty over the euro and future economic growth is having a dampening effect on the Dutch market. Home purchase is generally considered to be a good long-term investment in Holland, where there are considerable tax advantages to buying property.

The two main publications for housing adverts are *De Woningcourant* and *Huis Aanbod*. If you're determined to buy a house in Holland, you should remember that verbal contracts are binding and so most foreigners are strongly advised to work with an estate agent (*makelaar*) who's a member of the NVM (see **Rented Accommodation** below). The *makelaar* can do most of the negotiations for you and avoid expensive misunderstandings. *Makelaars* can charge whatever they like for their service, but most NVM members charge the recommended fee of 1.85 per cent of the purchase price. Be sure to ask what the fees are in advance and obtain them in writing.

You will need to have a residence permit, the deposit, and approval from the Department of Housing (*Gemeentelijke Dienst Volkshuisvesting*) to purchase property. If you're buying a house covered by housing permit regulations, you may need to show that you have a valid reason for staying in the area where you're buying (usually related to your work situation) and you must submit proof of good character (generally a police report showing you haven't been arrested) and adequate funds. Your *makelaar* will take care of most of the necessary paperwork.

The selling price is assumed to be negotiable and you usually make a starting bid somewhat lower than the price you expect to pay. 'Bidding' is done verbally until a final price is agreed, but note that this verbal agreement is fully binding. The sales contract is put into writing and signed by both buyer and vendor and the buyer must then make a deposit of 30 to 40 per cent of the purchase price with the notary. Fortunately, mortgages are relatively easy to obtain, and it's possible to borrow up to 125 per cent of the purchase price. Mortgage interest is also fully deductible from your income for tax purposes.

You should reckon on 10 to 14 per cent of the purchase price in fees, including the estate agent's fee, appraisal costs, loan initiation fee, a recording fee and 6 per cent registration tax (*overdrachtsbelasting*). Completion involves the notary making the transfer (*transport*) of the property into the buyer's name. The notary reviews all deeds and contracts connected with the property, in the presence of the buyer and the vendor, to determine whether there are any outstanding claims (*onbezwaard*) – generally for taxes – which must be settled before the new owner's name can be entered in the public registry (*kadaster*). Since it's usually the seller who engages the notary, you may want to have your own representative, possibly another notary, present to make sure everything is properly handled. The notary's fee is normally around 2 per cent of the purchase price of the property.

Note that if you wish to rent out your house (for example, if you're transferred out of the country), you first must check with the local housing authority, which will determine whether your property can be rented on the private market or only to housing permit holders.

Luxembourg: There's no shortage of housing in Luxembourg, although demand is greatest in Luxembourg city, where prices are not surprisingly at their highest. A studio apartment in the city generally costs over €125,000 and you should expect to pay over €200,000 for a one or two-bedroom flat with a floor area of around 75m². A flat or house described as 'of standing' means that it's luxuriously fitted out and will probably cost considerably more. Prices for detached houses are high, generally starting at around €300,000. Many Luxembourgers prefer to buy a plot of land in the countryside (but not too far from where they work) and build their own home.

Building land is also in plentiful supply and is often advertised by construction companies, which will build a house to order.

You should expect to pay a deposit of around 25 per cent, and estate agents fees are high but negotiable and normally calculated as a percentage of the selling price. There's a 6 per cent transfer tax on the sale of property in Luxembourg, and the transfer of ownership (conveyance) must be undertaken by a notary (*notaire/notar*), whose charges bring the total costs involved in buying a house to around 15 to 20 per cent of the selling price. Annual property taxes vary from less than 1 per cent to around 8 per cent of the selling price according to the commune (see page 273).

'For Sale' signs are rarely displayed in windows or yards in Luxembourg, where the most common sources of property advertisements are newspapers, e.g. *Marché de l'Immobilier/Immobilienmarkt*, and estate agents. As well as local agents, there are a number of international estate agencies in Luxembourg, e.g. ERA and Century 21. Many agents have websites listing homes for sale, which can be found via 🖥 www. luxweb.lu and www.achats.lu. Agents may also help or advise you concerning the financing, construction and management of a property.

RENTED ACCOMMODATION

If you're coming to live in one of the Benelux countries for less than five years, you will probably find that renting is the easiest (and in some cases, the most economical) solution. It's also the answer for those who don't want the trouble, expense and restrictions associated with buying property. Even if you're likely to be staying in the region indefinitely, it's wise to start in rented premises until you've got to know the customs and legalities of buying and owning property.

There are a number of ways to find a property to rent, including the following:

● Ask friends, relatives and acquaintances to look out for suitable accommodation, particularly if you're looking in the area where you already live. A lot of rental properties are found by word of mouth, particularly in cities with large expatriate or transient populations (e.g. Brussels, Amsterdam and The Hague).

● Look at advertisements in local newspapers (including free ones) and magazines.

● Visit accommodation and letting agents. Most cities and large towns have estate agents (*agences immobilières/makelaars in onroerende goederen* or simply *makelaars*) who also act as letting agents for owners. It's often better to deal with an agent than directly with owners, particularly regarding contracts and legal matters (especially in Holland – see below).

● Look at advertisements in shop windows and on notice boards in shopping centres, supermarkets, universities and colleges and company offices.

● Walk through neighbourhoods you think you might like to live in and look for 'to let' signs (*à louer/te huur*) on suitable properties.

● Read newsletters published by churches, clubs and expatriate organisations or ask at international schools or other places where expats and their families congregate.

Most rental properties in Belgium, Holland and Luxembourg are let unfurnished, which means that you must provide most fittings and fixtures, including ceiling lamps, kitchen cupboards, appliances and often floor coverings. Furnished properties (*meublé/gemeubeld*) are rare and often difficult to find except for short-term stays, generally less than a year. In some areas of Holland, you may be able to find partially furnished (*gestoffeered*) units, which include most of the basic fixtures (light fittings, floor coverings and curtains) plus basic kitchen appliances (sink, cooker and perhaps a refrigerator). Be careful, however, to determine exactly what is or isn't included in the rental, particularly if you view the apartment or house before the old tenants move out. You could be unpleasantly surprised to find that the wall-to-wall carpeting wasn't part of the deal.

Belgium: Rental housing in Belgium is plentiful and generally easy to find, thanks to rather generous (for Belgium) treatment of rental income. Despite recent changes to this popular tax loophole, rental property is still considered a good way for retirees to supplement their pension income. In larger cities such as Brussels, there's a constant changeover of diplomatic and corporate personnel, so that apartments and houses become available at all times of the year. You will see plenty of window signs with big orange letters on a black background proclaiming '*à louer/te huur*' and the phone number you can call for further information. It's sometimes possible to arrange an immediate appointment to see a property if you're touring an area with your mobile phone in hand, and 'sign hunting' is a popular means of finding living quarters in a specific neighbourhood.

There are two kinds of agencies that handle housing rentals in Belgium, although it isn't always obvious which is which, so you may need to ask. The first is a rental agency (*agence/makelaar*), which charges you a fee (generally around €50) to find properties meeting your requirements (i.e. essentially doing your 'sign hunting' for you). There's no central rental listing service in Belgium, so rental agents generally scour newspapers and other listings, then match up what they've found with the preferences of their clients. If you're registered with a rental agency, you will receive a list of addresses and phone numbers so that you can set up your own appointments to see the units. When you find a suitable place, you're on your own as far as negotiating a lease is concerned. The rental agency fee may entitle you to a certain number of referrals or to unlimited referrals over a set period of time, usually around six months. A few agencies will continue to provide you with listings until you've signed a lease.

The second kind of agency is an estate agent (*agence immobilière/ woningkantoor*), who charge the property owner a commission on the rental of an apartment and may perform some or all of the property management duties for the owner. If you're dealing with an estate agent, you shouldn't have to pay any fee. The estate agent will contact the owner and set up appointments for you to see the property and many will actually drive you to the appointment (saving you a considerable amount of money in taxi fares). An estate agent should also provide detailed information about a property and explain standard lease terms and clauses as well as negotiating a lease for you. Owners often list their vacant properties with several estate agents and pay the fee only to the one who arranges the lease. As a potential tenant, you may (and probably should) contact as many estate agents as you can. Be careful, however, to keep track of which properties you've already seen. If a second agent shows you a property you're thinking of renting, you could be setting the landlord up for a fee argument, in which case he may simply refuse to rent you the property at all!

Most apartments and houses are rented unfurnished, although the kitchen (*cuisine/keuken*) can vary as to how well equipped (*equipée/uitgerust*) it is. A semi-equipped kitchen probably has a sink and some built-in cupboards, but not much more. You will be expected to provide your own appliances or make arrangements with the prior tenant to buy theirs. 'Equipped' means that the basic appliances are included (cooker and probably a refrigerator, but not always), and 'super-equipped' indicates that the kitchen may have a dishwasher, microwave and/or other 'luxury' appliances, as well as all the basics. If the kitchen isn't equipped, you will have to provide all your own cupboards and appliances.

Holland: In a small country with a chronic housing shortage, finding a suitable property to rent can be a problem, particularly if you're a foreigner (and this is one situation where EU nationality won't put you on an equal footing with the natives). Roughly 45 per cent of all housing in Holland falls under various forms of government control, including who has the right to rent and purchase properties and how much can be charged for them. The remaining 55 per cent of housing is in private hands, and owners are free to charge what they want – or what the market will bear, i.e. a considerable amount!

In order to rent almost any low to mid-price housing in Holland, you need to be eligible for a housing permit (*woonvergunning*) from the local Department of Housing (*Gemeentelijke Dienst Volkshuisvesting*). Foreigners aren't eligible for housing permits until they've lived and worked in Holland for at least two years. Whether or not you're then granted a permit will depend on your family size, your income and your reason for wanting to live in a particular area (usually related to your work). Depending on the area you're interested in, the permit application process can take a further four to eight years! In practice, this means that foreigners are limited to renting from the private sector market, which is expensive. You should expect to pay at least €700 per month for the rental of a studio apartment (plus maintenance charges, utility bills, etc) and at least 900 for a one or tw-bedroom unit. Rents in Amsterdam, The Hague and other major cities can be much higher!

Holders of a housing permit sometimes offer desperate foreigners the opportunity to rent or sub-let a rent-controlled apartment or house 'under the table', charging them a higher rent than the statutory amount and pocketing the difference. Not only is this illegal but, if you agree to leave the property in the permit holder's name, you won't be able to register with the town hall or the Aliens Police, which can make it difficult for you to obtain a telephone or a bank account, or even to get paid by your employer. You will also be evicted as soon as the ruse is found out. If you don't use an estate agent (*makelaar*) to help you find a home, be sure to enquire at the local town hall about your eligibility to live at the address you're considering renting before you sign any agreements.

It's normally highly recommended to engage an estate or rental agent to help you in finding housing in Holland. A good *makelaar* can ask all the right questions and carry out the necessary negotiations for you, as well as confirm that a property is legally available for you to rent. Estate agents aren't strictly regulated in Holland, where individual agents are free to charge what they like. Most agencies charge around a month's rent, but be sure to ask what the fee is before you sign up, as some charge much more. For your own protection and peace of mind, make sure that an agent is a member of the *Nederlandse Vereniging van Makelaars in Onroerende*

Goederen (NVM), the Dutch real estate agents' foundation. All NVM agents must have a certain level of training and subscribe to the foundation's code of practice.

Another good reason for using a *makelaar* is that oral agreements are binding and fully enforceable in Holland. Your casual comment about how 'nice' an apartment or house looks could be taken to mean that you're agreeing to rent it at whatever terms the landlord suggests! Even a nod or a wink at the wrong moment could result in a binding lease costing you several months' rent. (On the other hand, making negative comments in front of an owner could get you thrown out with no chance of renting from that landlord ever again!) If you use a reputable estate agent, he will tell you to keep your hands at your sides and your mouth shut at all times while looking at rental properties. This isn't rudeness, just practicality. Let your agent do the talking and all the negotiations for you and you will minimise the chance of a costly misunderstanding!

Apartments and houses are rented either unfurnished or partially furnished. Unfurnished means stripped of light fittings, floor and wall coverings and all appliances. In Dutch homes, there are often separate water heaters connected to each sink or basin, with a larger one for the bath. These are regarded as appliances, and in an unfurnished rental you may be expected to provide your own (unless you're happy to wash in cold water). If there's wall-to-wall carpeting when you see the flat, don't be surprised to find nothing but exposed floorboards when you move in, as the Dutch take even the carpets with them when they move! A partially furnished apartment will have a few appliances and possibly carpeting, but be sure to check what's included before you agree to rent. In the kitchen, for example, there may be a hob but no oven. If you already have appliances, you should also measure carefully to make sure they will fit. Furnished apartments are almost impossible to find, other than for short-term rentals, as they fall into a legal category similar to that of hotels, where tenants can be evicted with little or no notice.

Luxembourg: Rental property in Luxembourg can be difficult to find, particularly at short notice, and rents are generally high. The expatriate community is a good source of information on houses and apartments for rent, especially if you want to avoid estate agency fees, which amount to as much as two or three months' rent. Estate agencies are open only limited hours and very often aren't open at all at weekends. If you do use agencies, make sure you keep track of the properties you've seen; if you view the same property twice with a different agency and decide to rent it, you could end up paying two agency fees! Unfortunately, you can't find a house for rent (or for sale) in Luxembourg by 'sign hunting', as owners don't normally post signs on available properties.

Most property in Luxembourg is rented unfurnished, which may mean there's a kitchen sink, but not much else. You must normally provide your own carpets, curtains, curtain rods, light fittings and most kitchen appliances. If you view a house or flat before the old tenants move out, you may be able to arrange to buy their appliances and fixtures. Furnished rentals are available (at higher rents) and include everything you need, right down to crockery, kitchen utensils and bed linen. If you rent a furnished property, make sure you understand who's responsible for insuring the contents (see page 241).

Leases

Once you've found a house or apartment to rent, you will have to negotiate and finalise a lease, or rental contract. The requirements and formats for valid leases vary considerably across the Benelux countries, although there are elements in common. You should read the lease carefully before signing it and, if you have doubts or questions about any of the terms, have them translated or explained to you.

A lease will identify the property you're renting, including both the street address and the apartment (either by number or location). If there are additional rooms or privileges included in the basic rental, such as access to a laundry room, garage, parking space or storage facilities, these should be noted in the lease. If you're renting a semi-furnished or partially equipped unit, this should also be noted, along with an indication of what equipment or fittings are included. (This may be part of the inventory – see page 90.)

A lease will indicate the amount of your monthly rent, the date it is to be paid and possibly the method of payment (many landlords require you to set up a standing order with your bank), plus any penalties for late payment. It should also include details of annual rent increases, which are usually indexed, as well as the procedure for increasing the rent above this amount. In addition to your rent, you will be required to pay an estimated monthly amount for common charges (see page 89).

Your lease should also include the amount and conditions of the damage deposit. When you move out, you will be expected to return the house or apartment to the condition it was in when you took over; if you fail to do so, the landlord can use your deposit to cover the cost of making any necessary repairs. The deposit will usually be held until the last common charges have been determined and settled, so it can be a year or more after you leave before you receive your deposit refund! Most landlords require a deposit of one to three months' rent. If possible, you should arrange to have this money held in an interest-bearing account, usually a blocked account that requires authorisation from both you and the landlord before the funds can be released. Some landlords will accept a bank guarantee for the amount of the deposit. You can arrange this through your bank, usually for a small annual fee. Beware of landlords who attempt to include a clause requiring you to return the property to 'perfect' condition rather than to the condition in which you received it. If you agree to such a clause, you could be faced with major renovation costs to cover previous tenants' wear and tear as well as your own.

Other terms and conditions that may appear in the lease include notice periods and penalties for breaking the lease. Tenants' rights are extremely well protected under most standard leases in Belgium, Holland and Luxembourg. Evicting a tenant, even one who has caused considerable problems, is a process that can take months or even years, and the circumstances under which a landlord may evict a tenant are severely limited. In most cases, he must give a long notice period and pay you substantial penalties (which doesn't mean you should make a habit of getting yourself evicted from rented accommodation!). For this reason, most landlords insist on verifying your employment, residence and income details before accepting you as a tenant. If you want to terminate the lease, there are standard notice periods and procedures to follow, and sometimes penalties to be paid. It has become common practice to include a so-called 'diplomatic clause' in the standard lease form. This permits you to terminate your lease at 30 days' notice if you have to move owing to your employment, i.e. you're transferred at short notice or you change jobs.

Belgium: A standard lease in Belgium runs for a period of nine years and is often referred to as a 3-6-9 lease. This is because the base rent can be increased only at the beginning of each 3-year period, and then only if written notice has been given. Under the standard lease, you must give at least three months' (usually six or nine months') notice in writing in order to break or terminate the lease. If you break the lease within the first year, you must pay a penalty of three months' rent. During the second year, the penalty is reduced to two months' rent, and during the third year to one month's rent. After the third year, there's no penalty provided you've given adequate notice. After each three-year period, the landlord may eject you if he needs the property for his own or a close family member's use, but he must give six months' notice and pay you a large penalty (equal to nine months' rent after three years and six months rent after six years). If the landlord fails to give proper notice, he must pay you 18 months' rent as a penalty. At the end of the nine-year lease period, the lease is automatically renewed for another nine years unless you or the landlord has given notice of an intention not to renew at least six months' in advance by registered letter.

It's always wise to include a diplomatic clause in a rental contract but, unless you're on amicable terms with your landlord, you may find that the Belgian courts won't enforce it. Instead, you can often persuade your employer to reimburse you for any rental penalties incurred as a result of a forced relocation.

While you can negotiate some changes to the standard contract, you may find that the Belgian courts are unwilling to enforce unusual provisions or non-standard lease clauses if a disagreement with your landlord results in legal action. Open-ended or indefinite term leases aren't permitted under Belgian law and, if you insist on negotiating a non-standard term lease, you run the risk of losing most of the legal protection that tenants enjoy in Belgium.

Leases in Belgium must be registered with the local office of the Receiver of Registrations, Ministry of Finance (*Enregistrement/Registratie, Ministère des Finances/Ministerie van Financien*) within four months of being signed. Technically, you can be fined for forgetting this formality, although it's in your own interest to remember to register the lease and any changes or codicils made during the term of the lease. Don't take any notice if your landlord attempts to discourage you from 'bothering' with the registration process: if the landlord wants to re-let the property, the new tenant can only be held to the terms of the existing lease if these have been properly registered; if you haven't registered your lease, the new tenant is free to evict you, raise your rent or change any of the other terms of your rental contract!

In Belgium, you must usually pay a deposit equal to three months' rent, either in cash or by obtaining a bank guarantee for the amount, and an inventory (see page 90) is generally done before the lease is signed and deposits paid. The Belgian Consumers Association publishes a booklet entitled *Guide de la Location/Huren en Verhuren*, which explains standard lease terms and clauses you should look out for. Contact Test Achats/Test Aankoop, rue de Hollande 13, 1060 Brussels (☎ 02-536 6411).

Holland: When renting property in Holland, it's customary first to strike a verbal agreement with the owner or landlord, which is then drawn up in writing. The advantage of using a rental agent is that he can handle both the verbal and the written negotiations for you. The basic rental contract is usually open-ended, although for foreigners a lease may be drawn up for a fixed term of a year or two. Rent is normally due on the 1st of the month, and many landlords insist on being paid by standing order. You must provide proof of your income and a letter from your employer, together with the appropriate housing permit (if necessary) and a damage deposit. Damage deposits are normally equal to one month's rent, although some landlords insist on two. Some landlords will accept a bank guarantee for the deposit. Usually, you're also required to pay the first month's rent in advance. If you're using an agent, your agent's fee is due when you sign the lease.

Rental property in Holland is subject to a variety of common charges (see below) and these should be detailed in your rental contract, along with an estimated monthly amount, which you must pay to your landlord in addition to your basic rental fee. Utilities are sometimes included in the lease, either as part of the common charges or as a separate payment. If possible, you should have the utilities bills for which you're responsible sent directly to you (and in your name) rather than paying them through the landlord. Besides the obvious possibility that he will fiddle the charges, if your landlord doesn't want to transfer the name on the telephone, cable TV or other utility bills, it could be a sign that the property is rent-controlled and consequently that you're being grossly overcharged!

A rental contract should state who is responsible for what kinds of repairs and maintenance. The usual arrangement is for the tenant to cover minor interior repairs only, leaving the rest to the owner. You should complete an inventory to document the condition of the apartment when you move in (see page 90), but before signing the lease make sure that all appliances included in the rental are listed in the contract and are in working condition. Beware also of clauses allowing the owner to reoccupy the property without adequate notice or compensation. You should always ask for a diplomatic clause to allow you to vacate at two months' notice if you're transferred by your employer.

Luxembourg: A standard rental contract in Luxembourg is written for a fixed term of three years. If you're on a shorter assignment, you can ask for a one or two-year lease or have a diplomatic clause inserted into the standard lease agreement. You're usually required to give three months' written notice to break or terminate a lease. With a diplomatic clause, you can shorten this to a month, but your move must be related to your employment, i.e. either a change of job or a transfer. Apart from the basic rent, you must pay a monthly contribution towards common charges (often even if you're renting a detached house). Tenants in Luxembourg are often subject to weekly or monthly cleaning duties if the building has no concierge or superintendent to take care of common areas.

COMMON CHARGES

Common charges are the monthly fees you pay for the services you share with your neighbours in the same building (or sometimes within the same complex or housing estate). Each month, you're required to pay an estimated amount towards the maintenance and repair of common areas (e.g. hallways, lobby, grounds, lifts), the cost of the concierge or building manager, water supplies and sewerage and other shared utilities, including heating and hot water if these are provided on a communal basis. At the end of the year, the actual cost of these services is assessed and each tenant is charged a share, based on the size of his apartment or other criteria stipulated in the lease. If you've paid too much, you will receive a credit on your following month's rent payment; if you've underpaid, you will be asked to make up the difference. Your estimated monthly payment is then adjusted for the following year. Common charges typically add 10 to 20 per cent to the base rent, depending on what is covered and how the allocation is determined. When you move out of your apartment, it's customary for the landlord to retain your damage deposit until the last of the common charges have been settled, which can take a year or more. Note that in Benelux there are no tenants' or owners' associations to which you can belong in order to have a say in how much you're charged.

HOUSE RULES

Most apartment blocks have house rules, some of which may be formulated by the local commune and be enforceable by law. You should receive a copy of the house rules on moving into an apartment or when you sign a rental or sales contract, but it's wise to review them before you agree to rent or buy a home, as they can affect your use and enjoyment of the common facilities. (Sometimes they will even restrict the colour of the curtains you can hang in your windows!) If you don't understand the rules, have them translated; ignorance is no excuse for breaking house rules.

Common house rules include restrictions on the use of hallways for storing bicycles or children's toys; noise (particularly late at night), including the flushing of toilets or running of showers after 10pm; use of lifts by unaccompanied children or for moving furniture or other large items; use of the balconies or visible terraces for hanging laundry or mounting satellite dishes; and parking by residents and guests. Rules may also cover the rotation of cleaning duties for hallways or common areas (particularly in Luxembourg) where there's no concierge or maintenance staff, responsibility for locking communal entrances at night and the collection of rubbish.

INVENTORY

One of the most important tasks on moving into a new apartment or home is to complete an inventory and condition report (*état des lieux/staat van de huis*). This includes the state of the fixtures and fittings (if there are any), the cleanliness and condition of the decoration and any items missing or in need of repair. The procedure varies among the three countries (see below), but in general all problems and damages are listed on a form which is signed by both the tenant and the landlord, or the vendor and the buyer in the case of a sale. Most leases require the tenant to restore the property to 'move-in' condition (see above), and it's the inventory report which establishes what that condition was. Any damages that aren't noted on the inventory list when you move in will be charged to you when you move out, so you should make sure that you check a property thoroughly and that the inventory list is complete before you sign it. Once you've moved in, it can be difficult (or impossible) to persuade the owner to repair anything, as you will be responsible for all interior maintenance and decoration. If you're buying a house or apartment, the inventory should itemise any unfinished work or repairs that the vendor has agreed to remedy. If possible, this list, along with deadlines for completing the work, should be submitted to the notary prior to the transfer of the property so that it becomes part of the sales contract.

Belgium: In Belgium, an inventory is normally carried out by a specialist called an 'expert' (the same word in French and Dutch), who is usually paid by the property owner. However, it's wise to hire your own expert if you have any reason to doubt the competence or objectivity of the person your landlord or vendor has engaged. Experts are listed in the telephone book under the same heading as surveyors (*géomètres/landmeters*). An expert is supposed to examine the empty property in minute detail, noting all imperfections and damage, from heel marks or scratches on the floor to broken or malfunctioning windows, doors or plumbing. You can (and should) be present during the inventory to make sure that everything is properly noted. Experts' fees amount to between €100 and €200, depending on how long the inventory takes, and are supposed to be split between the landlord and the tenant.

If you're purchasing any fittings or appliances from the previous tenants, be sure to obtain a receipt so that the landlord can't claim them as part of his property, either during the inventory or when you move out. If you've bought fittings or appliances as part of a sale, make sure that they're included in the inventory and correspond with what you thought you were buying.

Holland: Before you move into a new apartment, you should compile your own inventory, noting all defects or damage. If you're renting a partially furnished unit, note what fixtures and appliances are in place and their condition before you move your belongings in. You should also ask your landlord to check and sign the inventory to avoid any disagreements when you move out. You then have 30 days after moving in to notify the owner by registered letter of any other damage you notice if you want him to repair it.

Luxembourg: When renting property in Luxembourg, you should inspect the vacant house or apartment for damage or repairs that need to be made before you move in. Send a list to the landlord and ask for written confirmation in return, indicating when repairs or other work will be done.

HOME SECURITY

When moving into a new home, it's often wise to replace the locks (or lock barrels) as soon as possible and fit high security locks, as you have no idea how many keys are in circulation for the existing locks. Some apartments and houses may be fitted with high security door locks that are individually numbered. Extra keys for these locks cannot be cut at a local store and you must obtain details from the previous owner or your landlord to have additional keys cut or to change the lock barrels. At the same time as changing the locks, you may wish to have an alarm system fitted, which is the best way to deter intruders and may also reduce your home contents insurance (see page 241).

In many homes, door locks work only with keys and there's no handle or knob to turn from the inside. To lock your front door at night, you will need to have your key handy. Many people leave a key in the lock at all times so that if there's a fire or other emergency they can quickly unlock the door and escape. If you do this, however, you should be aware that the lock won't operate from one side of the door when there's a key in the other side. In fact, if someone tries to insert a key in the other side of the lock, both keys and the lock are likely to jam and you will have to call a locksmith to drill out and replace the lock, which will cost you at least €25 to €50!. The best solution to this problem is to install a key rack in the hall so that there's no temptation to leave a key in the door.

Another important aspect of home security is ensuring that you have early warning of a fire, which is easily accomplished by installing smoke detectors. Battery-operated smoke detectors can be purchased for around €10 to €12 and should be tested weekly to ensure that the batteries aren't exhausted. You can also fit an electric-powered gas detector that activates an alarm when a gas leak is detected.

MOVING HOUSE

Once you've found a home in Benelux, it usually takes only a few weeks to have your belongings shipped from within continental Europe. From anywhere else it varies considerably – e.g. four weeks from the east coast of America, six weeks from the west coast and the Far East and around eight weeks from Australasia. Customs clearance is no longer necessary when shipping your household effects from one EU country to another. However, when shipping your effects from a non-EU country to Belgium, Holland or Luxembourg, you should enquire about customs formalities in advance. Otherwise you can encounter numerous problems and delays and may be charged duty or even fined. Removal companies usually take care of the administration and ensure that the necessary documents are provided and correctly completed.

For international removals, you should use a company that's a member of the International Federation of Furniture Removers (FIDI) or the Overseas Moving Network International (OMNI), with experience in the Benelux region. Members of FIDI and OMNI usually subscribe to an advance payment scheme, which provides you with a guarantee: if a member company fails to fulfil its commitments to you, the removal is completed at the agreed cost by another company or your money is refunded. Some removal companies have subsidiaries or affiliates in your destination country, which may be more convenient if you encounter problems or need to make an insurance claim. Obtain at least three written quotations before choosing a company. If you're moving from overseas, you should give careful thought to the shipping of your belongings. Most employer-sponsored overseas moves will allow for a small air freight shipment of around 250kg (550lb), which should arrive at your new home within a week or two. Make sure you include in this shipment those things you will need to tide you over until the rest of your belongings arrive.

Make sure to fully insure your belongings during removal with a well-established insurance company. Insurance premiums are usually one to two percent of the declared value of your goods, depending on the type of cover chosen, and most insurance policies cover for 'all risks' on a replacement value basis. Some insurance companies require separate 'riders' for valuable artwork or jewellery, and most insurers won't cover fragile or breakable items unless they've been packed by the removal company. You should make a complete list of all the items you're shipping and insuring, along with the price you paid for each item, purchase dates and current replacement values. This may be required for the insurance company to issue the cover and will certainly be required if you make a claim. The same list may be needed by the removal company to clear your household goods through customs if you're moving from outside the EU.

If you plan to transport your belongings to Belgium, Holland or Luxembourg yourself, check the customs requirements of all the countries you must pass through. Unless your move is very simple, it isn't recommended to do it yourself. It's no fun heaving beds and wardrobes up stairs and trying to squeeze cupboards or sofas down narrow corridors. If you're moving into a 'traditional' Dutch house, note that using those beam and pulley arrangements takes considerable skill. (You don't want to deliver your piano to a neighbour by accident, especially if the neighbour's window hasn't been removed to receive it!) Removal companies in Benelux have an array of specialised equipment designed to hoist large pieces of furniture into upper floors and convey boxes through windows and balcony doors. You should have some light refreshments (soft drinks and biscuits or sandwiches) available for the removal men; a tip (roughly €10 per man) after the work is done is always appreciated.

Bear in mind that moving house rarely goes smoothly. It's a chaotic and stressful time for everyone involved. You're often entitled to a day off from work to move house under local law or company policy, and you should plan on taking it, if only to enjoy a well-deserved moment of calm and quiet once the removal van has departed.

ELECTRICITY

Electricity is generated in the Benelux region using a variety of fuels, from coal and oil to the uranium used in the region's nuclear plants; over half of Belgium's electrical needs are provided by nuclear power plants (most of them French). In Luxembourg, the national electric and gas company, CEGEDEL, provides both electricity and steam for heating homes and businesses. All three countries are moving toward liberalisation of electricity supply, as mandated by the European Union, although most progress to date has been in the industrial sector. Holland has been successful in encouraging the establishment of new power generating companies, including several using wind generators and other sources of so-called 'green' power, but only for industrial customers. It's reckoned that the residential electricity market won't see much change until around 2005.

In Belgium, you can look in the white pages of the telephone directory under 'Electricité/Electricteit' to find the company that provides electrical service in your commune. In the Brussels area this is likely to be Electrabel, the main distribution company in Belgium. In Holland, contact the local electric utility (gemeente engergiebedrijf) to arrange for service; in Luxembourg city, contact the Service Lecture des Compteurs (Centre Hamilius), 51 boulevard Royal, 2449 Luxembourg (☎ 47-962 924 or 47-962 990) and in the rest of Luxembourg CEGEDEL, rue Thomas Edison, 1445 Strassen (☎ 26-241).

You should arrange a final meter reading if you're taking over a property from a previous owner or tenant. Electricity is billed every two months, based on your estimated annual usage. Bills must normally be paid within ten days, and you can be summarily cut off if payment isn't received on time. It's generally best to arrange for payment by standing order so that bills are paid automatically from a bank account. Electric meters are read once a year, at which time you're billed for any additional amount due or credited any overpayment and your estimated payments for the coming year are adjusted. In some areas, particularly in Holland, you must enter your meter reading on a card and return it to the electricity supply company or simply report your reading by telephone or via the Internet; the reading is only checked if it's much lower than the previous year.

Based on an annual consumption of 3000kwh, electricity costs around €45 per month in Holland and around €40 per month in Belgium and Luxembourg (€0.18 and €0.16 per kwh respectively). If you use a lot of electricity, you can usually obtain a lower rate. Belgium and Luxembourg offer half price electricity at night – usually between midnight to and 8am.

The electricity companies don't install appliances or make repairs to the electrical system inside buildings or apartments. For this you need a licensed electrician. Look in the telephone directory under 'Electriciens – Installateurs/Elektricients – Installateurs'.

Power Supply

The electricity supply in Belgium, Holland and Luxembourg is delivered to homes at 220 volts with a frequency of 50 Hertz (cycles). If you're coming from the UK, most of your appliances should be usable simply with a change of plug (see below). Televisions and video recorders are the main exceptions: although you will be able to play back video tapes, you won't be able to receive television programmes because of the difference in transmission systems (see **Chapter 8**). If your video recorder uses anything other than the European PAL format, you won't be able to watch locally bought tapes either. North American or other 110V appliances won't be usable in Benelux unless they can be switched or converted to the higher voltage (see below).

Plugs, Fuses & Bulbs

Depending on the country you've come from, you may need new plugs or a lot of adapters. Electrical plugs in Belgium, Holland and Luxembourg have two or three round pins. The third pin is for the earth (ground) contact. On two-pin plugs, there may be earth contacts on the sides of the plug. Almost all electrical sockets are recessed into the wall (particularly in modern buildings) and have both an extra hole for the earth pin and two small earth contacts at the side which look like bent bits of wire. These recessed sockets can make it impossible to use standard travel-type plug converters. If you're bringing appliances from the US or another country with a 110V supply, you will need to buy transformers (see below), unless they're dual-voltage; some items, such as clocks, won't work even with a transformer. Cordless telephones may not work either.

Electrical plugs aren't fitted with fuses. Instead, the circuit for your home will be protected by either a fuse box (*boîte à fusibles* in French) or a circuit breaker panel (*coupe-circuit* in French). The Dutch refer simply to the 'electricity cabinet' (*aardlekschakelaar*) in both cases; the word for fuse is *zekering*. In modern buildings, you're likely to find a circuit breaker panel containing several switches, usually (but not always) labelled to indicate the circuits or apparatus they control. When there's a short circuit or the system starts to overload, the breaker is tripped and the power supply is cut off. To reset the circuit breaker, you first need to flip the switch all the way to the 'off' position, as the tripped switch moves only to the half-way point; then you can restore power by flipping the switch back to the 'on' position. But first ensure that you've switched off any heavy duty equipment on that circuit which may have caused the overload. If the power goes off while you're using a computer, you should switch off both the computer and the monitor before reconnecting the power. Make sure you know where the breaker box is located and keep a torch handy so that you can find it in the dark. If your home is equipped with a fuse box, you should have extra fuses (of the correct size and type) available. Both bayonet and screw-fitting bulbs are used in Benelux.

Converters & Transformers

If you have electrical equipment rated at 110 volts AC (for example, from the US) you will require a converter or a step-down transformer to convert the supply to 110 volts. Converters can be used for heating appliances, but transformers are required for motorised appliances. However, some electrical appliances are fitted with a 110/220-volt switch. Check whether there is one (it may be inside the casing) and make sure that it's switched to 220 volts before connecting to the power supply. Add the wattage of all the devices you plan to connect to a transformer and make sure that its power rating *exceeds* this sum.

Generally all small, high-wattage electrical appliances, such as kettles, toasters, heaters and irons, need large transformers. Motors in large appliances, such as cookers, refrigerators, washing machines, dryers and dishwashers, will need replacing or fitting with a large transformer. In most cases it's simpler to buy new appliances locally, which are of good quality and reasonably priced (see page 332). Note also that the dimensions of cookers, microwave ovens, refrigerators, washing machines, dryers and dishwashers purchased abroad may differ from those in Benelux, so they may not fit into your new kitchen.

An additional problem with some electrical equipment is the frequency rating, which in some countries, e.g. the USA, is designed to run at 60Hertz (Hz) and not Benelux's 50Hz. Electrical equipment without a motor is generally unaffected by the drop in frequency to 50Hz (except TVs). Equipment with a motor may run with a 20 per cent drop in speed; however, automatic washing machines, cookers, electric clocks, record players and tape recorders must be converted to 50Hz. If the label on the back of the equipment says 50/60Hz, it should be all right; if the label says 60Hz, you can try it, but first ensure that the voltage is correct as outlined above. Bear in mind that the transformers and motors of electrical devices designed to run at 60Hz will run hotter at 50Hz, so make sure that the apparatus has sufficient space around it to allow for cooling.

GAS

Mains gas is available in many areas throughout Benelux, particularly in and around the major cities and towns. Gas is widely used where available for cooking, central heating and heating water. In most areas, mains gas is supplied by the same utility company as electricity, and you will usually receive a single bill combining electricity and gas every other month. Where mains gas isn't available, mostly in rural areas, bottled propane or butane is often used. Bottled gas is available from local merchants, who will also deliver and install tanks. Mains gas costs around €0.27 per m³ in all three countries, although it's charged by the mega-joule in Belgium.

Gas appliances must be installed by a licensed plumber and should be regularly cleaned and serviced. Look in the telephone directory under '*Plombiers-zingueurs/Lood- & Zinkwerken*'. You should be particularly careful if your home has gas heaters or individual gas water heaters for each sink (some owners install a gas water heater intended for kitchen use in the bathroom); if these heaters are used for long periods in an area that isn't well ventilated, they can generate dangerous levels of carbon monoxide.

FUEL OIL

Fuel oil (*mazout/stookolie*) is often used for heating in the Benelux region, particularly in homes with central heating systems. If you're living in a home with oil heating, there will usually be an oil tank buried under the courtyard or garden, and there should be a long metal ruler in the cellar or garage. This ruler is used to dip into the tank to determine how much fuel it contains. When the level is low, you can have the tank filled by a local fuel company (there may be a telephone number on the tank). Don't forget to check your oil level regularly, as it can take a day or two to arrange a delivery. If you have oil heating, it's also likely that your water heaters will use oil, so don't forget to check your oil level during the summer as well as in the winter. Further information (in French and Dutch only) is available on 🖳 www.infor mazout.be.

Oil prices vary considerably according to the world market, but you should expect to pay around €0.34 per litre, which equates to around €860 per year to heat and generate hot water in an average home.

WATER

Water charges are included in the common charges (see page 89) for most rented accommodation in Belgium, Holland and Luxembourg. Home owners receive a bill directly from the commune, city or town agency, usually covering a number of municipal utilities. Like electricity, water is metered and meters are read annually. In most communities, you're billed in estimated quarterly or monthly instalments based on your previous year's usage. In some areas, particularly in Holland, you may be sent a postcard asking you to read your own meter and return the information to the appropriate agency. Meter readings can often be submitted by phone or via the Internet.

Mains water throughout the Benelux region is safe to drink but is generally hard, which means you will need to use plenty of 'descaler' to keep your kettle, iron and other equipment and utensils clean. There are a number of water filter systems available that can improve the quality of small quantities of water used in cooking and reduce or eliminate the calcium build-up on heating elements and in pots and pans. These normally require you to pour tap water through a filter into a jug or other container before you use it. Other systems involve having a small filter mounted directly on the kitchen tap. Filters for both systems are available in supermarkets and other shops and generally need to be replaced every month or two. It also pays to clean and decalcify dishwashers and washing machines regularly. Alternatively, you can use detergents which contain decalcifying agents. Dishwashers have built-in water softeners, which require the regular addition of salt tablets to clean and regenerate the softening filters. Rinsing liquid is also essential for dishwashers if you want to avoid streaky mineral stains on your glasses and crockery. Tap and shower fixtures must be decalcified regularly. Distilled water, or water melted from the frost build-up in your refrigerator or freezer, should be used in some electric steam irons, but check the manufacturer's instructions; some brands of steam iron are designed to be used with unfiltered tap water and have their own decalcification systems which should be periodically cleaned. It's also possible to install 'house-wide' decalcification equipment, but these systems are generally expensive and not practicable for rented premises.

REFUSE DISPOSAL

The local municipality arranges for the collection and disposal of household refuse and in most areas offers an impressive range of recycling services. The systems used vary from commune to commune but in most cases, you will be expected to sort your rubbish into containers that are colour coded to indicate recyclable and other waste. Containers must sometimes be purchased or rented from the local commune, or they may be provided 'free' to those who pay communal taxes (e.g. in Belgium – see **Chapter 14**). In many Belgian towns you must buy special rubbish sacks or stickers; the refuse men will only collect the proper sacks or sacks with the proper sticker, indicating that you've paid for collection. Sacks or stickers may be sold in shops (for €0.75 to €1.25), but be careful to purchase the correct stickers for your area, or you will have to take your refuse to another area for collection! In Holland, the municipality sends out a monthly bill for refuse removal, sewerage, water, an environmental tax (covering various kinds of recycling – see page 273) and sometimes a cable television service.

Make sure you check the regulations concerning refuse collection at your local town hall, as refuse crews will not pick up anything that isn't properly set out or marked. If you leave out 'unauthorised' containers, not only will they be ignored but you could be fined for littering the street! Some towns have strict ordinances covering how early you're permitted to put your bins or sacks out (usually no earlier than 6pm the night before a scheduled pick-up) and require you to take in empty bins shortly after the crews have passed or at least by the same evening.

In some communes, you will have to take certain types of recyclable waste to collection points. Many towns have special pick-up dates for large items at least a few times a year, or you can call the town hall to arrange (for a fee) collection of bulky items, garden rubbish or 'hazardous' materials, such as old paint and other chemical products.

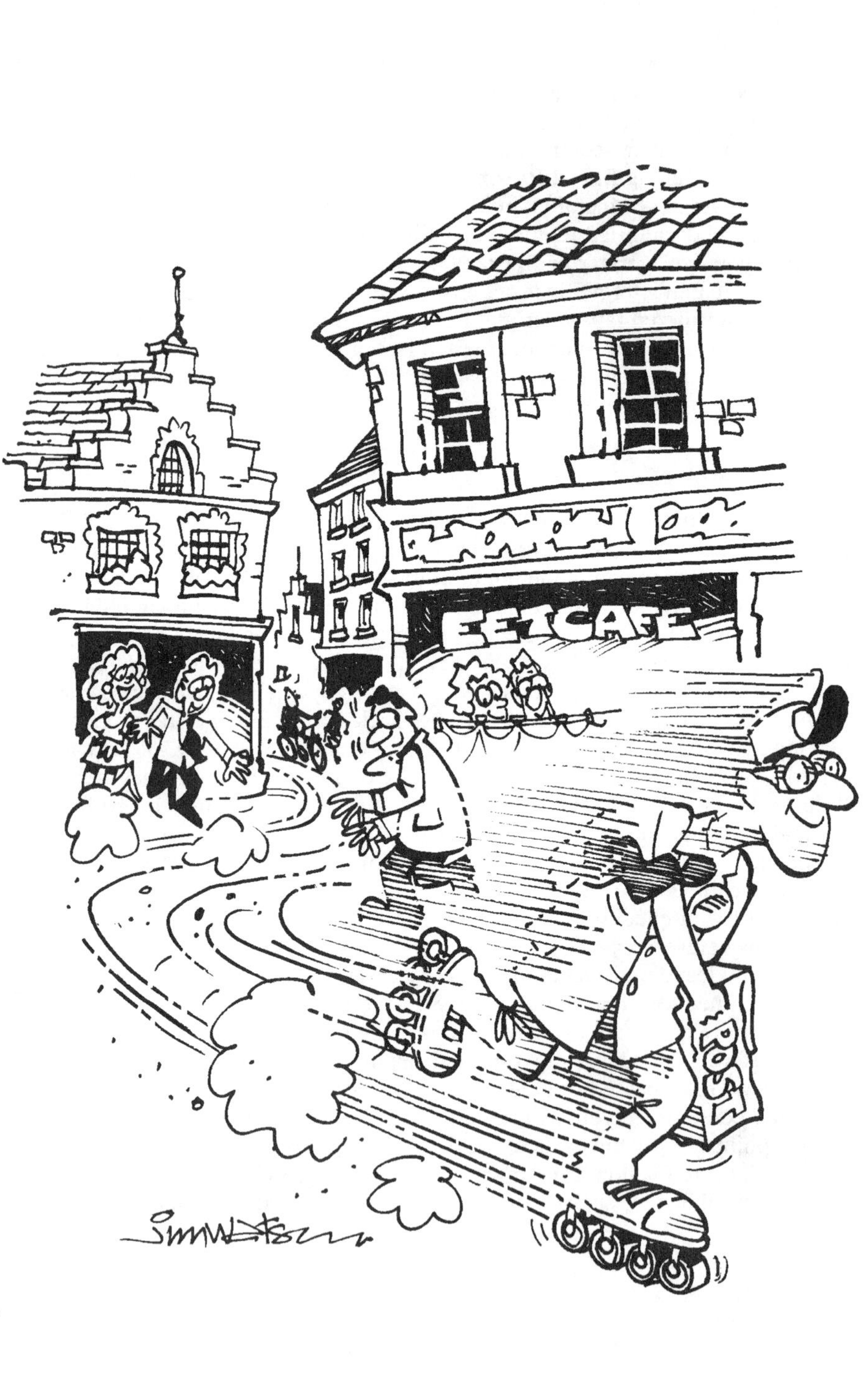
EETCAFE
POST

6.

POST OFFICE SERVICES

Post office services throughout Benelux are reliable and efficient. In fact, the Dutch postal service, PTT Post, is among the best in the world. This certainly wasn't the case 20 years ago, when service and standards had dropped to an all-time low, but the subsequent privatisation of PTT Post is considered a classic example of how privatisation ought to be carried out. Today, not only is PTT Post profitable, but it can guarantee overnight delivery of letters and most packages within Holland. Its shares are traded on several of the major stock exchanges and, since its purchase of TNT courier services, it has established itself as a leader in the field of logistics not only in Holland, but world-wide. Privatisation of the Belgian and Luxembourg post offices is also under way, and all three national post offices are constantly modernising and updating their facilities and operations in preparation for the opening of the postal marketplace to full competition in 2002.

There's a post office (*la poste/de post*) in almost every town and village in Benelux, where all three national post offices promise overnight delivery of standard letters and small packages within the country. They also offer various parcel and courier delivery services, both locally and internationally, as well as postal banking services, although in Holland these are operated by a separate company. Most post offices incorporate a shop selling post office products, although sometimes these are in a separate building (usually near the post office) or within other kinds of shop.

An increasing number of post office services are now available 24 hours a day, seven days a week via automated stamp vending machines, bank (ATM) machines and the Internet. All three national post offices have websites containing a variety of information:

Belgium: The La Poste/De Post site (🖥 www.post.be) offers information and most services in four languages (English, French, Flemish and German), although banking services are available only in French and Flemish.

Holland: The PTT Post site (🖥 www.ptt-post.nl) is in Dutch only but includes an online 'shop' selling stamps, postcards and packing material, and even enables you to track parcels and registered post. You can also download a list of rates for PTT Post's various services – all 50 pages of it.

Luxembourg: La Poste's website (🖥 www.postes.lu), available only in French, offers downloadable copies of most of the forms you might need, e.g. registered post, insurance declarations, customs forms and mail forwarding. You can also check most charges and fees online.

OPENING HOURS

Post office opening hours vary throughout Benelux, as individual post offices set their hours according to local demand, rather than adhering to standardised schedules. Many post offices open as early as 8 or 8.30am and generally stay open until 6pm most weekdays. Post offices in or near busy shopping centres may be also be open on Saturdays, at least until around 4pm. Those in small towns tend to close for an hour or so at lunchtime, although the practice is becoming less common. Opening hours are displayed outside post offices, and the national post office Internet sites (see above) include a list of post offices and their opening hours.

LETTER POST

Standard domestic letters posted anywhere in Benelux are normally delivered the next working day. Delivery times to neighbouring countries may add a day or two, although Benelux post offices claim that this is the fault of the receiving countries' postal system rather than theirs! A standard letter is defined as a sealed envelope no smaller than 90mm x 140mm (3.5in x 5.5in), no larger than 125mm x 235mm (4.9in x 9.25in), no thicker than 5mm (0.2in) and weighing no more than 20g (0.7oz). American 'business size' envelopes (i.e. 9.5 inches or 240mm long) fall just outside these limits, although you can often sneak them through as standard letters. A standard letter must also be rectangular; square, round or other shaped envelopes cost more to post. Benelux post boxes are for stamped post only. Franked post must be taken to a post office, as must any envelope or package that doesn't fit through the slot in a standard post box and any that qualifies for a special rate, e.g. printed material and bulk mail.

Belgium: A standard domestic letter costs €0.42. A non-standard envelope or one weighing between 20 and 50g costs €0.79. You pay €0.89 for letters weighing 50 to 100g, €1.24 for letters between 100 and 250g, and €1.44 for items between 250 and 350g. Items weighing between 350g and 2kg are called *maxipost*, to which a different scale of charges applies. (All La Poste/De Post's rates are shown on the website and in brochures available at post offices.)

For international mail there are two levels of service: priority and non-priority. Priority service is slightly more expensive, but delivery is guaranteed to be at least two days quicker than for non-priority items. Countries outside Belgium are divided into three zones: zone A includes all other EU countries, zone B the rest of Europe, and zone C the rest of the world. To send a letter priority, you must attach a blue '*prior*' sticker to the front of the envelope; otherwise it will be treated as non-priority. *Prior* stickers are available free at all post offices. Rates for priority and non-priority standard letters (i.e. those meeting the same requirements regarding size and weight as for domestic mail) are as follows:

Zone	Priority Rate (€)	Non-priority Rate (€)
A	0.52	0.47
B	0.74	0.52
C	0.85	0.57

There isn't a special rate for postcards, most of which are treated as standard letters.

Belgian post boxes are red and mail collection times are shown on each box. Provided a letter is posted before the last collection time of the day, you can expect it to be delivered (within Belgium) the following working day.

Holland: A standard domestic letter or postcard costs €0.39; letters weighing 20 to 50g cost €0.78, and the scale of charges for heavier items is similar to Belgium's (see above). International post can be sent either priority or standard, the standard service taking from two to ten days longer than priority, depending on the destination. Priority letters up to 20g cost €0.54 to European countries or €0.75 to any other destination. Non-priority mail costs €0.50 to Europe or €0.65 to the rest of the world. Postcards can be sent to any country for €0.54.

Dutch post boxes are red and rectangular, and are often found in pairs, one for local mail (*streekpost*) and the other for all other mail (*overige bestemmingen*). Be sure to check the list of destinations on the local post box, as in some areas this may be limited to specific postal codes. In metropolitan areas this may mean only certain parts of a city, while in other areas it may include several neighbouring towns.

Luxembourg: Standard letters can be sent for €0.45 within Luxembourg, €0.51 to other parts of Europe and €0.74 to anywhere else in the world. For letters weighing between 20 and 50g, the charges are €0.60 within Luxembourg, €0.74 for Europe and €1.12 for the rest of the world. As in Belgium and Holland, there's no special rate for postcards.

The post office's colours in Luxembourg are yellow and green, and post boxes are normally yellow. If you want to know where your nearest post boxes are and the collection times from each one, you can visit the La Poste website (: www.postes.lu), click on '*recherche*' (search) and go to '*localisation des boîtes à lettres*' (finding post boxes). Alternatively, you could go for a walk!

GENERAL INFORMATION

Note the following general information regarding postal services in Benelux:

- All three post offices produce a constant stream of special stamps (*timbres/zegel*) for collectors, as well as offering first-day covers. These can be ordered by post, online, and at any post office shop.

- In Holland you can even design your own stamps and have packages collected from your home or workplace. and all three national post offices offer online tracking of registered and priority items, mailing lists and mass mailing services.

- Certain items addressed to blind people can be posted free or at reduced rates. These include Braille texts and audio tapes weighing up to 7kg (15.43lb). Items over 7kg can also be sent at reduced rates. You should enquire at a post office for details, as each country has different requirements regarding the wrapping and marking of packets. In Belgium, this service is charged at one of the special rates for 'printed material', which includes audio tapes and Braille publications. The Dutch refer to it as *braillezendingen*, while in Luxembourg an item sent to a blind person is called a *cécogramme*.

Belgium:

- Post codes consist of four digits, often prefixed by 'B-', even on domestic mail (but not included in addresses shown in this book).

- Addresses in Flanders should be written in Flemish and those in French-speaking parts of Belgium in French. For Brussels addresses, either language may be used. The following is the correct way to address mail:

French	Flemish
Jacques Brel	Jacques Brel
Rue Brel 45	Brelstraat 45
B-1000 Bruxelles	B-1000 Brussel

Note that in both languages the street number follows the street name and that the post code precedes the name of the city or town.

- Mail with insufficient postage is returned to the sender if there's a return address on the envelope. If there's no return address, the item will be delivered to the addressee, who will be charged the balance of the postage plus a 'fine' of €0.42. (Don't do this to your bank manager!)

- There are a number of discounted rates for 'printed papers', which include Christmas cards, pre-printed death notices, photographs, and audio and video recordings. To qualify for these special postage rates, the material must be in an unsealed envelope and contain no personal message or greeting longer than five words. 'Printed papers' must be taken to a post office and cannot be deposited in a post box. (Rates and detailed requirements are available on the La Poste/De Post website, 🖳 www.post.be.)

- Your postman can sell you small quantities of stamps and can accept standard letters for posting, saving you a trip to a post office. He also has a supply of the most commonly used forms and can accept certain types of registered or declared value items (see below) and issue the necessary receipt. There's a small charge (around €0.42) for each item processed by a postman in addition to the normal postage or service fees.

Holland:

- Dutch post codes consist of four digits followed by a space and then two letters. (As in Belgium, the street number follows the street name and the post code precedes the name of the city or town.) A typical Dutch address is shown below:

V. van Gogh
Kalverstraat 152
1012 XE Amsterdam

Note that Dutch business addresses often include a street and a PO Box address, indicated by the word *Postbus*.

- The many and various services offered by PTT Post include several types of promotional mailing, bulk rates (by piece or by total weight) for small and large packages, mailing lists (either pre-prepared or compiled to order), and an array of logistics, freight and courier services, both domestic and international, including 24-hour guaranteed delivery and 48-hour delivery for most kinds of small packages.

Luxembourg:

- Post codes consist of four digits, often prefixed by 'L-', even on domestic mail (but not included in addresses shown in this book).

- Addresses in Luxembourg are generally written in French and in the French style, as follows:

Mr Jacques Santer
12 rue de l'Eglise
L-1012 Luxembourg

The house or building number appears before the street name, and usually has a comma after it (although not in the addresses shown in this book in order to avoid confusion). Luxembourg city is written simply as Luxembourg, preceded by the appropriate post code.

REGISTERED POST

Registered post is often used in Benelux when proof of posting is required. In many cases, you're required to use registered post for legal notifications, such as terminating a lease or giving notice to quit a job or cancel an insurance policy or other contract. A registered letter (*lettre recommandé/aangetekend schrijven*) will be delivered directly to the addressee or his authorised delegate, who must sign a form confirming receipt. You can also request proof of delivery (*avis de réception/ handtekening retour*), which is a copy of the signed receipt.

If you aren't at home (or work) to sign for a registered letter, you will be left a note requesting you to go to a particular post office and sign for it or to arrange for re-delivery at a more convenient time or to another address. In most cases, the post office will hold registered letters for up to 15 days and will automatically attempt to re-deliver them if they don't hear from the addressee within a few days.

To send a registered letter, you must take the letter and the relevant form to a post office, where you will be given a receipt confirming the time and place of posting. (In Belgium, your postman can process most forms of registered letter for a small service fee.) Registering a letter costs €3.72 in Belgium, around €1.15 in Holland and €2.50 in Luxembourg in addition to the normal postage charge. Proof of delivery costs an extra €0.50 to €1. If a registered letter is lost in the post or cannot be delivered for any reason, you can claim a refund and damages by presenting your receipt at a post office. Note, however, that damages are usually small and don't cover the value of any goods or documents lost. **If you want insurance for the contents of a letter, you must purchase it separately.** Rates vary according to the declared value of the contents and differ between the three Benelux countries; details are available on the national post office websites (see page 100).

PARCEL POST

The post offices of Benelux provide a range of parcel (*colis/pakket*) services, both domestic and international, and there are also a number of parcel delivery services offered by road transport, railway, airline and international courier companies such as DHL, UPS and Federal Express. The Dutch post office entered the market as a major competitor with their acquisition of TNT's parcel and courier services, which they have recently expanded, particularly in the business sector.

Generally, any item over 2kg (4.4lb) or exceeding the maximum size for letters is considered to be a parcel. All three postal services handle parcels up to 30kg (66lb), for both domestic and international delivery, and offer a variety of levels of service, e.g. economy, priority and express. Parcels should always be securely wrapped, and all three post offices sell a wide range of packing materials and boxes through their postal stores and online shops. Packing material is also available at stationery shops.

Belgium: Standard parcel post is called *kilopost* in the Belgian postal system and applies to any item exceeding 305mm (4.7in) in height, 381mm (15in) in length or 30mm (1.2in) in thickness. Domestic *kilopost* parcels are delivered within four working days. International *kilopost* delivery times vary from 2 to 15 days according to the destination. International service is split into six zones (numbered from 0 to 5). Sending a 2.5kg (5.5lb) package to Switzerland (zone 2), for example, would cost €38.42. Complete rate tables and information on requirements and restrictions are available at local post offices and on the post office website (: www.post.be). Information on the website is in English as well as French and Flemish, and you may also be able to obtain English-language leaflets at some post offices.

Belgium's express letter and parcel service, *taxipost*, is operated by EMS Taxipost, a subsidiary of La Poste/De Post. EMS Taxipost has its own website (: www.emstaxipost.be), which describes the various express delivery services. These include parcel (or letter) collection at your home or office, special handling, insurance, and electronic package tracking, which can be done from a computer. Taxipost offers several levels of express service, from 48-hour to overnight.

Holland: Since privatisation, and particularly since acquiring the TNT express service, the Dutch post office has become a world leader in parcel delivery, especially in the business sector. Parcel services are called *worldpack* or *worldpack special*, depending on the size and weight of the parcel and the level of service. *Worldpack* applies to parcels up to 2kg (4.4lb) and offers a choice of priority and standard delivery; *worldpack special* is for parcels up to 20kg (45lb). International parcel delivery is charged by weight and destination, using a three-zone system: EU countries, other European countries and outside Europe. *Worldpack special* parcels can be sent priority or standard to all three zones, and there's an additional economy option for destinations outside Europe. For example, sending a 2.5kg (5.5lb) parcel by *worldpack special* to a non-EU European country costs €20 priority or €17 standard.

The Dutch post office offers a wide range of supplementary services in connection with parcel delivery, including collection (from home or office), insurance, packing materials and various bulk mailing services. It also offers a special rate for books, which most other postal systems have eliminated in recent years. Parcels containing books and weighing up to 5kg (11lb) can be sent priority within Europe for €14.75 – a saving of €3.75 on the normal priority parcel rate.

Luxembourg: Parcels for delivery by the Luxembourg post office are limited to 2.5m (8.2ft) in length, and any package longer than 1.5m (4ft 11ins) must carry a 'bulky package' (*colis encombrant*) sticker. Domestic (*national*) delivery costs €3.60 for parcels up to 2kg (4.4lb), €4.30 for parcels between 2 and 10kg (4.4 and 22lb), and €4.90 for packages of 10 to 31.5kg (22 to 70lb). International destinations are divided into 12 zones, roughly according to distance. The first eight zones include all of Europe, except Russia. Zones 9 to 12 include Russia and the rest of the world. There are three scales of charges: basic (*Q'Pack*), which includes insurance of up to €180 based on the declared value of the parcel at the time of mailing; express (*Q'Pack+*), which guarantees delivery in two to five days and includes insurance up to €625 plus electronic tracking of parcels in transit (available only to certain European countries); and *E'Pack* for non-urgent parcel delivery to destinations outside Europe. Sending a 2.5kg (5.5lb) parcel to Switzerland (zone 4) by *Q'Pack*, for example, costs around €13. Details, including rates and conditions, are available at post offices and on the La Poste website.

MAIL DELIVERY & COLLECTION

If your postman calls with an item requiring a signature or payment of postage or other fees (e.g. VAT or import duties) and you aren't there to receive it, he will leave a form showing the address of the post office where you can collect the item and a phone number if you prefer to arrange re-delivery. To collect mail, you must present the form at the specified post office along with some form of identification (passport or national identity card) proving that you're the person to whom the mail is addressed. If you want to send someone else to collect registered mail addressed to you, you must complete an official authorisation (*procuration/machtiging*) in advance at your local post office. In Belgium, there's a charge of around €9 per year to process an authorisation for any member of your household to collect registered letters or sign for them in your absence. The Dutch and Luxembourg post offices don't charge for this service but require both you and your delegate to present identification when you complete the authorisation.

You can receive mail at any post office in Belgium, Holland or Luxembourg via the international *poste restante* service. If you live in a large town or city, you should have mail addressed to the main post office (*poste centrale/post centraale*) to avoid confusion. Letters should be addressed as follows:

Smith, John
Poste Restante
Poste Centrale
B-1000 Bruxelles
Belgium

Mail sent to a *poste restante* address is returned to the sender if it's unclaimed after 30 days. Identification (e.g. passport or national identity card) is required for collection, and there's a charge for each letter received of €0.30 to €0.50, depending on the post office. Mail can be forwarded from one post office to another. It's also possible to arrange for a post office box (PO box), if you need or want to collect your mail at the post office yourself rather than having it delivered to your home. Mail can also be held for limited periods, e.g. when you're on holiday, or forwarded to you at another address.

Belgium: A PO box (*boîte postale/postbus*) costs €7.81 per quarter (three months) and there's a €12.40 deposit for each key required. Most post offices install PO boxes in a separate room, which may be accessible at all hours or at certain times outside normal opening hours, e.g. Saturdays and Sundays. You can arrange for mail to be held for up to 60 days at a time, for which there's a charge of €8.68.

It's also possible to have your mail redirected or forwarded to another address, e.g. when you move house or if you're going to be away for longer than 60 days. For private customers, redirection within Belgium costs €8.68 for six months and can be renewed for a further six months at €17.35. If the forwarding address is outside Belgium, redirection costs €14.87 for the first six months and €29.75 for a further six months. Redirection for businesses is around twice the cost.

Holland: You can rent a PO box (*postbus*) for €114 per year, but these are intended primarily for business customers. Individuals who need or want to collect mail from a post office can make use of a service called *PostApart*, whereby your mail is held for you at the post office counter. Each day's mail is available for collection after 2pm. *PostApart* costs €5.45 per month, and you must pay for at least three months when you open an account. If you need your mail held for a short period, a holding service (*bewaarservice*) is available for €13.77 for the first two weeks and an additional €2 per week thereafter.

Redirection or forwarding of mail from one address to another is also available, but charges vary according to the reason for requesting it! When you move house, provided you contact the post office at least a month before your move, they will redirect mail to your new address, whether local or international, for one month free of charge. (PTT Post will also provide you with a kit to help you notify your correspondents of your new address.) After the first month, redirection costs €1.25 per week to a new address in Holland, €2.75 per week to anywhere else in Europe or €6.02 per week outside Europe. If you aren't moving house but want your mail redirected within Holland, you must pay €13.77 for the first three weeks and €2 for each week thereafter. Redirection elsewhere in Europe costs €16.27 for the first three weeks plus 3.50 per week thereafter, and the charges for redirection outside Europe are €24.55 plus 7.50 per week.

Luxembourg: You can rent a PO box at most post offices, although this service is generally used by businesses, many of which send an employee to pick up their mail first thing in the morning rather than waiting for the postman to arrive. There's no charge for this 'service', although you must collect your mail every working day. A list of PO box holders is included in the Luxembourg telephone directory.

Mail holding (*ordre de garde*) costs €5 per month plus €3.75 per month for each Luxembourg-based newspaper or journal you want held for you. If you prefer to have your subscription to local newspapers and journals temporarily suspended (*suspension temporaire*) while you're away, the post office will handle this for you free of charge when you place your hold order. You must notify the post office at least three working days before you want the hold order to take effect.

When you move house, the post office will redirect your mail for one year, after which you may renew the service annually for up to three more years. The first year of redirection costs €11.25 and each subsequent year €91.25.

POST BANK ACCOUNTS

The post office is one of the largest banking facilities in each Benelux country. Only the Dutch Post Bank is entirely private (owned and operated by ING Bank), but in all three countries the banking facilities offered by the post office are almost identical to those offered by most banks (see page 250). These include international money transfers, bill payments, cash and debit cards, insurance and investment plans, use of ATMs and other bank machines, and even online (Internet) banking.

Two advantages of banking with the post office are the vast number of 'branches' in each country and often longer opening hours than most banks. For those who prefer dealing in real money, the post office will accept cash payment of utility and other bills, even if you don't have a post office account. Simply take the bill you wish to pay to the post office, and they will make an electronic transfer to the supplier and give you a receipt as proof of payment. Most utility bill payments are handled free of charge and there's a small fee (generally no more than €1) for other bills.

International cash transfers, both telegraphic and electronic (e.g. SWIFT), can also be made via the post office. The Luxembourg P&T (see page 112) is one of Western Union's 50,000 agencies world-wide, through which you can send money to over 195 other countries (if you don't mind paying their high fees).

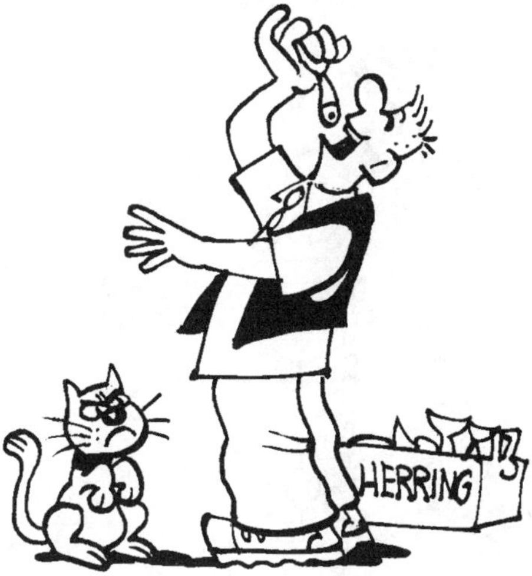
HERRING

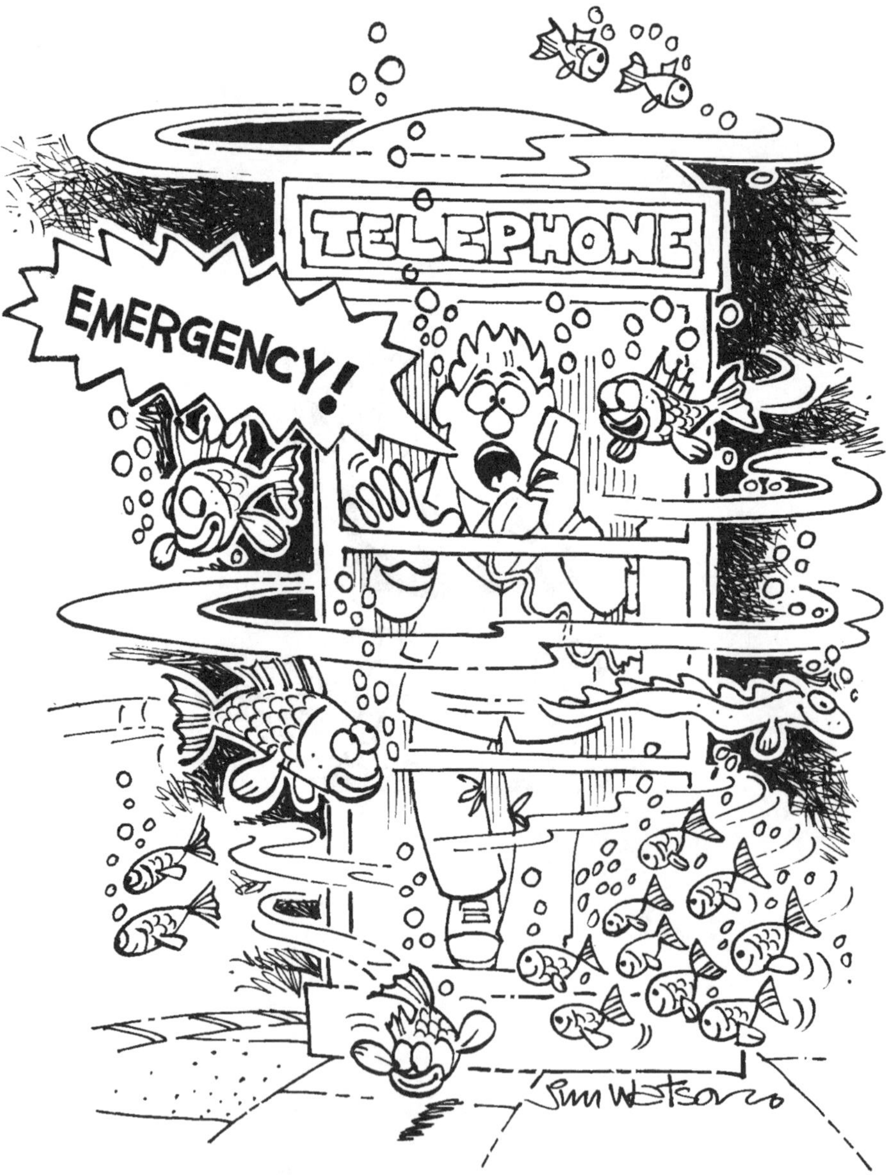
TELEPHONE
EMERGENCY!
Jim Watson

7.

TELEPHONE

Benelux telephone services provide state-of-the-art telecommunications in a wide range of areas, including both fixed line and mobile telephone networks, long-distance and international calling services, Internet services, and high capacity telecommunication lines (ISDN, ADSL and cable) for business and home use.

For decades, telephone services in Benelux were the province of state-owned and operated monopolies called PTTs (Post, Telephone and Telegraph). The PTTs were bureaucratic organisations, better known for creating rules than for anything resembling customer service. But since the early '90s, they have developed into modern and efficient service providers ready to meet the impending competition in an open telecommunications market. The three national telephone companies are: Belgacom in Belgium; KPN Telecom, known simply as KPN, in Holland; and Entreprises de P&T (EPT), known as P&T Luxembourg. These companies still have a monopoly over local telephone services, but for all other services there's a wide choice of operators and service providers, including the national phone companies of neighbouring countries. For example, KPN offers long-distance and mobile phone services in Belgium, and Belgacom does business in Holland as Ben Netherlands. All three Benelux phone companies have also recently expanded their activities in their home countries to include retailing through phone shops (*téléboutique/teleboetiek*) and via the Internet. Details of these services are given below.

Belgium: Belgacom has an extensive website (🖳 www.belgacom.be), with information in English, French and Dutch. You can shop online or find the address of your nearest phone shop.

Holland: KPN's website (🖳 www.kpn.com) contains information about its products and services, but only in Dutch. Phone shops operated by KPN are called Primafoon and are found throughout Holland. To find the address of your nearest Primafoon shop, click on '*klantenservice*' (customer service) to reach the caption '*Primafoon bij u in de buurt*' where you can enter your post code to receive a list of shops and their opening hours. It's also possible to order services and products online, using the Primafoon link on the home page.

Luxembourg: The EPT website (🖳 www.ept.lu) covers various services provided by P&T Luxembourg, including post, postal banking, stamps and Internet services, as well as telecommunications, but information is available only in French. There are four *téléboutiques*: at Luxembourg-Gare, Luxembourg-Cloche d'Or, Esch-sur-Alzette and Ettelbrück. Addresses, contact information and opening hours are listed on the website under the heading '*L'Entreprise – Activités*'. There's an online phone shop at 🖳 www.telecom.lu, which can also be accessed from the EPT website.

INSTALLATION & REGISTRATION

When moving into a new home in Benelux, the simplest way to arrange your telephone connection is by going to a phone shop. You'll need identification (passport or national identity card) plus evidence that you're the new occupant of the property (normally a copy of your lease or a rent or deposit receipt). If you're moving into a property without a telephone line, you will be notified (usually by post) of the date of installation and whether you need to be present. If you're taking over an existing line, it will simply be re-activated with your choice of services and features. However, you should be prepared for a bewildering (and ever increasing) range of options, including: the type of line you prefer (analogue, ISDN or, in some areas, ADSL); the number of lines you need for accessories such as a fax and Internet connection; the type of call charge 'plan' you want (see page 116); and the optional services (see page 115) you'd like. Except for the type of line, most services can be added or adjusted later without the need for another appointment.

Telephones, answering machines and most other forms of communication equipment can be either purchased or rented from the national telephone companies, or you can buy equipment at an electronics shop or other store. Equipment sold in the country is usually pre-registered for use on the national telephone system. Officially, telephones and other equipment imported from other countries must be registered with the phone company to ensure that they're compatible with the local network, but in practice few people bother to register foreign equipment. Most standard telephones, answering machines, faxes, modems, etc. should work in Benelux, although you may have to buy adapters to connect your equipment to telephone or electrical sockets. All three national phone companies have websites (see above), where you can order telephone equipment and make changes to your services.

Belgium: Belgacom operates over 120 phone shops throughout Belgium, where you can arrange connection or line installation. Alternatively, you can make arrangements through electronics stores such as FNAC and Exell. You must provide identification and complete a form, and you will be notified by post of your new phone number and the date and time of the installation or connection. Belgacom promises installation within five working days of receiving a request; if they fail to meet this deadline, they will give you two months' free service (i.e. no monthly line fee) as compensation.

If you opt for the basic, analogue service, there's a charge of €134.38 for installing a new line or €65.99 for re-connection of an existing line. A new ISDN line costs €182.97; to convert an analogue line to ISDN costs €101.98. ADSL is available in some areas, with a variety of installation packages from 'do-it-yourself' to 'have everything done for you'.

Wall sockets for telephone equipment take a large plug with five round pins, four arranged in a rectangle at the bottom and a single pin at the top. For phones and equipment with an RJ11 plug, which is standard on telephone equipment in many countries, you can purchase adapters at most electronics shops and do-it-yourself stores in Belgium. Further information (in English) regarding registration and installation is available on the Belgacom website (🖥 www.belgacom.be).

Holland: To arrange telephone connection or installation, you should go to your nearest KPN Primafoon shop. Most cities and towns have at least one. (You can use the KPN website to find your local shop – see page 112). You will need to produce identification and a copy of your home rental agreement. The charge for a new analogue line is around €45. A new ISDN line costs €102.10 unless you opt to do-it-yourself (*doe-het-zelf*), which can save you at least €65.

Dutch telephones use a four-pin plug, with the two top pins further apart than the lower pins. Adapters can be bought for equipment with an RJ11 plug at most electronics shops, do-it-yourself and hardware stores selling telephones and electrical equipment. Further information about registration and installation and the various line options available can be found (in Dutch only) on the KPN website (🖥 www.kpn.nl).

Luxembourg: Telephone connection can be arranged through EPT phone shops or online at 🖳 http://shop.telecom.lu, where you can also find a detailed list of charges for telephone services. Installation of a new line or activation of an existing line €57.50, but you must pay an additional €213.90 for wiring a new house and installing telephone points. This additional charge also applies if the re-connection of an existing line involves rewiring. Installation of an ISDN line for home use normally costs between €55 and €90, depending on the type of service you want and the kind of terminal connectors required.

In Luxembourg, new telephone installations use the standard RJ11 plug, but in older buildings you may find Belgian-style plugs still in use. Adapters can be bought at phone shops and electronics stores.

USING THE TELEPHONE

In Benelux, it's generally wise to dial the complete phone number, including the area code, irrespective of where you're calling from. Numbers are usually dictated in groups of two or three digits – for example, 'forty-three, twenty-five, sixteen' or 'four hundred and thirty-two, five hundred and sixteen' rather than 'four three two five one six'. They're often written with a full stop or space between each group.

Telephone numbers in Belgium have nine digits, all of which must be used when dialling from anywhere in Belgium. The first two or three digits used to be an area code (although they no longer function as such), and these are often separated from the rest of the number by a slash as follows: 02/123.45.67. In Holland, phone numbers have ten digits, the first three or four of which comprise an area code. For example, 020 is the area code for Amsterdam. The area code may be separated from the rest of the number by being written in parentheses. If you're calling from a number with the same area code, you can omit the code and dial only the rest of the number, but you can also dial the full ten-digit number. In Luxembourg, a telephone number can have anything from four to ten digits. Simply dial the whole lot and hope for the best!

Telephone numbers starting with 0800 are national or international freephone (toll-free) numbers. Numbers that begin with 0900 are usually premium rate lines, particularly in Holland. In Belgium, some premium numbers begin with 070, but these are gradually being changed to 0900 numbers. Charges for premium rate calls vary from €0.25 to €1 per minute for information and booking numbers, to several euros per minute for certain 'adult' services. All three Benelux countries use the prefix 06 for mobile phone numbers, for which there are special (i.e. expensive) call rates.

To dial a number in Belgium, Holland or Luxembourg from outside the country, you dial the international access code (00 from most countries in Europe), followed by the appropriate country code: 32 for Belgium, 31 for Holland or 352 for Luxembourg. Then omit the 0 for all Belgian and Dutch phone numbers. (Most Luxembourg numbers don't start with 0, so you should dial the whole number.) It's possible to direct dial most countries from both private and public telephones in Benelux. (A full list of country codes is included in the information pages of the phone book). All three countries use the standard international access code, 00, for international calls. To reach the UK, for example, you dial 00-44; for the USA or Canada dial 00-1 and then the area code (minus the initial 0, if applicable) and phone number. Detailed dialling instructions are included in most telephone directories, often in English as well as in local languages.

Telephone etiquette in Benelux is rather formal and it's considered rude to ask to speak to someone without first identifying yourself (and your company, if it's a business call). Many people answer their phone with a greeting such as 'good day' (*bonjour/goedemiddag*) followed by their name. You should return the greeting, introduce yourself and then state the reason for your call or ask for the person you wish to speak to. Except with friends, you normally identify yourself as Mr or Mrs (Smith), rather than using your first name.

If you have a voice mail system, either at work or at home through the local telephone company, it's usually possible to record your own message or choose a standard message in English (or sometimes other languages). To enquire about having a voice mail system on your home line, enquire at one of the local phone stores. It's becoming increasingly common for telephone companies to provide answering services or a voice mail system free of charge, often in conjunction with mobile phone or other services.

OPTIONAL SERVICES

All three national telephone companies offer a range of optional telephone services (as do most of the mobile phone companies – see page 115). There are two types of service: those for which you pay a monthly subscription, and those for which you're charged each time you use them. The most popular subscription services include the following:

● **Call transfer** allows you to divert calls to another telephone automatically, e.g. from home to office (or vice versa) or to your mobile phone.

● **Call waiting** lets you know when another caller is trying to contact you when you're already on the phone and allows you to speak to the other person without terminating your call.

● **Three-way calling** allows you to hold a three-way conference call.

● **Caller identification** displays the telephone number of the caller while the phone is ringing so that you know who is calling you. To make use of this service, you need to have either a phone with a display feature or a display box attached to your phone. Both phones with built-in displays and display boxes can be purchased at phone shops and most electronics and electrical appliance shops. Note that calls from outside the country may not be displayed correctly (or at all).

Charges for subscription services vary but in most cases are less than €1 or €2 per month. Packaged groups of services (such as Belgacom's 'Comfort Services' plan) are generally also available. Contact your telephone company or refer to their website, where many services can be ordered online.

Services for which you pay a fixed fee each time you use them include alarm call, which is available in all three countries. Details of how to set the alarm feature are included in the front of the phone book (usually in English) and charges are between €0.25 and €0.55 per call. (You might find it more economical to buy an alarm clock.)

CHARGES

Telephone charges may include a monthly line charge, equipment rental charges, monthly fees for any subscription services you've requested, and charges for other services such as alarm calls, in addition to call charges. Monthly line charges vary according to the call 'plan' you've chosen. For example, you may opt to pay a higher monthly line charge in order to benefit from cheaper calls. All three telephone companies offer a range of plans that may include discounts on certain types of calls, or discounted Internet or mobile phone services. (For international call charges, see below.)

Belgium: Monthly charges depend on the type of phone line you have. A basic, single analogue (i.e. normal) phone line costs €16.20 per month. There's also a two-line option for €28.33 per month. An ISDN service, complete with two ISDN lines and up to six separate phone numbers costs €36.29 per month. ADSL is available in two levels, 'Go' and 'Plus', at €39.54 and €54.41 per month respectively. (The Go service offers a maximum download speed of 750Kbits per second and a volume of 10GB, the Plus service 1Mbits/sec. and 15GB.) Domestic calls are charged at a single nation-wide tariff. (Belgium eliminated the notion of zones for calling within Belgium at the beginning of the year 2000.) Peak time calls, i.e. between 8am and 7pm Mondays to Fridays, cost around €0.05 per minute, and off-peak calls (at all other times, including public holidays) around €0.025, i.e. half-price. There's also a charge of €0.05 for all connected calls. Note that charges are calculated to the nearest second, so that a one-and-a-half minute peak time call will cost €0.075.

Belgacom offer a variety of discount plans costing from €1 to €6 and giving you discounts of up to 10 per cent on domestic calls and up to 28 per cent on international calls.

Holland: Monthly line charges vary in Holland according to whether you have an analogue line or an ISDN line and the level of service you choose. In general, the higher the monthly line fee, the lower your call charges.

The standard service, called 'BelBasis', costs €16.43 per month for an analogue line or €23.79 per month for an ISDN line. As in Belgium, you then pay a fixed fee for each connected call (*starttarief*) plus a per minute charge calculated to the nearest second. The *starttarief* for local calls is €0.035 and for long-distance calls and calls to mobile phones €0.045. Per minute charges vary from €0.01 per minute (Mondays to Fridays from midnight to 8am and all day Saturdays and Sundays) to €0.028 per minute (Mondays to Fridays between 8am and 7pm) with an intermediate rate of €0.015 per minute for calls made between 7pm and midnight on weekdays.

'BelPlus' service costs €18.72 per month for an analogue line but offers a reduced weekday evening rate of 0.0125 per minute (so you need to make at least 15 hours of weekday evening calls every month to make it worthwhile!). Both BelBasis and BelPlus services allow you to pre-select a certain number of domestic and international phone numbers (*voordeelnummers*), calls to which are then charged at reduced rates. (The reduction also applies to the *starttarief*.) You can set up or change your *voordeelnummers* at any time by dialling a special *zelf-service-lijn*.

There's also a 'BelBudget' service, available only to those with a single analogue line. The monthly line fee is €9.05 but there are no call discounts or *voordeel-nummers*.

Luxembourg: The monthly fee for an analogue phone line in Luxembourg is €18.57, and an ISDN line costs €25.53 per month. Calls within Luxembourg are charged at €0.031 per minute during business hours (Mondays to Fridays from 8am to 7pm) and at €0.015 per minute at all other times and on public holidays. Domestic calls are charged to the nearest whole minute, which means that if you speak for two minutes and 29 seconds you get 29 seconds free!

Long-distance & International Calls

Deregulation of the telecommunications market has resulted in an intense price war, and considerable savings can be made on long-distance (in Holland) and international calls by shopping around for the lowest rates. There's a wide variety of call providers and services for which you're charged on a per call basis, i.e. by dialling a special prefix or by programming your phone to dial it automatically every time you make a non-local call. It's even possible to buy a gadget that can be programmed to transfer each call to the 'best' provider, based on criteria you set! Call rates change constantly, and deciding which is the 'best' service for you depends on how often you call long-distance or internationally, which countries you call, and at what time. The three national telephone companies, Belgacom, KPN and P&T Luxembourg, also offer competitively priced long-distance and international call packages.

Belgium: There's no longer a 'long-distance' call rate in Belgium, where all domestic calls are charged at the same rate (see above). For international calls, Belgacom offers several discount plans whereby you can save up to 50 per cent on standard rates for calls made at certain times of day or to pre-selected numbers or countries. Their 'Benefit+' plan, for example, costs €1 per month and provides a 20 per cent discount on all calls to one pre-selected country, a 20 per cent reduction on connection charges and a 25 per cent discount on international calls made with a Belgacom Calling Card (see page 122).

Other companies offering international call services include Tele2, Global One, KPN Belgium, Mobistar and Versatel. A list of phone service companies can be found on the Belgian Institute of Postal Services and Telecom website (🖥 www.bpt.be).

Holland: KPN's long-distance and international call charges are competitive with the many alternative services available in Holland. These include Bel1600, NetSource, Scarlet, Talkline, Axxon, Ocean, Versatel, Budget Phone and Vocalis. Each provider has a different package, some offering reduced rates at certain off-peak times, while others offer a fixed price for each country at all times. If trying to calculate which package will suit you best is giving you a headache, you can visit the Spraakmaker website (🖥 www.spraakmakertele.com) where you simply input your calling habits and let a computer work it out for you! The site is all in Dutch, but it isn't difficult to follow with a basic knowledge of the language. (You could even put the savings you make on phone calls towards Dutch lessons.)

Each call provider has a four-digit code with which you can prefix any phone number in order to route the call through that provider. You must first register with the provider or providers you wish to use. Most people prefer to choose a single call provider and register its four-digit code with KPN so that all long-distance and international calls are automatically re-routed. KPN even has a freephone number (☎ 0800-1273) for registering an alternative carrier's code.

Luxembourg: As in Belgium, all domestic calls in Luxembourg are charged at the same rate. With international calls, there's less choice of providers than in Belgium or Holland. P&T Luxembourg's charges are based on a ten-zone system. Certain parts of Belgium, France and Germany are included in a 'neighbour zone' (*zone de voisinage*), to which calls cost €0.104 per minute. The UK, USA and Canada are all in zone 1, with call charges of €0.144 per minute at peak times (Mondays to Fridays between 8am and 7pm) and €0.12 off-peak. Calls are charged on a per second basis subject to a minimum of one minute. P&T Luxembourg also offers 'frequent number' and 'frequently called country' discounts. Alternative services are limited to call back companies and telephone calling cards such as MCI, AT&T and Sprint International, which offer better rates than P&T Luxembourg on most international calls.

BILLS

Belgacom, KPN and P&T Luxembourg all bill their customers bi-monthly, and you must generally pay bills within 10 to 15 days. All three telephone companies have low tolerance of late payment and, although they must go through a formal notification process before cutting you off, they will reduce you to 'minimal service' (meaning that you can receive incoming calls but can only dial emergency numbers) shortly after issuing the first late payment notice. It's possible to set up a direct debit from your bank account, which is recommended if you travel frequently or have a tendency to lose bills, or you can pay via the telephone using a special number.

Belgacom and KPN both offer online billing services on their respective websites. (P&T Luxembourg doesn't yet offer this service.) You can review prior bills, check to see what calls you've made in the current billing period (i.e. before you receive your bill) and analyse your telephone usage in a variety of ways. All three Benelux phone companies charge extra if you want or need an itemised bill (i.e. listing all phone numbers you've called, plus the time and duration of each call) but much of the same information is available free online. The KPN site, in particular, allows you not only to see details of all the calls you've made, but also to highlight your most expensive calls, longest calls or most frequently called numbers or countries. You can also pay your bill online and sign up for various special offers related to use of the online billing service (e.g. a rebate for downloading your billing information from the site instead of having the telephone company send you a bill every two months).

Most long-distance providers provide itemised bills for no additional charge, and some offer online billing whereby customers can refer to prior bills, download billing information and pay bills via the Internet.

DIRECTORIES

The telephone company to which you pay your monthly line fee will provide you with a free directory or directories (i.e. white pages and Yellow Pages) covering your local area. You're normally entitled to one set of directories for each telephone line you have. What constitutes a local area varies considerably from country to country. In Belgium there are 39 different areas, whereas the whole of Luxembourg is one area covered by a single telephone directory.

Directories are much more than lists of phone numbers and also contain information about telephone and emergency services, and about local attractions and public services. There's also an increasing number of online directories, produced by independent companies as well as the national phone companies.

Belgium: There are 39 telephone areas in Belgium, in most of which the white pages (*pages blanches/witte gids*) and the classified listings, usually referred to as the Yellow Pages (*Pages d'Or/Gouden Gids*), are published in separate volumes. All telephone subscribers within the area covered by a directory are listed in the white pages, unless they pay a monthly fee €2.63 to be excluded (ex-directory) – in Belgium you have to pay even to have a service withheld! At the end of the white pages, there are lists of 0800 numbers, including both local services and local companies, and international freephone numbers.

The Yellow Pages list products and services by category, and there's an index of categories – in both French and Dutch in most Belgian directories. The Yellow Pages for Brussels and Antwerp also include indexes in English and German. There's normally an extensive information section (*pages info/infogids*) providing information about everything from post codes to local recycling programmes, as well as listing town halls, government agencies and ministries, and street names (with maps). In another section, which usually has blue-edged pages, there's a list of the so-called 'liberal professions' (*professions libérales/vrije beroepen*), where you can find doctors, dentists, architects, attorneys, notaries and other licensed professionals who are otherwise prohibited from advertising.

You can obtain additional copies of your local directories, or directories for other areas, at Belgacom shops, where you can also buy a nation-wide directory, available only on CD-ROM at a price of €81.25. This is updated twice a year, each update costing an additional €48.75, and is also available from some post offices and stores such as FNAC which sell Belgacom products. You can look up any Belgian telephone number free on the Belgacom website (💻 www.belgacom.be) using an online version of the white or Yellow Pages. Other online directories for Belgium are available via 💻 www.belcast.be and www.infobel.be.

Holland: KPN's telephone directories are also available in three media: a printed version (*telefoongids*), a CD-ROM (*CD-foongids*) and an Internet facility (*telefoongids op Internet*). As in Belgium, the printed white and Yellow Pages are usually published in separate volumes, one for each area code (*netnummer*), and entries are arranged alphabetically by town (*woonplaats*). A standard entry includes a person's surname or a company's name, street, post code and the local phone number (i.e. without the area code). Where there are several people with the same surname, the entries are arranged alphabetically by street name rather than by initials or first names. Names beginning van, van de and de, which are common in Holland, are listed according to the first letter of the main part of the name and not under van or de, and names beginning with the letters ij appear under Y.

There's a charge of €5 to €10 per year for special entries (e.g. in bold type) or additional entries (i.e. for another person sharing the same phone number), or to be listed in a neighbouring area's directory (e.g. for a business number). As in Belgium, you must pay if you *don't* want your number to appear in the phone book! If you're a KPN mobile phone subscriber, you can also have your mobile number listed free of charge. The Yellow Pages (*Gouden Gids*) is a classified listing of businesses in the local area. Both printed directories include information about telephone services, local government services and post codes, as well as maps.

The CD-ROM version of the telephone directory contains all Dutch numbers, including mobile phone numbers, and e-mail and website addresses, and incorporates various search facilities. (The 2001 version even contains a route planner for driving in Holland!) The CD-ROM directory costs €26.77 and is available from phone shops and some computer stores. If you want to receive quarterly updates, you can take out a subscription costing €225. Monthly updates are also available, as are versions of the directory designed for business use.

KPN's directory is also available online, and it promises that the information is updated daily. You can use a link from the KPN website or go directly to 🖳 www.de telefoongids.com. On the site you can look up information by name (*zoeken op naam*) or by category (*zoeken op trefwoord*) and you can find area codes for towns and what towns are covered by which area codes (*zoeken op netnummer/woonplaats*). You can also enter a telephone number and find who it belongs to, but this facility is limited to business numbers. The site includes an international section, listing country codes and providing links to online directories for most foreign countries where they're available.

Luxembourg: Luxembourg can accommodate its 400,000 residents in a single telephone directory. The white pages (*annuaire*) lists all telephone subscribers under the town in which they live. If you prefer to remain ex-directory, you only need to notify P&T Luxembourg. There's no charge! As P&T Luxembourg is still part of the Luxembourg PTT, the information section at the front of the white pages contains information about the post office, post codes and postage rates, and even a list of PO boxes. There's a section listing government offices, their phone numbers, e-mail addresses and websites, and of course you can also find detailed information about P&T Luxembourg services, contact numbers and how to understand your telephone bill. The Yellow Pages (*Annuaire Professionnel*) list businesses and professional practices by category, with a separate section at the front for doctors, dentists and vets, plus a list of hospitals and pharmacies. The category headings are numbered and there are indexes in English, French and German.

The alternative to the printed directory is the online directory (🖳 www.annuaire. lu). There are both white page and Yellow Page search tools, and you don't need to know the town in which a person or company is located in order to search the database. The online directory also includes information about emergency numbers, hospitals and pharmacies, as well as a list of crisis hotlines.

MOBILE TELEPHONES

Throughout Benelux it seems as if almost everyone has at least one mobile phone (*portable/GSM telefoon*), including small children and pensioners. They've become a 'necessary' as well as sometimes a fashion accessory. (Some mobiles have interchangeable face plates so that you can match your phone to your outfit.) They're also fast becoming a public nuisance. Many cinemas, theatres, concert halls and even restaurants make an announcement requesting that phones be switched off before the start of a performance or service, and some trains have 'no telephone' carriages (although it isn't at all clear what penalty you might incur for forgetting to switch off your mobile phone or for making a call from a no phone railway carriage).

Note that in recent years there has been widespread publicity concerning a possible health risk due to the microwave radiation emitted by mobile phones. There's also considerable concern over car drivers who are distracted while talking on mobile phones, and the Benelux countries are among several European nations that have passed or are considering passing laws to prohibit or restrict the use of mobile phones while driving, even using 'hands free' systems.

The three national telephone companies provide mobile phone services under the names Belgacom Mobile, KPN Mobile and P&T Luxembourg, and they offer various packages including fixed line and mobile services, combined answering services, and special rates for transferring calls from a fixed line to a mobile or vice versa. Both they and the various independent mobile phone companies (KPN Orange Belgium and Mobistar in Belgium; Ben Netherlands, Dutchtone, Libertel Netwerk and Telfort in Holland; and Tango SA in Luxembourg) offer WAP, Internet and other advanced features. As in many other countries, it's normally best to purchase a mobile phone as part of a package including a network contract (usually for 6 to 12 months), where the phone itself is offered at a heavily discounted price and sometimes virtually free.

Mobile phone numbers throughout Benelux start with 06, and all calls made to mobiles are charged at a higher rate than calls to fixed line phones. Unlike in the USA, a mobile phone user pays only for the calls he makes and not for calls received. There's usually a discount on calls made from one mobile phone to another, particularly if they're on the same network. You can contract for mobile phone services on a monthly basis, whereby you receive a certain amount of calling time each month (sometimes limited to off-peak or other times), or you can opt for a 'pay as you talk' system, which requires you to insert a pre-paid card in the phone, as if you were using a public card phone. International calls made on mobile phones are billed separately, at rates as high as €1 per minute. However, many mobile phone service providers offer plans that treat the whole of Benelux as part of your 'national' calling area.

Buying a mobile phone is a veritable minefield, as prices, services and conditions change constantly. Be sure to shop around and compare the various offers, features and types of phones available. Check that the network coverage is adequate for your needs, especially if you will be making use of roaming or international services. If you plan to use your mobile phone for data connections (faxes, Internet links, etc.), make sure you understand how data calls are charged, as they aren't normally included in your monthly time allowance or charges may be based on other factors, such as the number of megabytes downloaded (which can add up quickly if you're surfing the web on a mobile phone).

Almost all mobile phone service providers have extensive websites where you can study and compare the terms and conditions of their different offers at your leisure. There's also a number of industry associations (which promote minimum standards and contract provisions), whose websites contain comparisons between the various packages on offer (e.g. the GSM Association website at ⌨ www.gsmworld.com).

PUBLIC TELEPHONES

Public telephones are becoming increasingly rare in Benelux, now that almost everyone seems to have a mobile phone. Nevertheless, you can usually find a public phone in post offices, hotel foyers, hospitals and restaurants, in pedestrianised areas of towns, and at airports and railway and bus stations. Hardly any public phones, however, are coin operated, and almost all require a phone card, a credit card or one of the local cash cards, such as Proton or Chipper (see page 254). Most public telephones allow you to make calls to emergency services and many freephone numbers without having to use a card or coins.

Phone cards are generally available at news stands, post offices, railway stations, phone shops operated by the national phone companies, and sometimes at banks and supermarkets. Cards can be purchased in various values from €5 to €20. After picking up the receiver, you should insert your phone card in the relevant slot. Note that many phones also take credit cards and may have separate slots for each type of card. The display on the telephone should tell you how much money you have left on the card before you dial as well as during a call, warning you when the card is almost exhausted that you should be prepared to insert a new one if you wish to continue the call.

Belgacom, KPN and P&T Luxembourg also offer a kind of phone card called a Calling Card, which can be used in most public telephones. Calls made with a Calling Card are charged to your home or office account and are included in your normal telephone bill. You can either insert the card or dial the number printed on it, followed by a PIN, before dialling the number you wish to call. Because you don't need to insert the card, Calling Cards can also be used from private phones.

INTERNET

The Internet is widely used throughout Benelux, where most banking operations and many interactions with utilities providers and the government can be conducted online, and the number of Internet service providers (ISPs) is constantly growing. It's possible to obtain 'free' Internet connection (i.e. without having to pay a monthly fee), although you will have to pay for calls to the ISP. However, many ISPs now offer plans that include telephone charges, often at reasonable rates, e.g. €20 per month for 20 hours online. All three national telephone companies offer Internet access services, often combined with ordinary telephone (especially ISDN and ADSL) or mobile phone services. Other call providers have also started offering Internet access as part of long-distance and international calling plans. Tele2, for example, offers Internet access in all three Benelux countries through its website (🖳 www.everyday.com). As an increasing number of mobile phones have WAP and other Internet facilities, many mobile phone companies have started offering Internet services in conjunction with mobile phone services. Internet services are also available through many cable television networks in Benelux, and cable-based Internet access has the advantage of being considerably faster than a telephone-line connection.

EMERGENCY NUMBERS

The European Union has established 112 as the Europe-wide emergency number, and this can be used to dial the emergency services (*urgences/noodgeval*) throughout Benelux, although Belgium and Luxembourg also have other emergency numbers. All emergency numbers are listed prominently in telephone directories, usually on the inside front cover or first page of either the white or Yellow Pages.

Belgium: Belgium has adopted the EU standard 112 as an emergency number, but you can also use 100 to contact the fire department or ambulance service, and 101 to call the police or *gendarmes* from anywhere in the country. Calls to all emergency numbers are free. Other useful emergency numbers are: 02-648 4014, an English-language crisis and information line operated by the Community Help Service in Brussels; and 070-34 4344, on which you can report lost or stolen bank or credit cards.

Holland: Holland has adopted 112 as its only emergency number, for the police, fire department and urgent medical assistance. There are a number of emergency helplines, called SOS Lines, for which the numbers vary by city or region, e.g. 020-675 7575 in Amsterdam, 070-311 0305 in The Hague, and 010-436 2244 in Rotterdam.

Luxembourg: The standard European emergency number 112 will connect you with ambulance, hospital, civil defence, fire and rescue services, as well as emergency vets. To reach the police, dial 113. A few other useful emergency numbers are:

- 12345 – a children's and young people's help line (*aide aux jeunes enfants et jeunes gens/kanner an jugendtelefon*);

- 54 66 77 – the Addiction Prevention Centre (*Centre de Prévention des Toxico-manies/Sucht-Telefon*);

- 45 29 67 – SOS Animals (*SOS Animaux/SOS Déieren*)

- 58 38 91 – a distress hotline (*SOS Détresse/SOS Hélief*)

Other hotline and social services numbers are listed on 🖳 www.luxweb.lu under *Infos Utiles* (Useful Information).

FAX

Fax (*télécopieur* or *téléfacsimilé/faxen*) is widely used throughout Benelux, and fax machines can be purchased or rented from national telephone companies (Belgacom, KPN and P&T Luxembourg) at any of their phone shops as well as from electronics stores. Before bringing a fax machine to any of the Benelux countries, check that it will work there or that it can be modified. It's also possible to send and receive faxes directly from your computer, using a fax/modem card and the appropriate software, although this requires you to leave your computer running in order to receive incoming faxes. You can now purchase 'all-in-one' machines that combine the functions of a fax, printer, photocopier and scanner.

If your fax machine is connected permanently to a phone line, you will probably receive a large amount of unwanted advertising material for everything from English-language lessons to travel and holiday packages and illegal radar detectors, which will waste paper and fax roll or toner. Most of these are more annoying than harmful, but beware of bogus fax bills (often for hundreds of euros) purporting to be from one of the national telephone companies. This is a Europe-wide scam offering you 'the right to inclusion in an annual directory of fax owners' in return for prompt payment. The give-away is usually the foreign address!

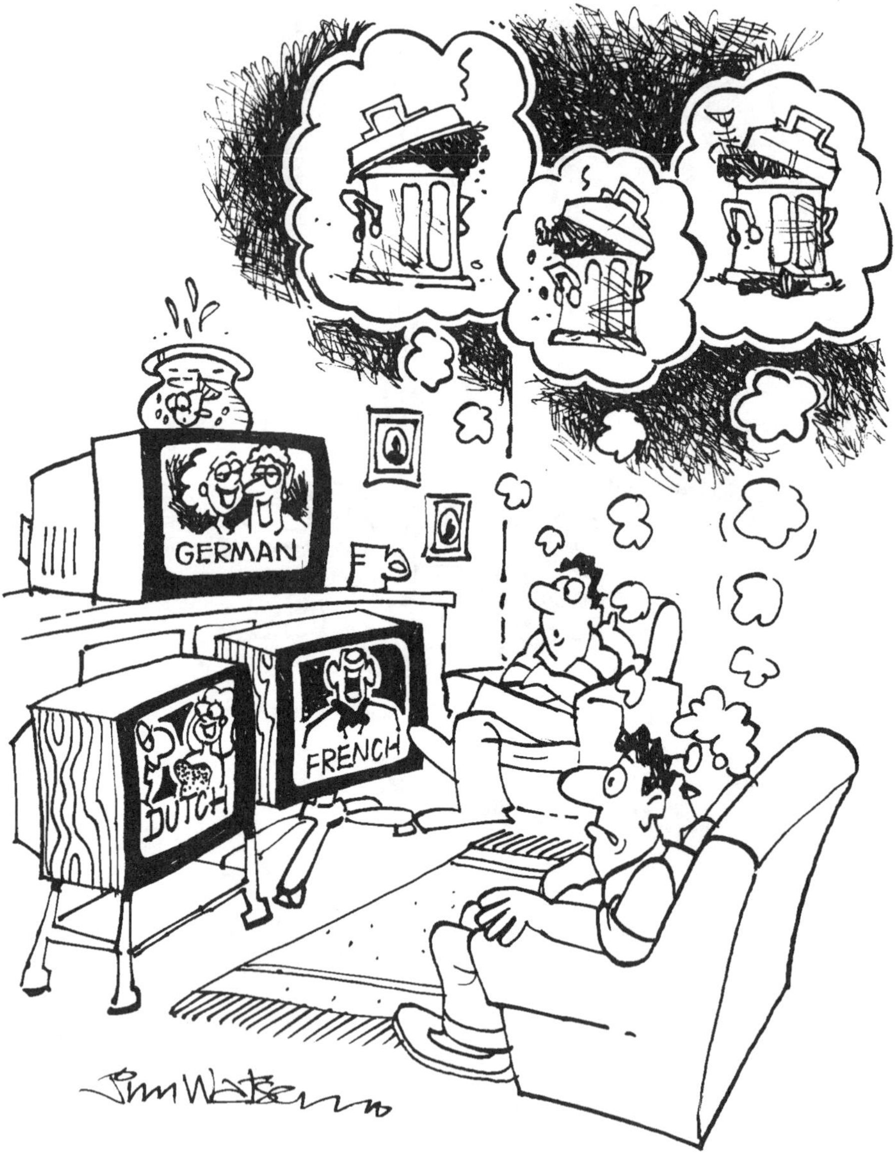
GERMAN
DUTCH
FRENCH
Jim Watson

8.

TELEVISION & RADIO

Both radio and television were strictly controlled by the national governments of Benelux until the '80s. Belgium and Holland operated state-run broadcasting companies, whose programming was of a largely 'public service' nature (i.e. dull) and contained no commercial advertising. In Luxembourg, however, the national monopoly for broadcast services was granted to a commercial company, *Radio en Télévision Lëtzebuerg* (RTL), which took advantage of the Duchy's location and linguistic diversity to broadcast commercial radio and television to Belgian, Dutch, German and French audiences. In fact, RTL was one of the first commercial broadcasters in Europe and is now owned by the German media giant Bertelsmann. Belgium and Holland continued to restrict broadcasting within their own countries, so that a number of pirate radio and television stations were started, on ships and former oil rigs in the North Sea, to provide more 'popular' fare. It wasn't until the late '80s that advertising restrictions were finally dropped and the Belgian and Dutch national broadcast companies were forced to compete openly for audiences (although most people still find their output dull!). Today, the full range of broadcast media is available in all three countries, including extensive cable and satellite services.

TELEVISION

Standards

Standards for television reception in Benelux aren't the same as in some other countries. Like most of continental Europe, the Benelux countries use the PAL-B/G standard, which differs from the PAL-I standard used in Britain, the SECAM-L standard used in France, the North American NTSC standard and SECAM-D/K used in Eastern Europe and many African countries. In general this means that if you're coming from any of these countries you may find your TV set of limited use (i.e. you can use it only to replay video tapes – foreign ones at that), unless it's multi-standard or equipped with a satellite receiver. In border areas, it's possible to receive French channels on a PAL-I TV, although they're in black and white, as colour transmission is the primary difference between the various systems.

Multi-standard TV and video recorders (VCRs) are widely available in the Benelux region (perhaps because the locals have been accustomed to taking advantage of neighbouring countries' programmes since television first started), where most TVs and video equipment accept both PAL and SECAM signals and some even accommodate the different versions of PAL and SECAM. The American NTSC standard poses more of a problem as far as TV is concerned, although there are few European stations broadcasting in NTSC in any case. However, many VCRs designed for use with PAL/SECAM televisions can play back NTSC tapes even on a PAL television. (This feature used to be available only in more expensive VCRs, but now it's common in all but the cheapest models.)

If you buy a TV in Benelux, you will find it advantageous to choose one with teletext, which allows you to display programme schedules and a wealth of other useful and interesting information. (Subtitles, otherwise known as 'closed captioning', are usually carried on one of the teletext channels and are an excellent way to hone your local language skills even if your hearing is normal!) An increasing number of films are broadcast in wide screen (16:9) format, and many new TVs allow you to change formats as well as providing enhanced sound quality and the facility to take advantage of various interactive services offered by cable and satellite companies. A basic 36cm (14in) portable TV with remote control can be purchased new for around €200 to €300. Larger models, such as a 55cm (21in) set, can cost over €500, depending on the make and the number of features. You can sometimes save up to 50 per cent in sales or at hypermarkets such as Auchan and Carrefour or large electronics retailers. Unless you want the latest model, you can buy equipment second-hand through expatriate clubs or advertisements in free newspapers.

Terrestrial TV

Owing to the size and location of the Benelux region, it's possible to receive many terrestrial TV channels from neighbouring countries, including some English-language programmes (as well as broadcasts in French, Dutch, German, Italian, Portuguese, Spanish, and sometimes Arabic and Turkish). Some British terrestrial TV channels (notably ITV, Channel 4 and Channel 5) can be received in coastal areas of Belgium and Holland. (Ask at your local electronics shop for the best antenna and a signal booster, if required.) In Dutch-speaking areas, films and some programmes are normally broadcast in their original language (sometimes marked in programme guides as VO for *version original*) with Dutch subtitles. American and British series are especially popular (and you can use the subtitles to improve your Dutch).

Belgium: Not surprisingly, there are two state-run TV networks in Belgium: RTBF for the French-speaking region, and VRT for the Flemish region, which are operated by the relevant linguistic communities. There are two RTBF channels, imaginatively titled *La Une* and *La Deux*. *La Une* is a general interest channel and broadcasts news, magazine programmes, and 'quality' films and series in French. *La Deux* focuses on live programmes, sport and cultural events (e.g. concerts), as well as showing films in VO (i.e. foreign-language films subtitled in French). VRT comprises three channels: TV1, Canvas and Ketnet. TV1, as its name implies, was the first channel and appeals to a general audience, with news, documentaries and other 'serious' programmes. Canvas offers cultural and sporting events, while Ketnet is aimed at children and young people.

The Belgian government also supports the Arte cultural channel, originally a joint venture between France and Germany, which offers cultural programming in both French and German. In French-speaking areas of Belgium, you can often receive TV5, the world-wide French-language channel, which re-broadcasts a variety of shows from many francophone countries (France, Belgium, Canada and some African nations) and is well known for its Sunday night films, broadcast in French with French subtitles (allegedly to help foreigners learn French, although many believe the subtitles are added to help the French understand Belgians, Canadians and other foreign French speakers!).

Holland: The availability of commercial funding to all television broadcasters has sparked considerable debate in Holland regarding the role of public broadcasting (i.e. the government-owned and operated networks), which currently consists of three national channels, TV1, TV2 and TV3 (plus a Dutch/Flemish satellite channel, BVN TV). Programmes are produced by associations representing various aspects of Dutch society, including the primary religious, political and social groups. These associations were originally supposed to represent the five 'pillars' of Dutch society but now number over 15 and represent groups as diverse as the Hindu community (OHM), liberals (VPRO), educationalists (Teleac/NOT) and youth (BNN). Each channel generally broadcasts programmes produced by a particular type of association. TV1, the most mainstream of the public channels, is associated with AVRO, KRO and NCRV, representing upper middle class, Catholic and Protestant interests respectively. TV2 focuses on live events and sports and is associated with NOS, a government-run association that produces news and sport programmes. TV3 is known for cultural and 'experimental' programming produced by OHM, VPRO, NOT and other associations.

Luxembourg: *Radio en Télévision Lëtzebuerg* (RTL) broadcasts a single channel specifically for Luxembourgers, *RTL Lëtzebuerg*, which is available only via cable and satellite (see below). Many other RTL channels are broadcast from Belgium, Holland, France and Germany and are also available via cable (see below). Otherwise, Belgian (see above), French and German terrestrial channels are all readily available in the Duchy.

Cable TV

Benelux is one of the most densely 'cabled' areas in the world, with over 90 per cent of households connected to cable services. Although there are numerous cable operators in each country, you're restricted to the one that serves your town or district. The local service provider is normally listed in the telephone directory or you can ask at your town hall. Most buildings are already wired for cable, although you may be charged a connection fee (referred to as an 'installation' fee) of around €25 plus a small deposit (around €10) for the necessary converter box. A basic analogue cable service costs between €10 and €30 per month, depending on your selection of channels and other services.

Most cable providers offer a 'standard' selection of 30 or more channels as their basic package, including the national public channels, those of neighbouring countries (depending on the language), commercial channels broadcasting in or to the country and a variety of European and international programmes, such as Eurosport, Euronews, CNN, CNNI, Cartoon Network, CNBC, Sky News and BBC World. Available channels vary from one area to another and it isn't uncommon for providers to change their selections with little or no notice. Many cable providers offer additional channels for an extra monthly fee, e.g. BBC Prime, Disney Channel, FilmNet, National Geographic and movie channels such as Premiere, CanalPlus and the Turner Movie Channel (TMC).

Digital cable is available in some areas, offering interactive services such as games and shopping, but is more expensive than analogue cable (around €30 or more per month) for a relatively limited selection of channels and features.

Belgium: There are local 'public service' (i.e. dull) channels available through most cable networks, such as ATV in Antwerp, Kanaal 3 in East Flanders, and ROB in East Brabant, all of which provide local information in Flemish, as well as Tele Bruxelles in Brussels and Tele Mons/Borinage in Mons/Borinage for local programmes in French. Commercial channels available include RTL Club (in

French), VT4 (in Flemish), and an assortment of channels from neighbouring Holland, France and Germany.

Holland: A popular independent TV channel (available via cable and satellite) is Veronica, which started as a pirate station operating from an abandoned oil rig in the North Sea. Veronica broadcasts primarily sitcoms, films and series, mostly from America, and was responsible for the Big Brother concept and a number of game shows which have been successfully adapted for other audiences, including British and American. Other popular channels that can be received in Holland include RTL4, RTL5, SBS6 and FOX8. RTL4 is a classic RTL channel, showing mainly series, soaps, films and general entertainment programmes. RTL5 is targeted at a slightly more upmarket but nevertheless general audience. SBS6 offers regional interest programmes along with the usual selection of soap operas, and FOX8 is part of the Murdoch empire, with popular American series in perpetual re-runs (and plenty of sex and violence to draw big ratings).

(Knowing what orderly people the Dutch are, broadcasters give their channels numbers which are intended to match the numbers assigned to each channel when a TV is programmed. In televised 'contests', camera teams arrive unannounced at viewers' homes to see whether they've programmed their sets 'properly', i.e. with RTL 4 on channel 4, FOX8 on channel 8, etc. Those who have receive prizes as well as a few moments of 'fame'!)

Luxembourg: RTL's only domestic channel, *RTL Lëtzebuerg*, broadcasts in Lëtzebuergesch around four to six hours per day, usually in the evening, and is available on all cable systems in the Duchy, as well as on the Astra satellite in unencrypted format (see below). If you're connected to the local cable system (as most residents are), you can also receive the French channels TF1, France 2 and France 3, as well as the German public channels, ARD and ZDF, and the Belgian RTBF1 and 2 (in French). You may also have access to many of the RTL channels braodcast in neighbouring countries, such as RTL2, RTL9 (in French), Super RTL (German), RTL-TVI and Club RTL (French), and even RTL4 (Dutch) in some areas.

Satellite TV

Although most people complain about the poor quality of television programmes in their home countries, many find they cannot live without it when they're abroad! Fortunately, the advent of satellite TV means that most people can enjoy their favourite programmes almost anywhere in the world. It was the Luxembourg-based *Société européene des Satellites* (SES) which triggered the European satellite revolution with the launch of the Astra 1A satellite in 1988. Since then, several more Astra satellites have been launched, increasing the number of available channels to 64 (or over 200 for digital TV). With a standard satellite dish, it's possible to pick up many unencrypted channels in a variety of languages, including English and even Turkish, Arabic, Japanese and Chinese. Most of the German commercial channels are available unencrypted via satellite. If you have a decoder box and subscribe to one or more of the pay satellite services (usually a monthly fee of €10 to €30), it's possible to receive many times as many channels in dozens of languages.

Satellite TV was slow to catch on in Benelux, largely because of the extensive availability of cable systems. In parts of Belgium it was actually discouraged when some communities began to impose satellite dish taxes (for 'aesthetic pollution') of up to €250 per year. However, in two separate European Court cases, satellite dish taxes were ruled illegal, and most of the towns that tried this scheme have quietly dropped it, although there are still a few areas in Wallonia where the authorities attempt to collect a tax (i.e. 'encourage' you to make use of the local cable network). Note that once you've paid the tax, you're unlikely to be able to talk local officials into giving you a refund, European Court rulings notwithstanding!

BSkyB Television: You must buy a receiver with a Videocrypt decoder and pay a monthly subscription to receive BSkyB or Sky stations except Sky News, which isn't encrypted. Various packages are available costing from around £12 to £30 a month for the premium package offering all movie channels plus Sky Sports. To receive encrypted channels via BSkyB, you must have an address in Britain. Subscribers are sent a coded 'smart' card (similar to a credit card), which must be inserted in the decoder to switch it on (cards are updated every few years to thwart counterfeiters). Sky won't send smart cards to overseas viewers, as they have the copyright to broadcast to a British-based audience only, so overseas homeowners need to obtain a card through a friend or relative in Britain. However, a number of satellite companies in Benelux (some of which advertise in the expatriate press) can supply BSkyB cards.

Equipment: A satellite receiver should have a built-in Videocrypt decoder (and others such as Eurocrypt, Syster or SECAM if required) and be capable of receiving satellite stereo radio. A 60 to 85cm (23 to 33in) dish suitable for receiving receive Astra stations costs around €200 to €400 plus an installation charge (which is sometimes included in the price). Shop around, as prices vary enormously and it's often possible to find deals combining equipment, installation and subscription to a satellite service. You can also install a motorised 1.2 or 1.5m (47 to 58in) dish and receive hundreds of stations in a multitude of languages from around the world. If you wish to receive satellite TV on two or more sets, you can buy a system with two or more receivers. To receive stations from two or more satellites simultaneously, you need a motorised dish or a dish with a double feed (dual LNBs) antenna. When buying a system, ensure that it can receive programmes from all existing and planned satellites.

Location: To receive programmes from any satellite, there must be no obstacles, e.g. trees and buildings, between the satellite and your dish, so check before renting or buying a home if you have your heart set on a particular service. Before buying or erecting a satellite dish, check whether you need permission from your landlord or the local authorities. Although satellite dish tax has been ruled illegal (see above), many communities have strict laws regulating where and how you can mount a dish, particularly on old buildings and in urban areas where dishes are considered an eyesore if visible from the street. Dishes can be mounted in a variety of unobtrusive positions and can be painted or patterned to blend with the background. It's possible to buy coloured, square and diamond shaped dishes, but you should check that these will receive the stations you want.

Programme Guides

Once you have access to hundreds of channels, the problem is working out what's on and when. Most newspapers and some weekly news magazines carry TV programme listings for both the public channels and those commercial channels most commonly carried by local cable services. There are also dedicated programme guides in each country, usually published weekly and containing programme listings, articles, interviews and sometimes reviews of films (including those being shown at the cinema!). Some guides focus on films or series or other kinds of programme. Most also include listings for a range of cable and satellite channels, including popular foreign-language channels as well as those in the local language. Your local cable service may publish its own programme guide or make a special channel or teletext service available for programme information. In addition, there are programme magazines dedicated to satellite TV, including the British publications *What Satellite*, *Satellite Times* and *Satellite TV* (the best), which are available from international news stands and by subscription.

There's a growing number of Internet sites offering complete TV programme listings for Europe, including the facility to construct your own viewing schedule, based on the channels you prefer or are able to receive, whether via cable or satellite. An advantage of online TV programme guides is that there's usually one in your own language, e.g. EuroTV (🖳 www.eurotv.com) for English speakers, where you can even find out when a particular series or film is being shown or join TV addict chat groups and newslines – if you aren't too busy watching television! Most TV channels and broadcasters also have websites where you can find programme listings and information about particular programmes.

TV Licence (Belgium)

Belgium is currently the only Benelux country that requires television owners to have a licence. (Holland abolished TV licensing in 2000 and Luxembourg's RTL has always been commercially funded.) Each household with one or more colour televisions must pay €184.20 per year. If your only TV is a black and white one (poor you!), there's a reduced fee of around €125. When you arrive in Belgium, you must register your TVs with the Radio and Television Licensing Authority (*Radio et Télévision Redevances/Kijk en Liustergeld*, Place Solvayplein 4, 1030 Brussels, ☎ 02-207 7411). The Authority has a number of regional offices, which are listed in the Yellow Pages. (Although NTSC televisions aren't subject to the licence fee, they must still be registered!) If you buy a new TV in Belgium, you must complete a registration form in the shop. If your surname begins with a letter between A and J, you must pay your licence fee in April, while those with surnames between K and Z pay in October. People with certain types and levels of disability are exempt from the licence fee.

Video & DVD

Video films and DVDs are readily available for rent and purchase in Benelux. To rent a video, you generally need to join a rental club and pay an annual fee or a deposit. Rental prices range from €1 or €2 per night for 'classic' films up to €5 to €10 for the latest Hollywood blockbuster. In Holland and in Flemish-speaking areas of Belgium films are generally in the original language with Dutch subtitles. In Luxembourg and French-speaking parts of Belgium most films are dubbed, although subtitled versions of major films are available from specialist shops and some large retailers such as FNAC. Video tapes and DVDs can be purchased in most hypermarkets and at many bookshops and news stands, as well as in specialist record shops. You can buy English-language DVDs and videos by mail-order and via the Internet, and you can exchange and buy second-hand tapes and discs through many expatriate clubs

DVD is becoming increasingly popular in the Benelux region. While both the players and the discs are considerably more expensive than video recorders and tapes, they often have added features such as multiple language soundtracks and subtitling (which you can switch off if you don't want it). Be careful, however, to buy DVDs for the correct 'zone', as films intended for an American audience (zone 1) won't play back in a European (zone 2) DVD player unless it has been modified, and zone 1 versions often don't contain as many alternative soundtracks and subtitles as those produced for European release. Multi-zone DVD players are available, although they're expensive, and it's also possible to modify many single-zone players to replay DVDs from other zones.

RADIO

The good news for radio enthusiasts is that radios have the same standard the world over, so there are generally few problems with equipment compatibility. Commercial radio was legalised in Belgium and Holland in the late '80s (RTL radio began broadcasting from Luxembourg a few years earlier) and Benelux airwaves are now almost saturated with radio stations, offering music of all kinds, sports coverage, news and talk programmes. The public broadcasters in each country have several radio channels offering a variety of programmes, from news and information to classical music, and there are numerous regional stations throughout Benelux. Both cable and satellite operators include a generous selection of radio channels in their basic packages, often including BBC and CNN stations as well as popular stations in neighbouring countries.

English-language Radio: In coastal areas it's possible to receive BBC Radio 4 (LW198) and Radio 5 (AM909 and 693). The BBC World Service can be heard throughout Benelux on MW648, and Talk Sport on MW1053 and AM1089. Details are available on the BBC and Talk Sport websites (🖳 www.bbc.co.uk and www.talksport.co.uk). In Belgium you can receive US AFN Radio (on FM101.7) and Voice of America (VOA), which broadcasts on a variety of frequencies (refer to their website at 🖳 www.voagov).

Belgium: In Wallonia, the RTBF has five stations: *La Première* (news), *Fréquence-Wallonie* (family programmes), *Bruxelles-Capitale* (focused on Brussels), *Radio 21* (aimed at 18 to 35-year-olds), and *Musique-Trois* (classical music). In Flemish areas, VRT offers a choice between Radio 1 and Radio 2, both general stations combining news and music, with Radio 2 devoting more time to regional information. Klara is an independent Flemish classical music station, while Studio Brussel (or StuBru) plays pop, rock and dance music and Radio Donna simply offers 'de fun, de hits'. (If you're something of a radio 'ham', you should note that instances of radio 'interference' are *always* investigated!)

Holland: The Dutch broadcasting service has five radio stations: Radio 1 (news and sport), Radio 2 (general), Radio 3 (pop music), Radio 4 and Radio 5 (both classical music). It also runs a number of regional stations, such as *Omroep Flevoland, Omroep Fryslan, Omroep Gelderland, Omroep Limburg* (*Omroep* being Dutch for 'broadcast'). There's also a range of independent provincial stations broadcasting mainly pop music on FM, including Sky Radio, Hot Radio, Radio Caroline (formerly an offshore pirate station), Jazz Radio, New Dance Radio, ConcertZender and Happy Radio.

Luxembourg: There's no shortage of radio stations in Luxembourg, where many towns have at least one local radio station, often transmitting via the cable television network. You can also receive most of the national and commercial stations from neighbouring countries, depending on which border(s) you're nearest to, and (of course) a number of radio channels are available via satellite.

Radio Licence

You don't need a licence for radios in your home anywhere in Benelux, provided you also have at least one television; if you *only* have a radio, you need to register it in the same was as for televisions (see **TV Licence** on page 133). In Belgium, however, you need a separate licence for your car radio. (You can't escape the tax man even when sitting in a traffic jam.) A car radio licence costs around €25 per year, and you must carry proof of payment when driving (along with your driving licence and registration and insurance certificates), as the police make random checks. If you buy a new car with a fitted radio, the dealer will ask you to complete a registration form. If you buy a car radio from a shop, you must register it in the same way as a television (see **TV Licence** on page 133). The Television Licensing Authority will send you a renewal notice every year.

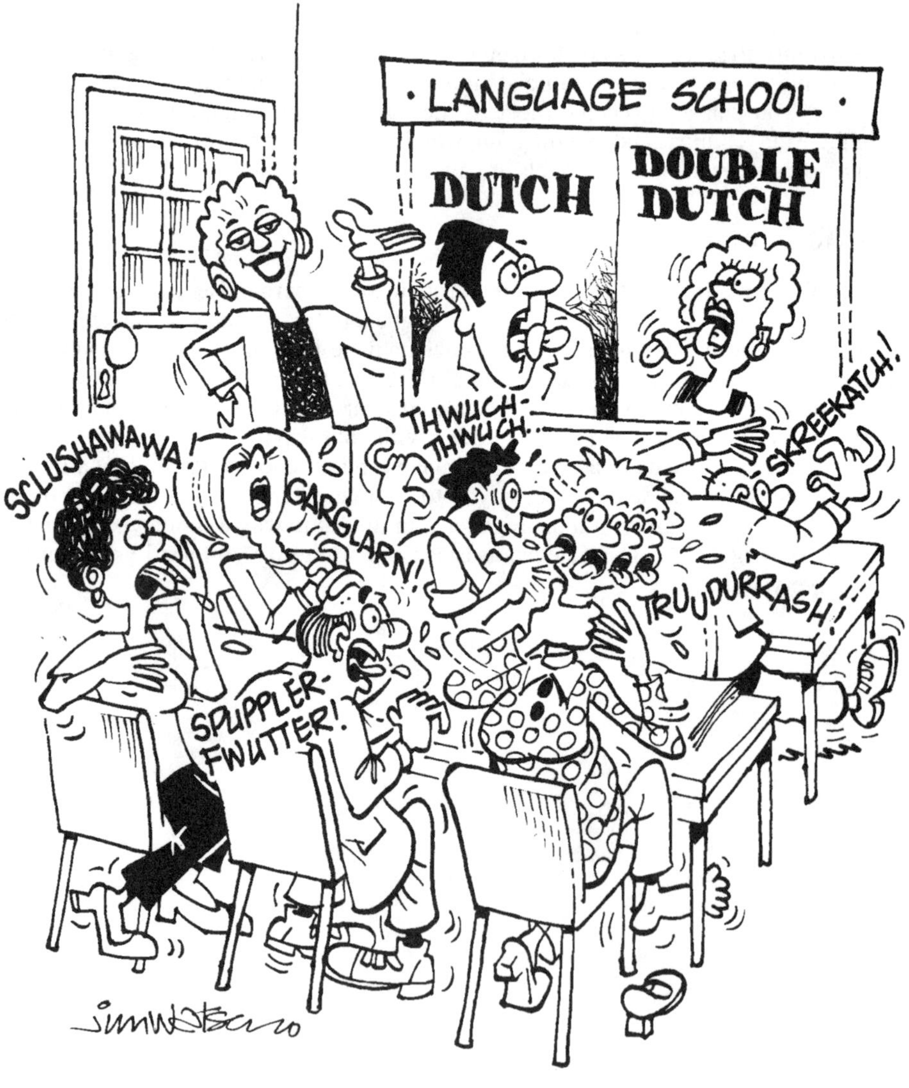
LANGUAGE SCHOOL
DUTCH
DOUBLE DUTCH
SCLUSHAWAWA!
GARGLARN!
THWUCH-THWUCH
SKREEKATCH!
TRUUDURRASH
SPUPPLER-FWUTTER!

9.

EDUCATION

The Belgians, Dutch and Luxembourgers are proud of their educational systems, which are unusual in that government funding is provided for both state-run schools and many forms of 'alternative' education, primarily schools organised by religious groups or orders. What would be private, fee-paying schools in many countries are integrated into the state system to provide a wide range of options available to all.

Education is compulsory in all three countries, starting as early as the age of three (in Luxembourg) and continuing for at least 12 years. During the compulsory period, schooling is free and parents can generally select from a range of schools, encompassing different religious, ethical and educational philosophies, as well as different curricula, i.e. oriented towards technical, vocational or academic goals. Higher and further education and vocational training programmes are also provided by the state, but fees must be paid, although subsidies are available for residents with limited funds. Free education is also provided for the children of foreign residents in Belgium, Holland and Luxembourg, although non-resident, non-EU students require a student visa (see page 62).

The three national governments have different approaches to the organisation of schools, and the degree to which the national curriculum is 'encouraged' or required in individual schools varies from country to country. In Belgium, certain educational policies are decided at national level, but the bulk of the curriculum and most administrative matters are determined by the linguistic communities (French, Flemish and German). Language is also an important consideration in both Dutch and Luxembourg schools, largely because of the influx of foreign immigrants over the last decade. All Benelux schools have made significant changes to their school policies in recent years for the benefit of pupils whose linguistic and cultural backgrounds aren't those of the local community.

Generally, the younger your child is when he enters the system, the more easily he will cope. Teenagers often have problems learning a new language and adjusting to school life in a different country, particularly children from America and Britain who haven't learnt a second language. In some Benelux schools, foreign children who cannot understand the language are simply expected to cope. In your early days in Belgium, Holland or Luxembourg, it's important to check exactly what your children are doing at school and whether they're making progress – not just with the language, but also with other subjects. You should be prepared to support your children through this difficult period, when they can experience feelings of frustration, inferiority or inadequacy. Note that it's also important to ensure that your children maintain their native language, which can easily be neglected – surveys show that children of English-language residents in non English-speaking countries gradually lose the ability to read and write English.

On the other hand, many children find living in a foreign country stimulating and challenging, and the experience can be culturally and educationally invaluable. Your child can become a 'world' citizen, less likely to be prejudiced against foreigners and foreign ideas. This is particularly true if he attends an international school with pupils from many different countries (many state schools, particularly in the larger cities, also have pupils from a number of countries and backgrounds).

Information about Belgian, Dutch and Luxembourg schools, both state and private, can be obtained from the respective embassies and consulates in your home country as well as from foreign embassies, educational organisations and government departments in Benelux. Local school information can be obtained from the town hall. A source of detailed (and objective) information about national educational systems in Europe is Eurydice, which is part of the EU's SOCRATES programme. The Eurydice website (💻 www.eurydice.org) offers publications which can be downloaded free or purchased in printed form as well as access to Eurybase, a comprehensive database on education in 30 European countries. The country studies are updated regularly and are available in English as well as in the local language.

In addition to details of the Belgian, Dutch and Luxembourg state school systems and private schools, this chapter contains information about apprenticeships, higher and further education and language schools. See also **Evening Classes** on page 304.

STATE OR PRIVATE SCHOOL?

Before making major decisions about your child's education, it's important to consider his ability, character and requirements. If you're able to choose between state and private education, the following checklist will help you decide:

● How long are you planning to stay in Belgium, Holland or Luxembourg? If you're uncertain, it's probably better to assume a long stay. Owing to language and other integration problems, enrolling a child in a state school is recommended only for a minimum of a year, particularly for teenage children who aren't fluent in the local language.

● Bear in mind that the area where you choose to live will affect your choice of school(s). For example, at primary level, you usually must send your child to the state school nearest your home or in your commune; if you choose a private day school, you will need to take into account the distance from your home to the school, as well as the available means of transport.

● Do you know where you're going when you leave Belgium, Holland or Luxembourg? This may be an important consideration regarding your child's language of tuition and system of education. How old is your child and what age will he be when you leave Benelux? What plans do you have for his subsequent education, and in which country?

● What educational level has your child reached and how will he fit into a private school or the local state school system? The younger he is, the easier it will be to place him in a suitable school.

● How does your child view the prospect of studying in Benelux? In what language should he receive tuition? Is schooling available in Benelux in your child's mother tongue?

● Will your child require your help with his studies and, more importantly, will you be able to help him, particularly with the local language?

● What are the school hours? What are the school holiday periods? Many state schools have compulsory Saturday morning classes. How will the school holidays and hours affect your family's work and leisure activities?

- Is special or extra tutoring available in the local language or in particular subjects, if necessary?

- Is religion (or the lack of it) an important aspect in your choice of school? Some state schools have compulsory religious education and many private schools are affiliated with churches or other religious organisations.

- Do you want your child to go to a single-sex or co-educational school? Nearly all state schools are co-educational.

- Should you send your child to a boarding school? If so, in which country?

- What are the secondary and further education prospects in Benelux or another country? Are local examinations recognised in your home country or the country where you plan to live after leaving Benelux? If applicable, check that the local secondary school examination or diploma is recognised as a university entrance qualification in your home country.

- Does a prospective school have a good academic record? Most schools provide exam pass rate statistics.

- How large are the classes? What is the pupil-teacher ratio?

Obtain the opinions and advice of others who have been faced with the same decisions and problems as yourself and collect as much information from as many different sources as possible before making a decision. Speak to teachers and the parents of children attending the schools on your shortlist. Finally, most parents find it pays to discuss the alternatives with their children before making a decision. See also **Choosing a Private School** on page 153.

STATE SCHOOLS

Within the three Benelux countries a wide range of terminology is used for the various types of state schools. In this book the term 'state' is used in preference to 'public' in order to avoid confusion with the term 'public school', which in Britain refers to a private, fee-paying school. The state school systems in Belgium and Holland, in particular, differ considerably from those in, for example, Britain and the USA, particularly regarding secondary education.

In all three countries state education is well organised and adequately funded (not that teachers would agree), and the state guarantees all children free education at the schools of their choice. In Belgium and Holland, the choice includes a wide range of denominational and non-denominational 'independent' (*libre/vrij*) schools. The state funds all schools, whether organised by governmental agencies (e.g. towns, communes or regions), religious organisations (e.g. the Catholic Church or local Protestant, Jewish or Islamic communities) or by private groups with particular philosophical or educational programmes. As long as schools adhere to the guidelines for curriculum and administration laid down by the state education authority, they're entitled to financial support.

State schools don't usually charge fees; if they do, they aren't permitted to exclude children who are unable to pay the fees but meet other requirements for admission. Many state schools in Belgium and Holland are run by religious orders, the Roman

Catholic Church operating a significant proportion of schools in many areas. The state system also encompasses institutions such as Montessori method pre-schools and primary schools, Steiner and Waldorf schools, and Jena Plan schools, which must accept all children who meet the entrance requirements. Even religious schools may not discriminate against children who don't practise a particular faith. This means that there are few private (i.e. fee-paying) schools in Benelux, apart from international and foreign curriculum schools, designed primarily to accommodate short-term expatriates, e.g. those in the diplomatic service (see **Private Schools** on page 153). Home schooling is also a recognised alternative and can even attract state funding, provided you have teaching experience and can demonstrate that your home schooling programme meets the requirements of the state curriculum in terms of subjects covered and duration.

Another feature of the three Benelux school systems is that some form of religious or 'moral' instruction is required at all levels. All schools must respect the religious backgrounds of their pupils, although in religious schools children may be required to attend classes in the faith espoused by the school as well as in their own religion. These classes are generally organised by local religious leaders. If a suitable religious programme isn't available during regular school hours or if children (or their parents) don't wish to participate in religious training, they must attend non-denominational classes in 'moral and ethical considerations'.

In the past, pupils were subjected to stringent examinations at the conclusion of primary school, the results of which determined their options for secondary education and thus for the rest of their lives. A school-leaving examination at the conclusion of secondary studies was similarly used to determine those eligible for university or other higher education. With the influx of immigrants and other foreigners to the region during the late '80s and early '90s the need for flexibility became apparent, and all three state school systems have since made major changes to their structure, requirements and approach to the 'tracking' of pupils for academic or vocational training. Although preliminary choices must still be made at the age of 12, specialisation is now introduced gradually over the first three or four years of secondary school; it's possible to select preliminary 'tracks' which leave a wider range of options (generally both technical school and university) and to change track during secondary school, at least until the last two years (generally ages 17 to 18). Examinations are still required at the conclusion of primary and secondary school, but the results of examinations are just one part of a broader evaluation of a child's progress which decides the awarding of school leaving certificates or diplomas. Parents have the right of appeal if a school's recommendations for further study conflict with their own aspirations or those of their children.

Language

There are many factors to be taken into account when choosing an appropriate school in Belgium, Holland or Luxembourg, not least the language of study. The only schools using English as the teaching language are a few foreign and international private schools. If your children attend a local state school, they must study all subjects in the local language, whether French, Dutch or Lëtzebuergesch. For most children, learning the local language as they go along isn't as much of a problem as it may at first appear, especially for those under the age of ten. In fact, language programmes in all Benelux schools are aimed at introducing 'foreign' languages (primarily English) as early as possible and children in state schools are generally expected to be at least bi-lingual (in Luxembourg, they're expected to be fluent in four languages) by the time they finish compulsory schooling. The majority of children adapt quickly and become reasonably fluent within three to six months (if only it were so easy for adults). However, all children don't adapt equally well to a change of language and culture, particularly teenagers, many of whom encounter language difficulties during their first year.

Most state schools in Benelux make resources available to help children whose mother tongue isn't the local language. In some areas, these resources are required by law and may include intensive language lessons or offering some subjects in the child's mother tongue until his local language skills are sufficiently developed for him to follow normal lessons. It may be worthwhile inquiring about the availability of extra language classes before deciding where to live, but note that while attending special language classes children may fall behind in other lessons. If your local state school doesn't provide extra language classes, you may have to pay for private lessons or send your child to a different (possibly private) school where extra tuition is provided. Some parents send their children to an English-speaking school for a year before enrolling them in a state school; others choose to throw their children in at the deep end. It depends on the character, ability and wishes of each child. Whatever you decide, it will help if your child has some foreign language lessons before arriving in Benelux.

Belgium: Language is a major issue in state schools in Belgium, where the linguistic community controls state education as far as curriculum and general administration are concerned. State schools in the Flemish region use Dutch as the language of instruction, schools in Walloon teach in French, and those in the small German community use German. It isn't only the language of instruction in the local schools that varies from one area to another but also, to some extent, the structure of the school programme and the available options. The bi-lingual areas of Brussels and the 19 surrounding communities have both French and Dutch-language state schools, and parents may choose which their children attend, generally according to the language they use at home. In families where neither French nor Dutch is used in the home, children will be assigned to a Dutch-language school.

Holland: Not surprisingly, the language of instruction in the Dutch schools is Dutch and the study of the Dutch language and its literature is required throughout the years of compulsory education. With the influx of non-Dutch speaking foreigners over the last decade or so, and in the traditional Dutch spirit of tolerance, schools where there's a certain number of non-Dutch speakers are required to provide both intensive lessons in Dutch and some lessons in the native languages of the foreign children. The Dutch government has also instituted a pre-school programme for non-Dutch speaking children, modelled on the American Headstart programme, to teach language and culture in a 'natural' environment before the child starts primary school. Information about these programmes is available from town halls.

Luxembourg: The language of instruction in Luxembourg schools is Lëtzebuergesch, a language you're unlikely to encounter anywhere but in the Duchy of Luxembourg. Lëtzebuergesch isn't really a written language (in fact some consider it a dialect of 'low' German, related to Dutch), although a written form has evolved. In effect, Luxembourg schools use Lëtzebuergesch as a means of introducing 'proper' German (*Hochdeutsch*) as a first foreign language at around the age of six, when children are taught to read and write. As it's important for children entering primary school to be able to speak Lëtzebuergesch fluently, compulsory education now starts at the age of three with pre-school, where the primary focus is on imparting fluency in spoken Lëtzebuergesch through games, songs and other activities.

By the time they finish school in Luxembourg, all children are at least tri-lingual (Lëtzebuergesch, German and French) and most will have some exposure to a fourth language, in many cases English. Foreign language study begins early: after graduating from Lëtzebuergesch to German at the start of primary school for the purposes of reading and writing, children start French lessons in the second half of the second year of primary school, with English or another foreign language starting at the end of primary school or the first year of secondary school. If you live near the Belgian border, you may enrol your children in the Belgian state school system, particularly if you prefer them to be educated in French.

Enrolment

If you've registered with the local authorities, they will usually contact you about registering your children for school; otherwise, information about registration for state schools is available from your town hall. In most areas, children are assigned to the primary school that covers the district where they live, which is normally the closest school to their home. To enrol a child, you must provide his national identity card, as well as your own, plus a medical certificate or other proof that the child has been vaccinated against all the usual childhood diseases.

Where there's more than one state school in the district, or if you're sending your children to a private school, you may be required to present proof of registration at the town hall. Truancy is a problem in some areas, particularly at secondary level. In Holland, for example, the authorities have introduced a special identity card system to track school attendance. Cards have a bar-code linked to the child's SoFi (social security) number, normally issued at birth to all Dutch nationals. Children of foreigners resident in Holland are issued with a special number, based on their parents' SoFi or other identification number, so don't forget to take your SoFi card when you enrol your child in a Dutch school. Some Belgian schools have also started using a bar-coded identity card system to track attendance in areas where truancy is a problem.

School Hours & Transport

Even within the state sector, school hours can vary considerably between different types of school as well as from region to region and from country to country. Some schools hold morning and afternoon sessions, even for pre-school children, until 4 or 5pm. Other schools have lessons six mornings per week (including Saturdays), but only on a few afternoons. Most children return home for lunch, although most schools have a canteen for those who live far away or whose parents work. A small fee is charged (generally per month) for school dinners. Alternatively, children may take a packed lunch if they want to remain at school during the lunch break but prefer not to eat school dinners.

Some schools provide minibuses to collect children from outlying regions and return them home at the end of the day. Otherwise, most public transport systems in the Benelux area make free or low-cost passes available to students for travel to and from school. In some cases, this can add considerably to the length of the school day and many parents prefer to drive their children to and from school or drive them to school and allow them to catch a bus or train home. State schools and communities usually provide an after-school nursery or other child-minding facility (often in the form of a 'homework school') for working mothers and during school holidays.

Belgium: Most schools in Belgium have classes from 8.30am until noon five days a week (Mondays to Fridays) and from 1.30 until 3.30 or 4pm four days a week, Wednesday afternoon being free in most parts of the country, particularly French-speaking areas. Some schools hold classes on Saturday mornings, although this practice is becoming less common. In secondary schools, afternoon lessons may run until as late as 5pm or the lunch break may be reduced to an hour (the legal minimum) to accommodate the additional course work required at this level.

Holland: In Holland, schools are free to set their own hours and weekly schedules provided they meet the minimum requirements for each 'cycle' set out by the Ministry of Education. Children in the first two years of primary school average around 22 hours per week. For the next six years, this rises to 25 hours per week. The maximum school day is 5 hours and 30 minutes, excluding breaks. All primary schools are required to provide lunch facilities, but children (or their parents) must pay for meals. Around 30 per cent of primary school children remain at school through the lunch period. Secondary school schedules are based on state guidelines regarding the number of instructional periods (each lasting 50 minutes) reckoned to be necessary to reach a certain level in each of the required subjects, but each school determines the length of the school day and lesson times. Most schools operate a five-day week (i.e. Mondays to Fridays), although some also schedule Saturday classes.

Luxembourg: The 'normal' school week in Luxembourg consists of six morning sessions (Mondays to Saturdays) from 8 to 11.45am and three afternoons (Mondays, Wednesdays and Fridays) from 2 to 4pm. In a few areas, local schools have eliminated Saturday morning classes, rescheduling the lost time during weekdays, in order to give children and their families a full weekend.

Holidays

The school year generally runs from September to July, except in Holland, where it officially starts on 1st August. Private schools in Belgium and Holland must adhere to guidelines issued by the relevant Ministries of Education or other centralised authorities, although they may add religious and other holidays to their schedule. Classes are normally suspended for national public holidays which fall on a school day.

Belgium: The school year in Belgium runs from 1st September to 1st July, with an eight-week summer holiday. Students generally receive a two-week holiday at Christmas and another two-week holiday in the spring. Although the spring holiday is referred to as the Easter holiday, most schools close for the first two weeks of April, irrespective of when Easter falls. The national holidays on 1st and 2nd November (see page 52) are generally extended to a week, making an autumn mid-term break, and there's another week's holiday at Carnival time, seven weeks before Easter.

Holland: The school year in Holland runs from 1st August to 31st July, and schools are free to fix their calendars as they wish, provided they accommodate local, regional and denominational holidays, as applicable. Summer holidays last six weeks for primary schools and seven weeks for secondary schools, but the holiday periods are staggered by region. Most schools close for one or two weeks at Christmas and at the beginning of May (around the Queen's Birthday and Liberation Day public holidays – see page 52). There are also recommended autumn and spring holiday periods, which vary from year to year.

Luxembourg: School schedules for Luxembourg are drawn up three years in advance and published each May. The school year runs from 15th September to 15th July, with a two-month summer holiday period. There are three 12-week terms, each with a one-week half-term holiday. The first term ends in time for the two-week Christmas holiday and the second ends with a two-week Easter break.

Uniforms & Equipment

School uniforms are the exception rather than the rule throughout Benelux, especially at state schools. In most cases, children devise their own 'uniform' of jeans, tee-shirt or sweatshirt and trainers. In some areas, the theft (i.e. by 'mugging') of designer clothes by gangs is widespread and has resulted in children being told not to wear expensive clothes to school.

Other equipment required varies with the country, region and type of school. In most areas, books and basic school supplies, e.g. paper and pens, are supplied for primary school pupils and usually also for secondary school children. However, almost all students will require some or all of the following:

- a school bag or satchel and a sports bag;
- a pencil case, pencils and pens, stationery, etc;
- gym shoes (plimsolls), shorts and a towel for games and exercise periods.

Books are generally provided by schools, but there's sometimes a small rental charge, particularly in secondary schools and for students on specialised courses. Most cities and towns provide grants to families that have difficulty paying school fees or buying uniforms or equipment.

Parents may be asked to pay for some non-academic activities, such as entrance fees to cultural or sporting events, transport for field trips, photocopying of projects where necessary, and a 'school diary' (a notebook often used for communication between teachers and parents).

Nursery School

Nursery school, pre-school (*prégardienne/peuter school*) or kindergarten (*jardin d'enfants/kleuterschool*) is in most cases voluntary, and parents may be required to pay for pre-school or child day care until a child reaches compulsory school age. In all three Benelux countries there are standards for pre-school programmes, which must concentrate on activities that develop local language skills, socialisation and cultural awareness. This means that children generally play games, sing songs and work on art and craft projects rather than being given formal lessons. Some nursery schools segregate children into age groups, while others group all pre-school children in a single class.

Belgium: Children aged two-and-a-half can be sent to pre-school or kindergarten, which is usually free even though attendance isn't compulsory. Over half of children this age attend pre-school, as the socialisation skills learned are widely believed to help them succeed in primary school and beyond. Most pre-schools are organised by local municipalities or church groups.

Holland: For children aged up to four, all pre-school or nursery school programmes are private and resemble crèche or child-minding services. In some areas, day care for very young children can be difficult to find and tends to be expensive. Compulsory school attendance starts on the first school day of the month following a child's fifth birthday, but most Dutch parents opt to enrol their children in primary school from the age of four.

Luxembourg: Pre-school is called *éducation préscholaire* in French or *Spillschoul* in Lëtzebuergesch. Compulsory school attendance in the Duchy used to start at the age of four but now begins at three, mainly because of the need to ensure that children entering primary school are sufficiently fluent in Lëtzebuergesch to deal with the demanding language curriculum. Intensive language classes are available to foreign children through the pre-school system.

Primary School

Primary school (*école primaire/lagere school* or *basisonderwijs*) is generally the start of a child's compulsory education. In Belgium and Luxembourg, primary school starts at the age of six and lasts for six years. Compulsory primary school in Holland starts at the age of five (but see **Nursery School** above) and also continues until the age of 12. The method of determining the exact age of entry to primary school varies, but all three countries make allowances for children born late in the year.

Schools are established and maintained by local communities, churches or religious organisations, and various state-approved groups that have set up programmes in accordance with national curriculum guidelines. Attendance at all state schools is free, although children attending a school outside their home district may be liable for transport costs if there's an alternative school nearer their home.

A primary school may have a director or head teacher, although in Luxembourg primary school teachers report directly to the district or regional school inspector. Primary schools vary greatly in the degree to which they encourage or promote participation by parents. Most schools have some form of parent-teacher association, although this is often a rather informal group concerned primarily with organising after-school activities. In some schools there's an elected board or advisory council, consisting of teachers, local officials and parents, which is responsible for certain aspects of after-school care, extracurricular activity and administration. All parents of children attending the school may be eligible for election to this board, or only those who are resident in the area (e.g. in Luxembourg). Most schools offer at least one or two opportunities a year for parents to meet teachers and discuss their children's progress, although most primary schools don't allow parents to sit in on classes except under extraordinary circumstances.

In primary school, a single teacher normally gives lessons in all subjects and the children remain in the same classroom throughout the school day, although special teachers may be brought in for art, music or religious studies. Children are usually grouped in classes according to their age, one year per class, although in smaller schools classes may contain children of different ages.

Belgium: In Belgium, the six years of primary school are divided into three 'cycles' of two years each. The controlling linguistic community (French, Flemish or German) sets attainment goals for each cycle in the main subjects, which include language, mathematics, expressive arts, environmental studies (nature, man, society, technology, and time and space), and physical education. There may also be goals within each cycle for 'soft' skills, such as learning to learn or social skills. There's strong emphasis on language and maths, and primary schools are increasingly being encouraged to introduce a foreign language in the early years. In French-language schools, the first foreign language offered must be Dutch; in Flemish schools, French is often offered in primary school, but isn't obligatory. Officially, the first foreign language classes begin in the last cycle (5th and 6th years) at age 10 or 11, but French-language schools in the Brussels area must begin teaching Dutch in the third year (age eight). Other required classes include religious studies (or the non-denominational 'ethics' option), road safety (apparently the Belgians are aware of their own reputation – see **Chapter 11**), geography, physical education, and arts and crafts.

Belgian schools issue regular reports to parents and are obliged to test pupils at the end of each cycle to determine whether the required attainment levels have been met. Tests can be developed by the schools themselves, but the diocesan council usually prepares standard tests for use in all Catholic schools. Most schools test their pupils at least once a year, combining the results of the tests with regular evaluations of class work. Teachers are generally free to develop their own teaching methods and to tailor these to the needs of their pupils provided they give at least the prescribed minimum number of lessons per week or per cycle in each subject. Extra tutoring is available to any school with a certain number of students lacking fluency in the official school language. Students who fail to meet attainment goals may be held back (i.e. made to repeat a year), although this is normally done at the end of only one of the two-year cycles and no child may be kept in primary school more than seven years.

At the end of primary school, there's sometimes a final examination, often standardised on a canton-wide basis or, in Catholic schools, prepared by an inter-diocesan council. The results of the final examination are combined with teacher evaluations of the pupil's last year (or in some cases last two years) of daily school work to develop a recommendation regarding the type of secondary school the child should attend. Children who have reached a certain standard of education are awarded a Primary School Certificate (*Certificat d'Etudes de Base/Getuigschrift van Lager Onderwijs*), usually referred to by its French acronym, CEB. This certificate is no longer required for admission to secondary school in Belgium but is useful for children who leave secondary school without a completion certificate, as without a CEB they may find it difficult to obtain employment.

Holland: Primary schooling (*basisonderwijs*) in Holland normally runs for eight years, from the age of four or five to 12 or 13, with 14 as the maximum age. Most schools are divided into eight classes, organised by age group, the first four classes being considered 'juniors' and the classes 5 to 8 'seniors'. Some schools divide classes into junior (1st to 3rd), middle (4th to 6th) and senior (7th and 8th) cycles and a few schools combine age groups according to pupils' level of attainment. Dutch regulations for primary schools set limits on class size, using a 'weighted' system of evaluating teacher load that assigns a higher weight to pupils likely to require greater assistance in the classroom, e.g. children from single-parent homes and non-native Dutch speakers.

Each school's 'competent authority' (usually the governing board) must prepare documents detailing the school's teaching philosophy, methods and policies, and these documents are available from the Ministry of Education to help parents select the appropriate school for their children. The Ministry of Education also prescribes a minimum number of lessons that must be given in each required subject and sets attainment levels for primary schools. Required subjects at primary school level include the Dutch language and literature, arithmetic and mathematics, sensory co-ordination and physical education, factual subjects (geography, history, science, social structures, and religious and ideological movements), expressive activities, social and life skills and healthy living. The study of English is compulsory in the last two years of primary school, although many schools introduce it earlier. Road safety education is also required for primary school pupils and includes bicycle safety – essential for survival in Holland!. There are plans to introduce technology studies, i.e. the use of computers, to the primary curriculum.

The Dutch Ministry of Education has an informative website (⌨ www.minocw.nl) containing further information about primary schools. The information is available in English and includes details of new projects and potential changes to the curriculum. The government also publishes a *National Guide to Primary Education* (in Dutch and English), which can be ordered via the website or by post from the Ministry of Education, Culture and Science, Postbus 25000, 2700 LZ Zoetermeer (☎ 079-323 2323).

Around 70 per cent of primary schools administer standardised tests at the end of the eighth year. Based on these tests and an evaluation of class work during the final two years, teachers prepare a school report (*onderwijskundig rapport*) for each child, detailing his level of achievement and an estimate of the child's potential, including recommendations for secondary study and career paths. Both the child's parents and local secondary schools receive a copy of this report. There's no national primary school certificate or diploma, although individual schools may award their own.

Luxembourg: The six years of primary school in Luxembourg are divided into three stages or cycles: lower, intermediate and upper. Some primary schools have separate classes for each year, while other schools group children in classes corresponding to the two-year cycles. Teachers follow the national curriculum, which includes German, arithmetic, art, music, physical education, science, and 'new technologies', i.e. computer studies. All pupils receive religious instruction, which includes preparation for First Communion in the Catholic Church, the predominant religion throughout Luxembourg. Children from non-Catholic families can elect to attend alternative 'moral training' classes.

Teachers are free to use their own methods and to schedule lessons as they consider appropriate, provided they meet the requirements of the national curriculum regarding subjects, textbooks and attainment levels. Oral French is introduced in the second half of the second year of primary school (age seven to eight), mostly through games and activities such as singing and story-telling. Reading and writing in French is introduced in the third year (age eight to nine). The teaching of English or another foreign language used to be reserved until the first year of secondary school, but an increasing number of Luxembourg schools are introducing a second foreign language (usually English) during the last two years of primary school.

Students are evaluated regularly, with reports sent to parents as frequently as every month. At the end of each school year, tests are administered (either standardised tests or tests developed by the classroom teacher) and a formal evaluation is made to determine the child's readiness for the next class. In the final year of primary school (6th class), a guidance council (comprising teachers and other educational professionals) is set up to evaluate each pupil's achievements and potential and to make recommendations regarding the type of secondary education for which he's best suited. If the pupil or his parents disagree with this assessment, they can appeal against it. Pupils must often sit an examination covering the subjects studied in the final two years of primary school.

There's a wide range of special services available in Luxembourg schools, including tutoring for 9 to 12-year-olds with academic problems, remedial classes (particularly in German) and *classes d'accueil*, special integration classes for children who arrive in mid-year. In schools where there are four or more children of the same foreign nationality, it's possible for them to have certain classes in their mother tongue.

Secondary School

Children are eligible for admission to a secondary school after completing primary school or when reaching the age of 13 or 14. There are no compulsory entrance examinations for state secondary schools, and children may attend any school in the state system provided they meet other entrance requirements. For example, some schools set their own entrance examinations, some require students to show certain aptitudes, and others require students to agree to attend religious services and in some cases to have some kind of religious training. It isn't uncommon for secondary pupils to travel large distances to attend a specialised school or one offering classes in a particular subject or field. Most secondary programmes run for six or seven years, with shorter options available to vocational students wanting to start their working careers or enter apprenticeship programmes.

In the past, pupils had to select their track or area of specialisation when admitted to secondary school and changing course later was difficult, if not impossible. Today, most programmes are designed to introduce specialisation in a more gradual manner and to leave open a greater range of options at each stage. There's a variety of programmes and types of schools available, whether for vocational, technical or general education. Nearly all programmes at secondary school level lead to some form of examination, but the granting of the secondary school completion certificate is no longer solely dependent on the results of these exams; student's grades in the last year or two are taken into account, as well as projects and portfolios of work compiled for evaluation.

Belgium: Schooling is compulsory in Belgium until the age of 18, and state secondary schools must admit all children who meet their entry requirements. Secondary schools may charge fees, but pupils who meet the entry requirements cannot be refused if they're unable to pay. At secondary level, pupils select a 'track' which leads to a course of higher education (i.e. university or professional school) or to training for a specific trade or job.

Secondary education (*éducation secondaire/secundair onderwijs*) lasts for six years and is divided into three two-year stages or cycles. The first cycle (*observation* in French-language schools) is a general one, based on a core curriculum that is essentially a continuation of the subjects studied at primary school: religious studies or ethics, Dutch, French, maths, history, geography, natural sciences, art, technical studies and physical education. A range of optional (elective) subjects is available, including English (or another foreign language), Latin, music, scientific and technical subjects, depending on the focus of the school. Pupils who didn't obtain a CEB in primary school (see page 146) may spend their first year in remedial classes and have another opportunity to earn their primary school certificate. On completion of the CEB, the pupil may either start the regular first-year programme (7th class) or go directly into a specialised vocational programme.

In the second cycle (*orientation* in the French system) pupils can begin to specialise, according to their selected track, and may select further options, such as Latin, Greek, modern languages (for general track students), supplementary maths (for technical or vocational students) or specific trades and job skills in the vocational programmes. In the third cycle (*détermination* in the French system) pupils make their final specialisation decisions, which determine the final examinations they will take and the type of school leaving certificate they will receive.

There are a number of different types of secondary school, some specialising in a particular track or type of education and some covering only one or two cycles. *Lycées* usually cover only the first cycle (i.e. the first two years of secondary school) but sometimes the first and second cycles (i.e. the first four years). *Atheneums* are generally upper level schools (second and third cycles) focused on pre-university and professional school education, although some offer six-year programmes. Technical institutes also focus on upper level courses for vocational and technical tracks, although some cover the full six years of secondary schooling.

In Flemish-language schools, the various tracks are identified by three-letter acronyms: ASO is the general or pre-university track (*algemeen secundair onderwijs*), TSO the technical track (*technisch secundair onderwijs*), and BSO the vocational training track (*beroep secundair onderwijs*). A few schools also offer an arts track (*kunst secundair onderwijs* or *KSO*), which allows pupils to study fine arts or a performing art as part of a general education.

The normal school week at the secondary level is 28 to 32 hours of classes, which may include an additional two hours of supervised revision. Students in the vocational tracks can choose a part-time option (*enseignement à horaires réduits/deeltijds beroep secundair onderwijs* or *DBSO*) when they reach the age of 15 or 16, combining work or an apprenticeship with classes until they reach the school leaving age of 18.

Pupils are given progress reports at least three times a year, normally before the Christmas holidays, before the spring or Easter break and at the end of the school year. At the end of each two-year cycle, pupils receive a graded certificate of completion. An 'A' certificate indicates that the student has successfully completed the cycle and includes teachers' recommendations for the courses the pupil should consider in the following cycles. A 'B' certificate indicates that the student has successfully completed the cycle but is being admitted to the next cycle with restrictions as to the courses or other options he may select. A 'C' certificate indicates that the pupil hasn't successfully completed the two-year cycle and lists the options available for further study. Pupils receiving either a B or a C certificate may take an extra year (in other words, repeat the last year of the cycle) to try to strengthen weak areas or correct any serious deficiencies before moving on to the next stage.

At the end of the third cycle (or on completion of a vocational qualification module) pupils usually sit a final or qualifying examination. Students successfully completing the programme are awarded a secondary school completion certificate (*Certificat d'Enseignement Secondaire Supérieur* or *CESS/Diploma van Secundair Onderwijs*) in either general, technical or artistic studies. Vocational students generally receive one or more qualification certificates (*Certificat de Qualification*) during the course of their studies. A 7th year secondary school programme is available for vocational students who wish to obtain a CESS or diploma for secondary studies. A few vocational schools, usually those run by the Catholic authorities, offer a 7th year vocational cycle with a specialisation in art, nursing or needlework. (Belgium is after all famous for its lace.)

Holland: After completing primary school, pupils in Holland may attend the secondary school of their choice, provided they meet the school's entrance requirements. Secondary schooling is free until the end of the school year in which a child reaches his 16th birthday. After that, state schools must charge a fee, which is set each year by the Ministry of Education. Financial aid is available through town halls for families who cannot afford the fees.

A major restructuring of the Dutch educational system was begun in the 1999/2000 academic year whereby the technical and vocational tracks have been recombined to allow pupils greater flexibility in changing direction in the early years, whereas previously there was no going back once you had embarked on a particular track. As in Flemish-language schools in Belgium (see above), the various options and tracks in Dutch secondary schools are commonly referred to by their acronyms, principally:

- **VBO** (*voorbereidend beroepsonderwijs*) – pre-vocational studies lasting four years;
- **MAVO** (*middelbaar algemeen voortgezet onderwijs*) – junior general secondary studies lasting four years;
- **HAVO** (*hoger algemeen voortgezet onderwijs*) – senior general secondary studies lasting five years;
- **VWO** (*voorbereidend wetenschappelijk onderwijs*) – pre-university studies lasting six years.

Both the MAVO and VBO tracks lead to further vocational study (MBO or *middelbaar beroepsonderwijs*) and are sometimes referred to as VMBO (*voorbereidend middelbaar beroepsonderwijs*). The HAVO track is designed to prepare students for non-university higher education (*hoger beroepsonderwijs – HBO*), including various kinds of professional school, e.g. business, law and medical. Pupils receiving an HAVO diploma may enter the sixth year of VWO in order to qualify for university entrance.

The first two years of all secondary school courses consist of general education, including Dutch language and literature, English language and literature, a second foreign language, general science, history and social studies, culture and the arts, and physical education. In addition to these, pupils may choose from a list of optional subjects according to their track and ambitions. For example, VWO pupils may start studying Latin or Greek. Within the technical and vocational tracks, pupils first select one of four general learning paths (*leerweg*): theoretical, pre-vocational training, a mixed path or direct vocational options. In the final two or three years of the VMBO, HAVO and VWO, students must choose a specialisation. Within the VMBO the choices are technology, health and welfare, economics, and agriculture. HAVO and VWO students must select from nature and technology, nature and health, economics and society, and culture and society. Pupils following the MBO or final VMBO programmes are also offered a choice of qualifying levels within certain skills or trades.

At the end of their secondary programme, pupils sit national examinations in their selected subjects as well as undergoing a school 'examination' usually consisting of a review of grades and projects or sample work compiled during the last two years of their secondary programme. On successful completion of these examinations, students are awarded a diploma indicating the track completed, the subjects passed and all school grades in the final subjects.

Luxembourg: At the conclusion of primary school, pupils must select whether to continue their compulsory education in the general track or enter a technical school.

Those who follow a general secondary education track normally attend one of the ten state *lycées* in Luxembourg, where they must first select between classical and modern tracks. The classical track requires the study of Latin, while the modern track leads to further study of one or more modern languages. At the end of the first two-year cycle, students must then select between language and science emphasis within their track. Those who choose a language emphasis may select languages and human science, human and social science, plastic arts, and music (normally performance oriented). Those electing a science bias are offered a choice between maths and physics, natural science, and economics. For the final two years of general secondary education, pupils select the subjects in which they will sit their school leaving exams.

General secondary school usually lasts seven years, although some of the vocational training programmes are designed to be completed in six years. At the end of the seventh year, all students sit examinations in their specialist area. These exams are national standardised tests, taken over a period of eight half-days. Successful completion of the exams leads to a secondary school diploma (*diplôme de fin d'études secondaires*).

There are 17 technical secondary schools (*lycées techniques*) in Luxembourg, some of them specialising in areas such as agriculture, catering, and health (the *Lycée technique pour professions de santé*, which has branches in each hospital district so that pupils can be given on-the-job training). There are three technical options available, a vocational track leading to qualification in a specific trade or *metier*, a technical training track leading to a technical diploma (*diplôme de technicien*), and a technical course leading to a technical general secondary studies diploma (*diplôme de fin d'études secondaires techniques*).

Technical school starts with a three-year general education cycle, which includes most of the subjects studied at primary school, including French and English or another foreign language. Emphasis in recent years has been placed on the languages of Luxembourg's largest foreign populations, so that options generally include not only English, but also Spanish, Italian and sometimes Arabic or Portuguese. On completion of the *diplôme de technicien*, students are eligible to enter advanced technical training, such as that for a BTS (*brevet de technicien supérieur*). Those who obtain a technical general secondary studies diploma can normally go on to either advanced technical training or university studies.

PRIVATE SCHOOLS

Because of the broad base of state funding and wide choice of schools within the state system, Benelux doesn't offer as many different types of private school as some other countries. Most religious (denominational) schools are integrated into the state system (see above), as are many of the 'alternative' schools such as those based on the philosophy of Rudolf Steiner and the Waldorf Schools. In Belgium and Holland in particular, the main alternative to state schools is foreign or international schools, which are described below.

International Schools

Because of the large number of international organisations in Benelux, there's a large number of international schools, from pre-school to secondary, many catering to the British and American expatriate communities. Most of them are concentrated in the areas immediately surrounding Brussels, Antwerp, The Hague, Amsterdam and Luxembourg city, and most provide transport to and from the main expatriate communities in the area. As well as British and American, there are Japanese, French and German schools in Benelux, with classes in all subjects conducted in the native language of the respective country. A few international schools offer classes in a variety of languages.

Schools generally adhere to the standards of the relevant national school systems and offer the appropriate standard school-leaving examinations and certificates with the aim of providing children with a similar education to that of their 'home' country. British schools teach the British curriculum including the GCSE and A-level examinations. American schools offer a US high school diploma, and students can sit American college entrance exams (ACT, SAT, achievement tests and AP exams). French and German schools teach to the *baccalauréat* and *Abitur* examinations. Some international schools award the International Baccalaureate (IB), an internationally recognised university entrance qualification. The IB, which originated in Switzerland, is taught in over 500 schools in around 65 countries and is accepted as an entrance qualification by the world's top universities. As an international examination it's second to none. Many North American universities grant students with an IB up to one year's credit.

Admission to international schools is generally open to all nationalities, although nationals of the relevant country may be given preference, particularly if space in a school is limited, and there's often a competitive admission process, which can include an entry exam, personal interviews (of both children and their parents) and evaluation of previous school grades or teacher references.

Your country's embassy or consulate can provide information on international schools in your area. American or British expatriate associations often publish lists of private international schools in the local area, with evaluations of each, as well as information on boarding schools in other countries.

European Schools: For EU nationals there are also European Schools in Brussels, Mol (near Antwerp), Bergen (in Holland) and Luxembourg city. European Schools are operated by the EU for children of their diplomats and other employees of the various EU bodies. There are classes in each language of the EU, and the curriculum is based on a European-wide standard, culminating in the European Baccalaureate, which is recognised as a university entrance qualification throughout the EU. The curriculum places a strong emphasis on foreign languages and requires certain subjects to be taken in the pupil's first or second foreign language at secondary level.

Any EU national may apply to a European School on a fee-paying basis. English-language classes, however, are extremely popular and usually filled by the children of EU personnel. The Brussels schools alone cater for over 7,000 pupils and there have been no vacancies in the English-language section for several years. For further information, contact the Office of the Representative of the Board of Governors of the European Schools, rue de la Loi 200, Bâtiment Belliard 5–7, office 1/8, 1049 Brussels (☎ 02-295 3746, 💻 www.eursc.org).

Choosing a Private School

The following checklist is designed to help you choose an appropriate private school:

- Does the school have a good reputation? When was it established?

- Does the school have a sound academic record? For example, what percentage of pupils receive good examination passes and go on to university?

- How large are the classes and what is the student-teacher ratio? Does the class size tally with the number of desks in the classrooms? What are the classrooms like? For example, their size, space, cleanliness, lighting and furnishings – including computer equipment. Are there signs of creative teaching, e.g. wall charts, maps, posters and students' work on display?

- What are the qualification requirements for teachers and what nationality are they? Ask for a list of the teaching staff and their qualifications.

- What extras (e.g. art supplies, sports equipment, outings, clothing, health insurance, textbooks and stationery) must you pay for? Different schools have different policies.

- What is the teacher turnover? A high turnover is generally a negative sign and suggests underpaid teachers and/or poor working conditions.
- Which countries do most students come from?
- Is religion an important consideration in your choice of school?
- What language is used? Are special classes offered to students who need tutoring in the language?
- What languages does the school teach as compulsory or optional subjects?
- What is the student turnover?
- What are the school terms and holiday periods? Note that they won't necessarily coincide with those of state schools.
- What are the school hours? Ask to see a pupil timetable to check the ratio of academic/non-academic subjects. Check the number of free study periods and whether they're supervised.
- What are the withdrawal conditions in case you wish to remove your child? One term's notice is usual.
- What does the curriculum include? What examinations are set?
- What sports instruction and facilities are provided? Where are the sports facilities?
- What are the facilities for art and science subjects, e.g. arts and crafts, music, computer studies, science, hobbies, drama, cookery and photography? Ask to see the classrooms, facilities, equipment and some students' projects.
- What sort of outings and celebrations does the school organise?
- What medical facilities does the school provide, e.g. sick room, resident doctor or nurse? Are medical and accident insurance included in the fees?
- How is discipline handled?
- What reports are provided for parents and how often?
- Last but not least, what are the fees?

Before making a final choice, it's important to visit the schools on your shortlist during term time and talk to teachers and pupils (if possible, also speak to former pupils and their parents). Where possible find answers to the above questions yourself and don't rely on a school's prospectus or director to provide the information. If you're unhappy with the answers, look elsewhere. Be sure to ask for advice and information from other expatriates in the community. Many expatriate women's clubs, especially American Women's Clubs, offer publications comparing the various private schools in the area, and some even host private school fairs or 'get acquainted' events, where you can meet staff and pupils from a range of local private schools.

Finally, having made your choice, keep a check on your child's progress and listen to his complaints. Compare notes with other parents. If something seems wrong, try to establish whether the complaint is founded or not and, if it is, take action to have the problem resolved. Never forget that you're paying a lot of money for your child's education (or your employer is) and you should ensure that you receive good value. See also **State or Private School?** on page 139.

APPRENTICESHIPS

Many young people look forward to starting work and learning a trade rather than preparing for higher education in the formal system. The secondary school systems in Belgium, Holland and Luxembourg all offer a two-tier system of technical education, with the 'upper' tier focused on preparing students for higher technical or professional education and the 'lower' tier directed toward job training. Within most technical secondary schools students may take an apprenticeship rather than continue full-time studies once they reach the age of 15 or 16 (see **Secondary School** on page 149 for country details).

An apprenticeship is a combination of on-the-job training and classroom education which is overseen by the educational authorities. The technical institute where the apprentice is enrolled is responsible for helping him negotiate a standard apprenticeship contract with an employer, which requires the apprentice to continue to take a minimum of 400 hours of class work per year, usually in modules tailored to the type of work the student is doing. An apprenticeship lasts from one to three years, depending on the type of profession and the qualification sought. It can be in almost any vocation from a carpenter to an electrician, a nurse or a waitress. Employers pay a small salary which increases with age and experience and also pay for apprenticeship schooling and in some cases travel to and from school.

HIGHER EDUCATION

Higher education in Belgium, Holland and Luxembourg is provided through two types of institution: universities and professional schools (*hautes écoles/ hogescholen*). Professional schools focus on practical training designed to prepare students for a profession requiring advanced study, such as law, medicine, engineering, architecture or agriculture. Universities are devoted to theoretical training in a subject area, and degrees or diplomas normally lead to teaching or doing 'pure' research in a university setting, although a few Belgian and Dutch universities have business, medical or law schools offering 'practical' degrees.

Belgium and Holland each offer a number of different types of higher education as part of the state educational system and, as with primary and secondary schools, there's a wide range of secular and denominational (mostly Catholic) institutes offering higher education to all graduates of the national secondary school systems. Unlike most other European countries, Luxembourg doesn't have its own university system, although there's a variety of options for post-secondary education within the Duchy.

In all three countries, admission to some form of higher education is guaranteed to all holders of the appropriate school leaving certificate. All three countries adhere to one or more of the European conventions regarding higher education qualifications and will admit students with British A-level or International Baccalaureate certificates. American students generally require one year of US college or university study before admission to a European higher education programme.

Belgium: The French and Flemish communities each operate their own system of higher education, the primary difference being linguistic. Institutions in the French-speaking part of Belgium conduct all classes in French, while those in Flemish-speaking areas may offer classes in either Dutch or English. Enrolment in most courses is open to all holders of the appropriate secondary school certificate, but certain areas of study, e.g. specialise medical courses and some civil engineering subjects, are subject to competitive entrance examinations. Foreign students must have the equivalent of the CESS (*Certificat d'Enseignement Secondaire Supérieur*) and may be required to pass an entrance examination, as well as demonstrating adequate knowledge of French or Dutch. Most universities organise summer language classes for foreign students before the start of the academic year. Belgian students pay annual tuition fees ranging from around €30 to €650. Foreign students may have to pay higher fees, up to a maximum of around €9,500 per year, and may be required to provide proof of adequate financial resources while they're studying in Belgium.

Belgium's universities offer four cycles of study. The first cycle (*candidature/ kandidaat*) covers a broad, multi-disciplinary field of studies and takes two or three years to complete. In the second cycle, students focus on a single subject or area of study for a period of at least two or three years. This second cycle can result in the award of a *licence/licentiaat* or a professional title such as pharmacist, medical doctor or veterinarian. The third cycle is usually that of a doctorate (*doctorat/doctor*), which requires five or six additional years of study and research in a specific discipline. At the end of this period, the candidate prepares a doctoral level thesis, which he must formally defend in a public presentation. The fourth cycle consists of an examination open only to students with a doctorate giving them a special qualification to teach at higher education level, although a doctorate is sufficient. (There's also a teaching certification curriculum, which is limited to local nationals.)

Non-university higher education normally consists of either 'short-cycle' or 'long-cycle' programmes. Short-cycle programmes run for three years and lead to qualifications in industry, commerce, agriculture, teaching, etc. Long-cycle courses run for at least four years and lead to diplomas or degrees. They may be divided into shorter cycles with intermediate certificates or qualifications.

To apply for admission to a Belgian university or institute of higher education, contact the institution directly. A list of Dutch higher education institutions can be found on the Dutch embassy website (🖳 www.netherlands-embassy.org/ c_univlist.html). The National Academic Recognition Information Centre (NARIC) provides information about recognition of foreign academic qualifications: for the French community, contact the *Direction générale de l'Enseignement supérieur, Ministère de l'Education et de la Recherché scientifique et de la Formation de la Communauté française*, Quartier des Arcades, 6ème étage, rue Royale 204, 1010 Brussels (☎ 02-210 5577, 🖳 www.cfwb.be/infosup): for the Flemish region, contact the *Ministerie van de Vlaamse Gemeenschap*, Henri Consciencegebous Tower A7, Koning Albert II Laan 15, 1210 Brussels (☎ 02-553 9819, 🖳 www.ond.vlaan deren.be).

Holland: Higher education in Holland consists of either university education (*wetenschappelijk onderwijs – WO*) or professional education (*hoger beroepsonderwijs – HBO*).

There are 14 universities in Holland, in Amsterdam, Delft, Eindhoven, Groningen, Leiden, Maastricht, Nijenrode, Nijmegen, Rotterdam, Tilburg, Twente, Utrecht and Wageningen. Some universities are affiliated to the Catholic or Protestant churches but, as in the state school system, all must conform to national guidelines and must accept students of all religions. The Dutch take great pride in the fact that all their universities are considered to be of equal academic standard and status. All universities charge the same fees, regardless of their area of specialisation, and receive the same level of state funding.

There are seventeen professional schools in Holland, including the Royal Conservatory in The Hague and the *Hogeschool voor de Kunsten* in Utrecht, as well as various polytechnics and University College in Utrecht, which offers an undergraduate course in English.

In theory, the Dutch higher education system consists of a four-year programme in both professional schools and universities. Only medical studies are scheduled to last five or six years. In practice, however, it isn't unusual for other courses to last this long. The system is based on 'credit hours', each year consisting of 42 credit hours. The first year of a higher education programme is referred to as the *propedeutisch*, which consists of general studies and results in the award of a certificate (*Getuigschrift van het Propedeutisch Examen*) which is required for admission to either an HBO or a *doctoraal* (not to be confused with a *doctoraat* – see below) but is essentially for those who drop out of higher education after the first year, so that they have some sort of qualification.

HBO studies last for four years (168 credits) and cover both the theoretical and the practical aspects of a profession, which is selected from one of seven sectors: technology, administration and economics, health care, fine and performing arts, education and teacher training, agriculture, and welfare services. All programmes in the HBO require both an internship (*stage*) and a major paper (*scriptie*) prepared in the final year of study. On completion of the programme, students are awarded the HBO certificate (*Getuigschrift HBO*) and may use the title *Baccalaueus* or *Ingenieur* (*Ing.*).

The university *doctoraal* programme is oriented towards research and in most universities takes three years (126 credits) to complete, although technical subjects such as engineering and certain mathematics and sciences are four-year (168 credit) programmes. Much of the final year is taken up with the preparation of a major paper (*scriptie*), which requires the student to conduct independent research. On graduation, students are entitled to use the title *Doctorandus* (*Drs.*), *Ingenieur* (*Ir.*) or, in the case of those completing the law programme, *Meester* (*Mr.*).

The highest academic qualification awarded in Holland is the *doctoraat*, which requires the candidate to write a dissertation based on his own research. Students can ask a professor to supervise their research or apply for a post as an assistant researcher (*Assistent in Opleiding – AIO* or *Onderzoeker in Opleiding – OIO*), which carries a small salary. The competition for paid research posts is intense, however, and they're difficult for foreigners to obtain. In a few fields, particularly in medicine, there are post-*doctoraal* training and research programmes that lead to other professional qualifications.

Admission to Dutch higher educational programmes is open to all holders of HAVO or VWO diplomas or the equivalent. Students with a fourth level MBO diploma may also be admitted to HBO programmes. Generally, a student holding a secondary school qualification can be admitted to any higher education institution, although there are entrance examinations and quotas (*numerus clausus*) in many medical fields of study. In fields that limit enrolment, no more than 2 per cent of new admissions can be foreign students. Foreign students must usually pass a test to demonstrate their ability to follow coursework in the Dutch language. Most universities offer summer language classes prior to the start of the academic year. Students at Dutch universities and polytechnics pay a standard tuition fee, set by the national government (currently around €1,400), and must pay their own living expenses. Grants and loans are available for both local and foreign students. Information on funding is available through the *Informatiseringsbank* in Groningen (💻 www.ib-groep.nl – the site is entirely in Dutch).

Admission to HBO and *doctoraal* courses is handled centrally by the CBAP, PO Box 30157, 9700 LJ Groningen. Applications to other courses in Dutch universities or professional schools are handled by individual institutions. For information in English about higher education opportunities and procedures in Holland, contact Nuffic, Kortenaerkade 11, 2518 AX The Hague or PO Box 29777, 2502 LT The Hague (☎ 070-426 0260, 💻 www.nuffic.nl – contains information in English).

Luxembourg: Because there are no institutions in Luxembourg which can award a degree, most of the business and professional people living and working in the Duchy have taken at least part of their post-secondary school training abroad. Luxembourg does, however, have a University Centre (*Centre Universitaire*), a technology institute (*Institut Supérieur de Technologie – IST*), an international institute (*Institut Universitaire International*) and two teacher training institutes (the *Institut Supérieur d'Etudes et de Recherches Pédagogiques – ISEEP* and the *Institut de Formation pour Educateurs et Moniteurs – IFEM*). These institutions offer a variety of courses, from first and second year university level programmes to a four-year technical diploma in industrial engineering. The two teacher training institutes specialise in training teachers for the Luxembourg state school system, and their programmes are open only to Luxembourg citizens. There are postgraduate programmes in law, economics and European studies, open to the international community, and a postgraduate course in European law. The *Centre Universitaire* also offers a variety of programmes and seminars in the humanities, law and economics throughout the year.

Each of the various programmes has its own requirements (for example, you must have a postgraduate law degree for admission to the programme in European law), and all higher education requires a secondary school completion certificate equivalent to those awarded in Luxembourg schools. Most higher education programmes require a perfect command of both French and German, although some of the shorter programmes and seminars are run in English. For further information about higher education in Luxembourg, contact the *Département de l'Enseignement supérieur, Ministère de la Culture, de l'Enseignement supérieur et de la Recherche*, 20 Montée de la Pétrusse, 2273 Luxembourg (☎ 478-6633). The *Centre Universitaire* has a website (💻 www.cu.lu – in French only) containing details of current courses.

FURTHER EDUCATION

Further education generally embraces everything except first degree courses taken at universities, technical institutes and other institutions of higher education, although the distinction between further and higher education is often blurred. Each year many thousands of students attend further education courses at universities alone. These are often short and job-related, although courses may be full or part-time and include summer terms. Belgium, Holland and Luxembourg have many private schools, institutes and other forms of training organisations, including some affiliated to foreign (mostly American) universities.

Many educational institutions offer American MBA degree courses, including the Universities of Rotterdam and Nijenrode in Holland, the University of Liege and the *Vrije Universiteit Brussel* in Belgium, and the Sacred Heart University in Luxembourg. Tuition fees are high and study periods strictly organised. Although most courses are taught in English, some schools require students to be fluent in one or more foreign languages for internship or research purposes.

Both the Belgian and Dutch ministries of education have developed their own versions of the UK's Open University (OU), providing distance learning programmes for adults. The Belgian and Dutch OUs are designed to allow adults to obtain secondary or higher education certificates or degrees they were unable to obtain while in the state educational system. Most teaching is done on a flexible timetable and makes use of distance learning tools such as video tapes, CD-ROMs and Internet-related tools. Whereas the Dutch OU is an autonomous institution, Belgian OU programmes are operated by the various universities and higher education institutes. Flemish-language OU courses are co-ordinated with the Dutch OU through an organisation called the *Stuurgroep Open Hoger Onderwijs*. Belgian and Dutch OU courses are normally conducted in the local languages (i.e. French or Dutch) and all examinations are conducted in either French or Dutch, usually at a local or regional centre. In French-speaking Belgium, information on OU courses is available from the relevant institutions. Information about Dutch OU courses is available via the Internet (🖳 www.ouh.nl – some information is in English).

UK Open University courses (in English) are also available throughout mainland Europe and the OU has offices in Brussels, The Hague and Rameldange (Luxembourg), where students can meet tutors and obtain information about courses and degree programmes. Most OU offices hold open houses or information sessions in June or September and information can be found on the OU website (🖳 www.open. ac.uk).

General information about local adult education and training is available in most towns and cities from town halls and libraries. See also **Day & Evening Classes** on page 304.

LANGUAGE SCHOOLS

If you want to make the most of your stay in Benelux and enjoy the Belgian, Dutch or Luxembourg way of life, it's essential to learn one of the local languages as soon as possible. For people living in Benelux permanently, learning the local language isn't an option but a necessity. French, Dutch and German may not be particularly easy languages to learn, but even the least linguistically-talented person can acquire a working knowledge of the language. All that's required is a little hard work, some help and perseverance, particularly if you have only English-speaking colleagues and friends. Note that your business and social enjoyment and success in Benelux will be directly related to the degree to which you master French, Dutch, German and/or Lëtzebuergesch.

If you don't speak at least one of the local languages (French, Dutch, German or Lëtzebuergesch) fluently, you may wish to enrol in a language course. Most people can help themselves a great deal through the use of books, tapes, videos and even computer-based language courses. However, even the latest interactive language-teaching programmes cannot answer your questions or correct your pronunciation. For most people, attending a course (combined with one or more of the other methods listed above) is likely to be the best solution. There's certainly no shortage of possibilities. Teaching the local language to foreigners is big business in Belgium, Holland and Luxembourg, with classes offered by language schools (including franchises of big corporations such as Inlingua and Berlitz), local and foreign colleges and universities, private and international schools, foreign and international organisations, local associations and clubs, and private teachers.

Tuition ranges from language courses for complete beginners, through specialised business-related or cultural courses, to university-level courses leading to recognised diplomas. If you already speak one of the languages but need conversational practice, you may prefer to enrol in an art or craft course at a local institute or club (see **Social Clubs** on page 299) or to try to find one of the many language circles, often sponsored by expatriate clubs. You can also learn a language via a telephone language course, which is particularly practical for busy executives and those who don't live near a language school.

There are language schools in all Benelux cities and many larger towns. Most run various classes suited to your language ability, how many hours you wish to study per week, how much money you want to spend and how quickly you want to learn. For those for whom money is no object (if you're lucky, your employer!) there are total immersion courses where you study for up to nine hours per day, five days per week. Rates vary, so shop around. Language classes generally fall into the following categories:

- **Extensive:** 4–10 hours per week
- **Intensive:** 15–20 hours per week
- **Total Immersion:** 20–40+ hours per week

Fees can range from a few hundred euros per week to several thousand euros for a total immersion course. You may prefer to have private lessons, which are a quicker, although generally more expensive, method of learning a language. The main advantage of private lessons is that you learn at your own pace and aren't held back by slow learners or left floundering in the wake of the class genius. You can advertise for a teacher in your local newspapers, on shopping centre/supermarket bulletin boards, university notice boards and through your or your spouse's employer. Also, don't forget to ask your friends, neighbours and colleagues if they can recommend a private teacher. Lessons cost between €15 and €50 per hour depending on the tutor's qualifications and experience. Another option is to find someone who wants to learn (or improve) his English and work out some kind of reciprocal arrangement. This can be an economical way of learning a new language, although it depends on your having the time (and inclination) to give 'lessons' as well as receive them.

In Luxembourg, you can take advantage of the newly re-configured Luxembourg Language Centre, a facility set up by the Ministry of Education initially to support language teaching and learning in schools. The Language Centre is affiliated with the official language training institutes of the various European nations, including the *Alliance française* (for French), the *Goethe Institut* (for German) and Cambridge University's programme in TEFL (teaching English as a foreign language). The centre offers classes in eight languages (English, French, Dutch, German, Italian, Lëtzebuergesch, Portuguese and Spanish) at all levels and in a variety of formats, from full-time intensive courses to evening classes held in secondary schools. In Belgium and Holland, schools and local governments often run French or Dutch classes in the evenings. Enquire at your town hall for details.

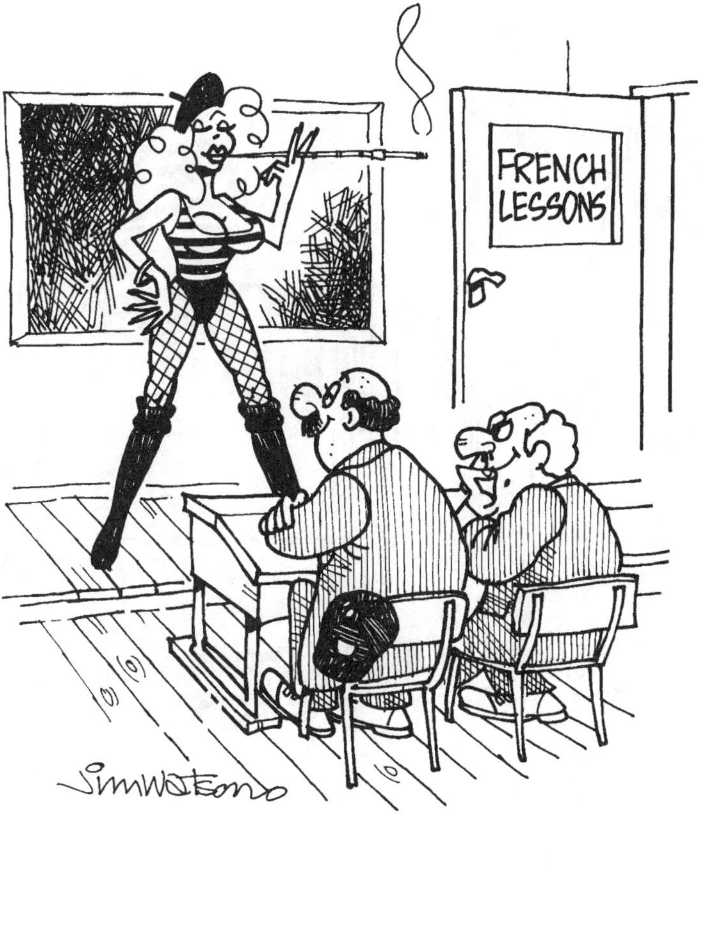
FRENCH LESSONS
Jim Watson

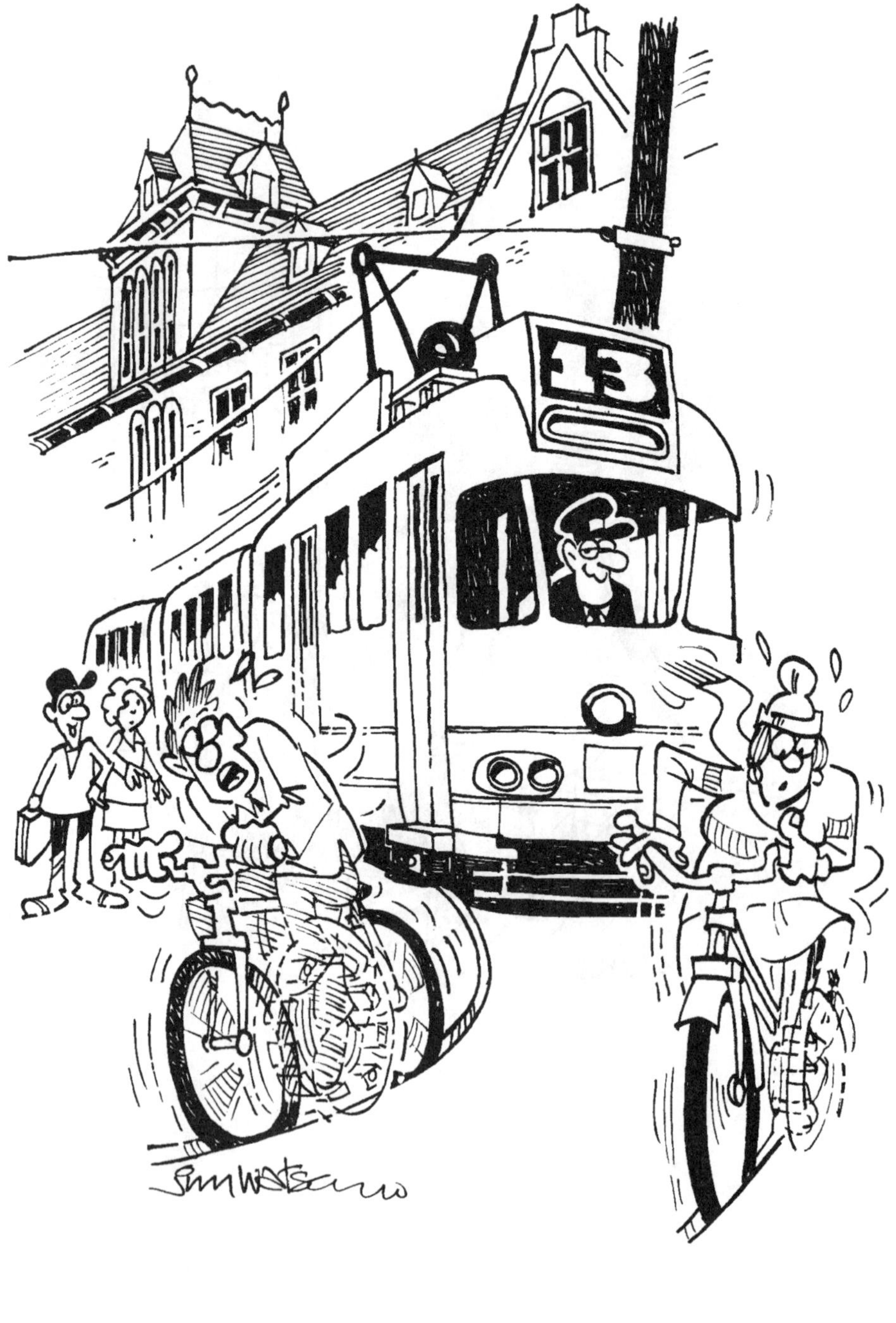
13

10.

PUBLIC TRANSPORT

The Benelux countries are enthusiastic proponents of all forms of public transport, which isn't surprising, as their roads and motorways are perpetually congested (see **Chapter 11**). Although the public transport system is operated quite differently in each country, most areas are well served by trains, buses, trams and other means of transport, which are modern, clean, efficient and generally good value.

TRAINS

Within the relatively small area covered by Benelux, trains have always been a popular method of transport and are often the quickest and simplest way to get around. It helps that the railway networks of Belgium and Holland are among the densest in the world. Belgium boasts 3,920km (2,450mi) of track serving both passenger and freight transport, while at 2,739km (1,702mi) Holland' rail network is only slightly less extensive than its waterway system. Luxembourg's railway system has been expanded to 275km (171mi) and comprises seven main lines, mostly connecting major towns with Luxembourg city. Although the country's population is a mere 425,000, its rail system accounts for almost 300 million passenger kilometres (176 million passenger miles) annually.

As in most other European countries, the railway systems of Benelux were originally government-owned public services. Belgium's SNCB/NMBS (*Société nationale des Chemins de Fer Belges/Nationale Maatschappi de Belgische Spoorwegen*) and Luxembourg's CFL (*Chemins de Fer Luxembourgeois*) remain mostly government-owned, while the Dutch NV NS (*NV Nederlandse Spoorwegen*) has been almost completely privatised, along with most other Dutch public services.

Types of Train

Passenger trains are classified according to the type of service they offer, and international train designations correspond to those used in other European countries:

- **EC** (Euro-City) – international long-distance trains for which you must pay a supplement (*supplément/toeslag*);
- **INT** – international trains for which no supplement applies;
- **IC** (Inter-City) – express trains operating between major cities at regular intervals (usually once or twice an hour);
- **IR** (Inter-Regio) – limited-stop trains connecting regional centres, usually at regular intervals at least once every two hours.

Each train has a unique number (similar to a flight number), which is prefixed by one of the above abbreviations. For local services, the prefixes vary by country but usually differentiate between trains that stop at all stations along the route and those that make only limited stops or different stops at peak hours (normally weekday rush hours) and over popular holiday weekends.

Most trains have a sign on each carriage giving the destination and route details (of the carriage), plus the train number, particularly international or inter-regional trains. Be sure to check the sign on the carriage you're entering if you don't have a specific seat reservation; on some long-distance routes, trains are divided at 'hub' stations and if you're in the wrong carriage you could find yourself in Copenhagen instead of Berlin!

Brussels is one end of the Thalys high-speed line (TGV/HST) from Paris and is also a terminus for the Eurostar train running via the Channel tunnel to London (see **Ferries & Eurotunnel** on page 173). There are 23 Thalys departures daily from Brussels Midi station to Paris Gare du Nord, making the trip in an hour and 25 minutes, plus four departures each day to Paris Charles de Gaulle airport and Disneyland. Once the special high-speed track is completed between Brussels and Amsterdam (some time between 2002 and 2005 according to various estimates), the Thalys service will connect Paris and Amsterdam via Brussels in little more than three hours (the trip currently takes just over four).

Tickets

In general, it's recommended that you buy your ticket before travelling anywhere by train within Belgium, Holland and Luxembourg. Although train conductors are often able to sell tickets on board (and some can even accept credit cards for payment), there's usually a surcharge for tickets purchased on the train. If you find yourself on a train where conductors don't sell tickets, you could be subject to a hefty fine, payable on the spot.

Most stations have a ticket office, and in main stations the national rail company often has a travel office, complete with travel agents and consultants ready to help you book an entire holiday, if you wish, including hotel and rental car (or bicycle). Most stations also have ticket machines, operating 24 hours a day, seven days a week, which accept cash (coins and sometimes notes), credit and local debit cards. Some machines offer touch screens, a choice of language and detailed instructions to prompt you through the process of purchasing tickets; others have a range of buttons to select the type of ticket you want (see **Fares** below), your destination and any other options that may be available.

For trains requiring a supplement or seat reservation, it's generally wise to purchase your ticket at least a day in advance. Long-distance trains can be fully booked at peak periods, and certain high-speed train lines (e.g. the Thalys and Eurostar) require seat reservations at all times. On most trains it's possible to make seat reservations, which are included with the supplement for EC and most TGV/HST trains. All three national railway companies have booking facilities on their Internet sites (see above). You need a credit card for payment and, in most cases, tickets will be posted to your home or office if you purchase them more than five days in advance. (Luxembourg's CFL website directs you to the German rail website for bookings and, in some cases, the Belgian SNCB/NMBS's booking is handled by the SNCF website – see **Information** on page 172.) If you book over the Internet less than five days in advance, you can usually collect your tickets from the station ticket office. Travel agencies in Benelux also book train travel, although you may have to pay a small service fee.

Ticket checks on all trains are routine and each train usually has a team of staff rather than a single conductor. On longer trips it's common to have your ticket checked two or three times, particularly if there's a crew change along the route. If you're found to be sitting in first class on a second class ticket, you'll be asked to pay the difference (plus a supplement for buying your ticket on the train) on the spot. Also, it does no good to hide in the toilet during ticket checks, as the conductor will knock on the door and wait outside until you emerge (evidently conductors have seen the same old spy movies as you).

Fares

Basic fares on all three rail systems are based on the distance travelled, and a return ticket (*aller-retour/heen en terug*) is normally twice the price of a one-way fare (*aller simple/enkel reis*). Children travel for half-price up to the age of 12, provided they're accompanied by an adult. (Unaccompanied children pay the full fare.) However, you hardly ever need to pay the 'basic fare', as all three railway companies offer a dizzying array of discounts, special programmes, package deals and rail passes designed to fit almost every possible itinerary. The programmes on offer vary with the seasons and the names of the passes or deals may change in accordance with the latest advertising campaign, but generally you obtain the cheapest fares if you travel at weekends or during off-peak hours, purchase tickets well in advance or travel with your family or in some other group. There are also discounts for young people, students and pensioners. Local trains (i.e. those that make lots of stops) are often cheaper than express trains, but it will take you longer to reach your destination. The following are some of the more popular (and enduring) discount fares in each of the three Benelux countries, but you should always check the current offers.

Belgium: Belgian railways offer an array of cards that allow you to buy train tickets for travel within Belgium at discounts of 25 to 50 per cent. On international routes, the discounts normally only apply to the Belgian part of the journey. The two most common discount cards are the 50 per cent discount card (*carte de réduction de 50%/reductiekaart 50%*), costing €15.87 and valid for a month, and the fidelity card (*carte de fidélité/getrouwheidskaart*), which gives you a 25 per cent reduction on all rail travel within Belgium for a year for €71.89. These cards can be combined with other discount cards, issued to children, students, handicapped people (and assistants accompanying them on trips), pregnant women and various other categories of travellers.

With all Belgian discount cards, only the 'variable' portion of the fare is subject to discount. Every second class ticket includes a 'fixed fare' of €0.62; for first class tickets, the fixed portion is €0.95. There are also rules regarding the order in which the various discount plans may be applied. (The Belgians are addicted to rules and regulations.) The SNCB/NMBS website explains the details (but only in French and Dutch) and offers examples for calculating discounts based on the various discount cards currently available. Station ticket office staff are also well practised in applying multiple discounts, but make sure you have your discount cards with you.

Another option is to buy a B-Tourrail Card for €51.50 that allows you unlimited train travel within Belgium on any five days in a month. If you're under 26 years old, you can guy a Go Pass for around €34 which entitles you to 10 one-way journeys within Belgium. Children under six travel free provided they're accompanied by a fare-paying adult, and there are other discounts available for large families (i.e. three or more minor children), groups, as well as a range of commuter passes for daily use on a single route. Ask at your local station or check the SNCB/NMBS website for details and current prices (🖳 www.sncb.be).

Holland: The array of full-price (*voltarief*) and discount tickets (*korting*) in Holland can be rather daunting at first. Besides having to decide between first and second class and single (*enkelereis*) and day return (*dagretour*), evening return (*avondretour*) or weekend return (*weekend retour*) tickets, you must choose between same day (*alleen vandaag geldig*) and undated (*zonderdatum*) tickets. Each of these options has its own button on ticket machines, and it's assumed you know what the various options require in terms of 'justification' if you're buying your ticket from a machine. If in doubt, go to the ticket office!

Undated tickets must be stamped before you board a train, either at the ticket office or by a machine which is usually located near the entrance to the platform. Single and day return tickets are valid on the date indicated on the ticket and up to 4am the next day. Weekend return tickets are valid between 7pm Fridays and 4am Mondays. With an evening (or 'cheap day') return, your departure must be outside rush hours, although you can usually return at any time the same day. These require a validating card (*vordeel-urenkaart* or *voordeelsurenkaart*), which costs €44.92 and must be presented in order for you to qualify for the discount.

If you're making the same journey regularly over a short period, you can buy a 'five return' ticket, valid for five return journeys to and from the same destination. For longer periods, it's better to purchase a monthly pass (*maandtrajectkaart*) or an annual pass (*jaartrajectkaart*), which can be used to obtain discounts on other train journeys during off-peak hours and can also be combined with a local transport pass covering one to three zones (see below). Because the rail system is integrated with other transport systems, there's also a variety of monthly and annual season tickets (*abonnementen*) available, combining rail travel with local bus and tram services at one or both ends of your journey. If you're planning a whistle-stop tour of Holland, there's a day card (*dagkaart*), which allows you unlimited rail travel throughout the country for a day (i.e. until 4 o'clock the next morning). For obsessive rail travellers, an *NS-jaarkaart* gives you unlimited train travel throughout Holland for a year, and an *OV-jaarkaart* allows travel on all public transport as well as providing discounts to many museums and other tourist attractions in Holland. In 2001, a second class *OV-jaarkaart* cost €2,776.68, a first class pass around 50 per cent more.

Children aged three or under travel free, provided they don't occupy their own seat, and those aged four to 11 travel at reduced rates (usually half price), provided they're accompanied by a fare-paying adult. There are discount passes for families and other groups. Details of all fares and discount tickets are available at railway stations and on the NV NS website (🖳 www.ns.nl), although the website has limited information in English. Many of the larger stations have brochures in a variety of languages explaining the various discounted tickets.

Luxembourg: A short distance (*courte distance*) ticket in Luxembourg costs €1.12 and a long-distance or network (*réseau*) ticket costs €4.46 for a single and exactly twice as much for a return – one of the few things that's simple in Luxembourg. For travel within the Duchy, CFL offers four kinds of season tickets or passes (*abonnements*): monthly short distance, monthly network, a 50 per cent discount card (*abonnement réseau comportant une réduction de 50%*) and a young person's annual pass (JUMBO-KAART). There's also a half-price network pass for old age pensioners (over 65) and large families. The CFL website (🖥 www.cfl.lu) includes route and fare information, but most tickets for travel within Luxembourg must be purchased at a station. Tickets for international travel can be purchased via the Internet using the German DB ticketing service.

Station Facilities

Railway stations throughout Belgium, Holland and Luxembourg offer a range of facilities, including a travel centre, luggage lockers (and sometimes a left luggage office), ATMs, a post office, one or more news stands and generally at least one bar, café or small restaurant. With the arrival of the euro, banks and currency exchange booths, which were common in larger stations, have mostly been replaced by bank machines. It's usually possible to purchase packaged sandwiches, drinks and snacks in or near stations, which is wise if you want to avoid the high prices of on-board food. Unlike those in some other countries, however, Benelux stations don't usually have extensive shopping facilities or even convenience stores.

A major problem throughout Europe, but particularly in the Benelux region, is that of pickpockets, who operate in railway stations and even on the trains themselves. It pays to keep your bags in sight and to be suspicious of any jostling you receive in stations or on trains.

Train Facilities

Most seating in Benelux trains is aircraft-style, particularly on express trains, but it's possible to find compartment-style seating on inter-regional and other long-distance trains. Most trains offer both first and second class seating. The difference between the two classes varies with the route and the railway company that operates the service, but generally first class offers a less crowded carriage, a guaranteed seat and not having to rub shoulders with the hoi polloi (e.g. students and tourists). Both first and second class carriages have smoking and non-smoking sections, although the number and size of smoking cars is being reduced. When booking, you may choose not only a smoking or non-smoking seat, but also a window or an aisle seat. Although half the seats face each way on most trains, a facing forwards or backwards option isn't usually available, as trains often reverse direction in the course of a journey.

Restaurant facilities are available on EC, IC and many IR trains, with a trolley service in second class and light refreshments (from the train conductor) in first class. IR trains often have a 'bistro' car, offering freshly cooked food, packaged sandwiches and soft drinks, beer and wine, as well as a trolley service. The quality of food varies. Some restaurant car meals can be excellent (as well as elegantly served), while bistro car fare tends to be limited to quickly prepared grilled dishes, sandwiches and other fast food. Prices tend to be high, although most bistro and restaurant cars accept almost any European currency, as well as major credit cards. Experienced locals generally take their own picnic lunch on longer trips – and some of these can be quite elaborate!

Most carriages on EC and IC trains and all TGV/HST carriages are air-conditioned. Most trains have toilets, including some specially equipped for use by disabled passengers.

Night Trains

A night train (*train de nuit/nachttrein*) is a train with sleeping cars (*couchettes*) consisting of single, double and quadruple compartments, including some with private shower and WC. Some trains even have bar-discos for those who cannot (or don't want to) sleep. Night trains run on certain long-haul routes, including those to Switzerland, southern France, Spain and Eastern Europe. Fares are based on the distance travelled, the type of accommodation and the time of year. Breakfast is included and it's usually possible to have the conductor wake you in the morning in plenty of time to prepare for arrival at your destination. If you want to indulge yourself totally, you can even order 'room service' so that you don't have to make your way to the restaurant or bistro car during the night. Further information is available from ticket offices or via the Internet (see page 167). Travel agencies also have information on night train services and sleeping car package holidays.

Car Trains

If you want to travel by train but have the use of your car when you arrive, you can use a car train. Most car train services in Benelux are operated in conjunction with night trains (see above). Simply deliver your car a couple of hours before your night train's departure to a designated station, where it's loaded onto a special carriage forming part of the train. When you arrive the next morning, so does your car. Schedules vary with the season, winter car trains heading mostly to ski resort areas, while summer trains go to coastal resorts and other holiday destinations. The price of the journey includes transport of your car plus a *couchette* or sleeping car accommodation for you and your travelling companions. All the usual night train facilities are at your disposal (see above), but note that you don't have access to your car during the journey, so don't leave your tickets in the glove compartment!

Discount cards are available to those who make frequent trips to the beach or ski slopes. Prices and conditions of use vary according to the season and the destination, as well as the level of sleeper accommodation you choose, and you should consult the relevant railway service or a travel agency for the latest information.

Bicycles & Luggage

Bicycles can normally be taken on local trains throughout Belgium, Holland and Luxembourg, and from spring to autumn some trains include a carriage exclusively for bikes, although there are restrictions on certain rush hour trains, and bicycles sometimes require a special ticket or pass indicating that the appropriate fare has been paid (around €1 in Luxembourg irrespective of the distance travelled). It's also possible to take your bicycle free of charge on many international trains (check the rail websites for a list, plus information about reserving a space for your bike), and you can take a bicycle (or two or three) on car trains, provided they're securely mounted on your car (and don't obscure your number plate). Alternatively, you can rent a bicycle at your destination. Rental bikes are available at many railway stations throughout the Benelux region, and some types of commuter passes, discount cards and package trips include discounts on bicycle rental.

As far as luggage is concerned, you're generally limited to what you and your travelling companions can handle. Airline-style baggage check-in isn't normally available for most forms of train travel. Belgian railways simply advise on their website that it isn't available 'any more' (although it's a moot point whether or not it ever was). Shipping large quantities of belongings by rail usually has to be arranged through a freight handling company, unless you're travelling by car train, in which case you can load up your car with as much stuff as you like. Under normal circumstances, you should limit your luggage to the number of pieces you can comfortably manage yourself.

Most long-distance trains have luggage racks at the ends of each carriage for stowing suitcases or other luggage too large to be placed in overhead racks. On crowded trains, luggage storage space fills up quickly. There's also a problem with theft on trains, so if you're seated at the opposite end of the carriage from the luggage rack, you should think twice before leaving anything valuable (such as a laptop computer) and be sure to lock all suitcases you stow in the luggage racks.

Information

Information about train services can be obtained at all main stations and smaller stations with a manned ticket office. The day's arrivals and departures are displayed on large electronic boards, although these don't usually list all the stops made by each train. If your train or a train you're meeting has been delayed, this will be indicated on the board. Large yellow timetables posted in the stations show all scheduled departure times and details of trains leaving the station. White posters give the same information for arrivals.

On the platform itself there's normally some sort of diagram or sign indicating the format of each train and showing you where to wait if you have seat reservations or need to find a particular carriage for your destination. Most stops last only two to three minutes, so there isn't time to walk up and down looking for your seat or carriage after the train has stopped.

All three national rail services maintain extensive websites containing general information about the railways, train services and ticketing. All three sites have information available in multiple languages (French, Dutch and English plus, usually, German) although the English language sections are rather limited. Many of the longer international routes are serviced wholly or partly by the rail services of neighbouring nations, particularly the French *Société nationale des Chemins de Fer français* (SNCF), which handles all Eurostar bookings, and *Die Bahn* in Germany, whose websites are also given below.

- 🖳 www.sncb.be (SNCB/NMBS)
- 🖳 www.ns.nl (NV NS)
- 🖳 www.cfl.lu (CFL)
- 🖳 www.SNCF.com (France)
- 🖳 www.bahn.de (Germany)

FERRIES & EUROTUNNEL

Ostend, Zeebrugge and Rotterdam and the main Benelux passenger ports offering a regular ferry service to Dover, Hull and other ports in the UK.The French ports of Dunkerque, Calais and Boulogne are easily reachable by train, bus and car and offer shorter and more frequent crossings between the European continent and the UK. The major ferry companies operating international services are P&O (operating as P&O Stena or P&O North Sea Ferries, depending on the route), Sea France and Hoverspeed, with its high-speed SeaCat service to and from Ostend. (Note that the service continues to be called Hoverspeed despite the fact that hovercraft were replaced by catamarans in 2001.) It's also possible to book an overnight 'cruise' from Rotterdam or Zeebrugge to Hull, and during the summer there are ferry services from Dutch ports to Denmark, Scandinavia and some of the islands in the North Sea.

Some ferry services operate during the summer months only, e.g. May to September, and the frequency of services varies from dozens per day on the Calais-Dover and Ostend-Dover routes during the summer to one per week on longer routes. Services are less frequent during the winter months, when bad weather can also cause cancellations. Most Channel ferries have a capacity of up to 2,000 passengers and 700 cars. Ferries carry all vehicles, while catamarans take mainly cars. All operators except Hoverspeed offer night services. Between Ostend and Dover, Hoverspeed offers its SeaCat service, which is for foot passengers only and can be combined with rail connections to and from Brussels and London Charing Cross station.

Berths, cabins and Pullman seats are available on longer crossings, and most ships have a restaurant, self-service cafeteria, children's play area and shopping facilities (although duty-free shopping within Europe ended in 1999). Generally, the longer the route, the better and more comprehensive the facilities, which often makes it worthwhile considering alternative routes to the Ostend-Dover or Calais-Dover crossings. Although these are the shortest routes and offer the most crossings, longer passages are generally less crowded and more relaxing.

It isn't always necessary to make a booking, although it's recommended when travelling during the summer period, particularly on a Friday or Saturday (and when you require a berth on an overnight service). Like aeroplanes, ferries are sometimes subject to delays due to strikes, out of service ferries or simply passenger or vehicle handling problems. Most of the ferry lines have websites and offer online credit card booking facilities. Hoverspeed's website (🖳 www.hoverspeed.co.uk) contains timetables and fare schedules in several languages. P&O North Sea Ferries' site (🖳 www.ponsf.com) includes complete information about its overnight services from Rotterdam and Zeebrugge to Hull.

Eurotunnel: Eurotunnel started operating its Shuttle car train service from Coquelles (near Calais) to Folkstone (near Dover) in 1995. It provides three to four departures per hour during peak periods and the journey takes just 35 minutes. Each train can carry around 180 cars and fares are similar to those for ferries (i.e. around £150 (€230) to £250 (€385) for a five-day return for a car and two passengers). Booking is recommended, particularly at weekends and during holiday periods. Note, however, that although you're given a departure time when you book, this isn't guaranteed and you may have to wait for the following train or even the one after that at busy times; on the other hand, it's possible to arrive early and catch an earlier train than the one specified. Trains carry all vehicles including cycles, motorcycles, cars, trucks, buses, caravans and motorhomes. Note that you may be asked to show that gas bottles have been disconnected and switched off, so don't stow them anywhere inaccessible.

An alternative to the Shuttle car train is the Eurostar passenger train, departing from Brussels Gare de Midi and arriving at London Waterloo just under three hours later (it would be quicker, but the French TGV trains must slow to a crawl on antiquated British tracks). It's possible to pick up the Eurostar at the Gare d'Europe in Lille, which is accessible from most of Belgium by rail, bus or car. If you're travelling by Eurostar, you must check in at least 20 minutes before departure in order to complete customs formalities.

BUSES, TRAMS & METROS

Almost all cities and towns in the Benelux region have a local public transport system, usually based on a combination of buses and trams. Four cities – Brussels, Antwerp, Amsterdam and Rotterdam – have an underground railway (metro) network, which is closely integrated with the above-ground public transport systems, particularly in Holland.

Belgium: Local bus and tram systems are run by the regional authorities and therefore tend to vary considerably from region to region. Public transport in the Brussels area is provided by the STIB/MIVB (*Société des Transports inter-communaux/Maatschappij voor het Intercommunaal Vervoer te Brussel*). In Brussels, the metro, tram and bus lines run from 6am to around midnight, with a limited night bus service (*bus de nuit/nachtbus*) on a few routes. Route maps and timetables are posted at most bus stops and are available at tourist offices and most railway and metro stations with a manned ticket office. On most routes, there are three or four buses or trams per hour, usually at regular intervals, with a reduced service (i.e. once or twice per hour) at weekends and on public holidays.

In Brussels, most stops have signs in both French and Flemish, but outside the city limits you may find only single-language signs. Many of the city's metro stations are beautifully decorated, including displays of paintings, sculpture and ceramics by local artists, and are worth a visit even if you don't plan to use the trains! Unfortunately, pickpockets and petty theft are major problems in metro stations, as elsewhere in Brussels. Otherwise, public transport is relatively safe, even at night.

Tram and bus stops are marked with a red and white sign and are mostly request stops (*arrêt sur demande/halte op verzoek*), which means you must hold out your hand as the tram or bus approaches if you want it to stop. On some buses the driver doesn't open the doors for you but you must push on the vertical strip in the centre of the doors to open them. If you already have a ticket, you may enter by either the front or back door. If you need to buy a ticket on the bus or tram, you must board by the front door. There are buttons in the bus or tram to signal to the driver that you want to disembark at the next stop; if the doors don't open automatically, check for a button to open the doors. In the metro, there's usually a latch on the doors that you raise to open them once the train has stopped.

Tickets have a magnetic strip on them and must be validated when you board a bus or tram and again when you change buses or trams. A ticket on the Brussels system is valid for an hour after its first validation. There are frequent ticket checks by inspectors, and if you're caught without a properly validated ticket you must pay an on-the-spot fine. When using the metro, you validate your ticket as you enter a metro station. Don't throw your ticket away until after you've arrived at your destination, as you may be asked to show a valid ticket anywhere along the route. At some metro stations you must use your validated ticket to exit the station, and there are usually ticket inspectors lurking just out of sight of the exit turnstiles, waiting to catch anyone unable to produce a valid ticket.

You can buy single tickets or multiple ticket packs (containing five or ten tickets) at any metro station, either at the ticket office or from a vending machine. Tickets are also available from tourist offices, news stands and even some food shops. Bus drivers sell single tickets and special five-journey tickets. It's also possible to purchase monthly or annual passes, plus a variety of discount cards for young people, senior citizens and families with three or more children under the age of 21. For these special fares, you must contact the Subscription Office (*Bureau des Abonnements/Abonnement Bureau*) at the Porte de Namur metro station. Most passes and some of the discount cards require two passport photos and some form of identification to prove you meet the age, family status or other requirements. For details or further information, contact the STIB/MIVB (☎ 02-515 2000).

Holland: The Dutch public transport systems (excluding the railways) carry an estimated 750 million passengers each year. Every city and town has some form of public transport system, usually consisting of a combination of buses and trams. Amsterdam and Rotterdam also have underground railway (metro) networks, and even the smallest towns (those with less than 2,000 inhabitants) generally offer a minibus service, staffed by volunteers and subsidised by the state. All local bus and tram systems use the same zone-based ticket and fare system, which includes a wide range of options for daily, monthly and annual passes covering multiple modes of transport. There's a single phone number (☎ 0900-9292 costing €0.34 per minute) for information about all public transport in Holland.

All local public transport systems in Holland are split into zones, each measuring approximately 4.5 km (2.5mi) across. Fares are based on the number of zones you must pass through as you travel to your destination and the whole system is regulated by the use of a uniquely Dutch invention, the National Strip Card (*Nationale Strippen Kaart*). A strip card consists of a series of blank strips, a number of which must be validated when you enter a tram or bus according to the length of your journey – one strip more than the number of zones you're travelling through. For example, a two-zone journey requires you to validate three strips. To validate the strips, you must fold over the required number of blank strips for your journey and then insert the card face up in the slot until you hear a bell, indicating that the last strip has been stamped with the current time and date.

Validated strips are valid for between one hour and three and a half hours, depending on how many of strips you've validated. Travelling on up to four strips (three zones), you have an hour to complete your journey; with 17 validated strips (a 16-zone trip), your ticket is valid for the full three and a half hours. If you don't want to fumble with the card, or you aren't sure how many zones your journey covers, you can have the bus driver or tram conductor validate your strip card for you when you board, simply by telling him what your destination is. If you have your card validated vertically instead of horizontally (which must be done by the conductor), it counts as a day pass. An eight-strip ticket allows you unlimited travel within the city limits, while two eight-strip tickets are valid for all journeys on public transport (excluding trains) anywhere in Holland.

You can buy cards with two, three, eight, 15 and 45 strips. Only the first three can be bought on buses and trams (and at metro stations) and cost around €1.50, €2 and €5 respectively. These can also be purchased at bookshops, tobacconists, post offices or at transport company ticket offices, which are the only places you can buy 15 and 45-strip cards. A 15-strip card costs the same as an eight-strip card, which is reason enough for remembering to buy one before you board a bus, and a 45-strip card costs around €16. There's also a special 15-strip card for those entitled to half fare, e.g. children and pensioners, costing around €5.

There's a range of reduced fares and monthly and annual passes for frequent travellers in Holland. Weekly, monthly and annual passes are all referred to as 'subscriptions' (*abonnementen*), and prices are based on the 'star value' (*starwaarde*) of the pass you purchase. The star value of the pass determines the number of zones through which you can travel, measured in relation to your 'home' zone. For example, a two-star pass permits unlimited travel within your home zone plus all adjoining zones. You must copy the number of your identity card (*stamkaart*) card onto each ticket and carry the ID whenever you use your pass; you can be fined if there's no number on the pass or it doesn't match the number on your ID card. If you also travel by train regularly, you might benefit from a combined rail and local transport passes.

Luxembourg: Most towns in Luxembourg have a bus service, and in most cases fares are reasonable. Luxembourg city has its own network of bus routes, most of which converge at the central bus terminal. Most buses run at least twice an hour, even on Sundays. You can purchase tickets from the driver when you board or buy a ten-ticket *carnet* at a reduced price at railway stations. A monthly pass is also available and can be used for the city's park and ride system, consisting of a series of car parks on the outskirts with a frequent bus service to the city centre operating between 7am and 7pm. For information on public transport outside Luxembourg city, contact your town hall or communal authority.

TAXIS

To hire a taxi, you need to go to the nearest official taxi rank or telephone a taxi company. Taxi ranks can be found at all airports and railway stations, as well as near major junctions, large hotels and principal tourist attractions. It's generally a waste of time to try to hail a taxi in the street, as most taxis are either already carrying a fare or on their way to pick one up in response to a call. In some cities (notably Brussels and Amsterdam) you may be able to hail a pirate (i.e. unregistered) taxi on the street, but these aren't recommended and can 'take you for a ride'. It's safer to use a registered taxi in which the fare is metered. Make sure the meter is set at zero when you enter the taxi; the driver will set any surcharges (usually for luggage or extra passengers) before he starts. Some taxis now take credit cards – look for credit card logos in the rear window.

In many cities and towns in Holland there's a special taxi service called a train taxi (*treintaxi*) operating to and from the local railway station. Train taxis charge a flat fee from or to anywhere within the city or town limits, provided you have a train ticket valid for that day. You can purchase a train taxi ticket at the station ticket office when you arrive (and you can buy a return ticket for the taxi service if you have a return train ticket). If you want a train taxi to take you to the station, you can buy a ticket from the driver on presentation of your train ticket. If you haven't bought a train ticket yet, the driver will charge you the normal train taxi fare plus a surcharge, in exchange for which you're given a coupon (*bon*) redeemable against the purchase of a train ticket on that day only. Not surprisingly, train taxis are popular, and in many areas it's necessary to book a day or two in advance.

AIRLINE SERVICES

The Benelux region is well served by airline services, both domestic and international. Until recently, each country had a 'national' airline – SABENA in Belgium, KLM in Holland and Luxair in Luxembourg – although these had largely been privatised. All three airlines began experiencing financial and operational difficulties in the late '90s due to increasing competition, both from other European airlines and from American and Asian long-haul carriers, and had to form alliances with other 'national' carriers in order to survive.

SABENA, formerly part of the SwissAir group of companies known as Qualiflyer airlines, went into liquidation in November 2001 but is likely to be replaced by a smaller, regional carrier backed by the Belgian government, which was a minor shareholder in SABENA. Unlike the large international airline 'alliances', the Qualiflyer group (comprising TAP Air Portugal, Turkish Airlines and several regional carriers, including Air Liberté and Air Littoral in France, as well as SwissAir itself) was the result of a cross-European merger, with SwissAir as the parent company. Problems in the process of assimilating the various airlines with their distinct corporate and national identities, however, have left the planned mega-group of airlines 'up in the air'.

KLM advertises itself as the 'world's first scheduled airline', having been established in 1919 and beginning a scheduled passenger service (to London) on 17th May, 1920. KLM has a joint venture agreement with Northwest Airlines and offers a large number of co-listed flights to and from the USA. KLM also operates several 'commuter services', such as KLM Cityhopper (which links smaller cities across Europe with the KLM hub at Schiphol) and KLM UK.

Not surprisingly, Luxair is the smallest of the three Benelux national carriers. With Luxembourg city as its hub, Luxair offers both passenger and cargo services, primarily within western Europe. Scheduled passenger services are targeted mainly at business travellers, while Luxair's subsidiary, Luxairtours, caters for holiday travellers and operates charter flights to destinations around the Mediterranean and in North Africa, the Canary Islands and Madeira. The Duchy of Luxembourg retains a 23 per cent share in the airline, and the German airline Lufthansa has a small (around 15 per cent) interest. The rest of the company is owned by various (mostly Luxembourg based) banks and insurance companies.

KLM and Luxair offer business and economy class travel within Europe, plus first class seating on intercontinental flights. KLM has an online booking service (🖳 www.KLM.nl), where you can also subscribe to its frequent flyer programme, consult flight schedules and find information about the airline. Tickets can also be purchased at travel agencies (or via the KLM website) and at ticket counters at airports. Luxair's website (🖳 www.luxair.lu) is less eye-catching but also allows you to book tickets and check flight schedules and fares.

The Benelux region is served by most European and international airlines, several of whom operate joint promotions with KLM. An increasing number of low-cost, no-frills airlines, e.g. Easyjet, Go and Ryanair, are offering flights to and from Benelux, generally from 'secondary' airports.

Airports

The main airports in Benelux include the Brussels National Airport at Zaventem and Amsterdam's Schiphol, which is rapidly becoming a major hub for travel within Europe as well as for international flights. Regional airports in Belgium include Antwerp (Deurne), Charleroi, Liege, and Ostend (Middelkerke). Some charter flights also operate out of nearby Lille (in France). In Holland, there are regional airports at Enschede, Groningen, Eindhoven, and Maastricht, mostly serving as 'feeders' to Schiphol airport. Luxembourg city's airport is the only airport within the Duchy that handles commercial flights, although there are a handful of smaller airports for private planes. Residents of Luxembourg often make use of the larger airports at Brussels, Paris (Charles de Gaulle/Roissy), Frankfurt or Düsseldorf, all of which are within easy reach by car, train and bus.

All commercial airports in the region have long and short-term car parks, including separate spaces for the disabled. Driving to the major airports, however, can be a nightmare, particularly in rush hours, at weekends and during popular holiday travel periods, so it's wise to use public transport, by which both Brussels and Amsterdam airports are particularly well served.

Brussels National Airport (Zaventem)

Brussels Airport in Zaventem, about 15km (9mi) north-east of the city, handled a record 21.6 million passengers in the year 2000. A new terminal building (Concourse A) is scheduled for completion in the spring of 2002, which will more than double the number of boarding gates as well as providing much needed shopping facilities. Existing facilities at Brussels airport include snack bars, restaurants, bistros, news stands, and rental car agencies. Directly beneath the main arrivals area is a large bus terminal, where you can catch city and regional buses as well as shuttle transport to nearby hotels. Some hotels offer a park and fly service, whereby secure short or medium-term parking is 'included' in the cost of a room. The airport is well-served by public transport and has good road access. Unfortunately, the airport terminal is frequented by pickpockets, and you should watch your possessions carefully at all times while waiting for your plane.

Like many European airports, Brussels hosts an extensive website (🖳 www. brusselsairport.be) where you can check the arrival and departure times of specific flights, check the traffic situation at the airport and even which car parks still have spaces. The website provides links to most of the major airlines operating into and out of Brussels, as well as to online travel agencies and Airstop, a Belgian discount travel agency that sells seats on charter flights up to two weeks before departure (🖥 www. airstop.be).

By Train: From the centre of Brussels there's a regular rail shuttle, called the Airport City Express, that runs every 15 minutes from 6am to midnight, seven days a week. The train stops at each of the main railway stations (South, Central and North) and a one-way ticket costs around €2.50 for second class or €3.50 for first class. The airport railway station also serves towns in the west and south of Belgium, including De Panne, Gent, Mons and Quévy/Quiévrain on the French border.

By Bus: There's an STIB/MIVB 'airport line' running from rue Ducale/ Hertogstraat in the city centre to the airport. There are only seven stops along the route, including Schuman (serving the EU facilities) and NATO, and buses offer comfortable seating as well as ample luggage space. There are usually three or four buses per hour and the service runs from 5am to midnight. De Lijn buses connect the airport bus terminal with the railway stations in nearby Zaventem and Vilvoorde.

By Road: From the Brussels ring road, you follow the green road signs for 'Zaventem' or 'Airport'. Traffic is usually heavy at the approaches to the airport, and both long and short-term car parks are often full, especially at peak times. There are a number of private car parks near the airport, including Car Hotel, Lock Park and VIP Park, all of which offer reasonable security, although it's usually necessary to book a space and you may have to pay extra for 'security'. For short-term parking you should expect to pay a minimum of €2; long-term parking are around €20 to €25 per day or €80 per week.

Other Access: Taxi fares from the centre of Brussels are around €25, but vary considerably according to traffic density and other factors. If you want to arrive in style (and money is no object) there's a helicopter taxi service from Antwerp, Gent and Kortrijk. On the airport website (🖥 www.brusselsairport.com) you can register with Airportstop, a car pool service for those travelling to and from the airport.

Amsterdam Schiphol

Amsterdam's Schiphol airport is rapidly becoming a major departure point for long-haul flights, particularly to the Far East. It's known throughout Europe as the 'see buy fly' airport on account of the array of duty-free (for those leaving the EU) and other shops in its large central terminal building. The motto is prominently displayed on black and yellow shopping bags, which identify passengers that have arrived from or travelled through Amsterdam. If you're in a hurry, you can order items via the airport website (🖥 www.schiphol.nl) and pick them up as you're dashing for your plane. Even if you aren't using the airport, there's a large shopping mall open to the public on the airport site. In addition to shopping, there's a business centre, a casino (yes, really), showers, a sauna and massage service, and just about every other service a tired traveller might need. (In fact, if you aren't careful, you could spend all your holiday money before you even take off!) The airport's single terminal design has the added advantage of making connections easier – at least for passengers; Schiphol has an unfortunate reputation for not always managing to transfer your luggage to your connecting flight.

Transport links to the airport, around 8km (5mi) south of Amsterdam, are extensive and, in typical Dutch fashion, extremely well integrated with the local and national networks of buses, trains and other forms of transport. There are even facilities at the airport for leaving bicycles, as well as for taking them on flights.

By Train: Schiphol boasts a railway station directly below the airport terminal, with a frequent service to and from the main railway station in Amsterdam. According to the NV NS, you can reach almost any station in the country from Schiphol without changing trains more than once.

By Bus: From Amsterdam, there are several bus routes to the airport, including nos. 192, 197 and 199. The Schiphol website (⌨ www.schiphol.nl) lists bus routes to and from Amstelveen, Hoofddorp and other nearby cities or you can call the public transport information line (☎ 0900-9292 costing €0.34 per minute) to find the best public transport route to the airport from anywhere in Holland.

By Road: The Dutch authorities are doing their best to discourage people from taking their cars to the airport, but if you're determined to drive, the route is well marked and easy to follow, although traffic around the airport can be heavy. At peak times, the road in front of the terminal is clogged with cars picking up and dropping off passengers. The Schiphol website shows you the current state of the roads surrounding the airport and of its short and long-term car parks, which cost around €3.50 per hour and €40 for up to 72 hours respectively. (For those with money to spare, there's executive valet parking, where your car is washed and waxed while you're away.)

Other Access: The Schiphol Travel Taxi is a service operating to and from the airport from anywhere in Holland. The charge varies according to the postal code of the address you're travelling from, and you must book at least 48 hours in advance. Bookings can be made either by phone (☎ 0900-7244 7465 or 0900-SCHIPHOL) or via the airport website (⌨ www.schiphol.nl). The evening before your departure, you'll receive a phone call telling you what time you'll be picked up the next day, based on the flight check-in time you provide. The taxi may pick up one or more other passengers en route, in which case the company guarantees that your travel time is no more than 50 per cent longer than if you were taken directly to the airport from your pick-up point. You can also book a Travel Taxi to meet your return flight.

Luxembourg International Airport

Compared with Brussels or Amsterdam, Luxembourg International Airport is tiny, with only 17 check-in counters and eight boarding gates. In fact the airport's relative tranquillity is its chief attraction – and Frankfurt and Düsseldorf are just over the border. Located 6km (4mi) outside the city, the airport is open from 6am to 11pm. Facilities include two shops, two restaurants and two news stands. There's a direct bus service (operated by Luxair) from the airport to the centre of Luxembourg city, and long-term parking at the airport costs only around €4 per day.

While Luxair, the national airline, operates the majority of flights, Luxembourg Airport is also served by KLM, SwissAir, British Airways and a number of smaller 'commuter' airlines serving cities throughout western Europe and North Africa. Airport information, including arrival and departure times for the day's flights, is available on the Luxair website (⌨ www.luxair.lu) or by calling the airport terminal (☎ 4798-5050).

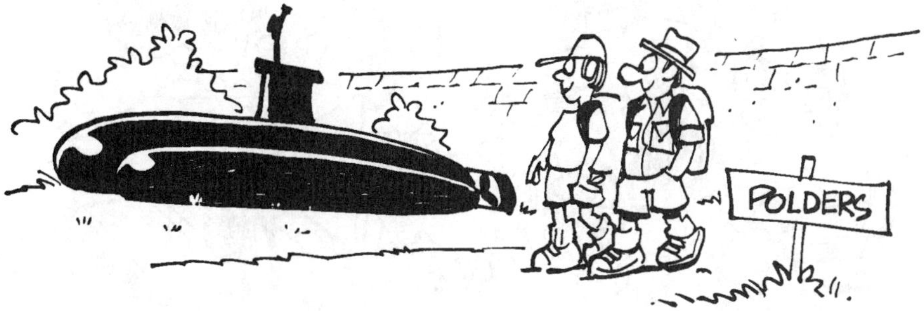
POLDERS

11.

MOTORING

Belgium, Holland and Luxembourg have a combined road network totalling around 272,000km (163,000mi) and including all kinds of roads from motorways to single-track dirt roads. Sharing these roads with HGVs, trucks, vans, motorcycles and visiting foreigners are over 10 million Benelux registered cars, so it's probably no wonder that traffic in most of the area is heavy and congested, particularly during rush hours and holiday periods.

Traffic laws and safety requirements are strictly enforced in Benelux; in addition to stringent (and often complicated) registration and regular inspection requirements, there are random check points, controls and road blocks where police can ask for your paperwork or search or inspect your vehicle. This is partly a reaction to previously lax licensing and safety regulations, which were until recently almost non-existent, especially in Belgium. Another factor is the standard of driving in Benelux, where drivers have had a reputation for being aggressive and reckless, particularly in their adherence to the 'priority from the right' (*priorité à droite/voorrang van rechts*) rule that causes drivers (and even bicycle riders) to dart out from side streets without so much as a sideways glance. In parts of their neighbouring countries (France, in particular) it's said that on seeing a Belgian or Dutch registered car approaching, you should simply pull off the road and let it pass. (Coming from the French, this may be intended as a compliment.) For many years, the three Benelux countries seemed determined to live up to their fearsome reputation by heading the league tables for accidents and deaths on both a per capita and a per kilometre basis. The consequence is that licensing and safety inspection requirements in the Benelux countries are now among the most stringent in Europe.

Perhaps as a result of this clamp-down, and thanks to stricter enforcement of drink driving laws, the number of accidents causing injury has been reduced by 40 to 50 per cent over the last couple of decades, but the Benelux region is still top of the table in the accidents per km category. This may be due in part to the driving hazards peculiar to the area. Bicycles are a common mode of transport in Holland, where riders are generally no less reckless than car drivers. The numerous canals and waterways in many Dutch and Belgian cities and towns offer opportunities for unwary drivers to end up 'in the drink' (irrespective of whether they have been drinking!). The cool, damp weather prevalent in the region can leave roads treacherously slippery and in winter 'black ice' is a common hazard, particularly in areas where cobblestone paving has been used (usually to encourage drivers to slow down – or *let op*, as they say in Dutch). In Luxembourg, you also need to look out for frog crossings (no joking!), which are marked by a triangular sign featuring a frog in the centre, and there are numerous accidents each year involving drivers and wild animals.

VEHICLE IMPORT

Importing a car, motorcycle or other vehicle into Belgium, Holland or Luxembourg can be an education in bureaucracy and red tape. Even if you're moving from another EU country, you'll need to go through a formal import process in order to obtain the documents necessary to register your vehicle in Benelux. Importing a vehicle from outside the EU may require payment of customs duties, but often these are waived if the vehicle is imported with your household goods (and within three months of your arrival). If you're using a removal company for your move, they should be able to handle most of the import formalities for you. If not, you may want to consider engaging a customs broker or agent to handle clearance of your car or other vehicles, particularly if you're moving to Belgium, where the process can be especially complicated.

UK residents making only a short stay in Benelux may find it far more convenient to sell or store their cars until their return. Apart from the fact that new car prices are significantly lower than in the UK (particularly in Belgium), most drivers find it easier to adjust to driving on the 'wrong' side of the road in a left-hand drive vehicle. Americans should think long and hard before importing US-built vehicles. Few American car manufacturers export to Europe, and even then only selected models, so replacement parts can be difficult or impossible to find in Benelux. Parts ordered from the USA can take two to three weeks to arrive, and you'll be charged import duty and VAT on both the parts and the shipping costs.

In general, motor vehicles can be imported without payment of duty or VAT if you're establishing residence in one of the Benelux countries and:

- you've resided outside the country for at least 12 months;
- you've owned and driven the vehicle for at least six months prior to import;
- VAT or sales tax on the vehicle have been paid in another country;
- you keep the vehicle at least 12 months after importing it.

If you decide to sell your car or motorcycle within the first year after importing it, you must pay import duty (if you arrived from outside the EU) and VAT and, in some cases, penalties.

Customs officials normally require the following documents when your vehicle arrives:

- invoice for the vehicle showing when and where it was purchased;
- title (registration) certificate in your name;
- receipt for VAT or sales tax paid on the vehicle;
- proof of residence outside the country for at least 12 months prior to your arrival in Benelux;
- proof of residence in the country, e.g. residence permit, certificate or ID card;
- shipping documents for your household goods and possessions.

The relevant customs authority determines whether or not you and your vehicle meet the criteria for being exempted from payment of duties or taxes. If any taxes or duties are due, you must usually pay them in cash. Import duty on motor vehicles amounts to around 10 per cent of the value of the vehicle at the date of import. VAT on motor vehicles varies between 15 per cent in Luxembourg and 20.5 per cent in Belgium, and the percentage is applied to the customs' estimate of the value of the vehicle, which may be different from the amount shown on the purchase receipt.

Once you've received either your exemption certificates or your receipts for duty and/or VAT paid, you must have your car or motorcycle inspected. All imported vehicles (including those from other EU countries) must meet local safety and equipment standards, and you're likely to have to make some kind of modification to your vehicle before being given a certificate of conformity (*certificat de conformité*). Once you've insured the vehicle (see page 195), you can finally register it (see below).

If you're staying in Benelux for less than a year or you're importing a vehicle that you'll be re-exporting within a year, you can apply for temporary import, which includes exemption from duties and VAT on import. In this case, you're issued with special registration plates that include the date by which you must re-export the car.

Each of the Benelux countries has certain specific requirements regarding vehicle import, as follows:

Belgium: In Belgium, you must provide a covering letter formally requesting exemption from import duties and VAT along with the documents listed above. Make sure you identify the vehicle in the letter, specifying the make, model, chassis number and registration number. The Belgian authorities also require evidence that you've insured your vehicle in your previous country of residence for at least six months prior to importing it. Before you import any vehicle into Belgium, check how much 'entry into service' tax (*taxe de mise en circulation/belasting op inverkeerstelling*) you'll be liable for (see page 190). If your car is in one of the highest categories, you could have to pay up to €5,000 just to put it on the road.

The Belgian requirements for a certificate of conformity are probably the strictest in Benelux. Among other requirements, your car must have white front indicator and side lights, a rear fog light and a speedometer calibrated in kilometres. Most imported vehicles will need new tyres and you're required to carry an approved fire extinguisher, first aid kit and red warning triangle at all times. The fire extinguisher must be mounted in a particular manner within easy reach of the driver. It's best to have any necessary modifications made after your arrival in Belgium and it's usually wise to consult the local main dealer for your vehicle in Belgium for advice on what modifications need to be made and where to have them done. After modification, your car must be inspected at a certified inspection centre, which will issue the certificate of conformity.

Holland: As with the importation of household goods (see **Chapter 4**) you must apply for an import permit for your car or other motor vehicles *before* your shipment arrives. Dutch customs authorities require most of the standard documents listed above, but make sure you don't pack them in your vehicle if it's being shipped! In addition to those, the Dutch require a car to have at least 6,000km (3,728mi) on the odometer before entering Holland for it to be exempted from 'new car' duties and VAT.

The initial vehicle inspection must be carried out by the RDW Centre for Vehicle Technology and Information (formerly the *Rijksdienst voor het Wegverkeer*, now an independent administrative body), and if you want to drive your vehicle to the centre you must request a one-day permit to drive on Dutch roads. Otherwise you're expected to have the vehicle towed or delivered on a flat-bed truck! Assuming your vehicle passes the inspection, you receive various certificates and documents, including a form for 'entry into service' or BPM tax (see page 190) and a one-time 'entry into service' tax (see page 190). After completing the BPM form and having it validated by the inspection centre, you must take it to the customs office to pay the tax, after which the customs office will notify the registration authority that it can process your vehicle registration – the registration authority just happening to be the RDW! (Bureaucracy knows no bounds in Benelux.)

Luxembourg: Compared to Belgium and Holland, customs clearance for a motor vehicle in Luxembourg is a breeze, although you should be sure to start the process as soon as possible after your arrival and in any case within three months. The customs authorities issue two documents: an IM4 customs declaration (if you're importing the vehicle from outside the EU) and a 705 form (*attribution de vignette*), both of which are necessary to register the vehicle (see below).

VEHICLE REGISTRATION

If you import a vehicle or buy a used car locally, you must register it and have registration plates made and fitted. If you purchase a new vehicle from a dealer, he will usually take care of the necessary paperwork – which may be one of the more compelling reasons to buy a new car after you arrive!

Belgium: To register your car in Belgium, you need to have the vehicle inspection certificate, proof of insurance and fiscal stamps to the value of €60. Fiscal stamps can be purchased at post offices and certain shops and must be stuck to your registration document by the relevant official (who obviously isn't trusted to handle actual money). Vehicle registration is handled by the DIV (*Direction de l'Immatriculation des Véhicules/Direktie voor de Immatriculatie der Voertuigen*), a section of the Ministry of Communications. The DIV accepts registration requests by post or you can go in person to the DIV office at Résidence Palace, Rue de la Loi 155, 1040 Brussels between 9am and 3pm. Written requests take around four days to process. If you decide to go in person, arrive early and expect to spend one to three hours in various queues.

The DIV issues a registration certificate, usually referred to as a 'grey card' (*carte grise/grijze kaart*) although it's actually a pink piece of paper, and one number (licence) plate, which is to be fitted to the rear of your vehicle. You must then have a front plate made at a motor spares shop or a Mister Minit stand. There are two sorts of number plates: those with adhesive numbers, which should be avoided, and embossed metal plates, which last much longer and cost only a little more. In Belgium, car registration plates belong to the owner of the car; if you sell a vehicle, you keep the plates for use on your next car. Road taxes (see page 190) are billed to the registered number plate holder, so you should return the official (i.e. rear) plate when you leave Belgium or no longer own a car.

Holland: Once you've paid your 'entry into service' or BPM tax (see page 190), the BPM office sends a form to the RDW (*Rijksdienst voor het Wegverkeer*), which then sends you your registration paperwork. This is in three parts (called *Deel I, Deel II* and *Deel III*). *Deel I* contains the title and description of the vehicle, while *Deel II* lists the owner's details. You must carry both documents with you at all times when driving. *Deel III* is the transfer document you must use when selling your car and is best kept in a safe place separate from the car and other registration papers until needed. The RDW website (🖥 www.rdw.nl) has an extensive section in English which includes explanations and examples of the registration documents. Take the registration forms, along with the vehicle's original, i.e. foreign, registration document and any customs clearance certificates (if you've imported the vehicle) to a recognised garage, which will relieve you of around €450 to make and mount the vehicle's number plates. (There's an additional charge of around €105 if you're registering the vehicle in a different name from that which appears on the original registration document – cars may be cheap in Holland, but registration certainly isn't.)

Luxembourg: The registration process in Luxembourg is unusual in that you first obtain your number plates and then have the vehicle inspected. It's the inspection station that issues your vehicle registration card (assuming the car passes the inspection). After your vehicle has cleared customs, contact the Ministry of Transportation (*Minstère des Transports, Numéros d'Immatriculation*) 11 route Luxembourg, 5230 Sandweiler (☎ 478-4482) to ask for a registration number. If you want a special number or 'vanity plate', it will cost you €50 and you must call a different number at the Ministry to make your request (☎ 478-4483). Once you have a registration number, take your car to Ateliers Jean Grün, 35 rue des Scillas, 2529 Howald (☎ 49-6162) to have number plates made and mounted. The fee for this is around €20.

Once you've obtained your number plates, go to the Bureau de l'Enregistrement, 1–3 avenue Guillaume, 1010 Luxembourg city (☎ 44-905 403) to purchase a tax stamp, costing around €12, and obtain a car registration request form (*demande en obtention d'une carte d'immatriculation*). Take all the paperwork you've collected, along with proof of insurance, to a test centre (see below) to have your vehicle inspected. After the inspection, the test centre issues your registration card (*carte grise*).

INSPECTIONS & EMISSIONS TESTS

In the Benelux countries, as in most other European countries, vehicles must be inspected whenever they're sold within the country as well as at periodic intervals. Motorcycles and mopeds don't usually need to be tested, but all cars and trucks do. A new car purchased in the country comes with an initial inspection certificate, valid for the first three or four years, depending on the country (see below), after which period you must have the car inspected annually. You can be heavily fined if you're found without a current inspection certificate, especially if it comes to light after an accident or during a police road check.

Annual inspections are thorough and cover essentially the same points in all three countries. All mechanical parts must be in working order, as well as front and rear lights, fog lights (if fitted) and indicators. Inspectors will check your tyres to make sure there's adequate tread and will inspect your brakes, exhaust system and check for rust or body damage. If you have any concerns about your car passing the test, you should have repairs made before going to the test centre. Procedures vary between the three countries, but if your vehicle fails the test, you forfeit the test fee and must have the car re-inspected after repairs have been made. It's possible to have your local garage or car dealer carry out a pre-inspection if you have any doubts that your car will pass the official test, and most motoring associations and automobile clubs provide some form of pre-inspection service (see page 205). The police in all three countries are permitted to make random safety checks, even on vehicles with a current safety certificate.

Belgium: The inspection certificate issued on the purchase of a new car is valid for four years in Belgium. Thereafter, the car must pass an annual technical inspection (*contrôle technique/technische controle*), and you must have a current certificate with you whenever you drive. Normally, you should be notified by letter a couple of months before your inspection certificate expires, but it's your responsibility to have the inspection carried out even if you don't receive a reminder. The expiry date is shown on the certificate.

The *contrôle technique* can be made by any certified inspection centre. If your car passes the test, the inspector issues a new certificate; if it fails, you're given either a Code 1 or a Code 2 temporary certificate. A Code 2 means that you have 14 days in which to have your car repaired and re-inspected. A Code 1 requires you to have it repaired immediately. (You're allowed only to drive the car directly home or to a garage.) In Belgium, you must notify your insurance company within 48 hours of failing an inspection; if you have an accident while driving on a Code 1 or 2 certificate, you may have to reimburse your insurance company for any amount it has to pay out, unless you can prove that the accident had nothing to do with the condition of the car.

Holland: Annual inspections are required in Holland from the third anniversary of a new car's first inspection. The annual inspection (*algemen periodieke keuring* or APK) can be carried out by any garage displaying the red and white striped RDW authorisation plaque, and you may have the inspection at any time during the two months prior to the date the certificate expires without affecting the expiry date. Each garage sets its own fee for the APK, but you may be able to find a garage that offers a maintenance package including the annual inspection. After the inspection, you receive an inspection report, stating the condition of the vehicle and whether or not it has passed. If it has failed, the report lists the things that need to be corrected and gives a deadline for having the necessary repairs made and a re-inspection performed.

If your car fails and you want to contest the judgement, you may take it the same day to a regional office of the RDW for a re-inspection. There's a charge of €45 for this service, which is refunded if the re-inspection finds that your vehicle should have passed. The RDW maintains strict control over the garages offering inspection services and carries out frequent random testing of its inspection sites. If you have a complaint about how the inspection was carried out, you should contact the RDW.

Luxembourg: All passenger vehicles in Luxembourg must be inspected when they're 42 months old and annually after that. Inspections are conducted by the *Stations de Contrôle technique pour Véhicules automoteurs* at Sandweiler and Esch/Alzette. You should receive an appointment card by post a few weeks before your inspection certificate is due to expire. You don't need an appointment to take your car to an inspection centre, but you may not have to wait so long with one. It's best to arrive first thing in the morning, whether you have an appointment or not. With an appointment, you can use designated lanes, which generally have shorter queues. If your car passes the test, you receive a new inspection certificate; if it doesn't, you receive a temporary certificate detailing the car's failings and giving you a deadline for having repairs carried out and the car re-inspected.

ROAD TAX

In addition to annual road tax (sometimes called excise tax) in all three countries, you must pay a one-off 'entry into service' tax when you register a vehicle in Belgium and Holland.

Belgium: 'Entry into service' tax (*taxe de mise en circulation/belasting op inverkeerstelling*) is due on all vehicles the first time they're put into use in Belgium, whether new, used or imported, and is based on the 'fiscal horsepower' of the vehicle, adjusted for age if a used car is being registered for the first time in Belgium. Fiscal horsepower is the government's determination of your engine's power and may or may not be related to the manufacturer's specifications. The tax is calculated in such a way as to discourage ownership of powerful cars, as the amount payable increases by 50 or 100 per cent between each engine power category. The highest category incurs a €5,000 tax, the second highest half as much, which is why so many Belgians choose cars with smaller engines!

About two months after registering your vehicle in Belgium, you receive a bill for the first year's road tax. The annual road tax (*taxe de circulation/verkeersbelasting*) is also based on the officially rated horsepower of your car but is a little easier on the pocket. The average car costs around €175 to keep 'street legal'. You must carry proof of payment for annual road tax in your vehicle at all times, as you can be stopped and asked to show it. (The same is true for the annual tax on your car radio.)

Holland: The entry into service tax in Holland is referred to as the BPM, although this acronym is sometimes also used to refer to annual road tax, and is even more crippling than its Belgian equivalent. When you first register a vehicle in Holland, you must pay BPM based on the car's 'list price'. The tax rate is a massive 45.2 per cent of the price, reduced by €1,540 for a petrol-powered vehicle or €960 for a diesel-powered car. To register a motorcycle, you must pay 20.7 per cent of its list price if it's over €2,100, or 10.2 per cent if the list price is less than €2,100.

Annual road tax in Holland is based on your car's 'fiscal rating', weight and fuel type and is paid in quarterly instalments. It's normally most convenient to pay by direct debit from your bank account.

Luxembourg: Luxembourg earns its reputation as a tax haven by minimising its dependence on indirect taxes such as the entry into service levies in neighbouring countries. There is, however, an annual road tax, and you must display a current sticker in your windscreen to prove you've paid it. When you sell your car or leave Luxembourg, you can remove the sticker and return it to the address on the back for a partial refund.

BUYING A CAR

Once you've discovered what's involved in importing and registering a foreign car, you may decide to sell or leave your car at home and buy another one in Benelux. There's a wide range of cars for sale in Belgium, Holland and Luxembourg; because the region has no automobile manufacturer of its own, all European makes and models are available, as well as many Japanese and even a few American cars.

New Cars

One of the advantages of buying a new car in Benelux is that most or all of the registration and certification procedures are taken care of by the dealer. New car prices throughout Benelux are considerably lower than in the UK and in many cases lower than in neighbouring countries. Making comparisons between new car prices in different countries can be difficult, owing to varying equipment standards, rates of VAT and import regulations. Within the EU, VAT on a new car is calculated according to the residence status of the buyer, and particularly in Belgium, you must make sure that a new car manufactured abroad can be registered without major modification.

New car prices are negotiable to a certain extent, but it may be better to ask a dealer to include one or more additional options for the list price. Americans should be aware that automatic transmission is still considered a rather 'exotic' (and therefore expensive) option, which can delay delivery of your new car by several weeks. Air conditioning is becoming increasingly common, either as a 'standard' feature or part of a package of options, which are often widely advertised. When discussing prices with a dealer, make sure you understand exactly what is included. VAT, delivery and 'preparation' are often added to the basic quotation. Don't forget to ask how much 'entry into service' tax you'll be liable for (see page 190), particularly if you're after a high-powered (Belgium) or expensive (Holland) vehicle.

Used Cars

All the usual caveats apply to buying used cars in Benelux, although the annual inspection system in all three countries means that vehicles must be kept in reasonable condition and you're unlikely to end up with a complete wreck. Used car dealers, other than franchised dealers, have the same dreadful (and well-deserved) reputation as in other countries, and caution must be taken when buying from them. On the other hand, a local garage or reliable mechanic often knows where to go for good used vehicles or can direct you to a long-time customer interested in selling a car the mechanic 'knows'. It's possible to find good value used cars, whether buying privately or from a dealer, although you should always check carefully:

- that the vehicle has a current safety inspection certificate issued within three to six months of the transfer of title (depending on the country).
- that the vehicle hasn't been involved in a major accident and suffered structural damage. A declaration that the vehicle is accident free should be obtained in writing.
- that the chassis number is the same as that indicated on the registration document, which should be in the name of the seller if you're buying privately.
- that the service coupons have been completed and stamped, and that service has been carried out by an authorised dealer.
- that the price roughly corresponds to that shown in one of the major car price guides or consumer publications (see below).
- that import tax and duty have been paid and that the vehicle has a valid certificate of conformity with local requirements (if applicable – i.e. in Belgium).

You must also obtain a written purchase agreement or bill of sale, even if you're buying the vehicle privately. The agreement should state the odometer (km) reading at the time of sale and identify the vehicle by its chassis number, make and model. Make sure you check that this information is accurate. Car dealers often give a limited warranty on used cars, depending on the age of the car and the model.

VAT is payable only when buying from a dealer, who must declare his mark up to the VAT inspectors. There's no VAT to pay when you purchase a used car privately in Benelux.

In each country, lists of standard new and used car prices are listed in car magazines. In Belgium, the two main sources are *Moniteur de l'Automobile* (in French) and *Auto Gids* (in Dutch). Similar magazines are available from news stands in Holland and Luxembourg. The main consumer magazines also publish regular information on both new and used car prices, as well as reviews of specific models.

SELLING A CAR

You can advertise a car for sale in local newspapers, in club and association newsletters, and on free bulletin boards in shops and offices. In Belgium, you can take a used car to the Saturday Car Market in Brussels or you can simply mention to your mechanic that you're interested in selling and see if he can send potential buyers your way. Depending on the make, model and condition of the car, you may want to consider listing it on one of the growing number of Internet advertising sites. It's necessary to have the car inspected as part of the transfer process, and in most areas the inspection certificate must be no more than three months old.

The main points to note when selling a car are:

● Prepare a bill of sale and make a copy (two copies if you want to keep one). This document should include the car's odometer (km) reading, the chassis number, the selling price and the fact that you're selling the car in its present condition (as seen) without a guarantee. Both you and the buyer should sign this agreement and you should give two copies to the buyer.

● In Belgium, the car's registration plates are your property and should be removed from the vehicle when you sell it. In Holland and Luxembourg, the plates normally stay with the car, although in Luxembourg you may keep your number plates, in which case the buyer must request new plates when he registers the car in his name.

● If you sell the car to someone you know and trust, it may be easier to let him register as the new owner of the car. However, if you have any doubts at all about the reliability of the buyer, you should transfer the registration yourself.

● Inform your insurance company as soon as the registration has been changed. You may be entitled to a partial refund of your last insurance premium.

● Insist on payment in cash – this is standard practice throughout Benelux and it's far safer than accepting a cheque.

DRIVING LICENCE

The minimum age for driving in Belgium, Holland and Luxembourg is 18 for a car or motorcycle over 50cc and 16 for a motorcycle (moped) below 50cc. Foreigners may continue to drive on a foreign licence for up to 90 days, provided they aren't resident in Benelux. If you're establishing residence, the situation depends on whether you hold an EU or a non-EU driving licence, although in both cases you may continue to use your home country licence for up to six months or a year after your arrival in Benelux (depending on the country).

The Second EU Driving Licence Directive provides, among other things, for the mutual recognition of driving licences issued by EU member states. While the advent of a standardised EU licence format was supposed to have heralded the end of national driving permits, member states are permitted to apply their own regulations regarding the validity period of driving licences, medical checks, taxes, and penalties or restrictions on driving, and in practice it's usually best to exchange your licence for a local one. Generally, you're expected to do so once you've established residence in the country. This is a simple process and is usually free or costs a nominal sum (plus the cost of any photos you must provide). You won't have to take another driving test or exam.

For holders of non-EU driving licences, the situation varies from country to country. Depending on where your driving licence was issued, you may be able simply to exchange your foreign licence for a local one, or you may be required to take a written or practical test – sometimes both. If there's no reciprocity between the country (or state, for Americans) that issued your licence and your adopted country, it may be necessary to complete the full road training course and pass the written and practical tests. You must also prove that you were resident in the country where your licence was issued at the time you obtained it. This is to prevent locals making holiday trips to the USA or other countries with less stringent (and less expensive) driver training and testing programmes, then returning home to exchange their foreign licence for a local one.

The requirements for obtaining a first driving licence in Benelux include the completion of an approved driving school (*auto école/autorijschol*) course and passing of a written theory examination. After a 'waiting' period of at least three months, during which you're expected to practise driving, you must take a practical road test (usually administered through a driving school). Some form of eye test or medical examination is usually required, along with two or three photos and the usual identification documents (passport, residence card or ID card). All three countries require you to pass the written or theory test before you can even start practising for the road test.

Belgium: Drivers holding licences issued by another EU member state may drive for one year in Belgium. At that point, you can simply exchange your licence at your town hall for a Belgian *permis de conduire/rijbewijs*. No tests are required and there should be little or no charge (some communes have a small service fee for all document preparation), although you must supply two passport-size photos.

Those with non-EU licences are expected to apply for a Belgian licence as soon as they receive their Belgian identity card. In cases where full reciprocity is granted (including most American states), you must present a valid driving licence at least six months old, your Belgian identity card, two passport-size photos, and fiscal stamps to cover the current driving licence fee (around €16). Some communes will ask you to have your foreign licence verified by the appropriate consulate or the issuing authority in your home country (see **Apostilles** on page 60). You may also be required to surrender your old driving licence, which will be sent back to the issuing country (usually via the local consulate or embassy). If you're planning to return to your home country before the licence expires, ask the commune to keep it for you until you leave Belgium.

If you hold a licence issued by a country or state not granted reciprocity in Belgium (e.g. Canada and some American states), you must take both the written and practical driving tests, although you should be exempt from the waiting period between the two. Note that both tests have a reputation for being very difficult, and it isn't uncommon for even experienced drivers to have to retake the written test a couple of times before passing, although you're only permitted to take it twice if you aren't enrolled on a driving school programme.

Holland: EU driving licences are valid for the first year you live in Holland. After that, you have the option of exchanging it for a Dutch licence or officially registering your EU licence at your town hall, which can be done when you enrol on the municipal population register. To exchange your EU driving permit for a Dutch licence, you need two passport-size photos, a valid licence and proof that you lived in the issuing country at least 185 days before coming to Holland. If you wait longer than a year before exchanging your EU licence for a Dutch one, you must also provide a medical certificate.

Holders of non-EU driving licences may only drive in Holland for six months, after which they must take a driving test in order to qualify for a Dutch licence. This 'special extra quick driving test' (as the Ministry of Transport refers to it on their website) is somewhat different from the one taken by new drivers, its main purpose being to ensure that you understand Dutch driving regulations and won't be a hazard to other road users. Although you aren't obliged to enrol in a driving school before taking the test, it's sensible to have a few lessons. Once you've passed the road test, you're given a certificate, which you must present at your town hall (along with two passport-size photos and proof that you meet the residence requirement) so that your new licence can be issued.

Luxembourg: As in the other Benelux countries, EU licence holders aren't obliged to exchange them for Luxembourg licences. If you decide to do so, you may ask the local authorities to look after your old licence until you leave the country, so that you don't have to repeat the process when you return home.

Holders of non-EU driving licences must exchange them for a Luxembourg licence within a year of their arrival in the Duchy. First you must go to the *Administration de l'Enregistrement et Domaines, Bureau des Actes civiles* (☎ 44-9051) to obtain an application form and a tax stamp, which costs around €12.50. You must have a health certificate from a doctor in Luxembourg (costing around €40), a certificate of residence from your commune (around €3) and an affidavit (*déclaration* or *casier judiciaire*) notarised by your embassy or consulate. (This is essentially a 'good conduct' certificate, stating that you haven't been arrested or involved in illegal dealings in your home country.) Take all the documents, along with a photocopy of your driving licence, to the Ministry of Transport, *Service des Permis de Conduire*,

23 boulevard Royal, 2449 Luxembourg (☎ 478-4461). You'll be notified by post in two to three weeks when your new licence is ready, and you must surrender your old licence when you collect your new one. Unless you ask the *Service des Permis de Conduire* to keep your old licence until you leave Luxembourg, it will be sent back to the issuing country via the embassy or consulate.

CAR INSURANCE

In theory, you may purchase insurance in any EU country, which should mean that UK automobile insurance, for example, is valid anywhere in Benelux (or any other EU country). Unfortunately, however, most EU insurers won't underwrite cover for vehicles registered outside the country, except perhaps on a short-term basis. It can also be almost impossible to find 'foreign' coverage that meets the particular requirements of your adopted country, so in practice you must usually find a local company to insure your car.

You must have at least third party liability insurance (*responsabilité civile/wetteligjke aansprakelijkheids verzekering*) in order to register your car in Belgium, Holland or Luxembourg (see **Vehicle Registration** on page 187). Third party cover includes 'unlimited' or high limit medical costs incurred by someone other than you and damage to third party property resulting from an accident. It doesn't include cover for injury to you or your passengers. It's wise to add some cover to the basic policy, usually in the form of a 'part comprehensive' (*tiers personne/mini-casco*) or 'full comprehensive' (*tous risques/volledig casco*) policy. Part comprehensive, sometimes called 'third party, fire and theft' cover, will pay the cost of damage due to fire, explosion, lightning, storm or theft and often includes breakage of glass and some legal expenses. Full comprehensive covers all of the above plus collision, overturning, malicious damage and violent acts, even if you aren't able to identify the person who caused the damage. Some full comprehensive policies provide for a rental car while yours is being repaired. Full comprehensive insurance can be expensive, although you may be able to reduce the cost by accepting a larger excess (deductible).

It's normally possible to take advantage of your foreign no-claims bonus when purchasing car insurance in Benelux, but you must provide written evidence from your present or previous insurance company, usually a letter on the company's letterhead. Most companies want to see more that just your last receipt showing your no-claims bonus level. The discount you're eligible for varies by country and insurance company, but with five years of claim-free driving you should qualify for the maximum bonus (from 50 to 75 per cent). Claims resulting from an accident where you were judged not to be at fault shouldn't count against you. When buying motor insurance, it's wise to shop around a number of insurance companies and compare rates and cover. Note that an insurer may offer excellent rates for certain classes of vehicle and/or driver but be uncompetitive for others.

All insurance companies in Benelux provide an automatic 'green card' extending your normal insurance cover to most other European countries. This doesn't, however, include cars insured in Britain, where most insurance companies (Prudential Assurance is one exception) usually provide a free green card for between 30 and 90 days per year. This is to discourage the British from driving on the continent, where they're a menace to other road users, most of them not knowing their left from their right (particularly the politicians). Nevertheless, you should shop around, as some companies allow drivers a green card for up to six months a year. If you're British and have full comprehensive insurance, it's wise to have a green card when visiting the continent.

Belgium: Car insurance is expensive in Belgium, which isn't surprising given the Belgians' reputation for bad driving and the high accident rate. Unlimited third party liability cover is the minimum requirement under the law, but most drivers add options such as collision, legal assistance, theft and car occupant cover. Rates are based on a car's engine size and power as well as on the insured driver's claims record. Some insurers will discount premiums according to the sex, age or residence of the driver. The maximum discount available for a five-year clean driving record is 46 per cent. In Belgium, a full comprehensive policy costs at least €750 per year and can be much more expensive on a new or customised vehicle. Some insurance companies may require you to have a car alarm if you want theft cover.

In Belgium, you must normally give three months' written notice if you want to cancel an insurance policy or change companies. However, you may be able to have a 'diplomatic clause' inserted into your policy giving you the right to cancel at shorter notice if you're obliged to do so by your employer, e.g. if you're transferred out of Belgium.

Holland: A peculiarity of the Dutch insurance system is that it's the vehicle which is insured, not the driver. What this means is that you can let anyone borrow your car without having to obtain permission from the insurance company first. (It also means that you risk paying higher premiums or losing your no-claims bonus if they have an accident while driving your car, provided they had your permission to do so.) You may qualify for a discount of up to 45 per cent depending on the age of your car, whether it's garaged and how many kilometres you drive a year. The maximum no-claims discount can be as much as 75 per cent.

Luxembourg: Luxembourg insurers are permitted to reduce the amount of compensation paid in cases where the insured contributed to the accident by failing to comply with one or more traffic laws.

RULES OF THE ROAD

The following general road rules may help you adjust to driving in the Benelux region:

- As you may know, the people of Benelux drive on the right-hand side of the road (most of the time); it saves confusion if you do likewise! If you aren't used to driving on the right, take extra care until you're accustomed to it. Be particularly alert when leaving lay-bys, T-junctions, one-way streets, petrol stations and car parks, as it's easy to look the wrong way and even pull out onto the wrong side of the road. It may be helpful to display a reminder (e.g. 'Think right!') on your car's dashboard.

- All motorists must carry a red warning triangle, first aid kit and fire extinguisher. You can be required to produce this safety equipment on demand at police checkpoints, and fire extinguishers may be subject to periodic checks (e.g. every two years in Luxembourg). In Belgium, fire extinguishers must be mounted in a particular manner and be accessible from the driver's seat, so don't leave it rolling around the boot.

- On main roads, make sure you look out for priority signs, which indicate that roads entering from the right DON'T have right of way. The most common priority sign is a yellow diamond on a white background, in use throughout most of Europe. The end of priority is shown by the same sign with one or more black diagonal lines through it. Priority may also be indicated by a triangular crossroads sign or one showing a broad vertical arrow with a thinner horizontal line crossing it or joining it from the right. On roads without priority signs and in built-up areas, you must give way to vehicles coming from your RIGHT. Drivers in Benelux consider priority from the right (*priorité à droite/voorrang van rechts*) to be a God-given imperative and, despite some changes to the laws in recent years, will often pull out from a narrow side street without bothering even to cast a sideways glance. If you have an accident where your car is hit from the right side, it's normally assumed that you were at fault, **so if in doubt, always give way to traffic coming from your RIGHT** – as well as to trams, buses and emergency vehicles (police cars, fire engines and ambulances).

- Traffic on roundabouts flows anti-clockwise rather than clockwise as in Britain and other countries where you drive on the left. To add to the confusion, this is one instance where the 'right of way from the right' rule usually doesn't apply. In order to be consistent with neighbouring countries (such as France), traffic rules in Belgium were changed in 1997 to give right of way to traffic already on a roundabout. Most roundabouts are also marked with 'shark's teeth' – a row of solid triangles pointing at approaching traffic – to remind drivers to give way, but it doesn't always work (particularly with Belgians).

- The sequence of traffic lights is red, green, yellow (amber) and back to red. Yellow means stop at the stop line; you may proceed only if the yellow light appears after you've started to cross the stop line or when stopping may cause an accident. In cities and towns, many intersections with traffic lights are fitted with hidden cameras to catch drivers going through (running) red lights. If you're caught, a ticket with instructions for payment will arrive a few days later at the address at which the vehicle is registered. If you're driving a company car, the ticket will be sent to your employer, but it's unlikely he'll pay the fine for you!

- The wearing of seatbelts is compulsory in Belgium, Holland and Luxembourg and also applies to passengers in rear seats where seatbelts are fitted. Young children must be provided with special seats or wear seatbelts adapted for their age and size. Infants may only be carried in the front seat if they're secured in a rear-facing safety seat. You can be stopped and fined for not wearing a seatbelt. Note that if you have an accident and aren't wearing a seatbelt, your insurance company can refuse to pay a claim for personal injury owing to your 'contributory negligence'.

- Don't drive in bus, taxi or cycle lanes (you can be fined for doing so) unless necessary to avoid a stationary vehicle or another obstruction. Make sure you keep clear of tram lines, i.e. outside the delineated area. Unless there's a central island, never overtake or stop to the right of a stationary tram with its doors open.

- The use of horns is forbidden in built-up areas unless necessary to avoid an accident. Flash your headlights to warn an oncoming motorist or pedestrian. If a motorist comes up behind you on a motorway and flashes his headlights, he could be trying to tell you that your exhaust pipe is falling off, but it's more likely to mean 'Get out of my $*@!# way!' It's illegal to flash your headlights at an approaching car to warn the driver of a speed trap or police road block ahead, but many drivers do so.

- Fog lights (mandatory on the rear of Belgian cars) should be used only when visibility is less than 100 meters. Dipped (low beam) headlights must be used in tunnels, fog, snowstorms, heavy rain and when visibility is less than 200 meters. There are fines for misuse of fog lights.

- Motorists must signal before overtaking and when moving back into an inside lane after overtaking, e.g. on a motorway. In fact, you should use your indicators before any sideways motion, even simply pulling out to avoid a cyclist or other obstruction at the side of the road.

- Take care when crossing railway lines, particularly at crossings with no barriers, which are very dangerous. Approach a railway level crossing slowly and STOP:
  - as soon as the barrier or half-barrier starts to fall;
  - as soon as the red warning lights are flashing or the warning bell is ringing;
  - when a train approaches!

- Be particularly wary of moped riders and cyclists. It isn't always easy to see them, particularly when they're in a 'blind spot' or are riding at night without lights. Cyclists are subject to the same road rules as motorists and, particularly in Holland, are likely to assert priority from the right. When overtaking mopeds or cyclists, give them a wide berth! If you knock them off their bikes, you'll have a difficult time convincing the police that it wasn't your fault; far better to avoid them (and the police).

- All motorists in Belgium, Holland and Luxembourg should be familiar with the local highway code, available from bookshops and news stands throughout the region. It's usually possible to obtain the highway code in English, either from a bookshop or through a driving school.

ROAD SIGNS

Standard international road signs apply in Belgium, Holland and Luxembourg, and almost all signs conform to the following shapes and colours:

- Warning – red triangle;
- Restriction – red circle;
- Requirement – blue circle;
- Guidance – square/rectangle;
- Priority – diamond;
- Stop – octagon.

Some of the signs you're most likely to come across are listed below:

Sign	Meaning
Allumez vos phares/Lichten aanzetten	Switch on lights
Attention/Opgepast	Caution
Toutes directions/Alle richtingen	All routes
Autres directions/Andere richtingen	Other routes
Brouillard frequent/Nevelvorming	Frequent fog
Danger/Gevaar	Danger
Déviation/Wegomlegging	Diversion
Files/Files	Stay in lane
Péage/Tol	Toll
Ralentir/Langzaam rijden or *Let op*	Slow
Route glissante/Slipgevaar	Slippery road
Sens unique/Eenrightingsverkeer	One-way street
Sortie/Uitrit	Exit
Sortie de secours/Nooduitgang	Emergency exit
Travaux/Werken	Roadworks
Verglas/Ijzel	Ice

Belgium: Because road signs in Belgium fall under the jurisdiction of the local government, they're normally only in the local language, i.e. French or Flemish but not both, except in and around Brussels, where bi-lingual signs are common. Most towns in Belgium have both a French and a Flemish name and it can be very confusing trying to follow signs as you cross from a French-speaking area into the Flemish part of Belgium or vice versa. Even motorway signs change languages abruptly, usually without any official recognition that you've crossed a linguistic border. Although some of the alternatives are relatively easy to recognise, e.g. *Bruxelles*/*Brussel* and *Bruge/Brugge*, some can catch you out. For example, *Gent* becomes *Gand* in French-speaking areas, while *Tournai* is known as *Doornik* to the Flemish, and *Bergen* is the Flemish name for *Mons*.

You may even run into this phenomenon with cities in neighbouring countries. The German town of *Aachen* is *Aix-la-Chapelle* in French and *Aken* in Dutch. If you're headed to *Lille* (in France) from the north of Belgium, you must follow signs for *Rijssel*. It may also be useful to know that, to French speakers, Holland is called *les Pays-bas* and will be indicated as such on most road signs in Wallonia (as well as in Luxembourg).

Good quality road maps often indicate alternative names, particularly if the maps are made for use in Belgium. When asking or taking down directions, make sure you check whether you've been given the French or the Dutch name.

SPEED LIMITS

The following speed limits are in force in Benelux:

● 120kph (75mph) on motorways and dual carriageways with at least two lanes in each direction;

● 90kph (56 mph) on main roads outside built-up areas;*

● 50kph (31mph) in built-up areas.

* Holland permits a maximum speed of 100kph (62mph) on main roads marked with a sign showing a white car on a blue background. All other roads outside built-up areas are limited to 80kph (50mph).

Speed restrictions in built-up areas such as small villages or towns often aren't indicated, but a 50kph (31mph) limit is understood to apply at the sign indicating the beginning of the town. Within cities and towns, speeds may be restricted to 20 or 30kph (12 to 19mph) in certain residential or other areas. A speed limit applies until you reach a sign showing one or more diagonal lines through the same limit. There are also reduced speed limits for lorries and vehicles towing a trailer or caravan.

The police are fond of setting up radar speed traps, and in many cases fines are payable on the spot. In Luxembourg, for example, the fine for exceeding the speed limit by up to 15kph (9mph) is €150, which is payable to the police officer who stops you. If you're resident in Luxembourg, the police may accept a cheque for the amount (or they may not), but foreign residents are expected to pay cash. In addition to the usual documents, you should always carry some cash with you when driving, especially if you have a tendency to speed!

TRAFFIC POLICE

In Belgium, Holland and Luxembourg, traffic police are empowered to stop any vehicle for virtually any reason, e.g. to check paperwork (either the driver's or the vehicle's). Police can and often do collect fines on the spot for minor violations, such as speeding or crossing the white line in the centre of the road. If you don't have enough cash to pay a fine, the police may offer to escort you to a bank machine so that you can withdraw the money, or in some cases you might be able to convince them to accept a cheque (assuming you have local identification). In some cases, the fine is increased (usually significantly) if you must be billed for it after the event.

Police in Benelux are also fond of setting up road blocks to conduct random checks, either for drink driving or simply to make sure that all your paperwork is in order and that your vehicle is in a safe condition. If you're stopped, you must be able to produce not only your driving licence, but also the vehicle's registration document, proof of insurance, evidence that you've paid your annual road tax (the receipt as well as the sticker in your windscreen), and your current safety certificate or proof of the car's having passed its last safety inspection. In Belgium, you must also carry proof of payment of the annual tax on your car radio if you have one. You should always carry at least one copy of the standard European Accident Report Form (see

Accidents on page 202) and make sure that you have all the required safety equipment with proper certification (e.g. for a fire extinguisher) where necessary.

Police also often check to make sure everyone in the vehicle has his seatbelt fastened, that children are secured in the proper safety restraint. You may also be asked to produce your passport and/or local resident identification card. There are certain times of year when roadblocks are more likely, e.g. around Christmas, when the major concern is drink driving, and just before or after deadlines for vehicle inspections. If you're caught without some piece of paperwork or safety equipment that's required, you generally receive an on-the-spot fine and may be required to return to the police station within a day or two with the missing item. The police can also search your car if they suspect you of carrying any form of contraband, usually drugs or illegal aliens. It doesn't pay to argue with police officers, as it can cause all sorts of trouble and even earn you a jail sentence! Be polite. Let the officers get on with their jobs and you'll minimise the time you spend at road blocks (or in the local nick).

BENELUX DRIVERS

Cars are an accepted status symbol and Beneluxers take great pride in owning and maintaining (generally in impeccable condition) large, state-of-the-art, usually German-made motor vehicles, which they tend to drive at high speed as close as possible to the rear bumper of the car in front. This may be attributable to the fact that, in Belgium at least, drivers weren't even required to have licences until the 1960s and, when licensing was finally introduced, it was thought that it would be insulting to submit 'experienced' drivers to a test, so existing drivers were permitted simply to register for a licence. It was the late '70s before Belgians were required to take a road test before being granted a driving licence for life, so most Belgian drivers over the age of 45 have never had to take a driving test. (Rumour has it that most older Belgians learned to drive by being tossed the keys to a lorry while doing their military service.) No wonder even the French consider Belgians to be bad drivers!

In recent years, the Belgian government has cracked down on licensing (to the point that Belgian driving tests are now quite difficult to pass) and introduced stringent and frequent safety checks. Although the accident rate has come down, the infamous reputation of the Belgian driver remains intact and Luxembourg still holds the title for the most murderous roads (on a per capita basis). Conducting business while en route to work is also a status symbol – to the extent that all three countries are moving to limit or ban the use of mobile phones while driving.

Both the Belgians and the Dutch take to the roads in huge numbers during holidays, particularly in summer, often towing caravans or driving large motor homes and heading south to sunnier and less crowded areas of Europe. This is no doubt also a factor in establishing their reputation as drivers to be avoided.

MOTORCYCLES

Motorcycles and mopeds are very popular throughout Belgium, Holland and Luxembourg, if only because they can weave in and out of traffic more efficiently than a car and are easier to park in crowded cities. A moped is essentially a motorised bicycle, categorised according to its maximum speed. A class A moped is one with a top speed of 25kph (16mph). These can be driven by anyone over the age of 16 without a licence or a crash helmet. (If you carry a passenger on your moped, you must be 18 or over.) A class B moped is one with a top speed of 45kph (28mph) and for this category of vehicle you're required to pass a written exam and wear a helmet. The minimum ages are the same as for a class A moped.

Any motorcycle more powerful than a moped (generally defined as having an engine greater than 50cc) is subject to regular licensing and safety requirements. You must be 18 to drive a motorcycle and have a special motorcycle endorsement on your driving licence, which involves passing both a theoretical and a driving test specifically geared to motorcycles. All three countries require both driver and passenger to wear approved crash helmets with chinstraps and, although motorcycles don't require regular safety inspections like cars, you're strongly encouraged (by the police) to use standard safety equipment on your bike and person: crash bars, safety glasses, leather boots, jackets, gloves and trousers. Headlights, rear lights and reflectors are required both for motorcycles and mopeds.

ACCIDENTS

Perhaps it has something to do with the high density of the population in Benelux or, more likely, with the reputation the region's drivers have for speeding, tailgating and asserting their *priorité à droite*, but you're far more likely to suffer an accident here than, say, in the UK. Luxembourg, in fact, has the worst per capita accident record in the EU, and Belgium isn't far behind. It's therefore worthwhile knowing the protocol in the event of an accident. This varies somewhat among the three countries, but generally involves the following:

1. Stop and make the scene of the accident safe, e.g. by moving vehicles and people to the side of the road (if safe to do so) and placing a warning triangle 100m (330ft) ahead of the scene to warn oncoming drivers.

2. Attend to the injured.

3. Report the accident in the appropriate manner, i.e. to your insurance company and to the police, if required.

There's no need to call the police if you're involved in a minor accident, i.e. one in which there's only slight damage to the vehicles and no injuries, provided you and the other driver(s) involved agree on what happened. For accidents where no one is injured, you must complete at least one copy of the European Accident Report Form (*Constat européen d'Accident/Europees Aanrijdings-Formulier*) that you should keep in your glove box. This is a standard form, which is available in various languages (including English), so it's sensible to carry a reference copy in English for your own use as well as one or more copies in the local language. You must fill in the form completely, giving information about the drivers involved (including their insurance information) and the accident. At the bottom of the form is a space for a diagram of the incident.

In Belgium, each driver fills out his own form and both must be signed by both (or all) drivers involved in the accident. In Holland and Luxembourg, only one copy of the form needs to be completed for a two-car accident. If more than two cars are involved, it may be necessary to fill out additional accident reports. The signed report (or reports) must be submitted to your insurance company within eight days.

Before signing an accident report, you should read what the other driver has written very carefully and make sure you understand and agree with everything, including the diagram. If you disagree with anything on the report, don't sign it, as the insurance company will base their settlement on the content of the form; you cannot change your story or explanation later. If the drivers involved in an accident cannot agree on the details, you should call the police, who will prepare their own report on the circumstances of the accident. Some drivers carry a (disposable) camera in their glove box, which can be used to document the scene of the accident and damage to vehicles.

If anyone is hurt in an accident or there's a spill of petrol or dangerous chemicals, you must call the emergency services, who will send an ambulance, police car or fire engine, as necessary. All drivers are legally required to lend assistance if there are injuries and you can be arrested or fined if you fail to stop to assist at the scene of an accident. There are 'good Samaritan' laws to protect those who render assistance. If your first aid skills are rusty, refer to the instruction sheet inside the first aid kid you're required to carry in your car.

If you're involved in an accident where the police have been called, make sure you collect as much information as possible, including the number of the police report, the branch of the police or *gendarmerie* involved, and the identity and insurance details of the other driver or drivers. If no assistance arrives at the scene of an accident involving injury within a reasonable time, you may leave the scene to take the injured to hospital for treatment, but you should leave your name and address with a witness or someone at the scene of the accident, telling them where you're taking the injured person and must return within 24 hours to report the accident to the police.

Should you hit an unattended vehicle, you're required by law to report the accident to the nearest police station, even if you don't think you've caused any damage. The law on fleeing the scene of an accident (*délit de fuite/vluchtmisdrijft*) in all three Benelux countries is extremely strict. You may not simply leave a note on a car giving your name and phone number 'in case' there was any damage. If anyone saw the incident and noted your registration number or any other identifying information, you could be arrested for failing to report an accident.

When a bus or tram is involved in an accident, it isn't necessary for the bus or tram driver to remain at the scene. If you're involved in this type of accident, you must remain at the scene until a representative of the transport company arrives.

DRIVING & DRINKING

All three Benelux countries take driving under the influence of alcohol (or drugs) extremely seriously and have cracked down on the practice in recent years. Breath tests can be carried out by the police at any time, and motorists who are involved in accidents or who have been caught violating any motoring regulation are routinely breathalysed. At weekends and on national holidays, the police often set up road blocks specifically to check for drunk drivers. You can normally ask to wait up to 30 minutes before taking a breath test; if the results are positive, you'll be required to take a blood test.

You're permitted to drive with 50mg of alcohol per 100ml of blood. The amount you can 'safely' drink depends on how regularly you imbibe, your sex and your weight. Fines increase with the level of alcohol in your blood and are generally accompanied by a suspension of your driving licence. In Belgium, the minimum fine for being apprehended with 50 to 80mg of alcohol per 100ml of blood is €125 and a driving suspension of three hours, i.e. the police will impound your vehicle and you must walk home or call someone to come and pick you up. With 80 to 120mg, the minimum fine rises to €375 with a minimum suspension of six hours, and from 120 to 150 mg of alcohol, the fine is €500. Over 150mg, you risk a fine of between 1,000 and €10,000, a prison sentence of 15 days to six months and the loss of your driving licence for at least eight days and up to five years.

The Dutch have a similar scale of fines, with an automatic licence suspension of six to twelve months if you're found to have more than 130mg of alcohol per 100ml of blood in your system. If you're involved in an accident while under the influence of alcohol, your car insurance may be nullified. This means that you must pay for any third party's car repairs, medical treatment and other damages.

PETROL

Leaded petrol is no longer sold anywhere in the EU. Unleaded petrol (*sans plomb/loodvrij*) is usually available in three grades: regular (93 octane), super (95 octane) and super plus (98 octane). Diesel fuel (*gasoil/diesel*) and liquid propane gas (LPG) are also available at most service stations. Note that *pétrole* or *fuel* is paraffin (in the British sense, kerosene to the Americans) and not petrol.

Although petrol prices will seem outrageous to North Americans, the Benelux countries are popular destinations for French and German day-trippers seeking 'cheap fuel' for the home bound run. Prices vary considerably according to the area, town and the particular petrol station, but are generally around €1 per litre. The cheapest sources are usually supermarkets, where prices can be 15 to 20 per cent lower than average.

Self-service petrol stations are common and include most motorway and supermarket stations. Manned stations are common in small towns and villages. Tips aren't expected for cleaning the windscreen and checking oil or tyre pressures, although they won't be refused. There are 24-hour petrol stations on or just off most motorways. When paying at self-service petrol stations, simply tell the cashier your pump number. Major credit cards are accepted by most petrol stations, and some have automatic pumps accepting credit cards when the station is closed.

GARAGES & SERVICING

As in most other European countries, for service and repair there's a choice of dealers, garages, petrol stations and chains of 'quick service' shops for oil changes, exhaust pipe replacement and other standard maintenance in most areas. There's also a growing number of automotive parts shops and discount centres for those who want to do it themselves. Most garages and service centres are open early, e.g. from 7am, for routine servicing, and you must usually collect your car by 6pm. Many service centres are open on Saturdays, at least in the morning, but all-day service on Saturdays is becoming the norm.

Prices vary, as does quality of service, and you should ask around for recommendations if it isn't an emergency. Be sure to obtain an estimate before allowing work to done or you could have a nasty shock when you pick up your car. Dealers are usually the most expensive option, although their work is guaranteed and you're assured that it has been done in accordance with your vehicle's warranty requirements. Many private garages offer guarantees on their work and may be considerably cheaper than a dealer. It pays to develop a relationship with a dealer or garage rather than simply accepting the cheapest quotation each time you need something done.

ROAD MAPS

Good road maps are available throughout Benelux at reasonable prices. All the major French, German and Swiss map publishers offer road maps of the region as well as individual city and area maps. Look for maps published by Hallwag, K&F and Michelin or ask at local tourist offices for free maps covering local sites or attractions. Several publishers, including Shell, offer hardbound books of maps, either by country or for the entire Benelux region or Europe. It's normally possible to find city maps at news stands and bookshops as well as in telephone books.

CD-ROM and online maps and driving instructions are becoming increasingly popular. Michelin (🖳 www.viamichelin.com), Microsoft (🖳 maps.expedia.com or AutoEurope software) and others offer both maps online and software you can use to generate your own maps or link to a global positioning system (GPS) in your car or motorhome. Some car manufacturers even include GPS and mapping systems in luxury cars, but these are otherwise expensive options.

MOTORING ORGANISATIONS

Belgium, Holland and Luxembourg each have their own motoring organisations offering detailed information about driving licences and driving schools, assistance with the purchase or sale of a car, road maps and route planning services. The mostpopular service is breakdown insurance, which can be extended to include medical care or repatriation in case of illness or accident when travelling abroad.

Most of the national motoring organisations are affiliated to international networks, so if you already belong to a motoring organisation in your home country, you should contact them before moving to Benelux to see if you can transfer your membership to the local affiliate. In the worst case, it's usually possible to sign up for a three month trial membership at your first breakdown. The Dutch automobile clubs, for example, charge around €85 for an 'on the spot' membership, renewable at the end of the trial period for between €30 and 90 depending on the level of service and coverage (e.g. national or European) you require.

Belgium: In Belgium, the main motoring associations are the *Royal Automobile Club de Belgique/Kininklijke Automobiel Club van België* (*RACB/KACB*), Rue de Trèves 828, 1000 Brussels (☎ 02-287 0900 or national rate 078-152 000 for the breakdown service), *Touring Club de Belgique/Touring Club van België* (*TCB*), Rue de la Loi 44, 1040 Brussels (☎ 02-233 2211 or 070-344 777) and *Vlaamse*

Automobilistenbond (*VTB/VAB*), St. Jacobsmarkt 45, 2000 Antwerp (☎ 03-253 6663 or 070-344 666).

Holland: The principal organisations are *ANWB*, Wassenaarseweg 220, 2596 EC The Hague (☎ 070-314 7147) and *Koninklijke Nederlandse Automobile Club* (*KNAC*), Postbus 446, 2260 AK Liedschendam (☎ 070-383 1612).

Luxembourg: In Luxembourg, contact the Automobile Club of Luxembourg, 54 route de Longwy, 8007 Helfenterbruck/Bertrange (☎ 45-00451).

CAR RENTAL

Car rental companies such as Avis, Eurodollar, Europcar, Hertz, Sixt and Thrifty have offices in most large towns and major airports. You can also rent cars at railway stations and at many hotels. Look in the local Yellow Pages under *Location de Voitures/Autoverhuringen*.

Car rental throughout Benelux can be expensive, particularly for short periods, and rental charges are subject to VAT (at 21 per cent in Belgium, 19 per cent in Holland and 15 per cent in Luxembourg). It's often possible to get a better deal if you book overseas, and some Benelux residents even telephone the US or UK office of a rental company in order to obtain the best rates. (The chances are you won't be asked where you're calling from.) It's usually cheaper to rent a vehicle over the weekend and often there are special rates for three or four days including a Saturday. For example, a three-day weekend rental for a small, manual transmission car can cost less than €120 in Antwerp or around €150 at Schiphol airport in Amsterdam.

To hire a car in Belgium, Holland or Luxembourg, you must be at least 20 to 25 years old (the terms vary by company and region) and have had your driving licence for at least a year. In some cases, if you're under 25, you may be asked to pay an additional charge to cover your 'increased risk'. Most international companies require you to book and pay for your rental using a credit card and you may be asked to show personal identification in addition to your driving licence when you collect your car.

Options include a portable telephone, a luggage rack, snow chains and child seats, all of which involve an extra charge. You can also hire a specialised vehicle, e.g. convertible, four-wheel drive, station wagon, minibus, luxury car or armoured limousine, as well as minibuses accessible to wheelchairs. Most basic cars have manual transmission and no air-conditioning. Automatic transmission and air-conditioning are available, but not always in all categories (for example, subcompacts or compacts may not be available with automatic transmission or air-conditioning). Most car rental companies have a website containing their terms and conditions as well as a complete list of options and prices.

Despite the high cost of car rental, many city dwellers in Benelux find it more economical to rent a car when needed for weekend trips than to own their own car and have to register, tax, maintain and find parking space for it (see below).

PARKING

Once you've deciphered the maps, successfully navigated the roads and reached your destination, you may be faced with a new challenge: finding a place to park. In many residential areas, on-street parking is limited to residents or holders of permits issued by the city or district traffic commission. In Luxembourg city, for example, parking vignettes are issued to city residents, giving them the right to park in their neighbourhood and priority over non-residents in certain areas of the city. Amsterdam has a severe shortage of parking places for residents and prices parking permits according to demand. If you live in the popular Binnenstad or Jordaan districts, you must pay up to €45 per quarter (€180 per year) to park outside your home – that's after you've been on a waiting list for four to five years! Waiting lists are shorter (or in some cases non-existent) in some less fashionable quarters, where charges are roughly half as much. Other cities in the Randstad (e.g. Rotterdam and The Hague) have similar resident parking permit systems. Enquire at your town hall when you register your residence.

It isn't only outside your home that you may have difficultly finding a parking space. Parking anywhere in major cities can be a problem. Legal on-street parking (where it exists) is usually indicated by signposting, but a number of standard rules apply:

- Don't obstruct driveways, garages or crossings.
- Don't park on railway or tram tracks or within 15 metres of a tram or bus stop sign.
- Don't park within five metres of a junction.
- Don't park where there's a yellow line on the kerb or a centre line on the road.

It's illegal to park on the 'wrong' side of the street, i.e. facing traffic, and unless there's a sign indicating otherwise, you shouldn't park with two wheels on the kerb or pavement. Where this is permitted, there should be a blue and white sign showing a car parked in that manner.

Brussels and several cities in Holland have thoroughfares known as 'red routes', which means all parking or stopping is prohibited during weekday rush hours, usually 7 to 9am and 4 to 6 or 7pm. These routes are clearly signposted and there may also be lights or other signals to indicate when these or other parking restrictions are in effect. In Amsterdam it's possible to buy a monthly permit allowing you to park in designated areas throughout the city, but you may decide that €360 is too high a price for the convenience!

In city centres, parking is normally controlled in a variety of ways, including meters, discs, tickets or stickers and sometimes by a system of alternating the side of the road on which parking is allowed. Meters limit parking to an hour or two. Make sure you have plenty of coins if you intend to use parking meters, as most meters don't give change or take credit cards. In most Benelux cities, it's illegal to 'feed' a parking meter (i.e. insert coins for extra time after your initial time has expired). 'Meter maids' or traffic police often mark tyres or note registration numbers to make sure you move on when you're supposed to. In some areas, instead of parking meters, there are machines that issue tickets indicating the amount of parking time you've paid for. The ticket, which is often self-adhesive, must be placed in the window of your car where a passing policeman or meter maid can see what time your parking privileges expire.

Parking discs (*disques bleus* in French) are required wherever parking spaces are marked in blue (*zone bleue/blauwe zone*) or where a blue sign indicates you must use a parking disc (usually a letter P with a parking disc pictured below it). Discs are available free from your insurance company, car dealer or motoring club and can be purchased at reasonable cost from news stands, petrol stations and garages. You must indicate on the disc the time you arrived in the parking space, and parking is usually limited to one hour, although there are a few two-hour zones. If you don't have a parking disc, you may get away with writing your time of arrival on a piece of paper and displaying it on your dashboard.

If you don't want to leave your car on the street, you can follow the blue and white signs bearing the letter P and an arrow to find car parks or indoor parking facilities (often indicated by a P with a 'roof' over it). Many cities with ring roads have automated signs indicating the number of parking places currently available in various nearby car parks. Most car parks are partly or fully automated, so that you must take a ticket in order to enter. In most cases, you should take the parking ticket with you so that you can pay at one of the machines near the pedestrian entrance on your return. You must insert a validated (i.e. paid) ticket in order to leave the garage or car park, and there isn't always a payment machine or attendant near the exit if you've forgotten to pay before fetching your car. Always make sure you note the closing hours of the car park before you spend a night on the town or you may have to wait until morning to recover your car. Only a few car parks are open 24 hours a day, and many are closed on Sundays and public holidays, when on-street parking is usually free and relatively easy to find.

Wherever you park in Benelux, you should always lock your car and put any packages, bags or personal items in the glove box or boot. In Holland, it's illegal to leave your car unlocked, so you could end up paying a fine *as well as* having your belongings stolen!

PEDESTRIAN ROAD RULES

All three governments have recently strengthened their laws protecting pedestrians, and in the event of an accident involving a pedestrian, the motorist is almost always held to be at fault. Nevertheless, you should take great care particularly when crossing the road in Benelux. Pedestrian crossings are indicated by broad white stripes across the road, and motorists are supposed to come to an immediate stop if you're waiting at a crossing. However, don't rely on them doing so, but give some indication as you approach the crossing that you intend to cross. Making eye contact with an approaching driver is the best method, as well as pausing to make sure the driver is slowing down and ready to stop. Cyclists are supposed to dismount and push their bikes if using a pedestrian crossing, but few do.

Many cities and towns in Benelux have pedestrian zones where motor vehicles are prohibited for much or all of the day. These are clearly marked, often with road blocks to prevent cars from straying into the zone.

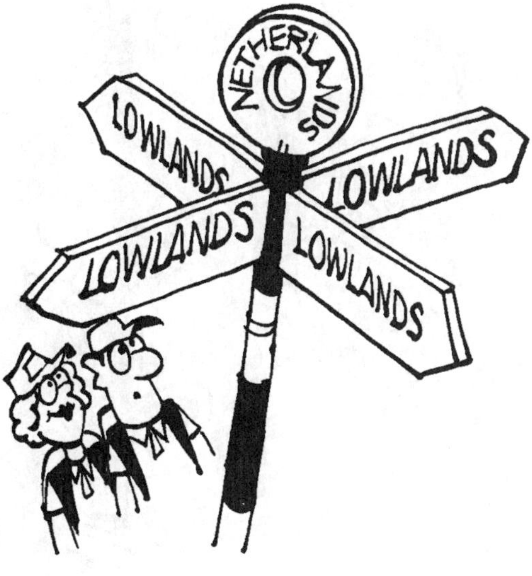
NETHERLANDS
LOWLANDS
LOWLANDS
LOWLANDS
LOWLANDS

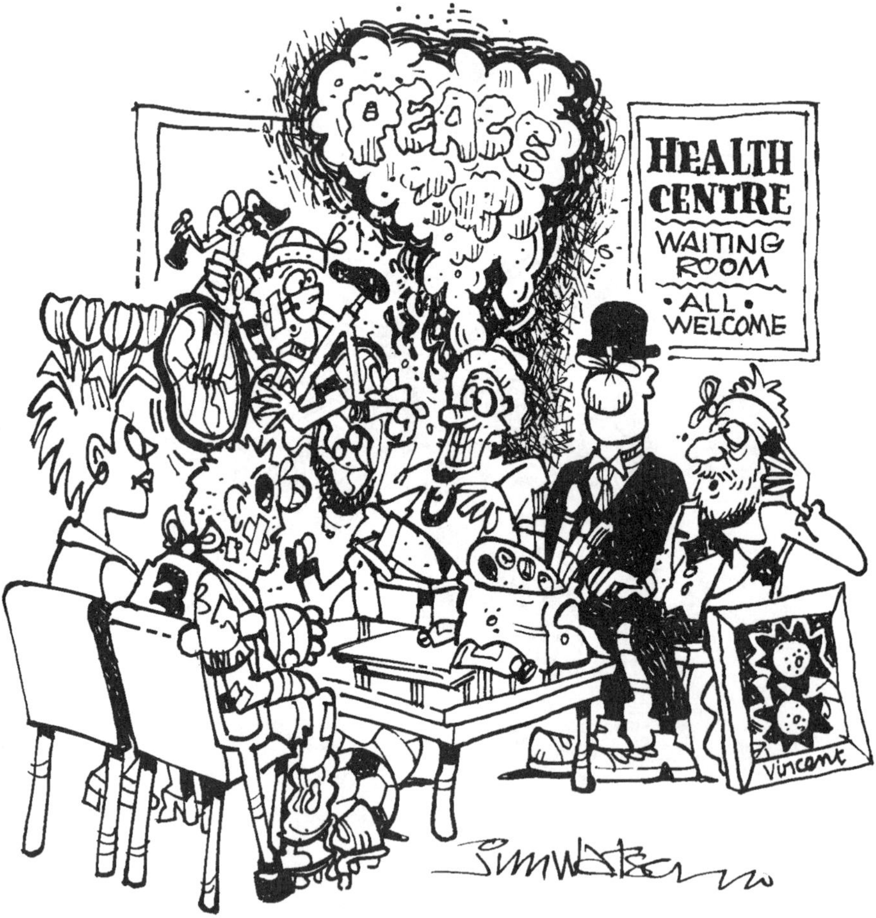
PEACE
HEALTH CENTRE
WAITING ROOM
• ALL •
WELCOME
Vincent

12.

HEALTH

Health care in Benelux is among the best in the world. The infant mortality rate is less than five deaths per 1,000 live births, and life expectancy averages 80 years for women and almost 75 years for men. As in most industrialised nations, the leading causes of death are circulatory disease (heart attacks and strokes) and cancer. The region boasts state-of-the-art research and treatment facilities, particularly in the areas of infertility, organ transplantation, hip replacement and certain kinds of cancer. It's probably no coincidence that Benelux is home to a large number of pharmaceutical and medical product companies as well as numerous private health insurers. Medical treatment is available to all, through a combination of public and private insurance programmes, with considerable emphasis on preventive treatment.

The open-mindedness of the Benelux region has led to pioneering (and usually highly controversial) experiments in the treatment of drug addiction, infertility and terminal illnesses, as well as in methods of birth control. Holland and Belgium have recently legalised euthanasia or assisted suicide (see page 223), the first countries in the world to do so. The Dutch were also among the first to consider drug use as a public health issue rather than a criminal matter by introducing schemes such as free AIDS testing and municipal sponsorship of needle exchange programmes.

EMERGENCIES

If you need a doctor outside normal office hours, you should first try contacting your regular doctor, either at home or through his answering service. (Keep the number near your telephone.) It's sensible to ask your doctor early on how emergencies (*cas d'urgence/spoedgeval*) should be handled, as some medical systems and insurers insist on doctor authorisation for emergency services such as ambulances and hospital admissions in all except life-threatening situations. Not all hospitals have emergency facilities, and even those that do may not be open all the time. It's obviously best to check these things before you actually need them.

Europe is gradually standardising the use of 112 as an all-purpose emergency telephone number, although some countries still have separate emergency numbers for contacting police, fire and ambulance services. The standard 112 number can be used to obtain assistance in any emergency, but you may want to use one of the specialised numbers where they're available (see below). Most emergency operators can speak English, although not necessarily fluently. In an emergency, no matter what language you're using, try to remember to speak slowly and distinctly, giving the operator all the information needed, such as your exact location and what assistance is needed. It's wise to practise giving your name, phone number and address and spelling critical details (like your street name) in the local language so as to avoid confusion – especially over the phone.

If you suffer from a condition that may need emergency treatment, you should carry a written description of the condition, the medicines you're taking, including doses, and any other relevant details. This can be in English or the local language and will save you considerable time (and possibly your life) if a medical emergency strikes and you're unable to speak for yourself.

Belgium: In Belgium, the emergency phone number for requesting an ambulance (*ambulance/ziekenwagen*) or reporting a fire is 100. If you can't stay on the line after calling 100 (e.g. if you're house is burning down), don't hang up; the emergency service will trace your call within a few seconds and send an ambulance and police to the site. An ambulance will take you to the nearest hospital with an available emergency service. In the Brussels area you can call 105 for a Red Cross ambulance that will take you to the hospital of your choice. In either case, you will be billed for the ambulance journey. This charge isn't reclaimable under the national health system, but you may be able to claim reimbursement under a private insurance plan if you have one.

Holland: Holland uses 112 as its general emergency phone number, whether for police (*politie*), fire (*bramdmelder*) or ambulance (*ziekenwagen*). Most emergency operators speak English (as well as several other foreign languages) or they will transfer you to an operator who does speak your language. Nevertheless, you should report your situation in simple terms, speaking slowly and distinctly, as English may be a second or third language for the operator, who needs to determine what sort of assistance to send. If the emergency isn't life-threatening, your first phone call should be to your general practitioner (*huisarts*), who can authorise and arrange hospitalisation or an ambulance for you. (Note that in Holland, you're supposed to select a GP whose office is no more than ten minutes' drive from your home.) Doctors will make emergency house calls or advise you of the nearest hospital and arrange to meet you there.

Luxembourg: The medical emergency phone number in Luxembourg is 112. You should describe the situation and your location carefully and answer any questions the operator asks you. Don't hang up until the emergency operator says that the call is complete. It's important that he understands the situation so that the proper emergency services are dispatched. Not all hospitals in Luxembourg have emergency services, and out of hours coverage is rotated among the hospitals in the area. Only the duty hospital can provide emergency services, so you need to know which it is. The duty schedule is published in newspapers and often posted in pharmacies and doctors' surgeries as well as at hospitals. The cost of ambulance services is reclaimable under most health insurance plans, but check your policy for specific conditions or limitations. If the emergency isn't life-threatening, you should try contacting your doctor first.

SOCIAL SECURITY HEALTH BENEFITS

All three countries include health benefits in their national social security systems and make provision to ensure that all residents have access to medical treatment. Health insurance coverage is mandatory, although at various levels, and is usually paid for through payroll contributions, shared between employers and employees. The self-employed must generally pay the equivalent of the employer's and the employee's contribution. Pensioners and those receiving unemployment or other benefits are also covered by social security programmes. Private insurance is available (and most residents contribute to some form of supplementary policy) to cover the portion of health care expenses not reimbursed under the compulsory scheme or to provide extended coverage for dental, optometric or other specialised treatment.

Belgium: The national health insurance system (*mutuelle/ziekenfonds*) is paid for by employers and employees and covers all dependent family members (see page 234). The basic cover includes a partial refund of medical and dental costs, hospital care, surgery, childbirth, medicines, home nursing and physiotherapy. The scale of reimbursements is set by the government to cover a percentage of the 'standard' fee for each service. A doctor who has agreed to base fees on the government standards is said to be *conventionné* or *gekonventioneerd*, which means that you will be reimbursed at the set rate (e.g. 75 per cent for doctor's visits). Doctors operating outside this scheme may set fees as high as they wish, but you will be reimbursed only up to the *ziekenfond* standard limits. Over 80 per cent of doctors (and other medical facilities) in Belgium are *conventionné*, but it pays to check before you discover (the hard way) that you won't be fully reimbursed. Most people also take out a supplementary policy to reimburse the portion of fees that isn't covered by the basic plan, and most supplementary plans include dental and eye care fees (not well reimbursed in the state system) as well as unlimited reimbursement for specialists, whether or not they're *conventionné*.

Holland: The government operates a two-tier health insurance system in Holland. The basic level is primarily preventative health care, and all workers earning less than a certain amount (currently around €31,000 per year – the amount is based on the national minimum wage and indexed twice a year) must enrol in one of the state run health insurance plans, known as sickness funds (*ziekenfonds*). There's optional supplementary cover for 'exceptional' medical expenses, called AWBZ (*algemene wet bijzondere ziektekosten*). If your earnings are above the limit, you must take out private health insurance (*particuliere verzekering*). Both forms of health insurance are paid for through payroll deductions combined with an employer contribution.

As the emphasis is on preventive treatmentroutine visits to general practitionersand dentists and most obstetric services are free. For other services, e.g. specialists, medicines and hospitalisation, the patient pays a portion of the charge (usually around 20 per cent) or a set amount such as the daily 'contribution' for hospitalisation. Make sure you take copies of your insurance certificates the first time you visit a doctor, pharmacy and other health care provider in order to establish your entitlement and determine whether your charges can be billed directly to your insurance company.

Luxembourg: Private health insurance in Luxembourg is usually offered by employers as part of a package of job benefits, and in many cases your employer pays most or all of the cost of a basic policy. Most people contribute to their own insurance scheme to supplement their employer's policy. It's normal practice to pay the doctor, hospital or other service provider directly and then submit the receipts for reimbursement. (See also page 237.)

DOCTORS

Doctors (*médecins/artsen*) throughout Belgium, Holland and Luxembourg are well trained and required to keep up-to-date with the latest medical developments. Nevertheless, you should choose your doctor as carefully you would in your home country. In Holland you're required to register with a general practitioner (*huisarts*), who's responsible for referring you to specialists or specialised treatment including hospitalisation. In Belgium and Luxembourg you aren't obliged to register with a GP, but if you incur treatment charges without obtaining a referral from your GP, these may not be reimbursed under some insurance plans, or will be reimbursed at much lower rates. Even in systems where you're permitted to book appointments or treatments directly with specialists, you will find that a good GP is invaluable in terms of guiding you through the system and helping you to find the right specialists or treatment facilities.

Doctors are listed in the Yellow Pages, but you're more likely to find someone who suits you and your family if you ask friends, neighbours and work colleagues for recommendations. Many Benelux doctors speak English or at least understand it reasonably well, as medical training in the region often involves the use of English-language text books or periods of study in the UK or USA. You may be able to obtain a list of English-speaking doctors from your local British or American consulate or embassy or by contacting expatriate clubs and associations. Benelux doctors aren't always particularly open to questions or discussion about your treatment or concerns, so if this is important to you it may take some searching to find a GP with whom you're comfortable. It's common practice to make an initial 'familiarisation' appointment with a doctor to determine whether you like his 'style', and this is recommended in Holland, where you may otherwise find yourself registered for a lengthy period with a doctor you don't relate to. The cost of such appointments is usually reimbursed by private health insurers, provided you don't meet every doctor in the area before making your decision! There may also be some restrictions on your choice of GP, depending on the health insurance system in which you're enrolled.

Once you've chosen a GP, you should ask about office hours and whether he makes appointments (*rendezvous/afspraak*) or holds 'walk-in' consultations or a combination of the two (which is most often the case). Being able to go to the doctor whenever you aren't feeling well can be convenient, although there may be a long queue. Some doctors operate a supermarket-style queuing system in their waiting rooms, so that everyone is seen in turn. If you prefer to make an appointment with your GP, it's normally possible to be seen the same day. On the other hand, it can take several days or weeks to see a specialist, most of whom work by appointment only. Doctors usually make house calls, and some prefer to attend to you at home by appointment rather than letting you share your 'germs' with everyone in the waiting room. Sometimes you need to call before a certain time, e.g. 9am, to secure a place on the house call schedule for that day, and house calls (other than for emergencies) may be limited to certain hours. Make sure you ask your new doctor what his system and preferences are for appointments and house calls.

Most Benelux doctors operate alone, without any administrative or nursing staff to handle phone calls or make appointments, which means that they often take phone calls in the middle of a consultation, which can be rather annoying at first. If you need to see a doctor outside normal surgery hours, at weekends or during holiday periods, your GP will have an answering service or recorded message giving you the name and phone number of the duty doctor (*médecin de garde* or *de nuit/wachtdienst*). The names and phone numbers of duty doctors are sometimes listed in local newspapers and neighbourhood publications, but it's generally best to call your GP first. In many cases the duty doctor will have access to your doctor's files or understand his preferences for treatment.

Doctors' surgeries are generally set up for consultations and general examinations. If you need to undress for an examination, it's unlikely that you will be given a gown or even a sheet to cover yourself, so dress accordingly. (For some reason, doctors' surgeries tend to be cold, so it's sensible to wear a loose shirt or top you can keep over your shoulders.) If the doctor determines that you need medication or a specialised examination or treatment such as x-rays, he will write a prescription for you to take to the appropriate facility. The doctor will normally recommend the closest or most convenient chemist or clinic, although in most cases you're free to choose where you go. Examination or treatment results are sent directly to your doctor, although you can ask to have a copy sent to you (either by the clinic or by your doctor). X-rays, scans and mammograms are generally given to the patient, along with a brief written description of any findings. You should take these with you on subsequent visits to the doctor, and keep them with your medical records in case they're required in future. If your doctor gives you an injection from his own store of vaccines, you will be given a prescription to purchase a replacement for the doctor's stock from a local chemist.

It's normal practice in most of the Benelux region to pay your doctor directly for both regular consultations and any services you receive. Doctors normally only accept payment in cash or by cheque. Clinics and chemists may take credit cards, but not all do. You will be given a receipt, which is also the form you need to complete to claim reimbursement. If you're covered by private insurance, particularly expatriate coverage, make sure you know what forms and information you require to claim any reimbursements due. In many cases, insurers insist on itemised receipts showing services rendered or indicating a specific diagnosis, which may not appear on a standard national health service form.

Belgium: Doctors in Belgium have trained for a minimum of seven years, in the case of a GP, and up to 12 years to become a specialist, and they're required to undergo additional training annually. Many Belgian doctors have undertaken at least part of their studies in English, so finding an English-speaking doctor shouldn't be difficult. Belgian doctors also have a reputation for taking time with their patients to answer questions and discuss treatment, which isn't always the case in other countries.

Under the Belgian national health care system, you can make an appointment directly with a specialist without requiring a referral from your family doctor, but your GP is often the best person to advise you on choosing a specialist.

Holland: Those covered under the national health scheme are given a list of general practitioners (*huisarts*) who will accept new national health patients. You're encouraged to choose someone close by, i.e. in the same postal district, as your GP must be able to reach your home within ten minutes. Under private insurance, you may be restricted to a list of approved or affiliated doctors, but are still encouraged to select a doctor close to where you live so that he will be available for house calls and in emergencies.

Under the Dutch health care system, visits to general practitioners, dentists and obstetricians are free, provided you meet certain criteria (e.g. regular check-ups) and don't exceed certain annual limits on the number of visits. You must present your insurance card (whether for the public health system or for a private insurance scheme) on your first visit. Your *huisarts* must sanction the use of ambulances, specialists and any hospital admissions in order for services or treatment to be covered. Check the terms of your policy if you're covered by private insurance; some companies require referrals, while others don't.

Luxembourg: In Luxembourg, you don't normally require a referral from your GP in order to make appointments with a specialist. Most doctors speak excellent English, but most aren't in the habit of offering much explanation to their patients or responding to a lot of questions or concerns. Ask among friends and neighbours or members of expatriate organisations for referrals to doctors who may have the approach you prefer. All medical fees in the Duchy are set by the state *Caisse de Maladie*, so all doctors must charge the same amount. You pay the doctor directly and are reimbursed by your insurance company. Doctors' surgeries are usually closed on Wednesday and Saturday afternoons (and Sundays!).

HOSPITALS & CLINICS

Hospitals (*hôpitaux/ziekenhuisen*) are identified by the international sign of a white H on a blue background. Local hospitals will be listed in the Yellow Pages, but it may be better to ask your GP, chemist or the English-language clubs and other resources in the area, as they will be able to tell you which hospitals have emergency services and how they function (see **Emergencies** on page 212). There are special hospitals or hospital sections for children, and it's usually possible for parents to stay overnight with a child.

Hospital care is generally very good throughout the Benelux region, although practices may differ from those in your home country. In most cases, hospitalisation must be arranged by your GP (see above) and there may be a waiting list for certain non-emergency treatments and services. When going to a hospital, you should take your own pyjamas, robe and slippers, as well as personal toiletries (soap, shampoo, toothpaste, etc.), towels and flannels. (If you're admitted in an emergency, you should ask a friend or family member to bring you these items.) You will also need a small amount of money to pay for telephone calls, television programmes and, in some cases, bottled water and other items offered by private services within the hospital.

Belgium: In Belgium there are two kinds of hospitals. A *hôpital* or *ziekenhuis* has its own staff on duty 24 hours a day. If you're admitted to one of these hospitals, you probably won't see your GP at all during your stay, as hospital staff are in charge of your case once you're admitted. A clinic (*clinique/kliniek*) is a private hospital with its own staff to provide patient services, but where your GP is usually in charge of your care during your stay. Most doctors are affiliated with at least one or two clinics and may give you a choice if you need to be hospitalised. Which type of hospital you attend will depend on the treatment you're receiving and whether your GP needs to oversee it.

Whichever kind of hospital you go to, you should bring your Belgian identification card or passport as well as your SIS (*Système d'Information Sociale*) card if you're being treated under the public health system or proof of insurance if you belong to a private health insurance scheme. Not all Belgian hospitals accept all insurance plans, so check in advance if you can. You will be asked to pay a deposit when you're admitted, and unless the hospital has an arrangement with your insurance company to bill them directly you will be asked to settle your bill weekly throughout your hospitalisation. Women in Belgium are admitted to hospital under their maiden names, so if you want to visit or contact a woman in hospital, make sure you know what her maiden name is.

Holland: Under the Dutch health care system, patients must pay a fee (known as a 'contribution' toward the cost of care) for each day in hospital. This may be covered by your private insurer. It's important that you notify your private insurer before being admitted to hospital or as soon as possible afterwards if you're hospitalised in an emergency. It's usually possible to have all bills sent directly to the insurance company. Most hospital rooms are shared between two or three patients, with private rooms reserved for cases where a patient needs to be isolated. If you insist on a private room, your hospitalisation may be delayed until one becomes available.

Luxembourg: There are no private hospitals in the Duchy. All hospitals are run by the state *Caisse de Maladie*, and all non-emergency hospital admissions must be arranged by your doctor. There are three classes of service, called first, second and third class. First class means you have a private room and you must usually pay part of the extra cost unless you have premium (i.e. very expensive) private health insurance. Second class, normally a shared room with two or three patients, is the standard service and is covered under most insurance plans in Luxembourg. Third class service consists of a ward, usually containing more than three patients, and is provided only under certain circumstances.

DENTISTS

There are many excellent dentists (*dentistes/tandartsen*) in Belgium, Holland and Luxembourg, and it shouldn't be difficult to find one who speaks English. Consulates, embassies and expatriate organisations can usually provide lists of English-speaking dentists in your area. You're normally free to choose any dentist, but you should check the conditions of your health insurance to see if they restrict reimbursement to dentists who are approved by the insurer or national health system. (In Belgium they may have to be *conventionné* – see page 214.)

Normally, you pay the dentist directly for his services and then submit your receipt for reimbursement. Under the Dutch *ziekenfonds*, with its emphasis on preventative treatment, you may be required to have regular dental check-ups in order to have certain types of 'curative' services covered. (Some private insurers are starting to add this requirement to their dental programmes.) Most major dental work, including crowns and bridges, require pre-approval whereby your dentist must submit a proposal to the insurance company or national health service before you have the work done.

OPTICIANS

If you need spectacles (*lunettes/brillen*), you must find an optician, optometrist or ophthalmologist to test your eyes and give you a prescription for glasses, which you can then have made at an optician's. Eye tests and glasses aren't nearly as well covered under most insurance programmes as other forms of health care, so you should be prepared to pay most or all of the cost of spectacles and contact lenses. Usually, only the doctor's appointment is fully reimbursed. There may be a limited range of spectacle frames that are fully reimbursable under national health care schemes, but sometimes these include only children's frames. There's generally only a nominal reimbursement against the cost of new spectacles when your prescription changes by a certain amount. If you want designer frames or special coatings or treatments for your lenses, you must pay for them yourself unless they're covered by your private health insurance. Contact lenses are usually covered by insurance only when there's a medical reason for choosing them in preference to spectacles, although you may be able to reclaim something against the cost of new lenses if your prescription has changed.

Both spectacles and contact lenses are generally expensive, although a few large French and German optical chain stores have started operating in the Benelux region and prices are slowly coming down in response to the increased competition. Look for Alain Afflelou, Grand Optical (French chain stores) or Fielmann and Apollo Optik (German chains) for the best prices and often same day or even one-hour service on spectacles. You may find it easier (not to mention cheaper) to have your eyes examined and new glasses made in your home country.

DRUGS & MEDICINES

The selling of drugs and medicines of all kinds is strictly regulated throughout the Benelux region, whether you want over-the-counter remedies or need a prescription (*ordonnance/voorschrift*) filled. A chemist or pharmacy (*pharmacie/apotheek*) is often the only place you can buy most kinds of medicines and health care products, including vitamins, contact lens solutions, cold remedies and even aspirin, although this is (slowly) changing. You may also be required to describe your symptoms before you will be sold these items. Note that, if you purchase non-prescription drugs from a chemist, you will pay full price, whereas if your doctor prescribes the same products (even aspirin), your health care insurer will usually reimburse at least a part of the cost.

In many ways, pharmacists have greater responsibility for your health and safety than your doctor in Benelux. If you're made ill (or worse) by taking a combination of medicines purchased from a chemist, the pharmacist can be held responsible for selling you the conflicting potions, even if they were prescribed by your doctor! Doctors cannot phone prescriptions in to a chemist, but pharmacists can process changes to prescriptions based on a telephone conversation with a doctor.

Both prescription and non-prescription items are sold in their original packaging, and the pharmacist normally writes the instructions for using or taking medicines on the box, so don't throw it away until you've finished taking the medicine. (It's sensible to keep the box even after you've finished the medicine, so that you can show it to a doctor or pharmacist if you need more of the same.) Most pharmacists speak at least some English and should explain to you exactly what a medicine is, how to take it, and any side effects to expect or watch out for.

If you're covered by the Dutch *ziekenfonds* or your private insurance requires it, you must designate an approved chemist close to your home as the place where you will have all your prescriptions filled and therefore where your medication records will be kept. Where this is the case, your insurer will give you a list of approved chemists in your area. When you have a prescription filled, you simply show your insurance card and the pharmacist bills the insurer directly. You pay only the patient contribution portion of the cost. Even if you aren't required to use an approved chemist, it's normally wise to select a single pharmacy close to your home to fill all your prescriptions and possibly supply all your medical needs.

Chemists are identified by a large green cross sign, often illuminated. Shops are generally small and carry only a limited selection of non-medical products, usually health and beauty care items. Chemists are generally open during normal shopping hours and in some areas only Mondays to Fridays. Outside these hours, one chemist in a town or region will be on duty and other chemists must display the name and address of the nearest duty chemist whenever they're closed. Local newspapers publish a list of duty chemists at least once a week and, in an emergency, the medical emergency services (see **Emergencies** on page 212) can direct you to a duty chemist at any time of the day or night. There may be a surcharge for medicines you obtain out of hours or from a chemist other than your designated one, and usually only private insurers will reimburse this additional cost.

CHILDBIRTH

The procedure for having a baby delivered in Belgium, Holland or Luxembourg may be rather different from that in your home country, and there are some significant differences between the three countries. Your first decision is whether to use the services of a midwife (*sage-femme/vroedvrouw* or *verloskundige*) or an obstetrician/ gynaecologist (*gynacologue/vrouwenarts*). In either case, your GP or gynaecologist can refer you to the appropriate specialist and explain the differences in treatment. Most of the costs of pregnancy and childbirth are well provided for under all three national health care systems and most private medical insurance, whether or not you're married.

Pre-natal care generally includes up to four or six scans during a normal pregnancy, and after the fifth or sixth month you may be prescribed physiotherapy or some form of exercise programme to prepare you for giving birth and help you get back into shape afterwards. In each of the Benelux countries, there's also a variety of 'support services', including English-language publications, volunteer help groups made up of young mothers and mothers-to-be, expatriate clubs and associations, and local health care agencies.

Another decision you must make is where to have your baby: in hospital, in a special maternity clinic or at home (a common practice, particularly in Holland). There's a general policy in Benelux to make giving birth as 'natural' a process as possible, so you should ask if you have special preferences or requirements. It's best to discuss all the available options with your doctor or midwife well in advance and to make sure that the services you require are available when you need them.

After a baby is born, you must register the birth with the local authorities in the town where the birth took place (not necessarily the town in which you're living) in order to obtain a birth certificate. Deadlines for registration vary by country (see below), although similar documents are required in all three. These include the record of the birth from the hospital, doctor or midwife, the local identification cards and/or passports of both parents and the parents' marriage certificate, if they're married. Generally you will be given two or three copies of the birth certificate and you may wish to obtain additional copies to send to insurance companies, government agencies, etc.

You will also have to notify your consulate or embassy of the birth and to register your baby as a citizen of your home country (if applicable). Children born in Benelux take their nationality from one or both of their parents, so only babies with at least one Benelux parent are automatically local citizens. It's usually advised to apply for a child's passport at the same time as you register the birth. This not only saves you having to do it later, when you want to take the baby home to show off to friends and family, but also avoids the difficulties that can arise when a child is put on one of his parents' passports and then travels with the other parent (or alone when older). Don't forget to register for birth and family allowances for your new family member. Everyone covered by a national social security scheme is entitled to benefit on the birth of a child, as well as a monthly benefit for a period thereafter (see page 229).

Belgium: The Community Help Service publishes a booklet in English called *Having a Baby in Belgium*, which contains information on pregnancy, giving birth and hospitalisation. Most babies are born in hospital and if there are no complications mother and baby are released around a week later. In some parts of Flemish-speaking Belgium (e.g. Leuven) you may be entitled to the services of a *kraamverzorgster* (see **Holland** below), normally through a local medical service agency. Births must be registered within 15 days at the town hall of the commune where the baby was born, and you can be fined for failing to meet this deadline. In Belgium, it's recommended that you obtain as many as a dozen copies of the birth registration certificate, particularly if you're on the national social security system and wish to obtain birth and family allowances. (Perhaps this is also Belgium's method of preparing children for the local bureaucracy!)

Holland: Most babies in Holland are born at home, and if you want to have your baby born in hospital you must ask a gynaecologist to arrange for a maternity bed in a hospital. Even hospital births in Holland take place in an outpatient facility (*polikliniek*), where mother and baby are normally discharged within a few hours of the birth. Births must be registered within three days, although a nurse or home care assistant (see below) may do this for you.

Wherever you choose to have your baby, you should register with a medical service association, often called a cross association or home care organisation (*kruisvereniging* or *thuiszorg*) early in your pregnancy. These organisations provide pre-natal exercise classes, general information and even instruction on child care, for a small monthly membership fee. Members of a cross association are also entitled to the services of a home care assistant (*kraamverzorgster*) during the first week after the birth, provided you enrolled in the association during the first three months of your pregnancy. The assistant will make sure that both you and the baby are well and carry out small chores, errands and housework for you. You can also make use of a cross association during the first few months for 'well baby' services and check-ups, including most immunisations, which is considerably cheaper than employing a private paediatrician.

Luxembourg: Babies are usually born in hospital in Luxembourg. In Luxembourg city, expectant mothers are normally referred to either the Maternité Grand Duchess Charlotte or the Clinique Dr Bohler. Obstetricians provide exercise classes, both pre-natal and post-natal, which are a good opportunity to meet other expectant mothers. You normally stay in hospital around five days for a delivery without complications, ten days for a caesarean section delivery. In hospital you're given a *carnet de santé,* a record book for keeping track of your baby's immunisations and check-ups, and a *demande d'une allocation postnatale* (to register for your social security payment).

All births must be registered within five days at the local town hall, and you must take your baby to a paediatrician between five and ten days after birth for a general check-up, which will be recorded in the *carnet de santé*. A curious aspect of giving birth in Luxembourg is that each commune maintains a list of approved babies' names, and you must choose a name from this list unless you can produce a statement from your consulate or embassy declaring that the name you want to use is 'acceptable' in your home country. Most consulates are happy to provide this assurance, unless you want to name your baby something outrageous.

COUNSELLING & SOCIAL SERVICES

Counselling and general welfare assistance are widely available in all three Benelux countries. In all major cities and many larger towns you can find social service organisations dealing with problems such as alcoholism (Alcoholics Anonymous or Al-Anon), drug addiction, compulsive gambling, marriage and relationship problems, as well as support groups for cancer patients, AIDS victims and their families and those with emotional or mental problems. There's a variety of phone lines for those in crisis situations, e.g. contemplating suicide, and there are special centres for women and children suffering abuse. These are listed in the Yellow Pages (and often at the front of the telephone directory, along with other emergency numbers). Your GP can normally refer you to relevant professionals, and many insurance companies have lists of specialised services fully or partially covered under health care or other plans.

Most local service centres have English-speaking staff, but there are also specialised services available in some areas for the English-speaking community and expatriates who may be unfamiliar with local services and agencies. Expatriate organisations and clubs often have lists of counselling and social service agencies with English-speaking staff, and some consulates and embassies may also provide lists of social services and crisis telephone numbers. Many of the larger expatriate clubs (particularly American Women's Clubs) have sub-groups that offer counselling or support for a variety of problems and concerns. Details of AWCs can be found on the Federation of American Women's Clubs website (🖳 www.fawco.org).

Belgium: Community Help Services (☎ 02-648 4014) is a volunteer organisation that offers a 24-hour crisis and information line for English-speakers in Belgium.

Holland: ACCESS (☎ 070-346 2525 during the afternoon and early evening only) is an all-purpose counselling and referral agency for English-speakers in Holland. SOS Help Line, run by the *Stichting Algemene Christelijke Hulpdienst*, is available 24 hours a day and most of their volunteers speak English. SOS Help Line phone numbers are listed in all telephone directories. In addition, the various cross associations (see **Childbirth** above) in larger cities and towns provide a variety of medical and social services and can refer members to other support groups. Monthly membership fees are reasonable, considering the variety of services on offer.

Luxembourg: Most social service organisations in Luxembourg are reachable through either the Ministry of Health or the Ministry of the Family. Just call the central government switchboard at 4781 and ask for the ministry you need. Social service and support groups are listed in the telephone directory, or contact the American Women's Club of Luxembourg (or their 'Living in Luxembourg' publication) for a complete list or services and contacts.

DEATHS

All deaths in Benelux must be certified by a doctor. If a death occurs in hospital, the hospital staff will usually handle most of the official paperwork, but if it occurs at home or elsewhere you must first contact a doctor, who will issue a death certificate. All deaths must be registered within 24 hours at the town hall (*mairie/gemeentehuis*) of the commune where the death occurred. You should take the local identification card and passport of the deceased along with the death certificate issued by the doctor. Make sure you obtain several copies of the death registration document, as they will be needed in the administrative procedures (especially in Belgium, where you should probably obtain at least 12 copies). If the deceased is a foreign national, youmust also notify the embassy or consulate of their home country. In fact, the embassy can often help you with funeral arrangements or shipping a body abroad.

Anyone resident in a Benelux country for more than six months is assumed to be an organ donor. If you or a member of your family objects to the possible donation of his organs after death, you will need to contact a notary to formally declare your objection and register it with the authorities. **If no such declaration by the deceased is on file at the time of death, the family cannot object to a hospital removing organs for research or transplant.**

Funeral customs vary by region, but bodies are often laid out for viewing at home so that friends and neighbours can pay their respects to the family. Burial is usually in the town cemetery, and cemetery plots can be leased from the local commune for a period of two to 50 years, after which time the remains are removed to a common grave. Cremation is an alternative, although there are strict regulations regarding the storage, scattering, and shipment of ashes.

Should you decide to ship the body home, ensure that you consult your home country's consulate or embassy. This is an expensive and strictly regulated procedure, and you may need additional documents from both your doctor and the undertaker, including reports on the cause of death and certification of the treatment of the body for shipment.

Euthanasia: Holland became the first nation to legalise euthanasia in 2001, although Dutch doctors had been participating in 'assisted suicides' for some time. The legal guidelines for euthanasia are strict: the idea of terminating a life must come from the patient; a doctor must be convinced that the patient is suffering intolerable physical pain, is mentally competent to make such a decision and has been advised of all possible alternatives; a second doctor must examine the patient and concur with the first doctor's conclusions. An inquest is held after the death to ensure that all necessary evaluations were properly made and that there's no cause for legal action. Dutch officials insist that terminally ill foreigners aren't able to come to Holland 'simply' to end their lives, as the guidelines require there to be a 'close and long-term' relationship between doctor and patient before a decision can be made to resort to euthanasia. A similar law was passed in Belgium in October 2001.

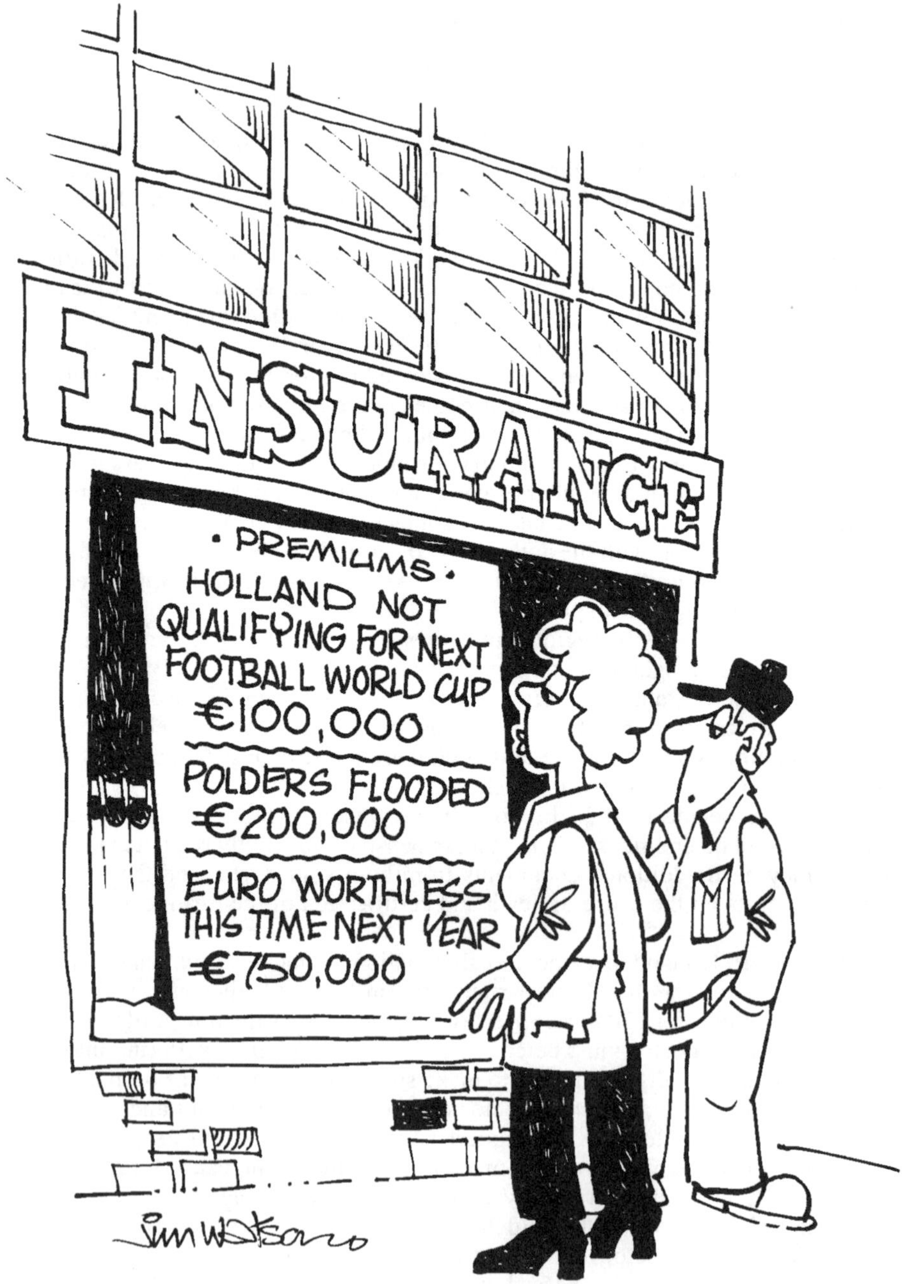
INSURANCE
• PREMIUMS •
HOLLAND NOT QUALIFYING FOR NEXT FOOTBALL WORLD CUP
€100,000
POLDERS FLOODED
€200,000
EURO WORTHLESS THIS TIME NEXT YEAR
€750,000
Jim Watson

13.

INSURANCE

The governments of Belgium, Holland and Luxembourg provide various state insurance schemes as well as requiring employers to contribute to employees' insurance. Although details vary across the three countries, national insurance generally covers sickness and maternity, work injuries, disability and unemployment and provides basic and supplementary pensions. Most employees and their families receive free health treatment under a national social security system and enjoy additional protection and benefits that are among the best in the European Union (EU). Cover isn't cheap, however, and national insurance contributions amount to between 29 and 38 per cent of salary, each government spending over 30 per cent of GDP on 'welfare'. Despite the high level of social security cover in all three countries, it's unwise to rely solely on state insurance, which in most cases doesn't cover all medical costs or provide generous pensions or other benefits.

You should ensure that your family has full health insurance during the interval between leaving your last country of residence and obtaining insurance in Benelux. One way is to take out a travel insurance policy, but it's usually better to amend your current health insurance policy (most policies can be extended to provide international cover where this isn't included in the basic policy). This is particularly important if you have an existing health problem that won't be covered by a new policy.

As in many other countries, there are certain kinds of insurance that are compulsory in Benelux, including health insurance (whether state or private – see page 234) and third party liability car insurance (see page 195). Third party liability insurance for tenants and homeowners is also recommended, particularly in Belgium and Holland, (see page 242), and life assurance may be required if you have a mortgage (see page 256). If you lease a car or buy one on credit, a lender will normally insist that you have comprehensive car insurance. Benelux law is likely to differ from that in your home country or your previous country of residence, so never assume that it's the same, and **note that it's your responsibility to ensure that you and your family are legally insured.** Voluntary insurance includes supplementary pensions, disability, health, household, dental, travel, car breakdown and life insurance.

It's unnecessary to spend half your income insuring yourself against every eventuality from the common cold to being sued for your last euro, but it's important to insure against events that could precipitate a major financial disaster, such as a serious accident or your house falling down. As with anything connected with finance, it's important to shop around when buying insurance. Simply collecting a few brochures from insurance agents, making a few telephone calls, or surfing the Internet for a few minutes could save you a lot of money. Regrettably, you cannot insure yourself against being uninsured (nor sue an insurance agent for giving you bad advice).

Bear in mind that if you wish to make a claim against an insurance policy, you may be required to report an incident to the police within 24 or 48 hours (in some cases this may be a legal requirement). Obtain legal advice for anything other than a minor claim.

For details of car insurance, see page 195.

INSURANCE COMPANIES & AGENTS

Luxembourg is one of Europe's 'insurance capitals' and there's a plethora of insurance companies to choose from, most offering a complete range of insurance services. Besides the 200 plus banks, 1,200 investment funds and over 340 insurance companies based in Luxembourg, there are subsidiary offices and holding companies of many international insurance organisations. The major insurance companies also have offices or agencies throughout Belgium and Holland. Some of the larger and better known companies are AXA, Dexia, Swiss Life, Winterthur and Zurich, but there are plenty of others.

In most cities and towns you can also find many independent insurance agents and brokers (*agence indépendante/makelaar*) who 'represent' several insurance companies and allow you to compare a number of different policies. There are also a number of independent insurance consultants (*conseils d'assurance/verzekeringsadviseur*) who will (for a fee) advise you on your insurance requirements in addition to finding you the best policies and rates. Unlike many brokers, consultants don't represent insurance companies or accept commissions from them. However, be sure to ask about charges before you engage an insurance consultant. Most banks sell insurance as part of their financial advisory services, which are usually free of charge to customers. It's also possible to purchase most kinds of insurance over the Internet, and a number of independent sites run by the insurance industry allow you to make comparisons between products. Sites are listed in online telephone directories (see page 118), as are insurance companies, brokers, agents and consultants, which are also listed in telephone books under *Assurances/Verzekeringsensmaatschappijen*.

When buying any form of insurance, consult friends and neighbours and be sure to compare not only prices, but cover, terms, benefits and any tax implications before you decide on a policy. Since mid-1994, the European insurance market has theoretically been open to permit insurers to offer cross-border policies. This means that if you're coming from another EU country, you may be able to retain many of your existing insurance policies (particularly life assurance and private pensions). Before you leave, check with your insurance company whether you're covered in Benelux and whether cover is adequate or can be adapted to meet local requirements. (Note that many car insurance companies won't insure you if you're living abroad – see page 195).

INSURANCE CONTRACTS

Read all insurance contracts carefully before signing them. If you cannot get an English version and you don't understand everything, ask a friend or colleague to translate it or take legal advice. Like insurance companies everywhere, some Benelux companies will do almost anything to avoid paying out in the event of a claim and will use any available legal loophole. It therefore pays to deal only with reputable companies (not that this provides any guarantee). Terms and cover can be difficult to compare, as insurers now offer a whole range of excesses (deductibles), co-payments, special conditions and exclusions on what used to be standard policies.

Always check the notice period required to cancel (*résilier/annuleren*) a policy. In Benelux, most insurance policies will automatically be extended (usually for a year at a time) if they aren't cancelled in writing by registered letter two or three months before the expiry date. If you don't pay, you can be sued for the whole premium plus the credit agency's fees and interest. In most cases, your insurance broker or consultant can provide you with a standard cancellation letter. You can generally cancel an insurance policy before the term has expired if the premium is increased, the terms are altered, or an insured object is lost or stolen. This must also be done in writing, however, and usually by registered letter. Cancellation is also permitted at short notice under certain circumstances, including changing jobs, redundancy, retirement, marriage, divorce and death.

If you wish to make a claim, you must usually inform your insurance company in writing by registered letter within two to five days of an accident or within two to four days in the case of theft. Thefts must also be reported to the police before making a claim, as a police report usually constitutes irrefutable evidence of your claim. For some claims you may be required to obtain two or three estimates for repairs (e.g. to your home or car) before having work approved.

SOCIAL SECURITY & HEALTH INSURANCE

Belgium, Holland and Luxembourg each have comprehensive systems of social security, which apply to all residents. These cover family benefits, unemployment insurance, work accident insurance, health care, old age and invalidity pensions, and long-term care insurance. All three nations take great pride in their benefits systems and the quality of their social security services, although the high cost of providing those services and benefits (employer contributions of up to 40 per cent plus employee contributions of up to 20 per cent of gross pay) has recently prompted all three governments to consider changes to their social security systems in an attempt to encourage individuals to assume greater responsibility for the costs of retirement, disability and even health care. There were major reforms to Dutch social security in the '80s and it's likely that more changes are on the way, particularly in the area of supplementary pensions.

Eligibility

All employees and self-employed people in Benelux are automatically enrolled in their respective state social security system. Foreigners taking up residence and employment in Benelux are normally enrolled in the social security system by their employers, who will obtain a social security number (a SoFi number in Holland) and card, which is required for claiming benefits. Social security benefits extend in most cases to family members, i.e. spouse, children and other dependent family members in the household. Even non-family members, e.g. an au pair, can be covered under certain circumstances. Special rules apply to students, trainees and apprentices if they aren't included in their parents' cover. Those drawing wage replacement benefits (unemployment, disability or old age pensions) continue to be covered by social security. The benefits authority makes the 'employer' contributions, and the 'employee' contributions are deducted from the benefits you receive.

Social security agreements exist between the Benelux countries and many other nations, including all EU countries and the USA, whereby expatriates may remain under their home country's social security scheme for a period. If you qualify for 'non-resident' tax status (see page 261), you may be able to continue making social security contributions in your home country while working temporarily (i.e. for up to five years) in Benelux. EU nationals must obtain forms E101 and E111 from their home country. Americans should be aware that US social security agreements cover pensions only, and that medical and some survivor benefits (particularly Medicare) aren't payable to those living outside the USA.

If you or your spouse work in Benelux but are insured through the social security system of another EU country, you can claim social security benefits from that country. If you wish to claim benefits in Benelux, your contributions to the foreign scheme are taken into account when calculating your eligibility. Contact your country's social security administration for information. In Britain, information is provided by the Department for Works and Pensions (formerly the Department of Social Security, 🖥 www.dss.gov.uk/dfwp). An information guide entitled *Your Social Security Rights When Moving Within the EU* is available on the European Union website (🖥 http://europa.eu.int/comm/employment_social/fundamri/movement/ guide_en.htm).

Contributions

Most social security contributions are divided between you and your employer and are calculated as a percentage of your gross income, usually up to a certain salary level. In each country some social security contributions are collected through the income tax system.

Belgium: In Belgium, 13.07 per cent of employees' salary is withheld and a further 25 to 30 per cent of salary contributed by employers. The 3 per cent 'crisis surcharge' (see page 269) also contributes to social security funding.

Holland: Dutch tax rates for the two lowest income brackets (up to annual earnings of €27,009) include a social security contribution of 29.4 per cent. This means that certain non-salary income is also subject to a social security deduction. If you're aged over 65, your social security contribution is reduced to 11.5 per cent in recognition of the fact that older taxpayers aren't eligible for certain social security benefits.

Luxembourg: In Luxembourg, the 2.5 per cent 'solidarity surcharge' levied on your net taxable income (see page 263) goes towards unemployment benefits, in addition to an overall social security contribution of around 31 per cent of the first €7,000 of an employee's gross income (11 per cent deducted from salary and the remainder contributed by the employer and the government).

Family Benefits

All three countries pay benefits to families with children, including a birth payment, regular child benefit payments up to the age of 18 or beyond, and supplementary benefits according to the children's ages and for handicapped children. After health care, family benefits are one of the largest social security costs, but all three governments appear to be committed to maintaining them. There are no means tests for most child benefits, and all families, including immigrants, are eligible to receive payments provided they meet certain residence requirements.

Belgium: In Belgium, family benefits are funded entirely by employers at a rate of 7 per cent of employees' gross salary. Benefits are paid to the mother or guardian of each child born and being raised in Belgium. Children or families living temporarily outside Belgium may also be eligible for Belgian child allowance. There are five categories of family benefit:

- **Birth or maternity benefit** is a flat amount, currently around €920 for the first child and slightly more for each additional child. (If you have twins, you can claim double the first child benefit.) Parents may apply for and receive the birth benefit any time after the sixth month of pregnancy.

- **Adoption benefit** is paid at the same rate as birth benefit, but always at the first child rate irrespective of the child's 'rank'.

- **Ordinary family benefit** (also known as child allowance) is a monthly benefit for each child living at home, currently around €68 per month for the first child, €125 for the second child and €187 for the third and each subsequent child. (When the oldest child leaves home, the remaining children are 'demoted' and their monthly benefit reduced accordingly.) Benefits may be continued up to age 25 for apprentices, students and recent graduates who haven't found a job but aren't yet eligible for unemployment benefit (see below).

- **Orphan's allowance**, currently around €260 per month, is paid to children who have lost one or both parents instead of ordinary family benefit. Where one parent has died, the family is eligible for orphan's allowance provided the surviving parent has no new partner living in the household.

- **Supplementary allowances** are amounts added to ordinary family benefits each month in recognition of certain family circumstances. There are age allowances for children in certain age groups (6 to 12, 12 to 18, and over 18) related to the costs of providing for children of different ages, and social allowances are added to individual benefits where a parent or guardian is retired, unemployed or disabled. Various other supplements are added to child allowances where a child is handicapped, depending on the nature and extent of the handicap.

Holland: Family benefits are often referred to as AKW for *algemene kinderbijslagwet*, the title of the legislation that covers this category of benefit. There's no birth benefit, but self-employed women are entitled to payments during their statutory 16 weeks' maternity leave. (Employed women are entitled to paid leave.) Parents are eligible for a quarterly payment for each child under the age of 18, provided they're legally responsible for the child and the child doesn't have significant income from employment or other sources (e.g. unemployment benefit or student financing).

Handicapped children are eligible for a separate benefit depending upon the nature and extent of their disability; those qualifying for high payments may not be eligible for general child allowance. The Dutch government has made frequent reductions in handicap benefits in recent years, and there's currently a two-tier system of benefits: one applies to children born before 1st January 1995 and the other to those born after this date. Under the first system, quarterly benefits range from €203 for a first child aged 6 to 11 to €360 for a tenth child aged 12 to 17. Under the new system, benefits start at €167 per month for children under the age of six and increase to €203 for children aged six and over, irrespective of their 'rank'. All benefits are adjusted annually for inflation.

Luxembourg: The *Caisse Nationale de Prestations Familiales* (CNPF) in Luxembourg pays family benefits to around 90,000 families. As in Belgium, there's a birth benefit (*allocation de naissance*), which totals €1,576 and is paid in three equal stages: one after the mother-to-be has completed the requisite pre-natal tests, the second after the new-born baby has undergone the required examinations and the third on the child's second birthday. There's also a monthly benefit for each dependent child, irrespective of whether they live at home (e.g. even if they're at boarding school). A family with one child receives a basic allowance of €145 per month, which is increased for each additional child, e.g. €653 for three children and €3,380 for a family with 12 children. (Yes, Luxembourg benefit tables allow for families that large!) Once a child reaches the age of six, his allowance is increased by €14.65 per month and from the age of 12 he's entitled to a further €29.31 per month.

In addition to these allowances, there's a 'back to school' benefit (*allocation de rentrée scolaire*), intended to cover the cost of school equipment and clothing, which is paid each August for each child attending school or college. The benefit ranges from around €100 to €300 per child, depending on the child's age and the number of students in the family. All children up to the age of 18 qualify for child benefits; if they continue to study, they're eligible for benefits until the age of 27. Handicapped children receive family benefits for as long as they're dependent upon their parents (i.e. earn less than a certain amount).

Foreigners living legally in the Duchy are eligible for family benefits the month after their arrival if they're from another EU country or one with which Luxembourg has a family benefits treaty. Those from outside the EU must generally wait six months before being eligible for family benefits, although this waiting period is waived if either parent is legally working in Luxembourg. Family benefits aren't subject to income tax or social security contributions. You should apply for family benefits at your town hall.

Unemployment Benefit

Unemployment insurance is mandatory for all employees in Benelux. In Belgium and Holland contributions are shared between employers and employees, whereas in Luxembourg all taxpayers contribute to the unemployment insurance programme through an income tax surcharge (see page 271). Unemployment benefits are paid only when you become unemployed involuntarily, e.g. if you're made redundant, and not when you quit your job voluntarily. If you're sacked, you may still be eligible for unemployment benefit after a certain period. To qualify for benefit, you must be fit and available for work (which usually means you must enrol with the national employment office), and register with your local benefits office on a regular basis.

If you're an EU citizen and move from a Benelux country to another EU country to seek employment, you may be entitled to up to three months' unemployment benefit from the country you've left. To qualify, you must notify the benefits office of your move and register with the unemployment office in your new country within seven days of your arrival. Further information is available on the EU website (⌨ http://europa.eu.int/business/en/legal/index.html).

Belgium: Unemployment benefits in Belgium are subject to complicated requirements and restrictions (no surprise!), depending on your age, work experience and family situation. You must have worked for a total of at least 312 days in the 18 months prior to losing your job if you're under the age of 36, 468 days in the last 27 months if you're 36 to 50, and 624 days in the last 36 months if you're aged over 50. There are special benefits for those over the age of 50 who take part in early retirement schemes, and all unemployment benefits cease when you reach the legal retirement age of 65.

To apply for benefits, you can go to one of the many trade union-run unemployment agencies (even if you aren't a union member) or to the state-run Auxiliary Fund for Payment of Unemployment Benefits (*Caisse auxiliaire de Paiement des Allocations de Chômage/Hulpkas voor Werkloosheidsuitkeringen*), and you're free to change agencies at any time. Benefits normally start immediately unless you're receiving a redundancy payment or compensation from your previous employer. If you were sacked, you must wait 4 to 26 weeks before receiving unemployment benefit, and young people who have just left school must also wait several months, although they're still eligible for child benefit during the waiting period (see above).

You must register with the state employment service (VDAB in Flemish-speaking areas, FOREM in Walloon or BGDA/ORBEM in the Brussels region) and go to the unemployment agency twice a month to 'discuss' your job hunting progress (i.e. to show that you're making an effort to find work). While receiving unemployment benefit, you aren't permitted to work, and this means any activity that might bring a material advantage to you or your family, including home improvements! If you have a secondary profession, you may resort to this only if you were practising it at some time during the three months prior to losing your principal job and had declared it for tax purposes. Even then, you aren't allowed to engage in this profession between 7am and 6pm, as this is when you're supposed to be looking for a job in your main line of work!

The amount of unemployment benefit you receive depends on your family status. If you're single or have a family which is dependent on your earnings, you're entitled to 60 per cent of your previous salary. If your spouse or partner has income, you may claim only 55 per cent. After one year, single claimants are reduced to 42 per cent of previous earnings, whereas those with dependants and no other wage earner in the family continue to receive 60 per cent benefit, in both cases for as long as they're unemployed (provided you continue to meet other criteria). If your spouse or partner is earning, your benefit is reduced to 35 per cent of your previous salary after one year, and this reduced amount is paid for three months only, plus an additional three months for each year you had been in work before you became unemployed. After that period, your benefit is further reduced to around €13 per day (to encourage you to get a job!).

Holland: Unemployment benefit is referred to as WW for *Werskloosheidswet*, the name of Dutch unemployment legislation. To be eligible for benefit, you must have worked for at least 26 weeks within the last 12 months or at least 52 days per year in four of the last five years. To apply for benefit, you must first register with the employment service (*Arbeidsbureau*), which will help you to find a job. You must then take proof of registration to the unemployment association to which your former employer belongs. Your health and other benefits are continued while you're unemployed, and you must notify the benefits agency if you fall ill while receiving unemployment benefit. (The Dutch government's success in reducing unemployment rates over the past decade has been at least partly attributed to their eagerness to transfer those on unemployment benefit to invalidity pensions and benefits!)

The basic unemployment benefit is 70 per cent of your salary immediately prior to losing your job. This continues for between six months and four and a half years, depending on your age, the type of work you were doing, and how long you had worked before becoming unemployed. Under most circumstances you can continue to receive benefit for up to two more years, but this is limited to 70 per cent of the statutory minimum wage for your profession and age. As in Belgium, unemployment benefit ceases when you reach the age of 65.

Luxembourg: Under the Luxembourg system, you're supposed to register with the local employment authority (i.e. to find work) the day you become unemployed. You must then submit an application for unemployment benefit to the *Administration de l'Emploi* within two weeks. You must have been employed for at least 26 weeks during the last 12 months. There's also a benefit available for partial unemployment, i.e. where your working hours are significantly reduced as a result of a company reorganisation or a decrease in production. Benefit starts the day you become unemployed, provided you submit your application within two weeks. If you apply late, benefit is backdated 14 days before your application. Young people who have completed vocational training are eligible for unemployment benefit at a special rate, according to their age, the school-leaving or technical certificates they've received, and the statutory minimum wage applicable.

Normal unemployment benefit is 85 per cent of your gross salary in the three months immediately preceding unemployment if you have dependants, or 80 per cent if you don't. If your spouse earns more than a certain amount, your benefit is reduced accordingly. The maximum duration for unemployment benefit is 365 days in a 24 month period (to encourage you to find part-time work), but this can be extended by up to 182 days, depending on a number of factors related to your expected chance of finding a job, e.g. your age, profession and family situation. Those over the age of 50 can further extend the benefit period by up to 12 months if they have a certain number of credits toward a pension plan.

Work Accident Insurance

Work accident insurance pays all medical and rehabilitation costs associated with an injury or illness caused by your job or an accident on your way to or from work. If you die from a job-related injury or illness, your survivors receive a funeral allowance and pension benefits. Work accident insurance contributions are paid entirely by employers, according to their health and safety record and that of the industry or profession in which they're engaged. The scheme requires employers to monitor and improve health and safety conditions in the workplace. If you're self-employed, you aren't legally required to have work accident insurance, but you can obtain cover through the state system or take out a private insurance policy.

If you suffer an injury at work or on the way to or from work, you must immediately notify your employer, who's responsible for filing a claim with his insurance company. If you're unable to work as a result of an injury or illness covered by insurance, your wages will be paid after your contractual period of sick pay (see **Salary Insurance** on page 51). Under most schemes, you continue to receive full wages until you can start work again. If you're unable to resume your previous job as a result of the injury or illness, the insurance company will assess your level of disability and pay a benefit relative to the extent to which your work capacity has been reduced. Statutory work accident insurance provides benefits regardless of whose fault the injury or illness was and exempts your employer from liability (no US-style lawsuits in Benelux!).

Health Insurance

Health insurance is mandatory in all three countries, and basic cover is generally provided by the national social security systems. Contributions are paid by both employers and employees, and most forms of public assistance (unemployment benefit, old age pensions, certain forms of sickness and maternity benefits) are paid net of withholdings for health insurance, the benefit authority effectively paying the employer contributions.

Foreigners coming to live in Benelux without working (e.g. retirees and the 'idle' rich) must generally produce proof of health insurance in order to obtain a residence permit. There are special health insurance plans, valid in a number of countries, designed specifically for the needs of expatriates and those who travel frequently. If you qualify for 'non-resident' tax status (see page 261), you may not be required to contribute to national social security, in which case you will probably be covered by your employer's health care plan. (You should check!)

Belgium: All employees and self-employed people in Belgium must contribute to a health insurance fund (*mutuelle* or *mutualité/ziekenfonds* or *ziekenkas*) as part of the normal social security enrolment process. Some funds are restricted to members of various religious, political or professional organisations for historic reasons, but most are open to all. Your employer should be able to provide you with information about available funds, and you should ask neighbours or colleagues for recommendations. All funds charge the same basic contribution and pay similar benefits, but some take longer than others to make reimbursements. Health insurance contributions are made by your employer directly to your chosen fund. These amount to 7.35 per cent of your gross salary, of which 3.55 per cent is withheld from your pay and the remaining 3.8 per cent contributed by your employer. If you're self-employed, you contribute the full 7.35 per cent through your quarterly social security payments. Cover is automatically provided for dependent family members, including spouses (if they don't have their own cover) and children up to the age of 18.

When you enrol in a Belgian health fund, there's a six-month waiting period before you can claim benefits. This waiting period can be waived if you were previously included for at least six months in another person's health cover (i.e. as a dependant) or, in many cases, if you were covered by a state health care plan (or the equivalent) in another EU country for at least six months before your arrival in Belgium. For most medical services, you must pay the bill and then submit the receipt for reimbursement. Reimbursements are usually less than the charges incurred, and most Belgians take out supplementary health insurance to cover the unreimbursed portion or to upgrade their cover from the statutory level. Many employers provide supplementary health insurance cover as an employment benefit, or you can purchase individual cover. Supplementary health insurance is also available to self-employed people through professional associations and private insurers.

In typical Belgian fashion, the exact nature of what is and isn't covered by the state system is rather complicated. Services rendered by most doctors and specialists, hospitalisation, prescriptions, pregnancy and childbirth, rehabilitation and other forms of therapy are normally covered, although the self-employed are covered only for 'major risks', which include mental illness, tuberculosis, cancer, hereditary diseases and birth defects, most types of surgery and childbirth. There are no fewer than 18 categories of medical procedure and service, each with its own reimbursement level, varying from 0 to 100 per cent (although the number of items qualifying for 100 per cent reimbursement is constantly diminishing because of funding problems). There are also certain 'preferred' categories of people who are entitled to a higher level of reimbursement for many items, including widows, orphans and those receiving certain forms of public aid (e.g. the blind). A standard doctor's appointment, for example, is normally reimbursed at 75 per cent, whereas those in a preferred category may be reimbursed at 85 or 90 per cent, depending on their circumstances.

It's wise to keep copies of all receipts and any other documents you send to your health insurance fund in case anything is lost. Rather than sending each receipt separately, it's often better to collect all receipts for a given illness or accident or all receipts during a three or six-month period before submitting them for reimbursement. If you have supplementary insurance, your health fund usually forwards information to your private insurer, and both insurers normally pay reimbursements directly into your bank account.

If you're hospitalised, you must usually pay a fixed daily accommodation fee, either in advance or when you're discharged, but the hospital normally sends all other bills directly to your health insurance fund. In the case of prescriptions, if you take most of them to the same chemist, it's usually possible to register with him so that he bills your health insurance fund directly. In this way you pay only the unreimbursed portion of the prescription fees, as well as saving yourself the headache of keeping track of your payments. Prescriptions are subject to a particularly complex scale of reimbursement percentages, according to the 'social and medical usefulness' of each medicine and whether it's available 'off the shelf' or must be made up by a chemist. Certain types of medicines have maximum patient contribution levels, where 100 per cent of charges are reimbursed after a certain period.

Holland: Health insurance in Holland is provided through a combination of public and private programmes. All Dutch residents are automatically covered for certain kinds of otherwise uninsurable (in Holland) medical care through the Exceptional Medical Expenses Act (*Algemene Wet Bijzondere Ziektekosten*, usually referred to as the AWBZ). This cover is paid for by a 29.4 per cent social security levy on all taxable income up to €27,009 and includes nursing home or extended care facilities, many home care costs, rehabilitation or therapy for those with physical or mental disabilities, psychiatric and mental health care and treatment, preventive health care (including children's vaccinations), dietary advice and physiotherapy. You may be required to contribute to certain services, depending on your household income.

Enrolment in the statutory health insurance scheme (*wettelijke ziekenfondsverzekering*, known simply as *ziekenfonds* or 'sickness funds'), is mandatory for all employees earning less than €27,009 per year and for all self-employed people with less than around €18,700 of annual taxable income. (These figures are indexed each year for inflation.) You must enrol for *ziekenfonds* cover within 60 days of starting work and may choose between a number of insurers offering this type of cover. Your employer will be asked to confirm the extent of cover you're eligible for (i.e. your salary) and is responsible for deducting the appropriate contribution from your pay and remitting it to the insurer. Contributions consist of a fixed fee (set by the insurer), averaging around €12 per month, plus a percentage of your income, currently 8.1 per cent of the first €27,009 of your gross salary. You and your employer share the percentage-based portion of the cost, although the split is determined by your employer, whereas you pay the whole of the fixed portion. Self-employed people pay the entire contribution (fixed fee and percentage) as part of their quarterly estimated tax payments.

Once your application for *ziekenfonds* is accepted, you're sent a registration card, which you use to obtain health care services covered under the programme. You must register with a doctor, usually a general practitioner (GP), who acts as 'co-ordinator' of your health care, referring you to specialists, clinics, hospitals and for various testing and ancillary services as required. *Ziekenfonds* cover most normal medical care and treatment, including doctor's appointments (both GPs and most specialists, although a referral from your GP may be required), hospitalisation up to 365 days, medical devices (purchase or rental for temporary use), obstetric services (although most Dutch women give birth at home with a midwife in attendance unless hospitalisation is advised – see page 220), transport to hospital and prescriptions (limited to the cost of generic medicines, where available). Dental care is covered for children up to the age of 18, including fluoride applications twice a year and orthodontia. For adults, cover of dental services is limited to 'preventive maintenance' and, provided you have at least an annual check-up, X-rays and certain kinds of surgery.

Most services are provided free, although some (notably prescriptions) require a non-reimbursable patient contribution or co-payment, usually a flat fee of €2 to €5. *Ziekenfonds* also provide cover, in the form of reimbursement, for medical treatment you receive outside Holland, and in some cases repatriation costs. If the insured person is the main wage earner (providing at least half of the household income), all dependent household members under the age of 65 are covered by *ziekenfonds*, including partners and children, unless they have their own health insurance.

All *ziekenfonds* make supplementary cover (*aanvullende verzekering*) available to their members, sometimes at two or more levels (and prices). Supplementary cover is optional, but can include alternative medicine (osteopathy, acupuncture, chiropractic or homeopathic treatment), eye care (spectacles and contact lenses), extended dental coverage and upgraded hospitalisation (i.e. a private or semi-private room instead of a bed in a ward) and other benefits not included in the statutory plan. The cost is normally €5 to €10 per month for each person insured (e.g. your spouse, children or other dependants), and payments are usually made through payroll deduction.

Around 70 per cent of the Dutch population are members of *ziekenfonds* or some other public health scheme (usually in the process of being phased out). The remaining 30 per cent are covered by private insurance, which is mandatory for all residents earning more than €27,009 per year. Many employers provide private health insurance as a benefit of employment for all employees earning over the *ziekenfonds* limit, although some employers share the cost with employees or require them to pay for dependant cover.

There's an almost infinite variety of private health insurance plans in Holland (in terms of both conditions and cost), but the government has defined a standard policy that must be made available by all private insurers at a standard price to any resident who is ineligible for *ziekenfonds* cover. The cost of the standard insurance policy is €125.29 per month per person. Children under the age of 18 and full-time students under the age of 27 can be added to a parent's policy for half the basic per person cost. Insurers may charge more if they provide services or benefits in addition to those required by law. The basic level of cover is the same as for the *ziekenfonds* plan, although patient contributions for certain procedures are allowed. You may be asked, for example, to pay €1 or €2 towards each doctor's appointment, or €5 towards a laboratory test or operation.

Officially, you're supposed to pay for services and then send the receipts to your insurance company for reimbursement. In practice, however, many hospitals, chemists, clinics, laboratories, and even doctors will bill your insurance company directly, requiring you to pay only the patient contribution. Under most private insurance schemes (including the standard plan), you can be reimbursed only for certain types of specialist treatment if you were referred by your GP, dentist or other specialist. Medical treatment received abroad is covered up to certain limits (which vary by country), although you won't be reimbursed if the insurance company can prove that you went abroad specifically to obtain treatment. Normally, Dutch health insurance covers foreign treatment only until you can be returned to Holland for local treatment (at Dutch approved rates!).

If you're privately insured and under the age of 65, the government requires you to pay a 'contribution' towards the cost of making the standard health insurance policy available to all. This contribution, which is added to the cost of your plan, is €90 per year for those under the age of 20 and twice as much for those aged 20 to 65. If you're insured under a standard policy and were formerly a *ziekenfonds* member, you must pay an additional contribution of €91.32 per year. If you're covered by a company insurance plan, the additional contribution is usually paid by your employer. Pensioners over the age of 65 normally continue with the health plan (*ziekenfonds* or private insurance) they had at retirement but can switch from a private plan to *ziekenfonds* if their total household income at retirement was below €18,700.

The Ministry of Health, Welfare and Sport (*Ministerie van Volksgezondheid, Welzijn en Sport* or VWS, PO Box 20350, 2500 EJ The Hague, ☎ 070-370 7911) publishes a booklet in English called *Health Insurance in Holland*, which is also available on its website (🖳 www.minvws.nl).

Luxembourg: Employees and the self-employed must contribute to the appropriate health fund (*caisse de maladie*) according to their profession. Both employer and employee contribute towards health insurance, and it's the employer's responsibility to withhold the appropriate amounts from your pay and remit them to the relevant health fund. The normal contribution amounts to 5.44 per cent of gross income, up to a maximum contribution of €6,225, divided equally between employers and employees. Self-employed people must pay the full contribution. Manual workers in certain trades pay a higher rate (9.9 per cent), split evenly between employee and employer, and those on public assistance usually pay a reduced rate of 5.2 per cent (half paid by the benefit authority). Those on unemployment benefit, old age pensions and other kinds of income-replacement benefit have health insurance contributions deducted from their benefit payments.

Cover is for all dependent members of your household, including children up to the age of 27 if they're full-time students or unemployed, and includes most treatment by GPs and specialists, laboratory tests, prescriptions and hospitalisation. As in the other Benelux countries, the Luxembourg health care system works on a reimbursement basis whereby you submit receipts for consultations, treatment and medicines to your *caisse* for reimbursement at the appropriate rate, which varies from 80 to 100 per cent. Your first consultation for a given illness is reimbursed at 80 per cent and subsequent consultations within 28 days at 95 per cent. Prescriptions are normally reimbursed at 78 per cent, although there are four categories of prescription with reimbursement levels ranging from 0 to 100 per cent. Dental treatment and eye care are also included, although some services are subject to pre-approval and you may be required to have regular annual check-ups. The *caisse* normally reimburses you for emergency medical treatment abroad (provided you haven't travelled expressly for that purpose) at the same rates as for equivalent services in Luxembourg.

There's a separate insurance for long-term care, called *assurance dépendence*, financed through a 1 per cent withholding tax on employees, professional revenues and income-replacement benefit payments. This provides benefits toward the cost of long-term care in nursing homes or other extended care facilities in Luxembourg.

Many people in Luxembourg take out supplementary insurance with one of the non-profit health insurance agencies or mutual associations (*mutuelles*) affiliated to the Ministry of Social Security. Many employers offer supplementary cover as a benefit of employment, either at cost to the employee or on a shared fee basis. A *mutuelle* pays the portion of your medical fees that isn't covered by your *caisse* and may offer extended coverage for such things as hospitalisation (i.e. private rooms), eye care (spectacles and contact lenses), dental treatment and medical services outside Luxembourg. The cost of supplementary coverage is normally low, but it applies on a per person basis (i.e. you must pay extra to insure your spouse, children or other dependants). If you have particular needs or circumstances or if you want to use doctors or medical facilities in other countries, it's possible to purchase private supplementary health insurance through an insurance agent.

Old Age & Invalidity Pensions

All employees and self-employed people in Benelux pay compulsory contributions to state funds for old age and invalidity pensions. Contributions vary from just over 16 per cent of gross income in Belgium (split between employee and employer) to 24 per cent in Luxembourg (split three ways, with the government contributing a portion). Pension cover is continued while you're on unemployment or other forms of income-replacement benefit, the agency usually paying contributions on your behalf.

In order to claim an old age pension, you must have reached a certain age (normally 65) and have made contributions for a minimum period. Special conditions often apply to civil servants, miners, railway company employees and other groups. Under EU regulations, you must be given credit for contributions made to the state pension systems of other EU countries, and Benelux has social security treaties with some non-EU nations (e.g. the USA) that may allow you to receive full or partial credit for contributions made in those countries. Further information on EU pension regulations can be found in the 'Dialogue with Citizens' section of the EU website (🖳 http://europa.eu.int/business/en/legal/index.html). Information on social security treaties with non-EU countries can be obtained from your embassy or consulate.

Belgium: Old age pensions under the Belgian state system are based on retirement at 65 after 45 years of contributions (including periods on unemployment or disability benefits). Women are permitted to retire at 60, with 40 years' contributions, but these limits are gradually being increased and will be the same as for men by the year 2009. It's possible to apply for reduced early retirement benefit at the age of 60 under certain circumstances, although the government 'encourages' those needing or wishing to take early retirement to contribute to private 'bridging pensions' (*prépensions conventionnelles*).

The basic state pension is 75 per cent of average lifetime wages for those with a dependent spouse, and 60 per cent for all other retirees. You should apply to the administrative offices in the commune where you live around a year before you reach retirement age, as it can take this long to process the paperwork (this is Belgium!), especially if you've made contributions in other countries that need to be taken into account. Pensions are paid monthly by direct deposit into your bank account. You may continue to work after the age of 65, although your pension may be 'adjusted' (i.e. reduced) for earnings above certain levels.

Everyone enrolled in a health insurance plan in Belgium is automatically covered for invalidity, provided they've worked for at least 120 days in the six months immediately preceding the accident or illness causing the disability and are incapacitated by a minimum of 66.66 per cent. (Even disability is calculated to two decimal places in Belgium!) Benefits are equivalent to 65 per cent of previous earnings if you have dependants, or 45 or 40 per cent if you don't (the lower figure applies if there's other income in the household), and are payable until you reach the age of 65, when the standard old age pension replaces them.

Holland: Pensions in Holland are regulated by legislation called *Algemene Ouderdomswet* and, in typical Dutch fashion, are often referred to as AOW. All Dutch residents are eligible for a state pension when they reach 65, provided they've made some social security contributions while employed. The standard pension is based on a guaranteed minimum income, which varies with age, family status and other factors, and the assumption that you've been resident in Holland from the age of 15 (i.e. for 50 years). In other words, for each year you've been a Dutch resident, you earn an entitlement to 2 per cent of the full standard pension, so with 10 years of Dutch residence, you would be entitled to a 20 per cent pension.

You're advised to apply to the Social Security Bank (*Sociale Verzekeringsbank*) several months before your 65th birthday, where you must complete a form listing all the EU countries in which you've worked. The Bank then contacts the relevant pension authorities to confirm your contributions there and ascertain whether you're eligible for a state pension in any of those countries. Benefits begin on the first day of the month in which you turn 65, and a supplement is paid in May each year, which is intended to be put towards a summer holiday. (Escaping the grey skies of Holland at least once a year is obviously considered essential to Dutch well-being.) Many employers make supplementary pensions available and the government encourages both employers and employees to take advantage of these programmes. If your total pension is less than the guaranteed minimum income, you may be eligible for other social benefits.

Invalidity pensions, known as WAO (*Wet op de Arbeidsongeschiktheidsver- zekering* – no wonder it's abbreviated), are available to those unable to return to work or able to earn only 85 per cent or less of their former wages after one year of sickness or injury leave. The initial benefit varies from 14 to 70 per cent of previous earnings, depending on the level of disability, and is paid for six months to six years, depending on your age. After the initial benefit period, a flat monthly benefit is paid until your condition changes or you reach the age of 65, when you become eligible for an old age pension. While on invalidity benefit, you may be eligible for a variety of cash grants for rehabilitation, therapy or necessary alterations to your home (e.g. to accommodate a wheelchair). Invalidity pensions are administered through the *ziekenfonds* (see page 234).

Luxembourg: To be eligible for an old age pension in Luxembourg, you must have made contributions in Luxembourg or another EU country for at least 120 months. If at retirement age you haven't made sufficient contributions, you don't receive a pension; instead the contributions that you've made in Luxembourg are returned to you, *excluding* any employer contributions that have been made on your behalf. Normal retirement age is 65, although early retirement is permitted at 60 or 57 under certain circumstances, provided you've made pension contributions for a minimum of 480 months.

The standard pension is around 71 per cent of your average salary during the years you contributed, up to a maximum of €6,000 per month, with a minimum benefit (after 480 months of contributions) of around €890 per month. Payments are indexed annually for inflation and revised every second year in the light of salary trends. Employees of private companies must apply to the *Caisse de Pensions des Employés privés* in Luxembourg city a few months before reaching retirement age to allow time for processing the necessary paperwork and verifying any foreign contributions.

To qualify for an invalidity pension, you must have been insured (i.e. working in Luxembourg and making social security contributions) for at least 12 months during the three years immediately prior to your disability. This requirement may be waived if the disability is due to an accident or occupational illness. Unlike in Belgium and Holland, no minimum degree of disability is required in order to receive a pension, the main criterion being that you're unable to practise your normal occupation. Invalidity pension payments begin around six months after the injury or the onset of illness, when standard employer sickness benefit expires (see **Salary Insurance** on page 51), and continue until there's a significant improvement in your condition or you reach the age of 65, when you're entitled to an old age pension. Anyone under the age of 50 who is receiving a disability pension must agree to undergo all recommended forms of rehabilitation. The amount of benefit paid is based on your previous income and is calculated in much the same way as for an old age pension, although there's no minimum contribution period.

SUPPLEMENTARY PENSIONS

Although all three Benelux countries have traditionally attempted to provide adequate pension income for retired residents, the cost of pension benefits have become prohibitive. With the population ageing and unemployment levels uncomfortably high, governments are putting pressure on employers to relieve them of benefit costs, particularly that of pensions. The result is an increasing need for private supplementary pensions (*retraite complémentaire/aanvullende pensioenregelingen*). If you already have private pension insurance in another country, it may not be necessary (or, in some circumstances, wise) to buy a supplementary pension policy in Benelux, particularly if you will be living there for only a few years. In Luxembourg, it's possible to purchase supplementary pension cover as part of an individual life assurance policy (see page 243). In Belgium and Holland, your bank or insurance broker or consultant will be only too pleased to show you a range of investment vehicles suitable as supplementary private pension schemes.

Because of the growing need for private supplementary pensions, it's becoming increasingly common for employers to offer them as a benefit of employment. In Belgium and Holland, many schemes are organised on an industry-wide basis through professional associations, unions or insurance funds (similar to those that offer statutory health and unemployment insurance). Some collective agreements require employers to offer supplementary pension cover. Costs are either paid by the employer or shared between employer and employee. In Luxembourg, supplementary pension insurance is also available through employer-sponsored plans.

HOUSEHOLD INSURANCE

Various kinds of household insurance are available to both renters and homeowners in Benelux. Homeowners are generally required by their mortgage lenders to have insurance for the building itself (*assurance de bâtiment/opstalverzekering*), which costs around €2.50 to €3.50 per €1,000 of estimated reconstruction cost per year. In Holland, owners of houses by waterways often take out separate insurance to cover the wooden pile foundations, which normally last around 20 years and are expensive to replace. With standard building insurance, you're protected against most kinds of disaster except flooding. The general rule is that building insurance pays for damage caused by water 'coming down' (i.e. heavy rain or a burst pipe) but not by water 'coming up' (see below). If you're renting a property, building insurance is normally the responsibility of your landlord.

Both renters and homeowners need to insure the contents of their homes (*assurance contenu/inboedelverzekering*), often referred to as fire and theft cover. If you're renting, you may be required to insure items belonging to your landlord (e.g. appliances) as well as your own property. Note that most contents policies cover only property that's normally stored in a home, and most insurers won't pay if they can prove that loss or damage was due to negligence on your part. You should therefore take out separate insurance for any valuable items you're keeping temporarily in your home and make sure that you don't leave the front door unlocked or a window open while you're out. If you have bicycles that you keep in a garage, a public hallway, or outside (including a balcony or patio), you should enquire about insuring them separately, as bicycles are rarely included in home contents policies. A separate policy or extension may also be required for high value items such as jewellery or antiques. Financial documents (share or bond certificates) and cash are rarely insurable against loss, and important documents should be kept at a bank, in either a safety deposit box or a custodial account.

Floods are a constant danger, particularly in Holland and parts of Flanders where homes are built on reclaimed land, although flood insurance is rarely available from local insurers. In the event of widespread flooding, the national government usually provides a relief fund, although this is rarely sufficient to pay for all damage. It's sometimes possible to obtain flood insurance through foreign companies, so if you're living in an area liable to flooding, you may wish to contact an insurance agent specialising in foreign-based insurance or insurance for expatriates.

Most building insurance also excludes damage to glass, so it's worthwhile considering a glass insurance policy (*bris de glace/glasverzekering*), whether you're renting or living in your own home. (Most landlords expect you to pay for the repair of any broken windows or doors.)

THIRD PARTY LIABILITY INSURANCE

It's customary in Benelux to have third party liability insurance (*assurance pour la responsabilité civile/aansprakelijkheidsverzekering*), which is often required of those renting a property. Third party liability insurance covers all members of a family and includes damage caused by your children and pets, e.g. if your dog or child bites someone or runs out into the street and causes a car accident. Most policies also cover damage done to third parties by your guests. Premiums are usually no more than €35 to €50 per year. Because most people have third party liability insurance, it's common for neighbours to 'sue' one another for minor damage, such as broken windows or dog bites (particularly in densely populated areas of Belgium and Holland). Provided both you and your neighbour are insured, the matter can be dealt with by your insurance companies with no hard feelings. The good news is that settlements are limited to the cost of repair or replacement, with no 'allowance' for pain, suffering or the theatrical talents of a lawyer! However, most third party liability policies also include cover for legal assistance, in case your neighbours aren't as accommodating as you expected.

HOLIDAY & TRAVEL INSURANCE

Holiday and travel insurance is available from a variety of sources, including insurance companies, banks and travel agencies, and at airports and railway stations in all three countries. Before taking out travel insurance, you should carefully consider the level of cover required and compare policies. Most policies include loss of deposit or holiday cancellation, missed flights, departure delay at both the start and end of a holiday (a common occurrence), delayed or lost luggage, loss of money or other belongings, medical expenses and accidents (including repatriation if necessary), personal liability, legal expenses, holiday curtailment and a tour operator going bust.

Your (compulsory) health insurance covers you for medical emergencies throughout Europe, although when travelling further afield you must take out additional insurance. Note also that state health insurance reimburses you for medical services at 'official' domestic rates, which may be far lower than your actual costs, particularly if you need emergency treatment abroad. Many people find it more economical to have an annual travel policy with world-wide cover including health insurance than to purchase a travel health insurance policy for each trip abroad. Annual policies are available from insurance companies that specialise in travel insurance, and some expatriate organisations also offer attractively priced policies to members. Travel health policies may also cover evacuation or repatriation of family members who fall ill or are injured while on holiday.

MOTOR BREAKDOWN INSURANCE

Motor breakdown insurance is provided primarily through the national motoring organisations (RAC/TCB in Belgium, ANWB and KNAC in Holland and the Automobile Club of Luxembourg). If you are or have been a member of a motoring organisation in another country, check with them before leaving to see whether they have a reciprocal agreement with the motoring organisation in the country you're moving to. In Benelux, you can join a motoring organisation on the spot at the scene of your first breakdown (see Motoring Organisations on page 205). Some car manufacturers include motor breakdown insurance as part of their warranty service, at least during the first year you own a new car, and some credit card companies (e.g. American Express and Diners Club) offer breakdown insurance for their members.

LIFE ASSURANCE

Although often referred to as life insurance, life policies are usually for life assurance. Assurance covers an eventuality which is certain to occur (like it or not, you must eventually die!). Thus a life assurance policy is valid until you die. An insurance policy covers a risk which may happen, but isn't a certainty – for example, that you will be hit by a falling tree. In Benelux, as in much of continental Europe, life assurance (*assurance vie/levensverzekering*) is considered a type of long-term investment, often connected with estate planning rather than providing for dependants' day-to-day needs after your death, as in Britain or the USA. You can take out a life assurance policy with numerous companies, particularly the many insurance companies based in Luxembourg. Life assurance is also available through most banks. If you already have a life assurance policy in your home country, it may be easier to maintain it, particularly if you're likely to be moving on after a few years in Benelux.

With most life assurance policies in Benelux, you're actually making an investment. You pay premiums for a certain number of years and at the end of the agreed term receive the capital accrued, either as a lump sum or over a period of time as an annuity, whether or not you die!. In many cases, life assurance policies are designed to mature at retirement age in the form of an annuity that will supplement a state pension plan. In other cases, life assurance is purchased primarily to cover the estimated amount of inheritance taxes, so that your beneficiaries aren't forced to sell their inheritance to pay the tax man.

Insurance companies promise different rates of return over the term of the policy so it's important to evaluate not only the rate you're being promised but also a company's performance over the last five or ten years. If the insured person dies before the end of the term, the proceeds are paid to his beneficiaries. In some cases, annual premiums on a life assurance policy are tax deductible and the proceeds are at least partially exempt from taxes, whether paid to the insured or to his survivors. Most life assurance policies must have a term of at least eight to ten years, or they're treated like any other form of investment for tax purposes. A number of insurance companies specialise in life assurance cover for expatriates and their families; many advertise or promote their services through expatriate organisations.

Note that you should leave a copy of all insurance policies with your will and another copy with your lawyer. If you don't have a lawyer, keep a copy in a safe deposit box. A life assurance policy must usually be sent to the insurance company upon the death of the insured, with a copy of the death certificate.

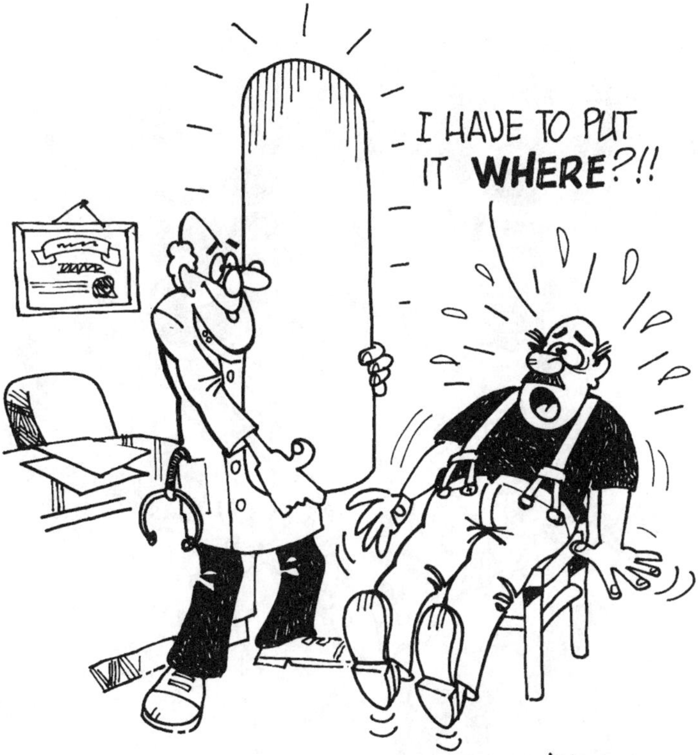
I HAVE TO PUT
IT WHERE?!!

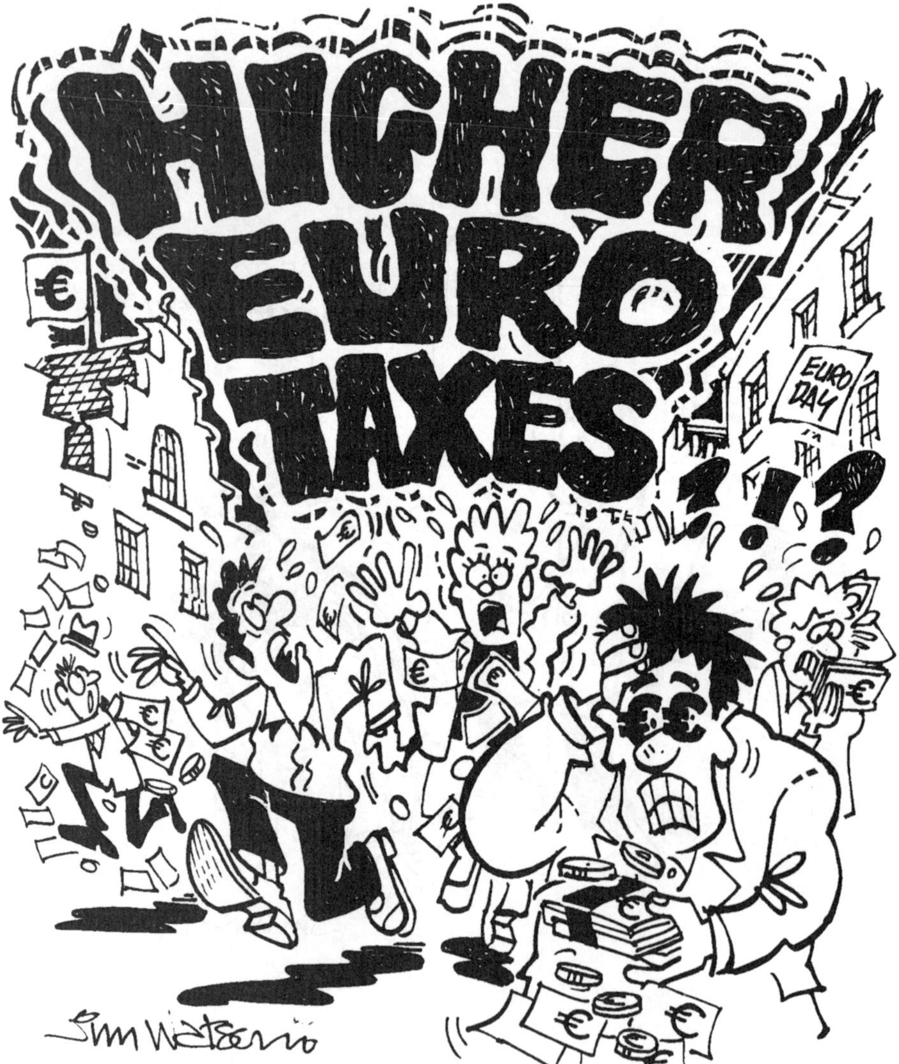
HIGHER
EURO
TAXES !?
EURO DAY

14.

FINANCE

The Benelux region is one of the wealthiest areas in the European Union with per capita gross domestic product (GDP) averaging around $22,000. The economies of Belgium, Holland and Luxembourg are among the most open in the world, with almost total integration with neighbouring France and Germany. The region is noted as a centre for the financial, banking and insurance industries, and Luxembourg boasts over 200 banks, including subsidiaries and holding companies of many of the world's largest and best known banking organisations, such as Crédit Lyonnais, Deutsche Bank, ING Bank, Dexia and HSBC. All three countries have sophisticated banking systems and are among the world leaders in electronic banking, including the use of cash cards (sometimes called electronic purses), which are rapidly creating a cash-less society – ironically, at the same time as new euro coins and banknotes are being introduced (under the guidance of a Dutchman, Wim Duisenberg, first president of the European Central Bank).

The Benelux region is also famous for its taxes, which are generally high and complicated. All three countries have been trying to reduce both their rates of taxation and the complexity of their taxation systems, and the rules are constantly changing. On the other hand, Luxembourg has attracted banking and insurance business from neighbouring Germany, France and Belgium by its refusal (at least so far) to withhold taxes on foreign accounts and to share private account information with other governments. Belgium has become something of a tax haven for individuals seeking to escape wealth taxes in both France and Holland.

When you arrive in Belgium, Holland or Luxembourg to take up residence or employment, ensure that you have sufficient cash, travellers' cheques, luncheon vouchers, coffee machine tokens, gold sovereigns and diamonds to last at least until your first pay day, which may be some time after your arrival. During this period you may also find an international credit card useful.

CURRENCY

The era of individual national currencies has drawn to a close in the 12 nations that make up the European Monetary Union: Austria, Belgium, Finland, France, Germany, Greece, Ireland, Italy, Luxembourg, Holland, Portugal and Spain. Until the advent of the euro, the official currency of Belgium and Luxembourg was the franc, and the Dutch used the guilder (*gulden* in Dutch). On 1st January 1999, the euro (€) became the official unit of currency in Belgium, Holland and Luxembourg, as well as in eight other European countries (Greece joined the so-called euro-zone in June, 2000, bringing the total membership to 12), and from 1st January 2002 euro bank notes and coins begin to replace francs and guilders. For a brief transition period, ranging from one to two months, it's possible to use the old national currencies in shops, although change on all transactions will be paid in euros only. Banks will exchange old bank notes and coins without charge, but only until the national cut-off date (see below). After that, you must take old notes and coins directly to the national central bank or treasury for exchange. It's likely that dual pricing will continue for some time after francs and guilders are no longer in circulation, as an accommodation to clients and customers still adapting to the new currency.

The euro, which is equivalent to 40.3399 Belgian francs or 2.20371 Dutch guilders, is divided into 100 cents, sometimes still referred to in French as *centimes*.

Coins are minted in 1, 2, 5, 10, 20 and 50 cents and 1 and 2 euro denominations. Coins have a common European face, showing a map of the EU and the stars of the European flag. The obverse will be different, depending on the country where the coin was produced, although euro coins may be used anywhere in the 12 member countries irrespective of where they were minted. Belgium, Holland and Luxembourg will each continue to feature their current monarch on euro coins.

Euro banknotes are printed in 5, 10, 20, 50, 100, 200 and 500 euro denominations. The design of the notes aroused considerable controversy, as the member countries each wanted their own national heroes and historic monuments depicted on the notes (especially the high value notes). In a typical EU compromise, it was decided that the notes should depict only 'hypothetical' architectural elements and 'symbolic' representations of bridges of the sort that 'could be' built anywhere in Europe. As a result, the euro will be the only major currency not to have faces or portraits on its bank notes. On the other hand, the notes are being printed in vibrant colours and varying sizes, with Braille markings for the blind and using a host of the latest, most sophisticated, anti-counterfeit devices.

Belgium: Within Belgium, both Belgian francs and Luxembourg francs are acceptable until the cut-off date of 28th February 2002. After that, you can exchange your old currencies for euros free of charge at any bank only until 31st December 2002. The National Bank of Belgium (*Banque Nationale de Belgique/Nationale Bank van België*, boulevard de Berlaimont 14, 1000 Brussels, ☎ 02-221 2111, 💻 www. bnb.be) will exchange Belgian franc bank notes indefinitely, but you can only exchange franc coins until the end of 2004. The website contains a list of branches as well as details of special opening hours for the introduction of the euro during 2002.

Holland: The Dutch will only accept guilders in the shops until midnight on 28th January 2002. All banks are supposed to accept guilders for exchange until the end of 2002, but they're permitted to charge a conversion fee from 1st April. After 2002, old currency will be exchanged only by the National Bank of Holland (*De Nederlandsche Bank*, Westeinde 1, 10017 ZN Amsterdam or PO Box 98, 1000 AB Amsterdam, ☎ 020-524 1999, 💻 www.dnb.nl), which has set up a special euro-line (☎ 0800-1521) to answer general questions about the new currency. There are branches of the National Bank in Eindhoven, Hoogeveen and Wassenaar. Addresses and opening hours can be found on the DNB website in English as well as Dutch.

Luxembourg: Like Belgium, Luxembourg will accept old currency (both Belgian and Luxembourg francs) in shops until 28th February 2002. Banks will exchange francs for euro until 30th June 2002, after which you'll have to go directly to the National Bank of Luxembourg (*Banque centrale du Luxembourg*, 2 boulevard Royal, 2983 Luxembourg, ☎ 04-7741, 💻 www.bcl.lu), which has also set up a euro-hotline for queries (☎ 8002-0101) as part of its Euro Campaign 2002, and also contains detailed information about the euro and the conversion process on its website.

FOREIGN CURRENCY

The three countries of the Benelux have no currency restrictions and you may bring in or take out as much money as you wish in any currency, although banks must report all movements of cash into or out of a country when they exceed a certain level (normally around €5,000, although levels are changing with the attempt to harmonise financial policies within the euro-zone).

Until 2001 you could buy and sell foreign currency at most banks throughout Belgium, Holland and Luxembourg, even in fairly small towns. It's difficult to predict how the transition to the euro will affect this situation, but clearly there will be less need for exchange facilities from 1st January 2002. During the transition period (see above), all 'old' currency exchange to the euro should be done free of charge and at the official rates. If you're changing sterling, dollars or other non-euro currencies, most banks add a service charge of 2 to 2.5 percent to the transaction or weight their exchange rate to include a service fee. Banks generally give a better exchange rate for travellers' cheques than for banknotes. Note also that most banks exchange only banknotes and not coins. (You can donate any spare change to a variety of worthy causes when you pass through most airports in Europe.)

Foreign currency can also be purchased from machines at some banks and in shopping centres, airports and railway stations. Many bank machines throughout Benelux accept foreign bank cards, provided your bank subscribes to one of the major networks, e.g. Visa, Mastercard, Switch, Cirrus or Maestro. Look for the network logo displayed on the bank machine to see if you can use your debit or credit card, and note that many networks charge a service fee of €1 to €5 for the use of another bank's machines. Many hotels and shops also accept and change foreign currency, but usually at less favourable exchange rates than banks. Exchange rates for most international currencies are displayed in banks and published in daily newspapers as well as on financial websites, including those of most banks and news services (e.g. CNN). Euro exchange rates against both the British pound and US dollar are also reported on radio and TV news programmes.

BANKING

Banking is a major industry throughout Benelux, and there's no shortage of banks to choose from. Belgium claims to have the largest number of bank branches per capita of any country in the world and Luxembourg is home to over 220 different banks employing 10 per cent of the population! The banks in the region have long led the world in the field of electronic banking, and there are few transactions you can't do either from an ATM (automatic teller machine) or from your home computer. Benelux banks offer a wide range of services, including personal and commercial banking, investment and insurance services, and personal, commercial and mortgage loans. Most larger banks have websites containing information about the services they offer, including online banking, and in some cases application forms.

Despite the spread of electronic banking, it's still necessary to have at least a current account (*compte à vue/zichtrekening*) in your country of residence, as cross-border bank transactions can be expensive and complicated, even when everything is denominated in euros. Online banking, using bank-supplied software or via the Internet, is gaining in popularity, but only in Belgium are there 'genuine' e-banks (banks operating entirely online, where you can open an account from the comfort of your home and never actually see your banker). Some online banks offer a full range of investment and loan services, complete with downloadable application forms (e.g. Fortis Bank, ⌨ http://be.fortisbank.com).

Personal accounts are generally more expensive in Benelux countries than in the UK or USA. You should expect to pay between €50 and €100 per year for a standard current account that includes debit and credit cards, plus ATMs and Internet banking facilities. Benelux banks usually charge for every service separately, as well as for each transaction, although they may offset charges by paying a (very small) rate of interest on your average account balance each month (provided you remain in credit). Most banks offer a variety of 'package programmes' which include the fees for the various bank cards, online banking access, a number of transactions at bank machines and often some form of account insurance, all for a single annual fee.

You can arrange to receive bank statements at regular intervals (daily, monthly, quarterly or annually) or to pick them up at your branch (in which case you avoid being charged a mailing fee plus postage) or simply print them at a bank machine or from your home computer (and not be charged at all). Bank fees are usually deducted directly from your account either quarterly or at the end of the year.

Belgium: Traditionally there have been three major banks in Belgium, although recent buy-outs and mergers have changed some of the names, which are currently *Fortis Banque/Fortis Bank* (formerly *Générale de Banque/Generale Bank*), *Banque Bruxelles Lambert/Bank Brussel Lambert* and *Kredietbank*. Bank account numbers are standardised in Belgium, the first few digits indicating the bank and branch to which the account belongs.

Holland: The big names in Dutch banking are ABN-Amro, Rabobank and ING Bank (which now owns and operates the Post banking system). The largest of the three banks is ABN-Amro, which many expatriates find convenient because of the large number of branches and automatic teller machines (ATMs) throughout the country, as well as having a special foreigners' department at the Amsterdam branch on the Rembrandtsplein. There are also many smaller banks offering essentially the same services and facilities as the larger, better known institutions.

Luxembourg: Wandering through central Luxembourg city, you'd be forgiven for thinking that every bank in the world has a Luxembourg branch – in fact you'd probably be right! If you wish, you can deal with banks based in your home country, although their accounts, terms and services are often quite different from what you're used to. The major indigenous banks are *Banque & Caisse d'Epargne de l'Etat* (BCEE), also known as *Spuerkeess* in Lëtzebuergesch, the *Banque du Luxembourg* and the *Banque Générale du Luxembourg*. The Luxembourg banking industry maintains an informative website (🖳 www.bank.lu) where you can find information about all the banks in the Duchy, including the services they offer to individuals and corporations. The site has a search engine that you can use to draw up lists of banks offering particular services.

Opening Hours

Bank opening hours vary by country and are generally somewhat shorter than shop opening hours, although one of the advantages of electronic banking is that you can make transactions at any time.

Belgium: Most banks are open from 9am to 4 or 4.30pm Mondays to Fridays and a few are open on Saturdays. Many smaller branches close for an hour at lunchtime (usually 1 to 2pm).

Holland: Banks in Holland are usually open from 9am to 4 or 5pm, with branches in shopping districts often open until 7pm on late shopping nights. Most branches are closed at weekends, except for those at airports and railway stations.

Luxembourg: Most banks are open Mondays to Fridays from as early as 8.15am to around 5pm. Most branches close for lunch from 11.45am to 2pm. A few banks in and around major shopping centres stay open through lunchtime and some are open on Saturdays.

Opening an Account

One of your first acts on moving to Benelux should be to open a bank account. The degree of difficulty and amount of bureaucracy varies among the three countries, but generally you'll be asked to provide standard identification (your passport), your residence permit or proof that you're registered with the local authorities, and a letter from your employer or a copy of your employment contract. It isn't always necessary, but it often helps to have a letter of reference or introduction from your home bank.

Belgium: Opening an account is generally a quick and simple process in Belgium. Banks usually require only your passport or other identification in order to open a current account (*compte à vue/zichtrekening*). You can even open an account online without having to set foot in a bank. It will be anything from a few days to two weeks before you receive the various transfer forms, cards, code numbers and passwords necessary to manage your account.

You can receive statements as often as you like, e.g. monthly, weekly or even daily if you want to keep a close check on your account. There is, of course, a charge for this service and the more frequently you want statements, the more expensive it will be. If you don't specify otherwise, you will normally receive one or two statements per month. You can also use your bank card or Internet connection to review your account balance and check recent transactions at any time.

Holland: Opening an account in Holland takes a certain amount of time and patience (not to mention a sense of humour) despite all the high-tech innovations of the Dutch banking system. It's the start of a business relationship and can't be rushed. First you must contact a bank to make an appointment to open an account, at which time you should ask which documents you must take with you. Dutch bankers normally require all the documents mentioned above, and it can be most helpful to have a letter of introduction from your last bank, indicating what a marvellous customer you are, how rarely (if ever) you overdraw your account, and how promptly you repay loans. Once your account has been approved, you must return to the bank to deposit funds and pick up your cards and the forms and other information you need to start using your account (and to shake hands again with your new banker to cement your relationship).

Luxembourg: In theory, all you need to open a bank account in Luxembourg is your passport (or other identification) and a smile. (A suitcase full of cash is also a great ice breaker.) Any teller in the bank should be able to give you the necessary forms and help you to complete them. Some banks like to delay issuing credit cards and offering you some of their other services until you've established a good record. This is where it helps to have a letter of reference from your former bank or current employer. The right introduction can put a credit card in your hand that much sooner.

In some cases, if you open a personal account in the bank your employer uses, you're eligible for special rates or services or a discount on certain bank charges.

Bank Transfers & Standing Orders

The usual method of making payments in Belgium, Holland and Luxembourg is a direct bank transfer. Cheques are hardly ever used, owing to the risk and expense of processing them, and you may have difficulty persuading your bank to issue cheques. There are two kinds of bank transfer, depending on whether you're instructing the bank to pay money to someone else from your account (*virement/overschrijving*) or authorising the bank to let someone take money from your account (*domiciliation/domicilie*), and slightly different forms are used to process the two types of transfer.

If you want to make a payment from your current account, you fill out a transfer form to instruct your bank to transfer money from your account to the account of the person or company you wish to pay. Bank transfer forms are similar (except for the language) in all three countries. Your bank usually provides you with a number of these forms, pre-printed with your name and bank account number. You fill in the spaces for the name of the payee, his bank account details and the reason for the payment, along with the amount to be paid. You must sign the form, and keep the stub or carbon copy as evidence of payment. You then send the transfer form to your bank, not to the payee, and the bank makes the payment for you. Most banks will give you freepost envelopes for sending transfer forms or you can take them to a bank yourself. Payment is usually made within a few business days of the bank's receipt of a transfer order, but most banks recommend that you allow five days for payment.

Often when you receive a bill (*facture/rekening*) in the post, it includes a transfer form with the company's bank details and the amount to be paid already filled in. You simply need to insert your own bank details and sign the form before giving or sending it to your bank (not back to the company).

To arrange for a standing order (*ordre permanent/bestendige opdracht*) contact your bank with the relevant payment information, including the bank account number of the person or company you want to pay. Standing orders are particularly handy for recurring payments such as your rent (in fact, your landlord may insist upon it) and utility bills. Where the monthly amounts vary, you can arrange to be sent a copy of the bill about a week before the scheduled payment so that you can contact your bank if you dispute the amount to be paid.

All forms of transfer can be made through a variety of 'self-banking' services now offered by most banks in the Benelux region. You can set up, authorise and change direct transfers, pay your bills and make transfers between accounts (including international transfers via the SWIFT system) using the phone, fax, bank machines or your home computer. Some banks require you to download their software for generating payments or making other sorts of transaction that require validation. Other banks have secure websites where you can make almost every kind of transaction normally possible at a bank machine, except of course withdraw or deposit cash.

Savings Accounts

In addition to a current account, you can open several different types of savings accounts with most banks. Your employer may also offer a form of tax protected savings account at your own or another local bank. Belgium, Holland and Luxembourg each exempt a certain amount of savings account interest from income taxes (see page 264), and there's a variety of savings plans available designed to permit you to save money for a deposit on a house. With deposit accounts (term deposits) you must be prepared to invest for a period of up to 12 months, and some employer-related savings plans require you to invest for several years before you can make withdrawals. In general, the longer the term, the higher the return. You receive a pass book for a savings account, where all deposits and withdrawals are recorded. Under some employer savings plans, you must take your pass book to the bank every few months to have the balance updated, or wait until the end of the year to receive your tax documents, telling you how much interest has been added to your account.

Debit & Cash Cards

Banks in Benelux are leading the way towards a 'cashless society' with the various types of cards they issue to their customers. Initially, you will probably be issued with a debit card, which permits you to use your bank's ATMs (*distributeurs automatiques/betaalautomaten*) for deposits, withdrawals, transfers of funds and, in most cases, bill payments and other standard forms of transfer between accounts. Most debit cards also give you access to any ATM that's part of the related debit card network (such as Maestro or Cirrus), although some banks make charges for use of another bank's machines. You can also use debit cards to make purchases at many shops and petrol stations. Debit cards are often preferred to credit cards, as the money is credited almost immediately to the vendor's bank account.

Debit cards normally have an electronic chip embedded in them, which allows them to be read by special machines. You need a four-digit code (referred to as a *PIN* in both French and Dutch) to validate a transaction or to use your card in a bank machine. In Belgium, the major types of debit card are Bancontact, Mister Cash and Maestro, which are accepted wherever the relevant logos are displayed. In Holland, debit cards are called Europas and often also function as credit cards outside the country. In Luxembourg, the S-Card is common, as are the major debit cards of neighbouring countries (Maestro, Cirrus, Bancontact).

It's also possible to make small cash purchases in Benelux using a cash card, which you can use like a phone card. There's an initial charge for the card (normally no more than €5 to €10), after which you can load the card with up to €120 of electronic 'cash' at either your bank machine or any telephone booth displaying the cash card symbol. (Some banks are now offering a machine that can be used with your home computer for this purpose.) At a store where cash cards are accepted, you can pay by inserting your card in a special machine and confirming the amount you wish to pay. Note that no PIN is needed for cash card transactions, so if you lose your card it can be used by the person who finds it (just like cash). The Belgian version of the cash card is called a Proton card, the Dutch call theirs a Chipknip and in Luxembourg your S-Card, Maestro or other debit card may work as both a debit card and an electronic purse, depending upon your bank. Cash card functions are increasingly being incorporated within both credit and debit cards.

Credit & Charge Cards

Credit and charge cards are referred to collectively as credit cards throughout Benelux. (In French-speaking areas, they may be called *cartes de crédit* or simply referred to by their 'brand' name; the Dutch use the English term *credit card*). Most so-called credit cards issued in the region function like charge cards, in that payments for purchases are due when billed and cannot be spread over several months or years. Both Visa and Mastercard are generally available through your bank in conjunction with your current account. American Express and Diners Club are also popular, although these cards are issued directly by the respective companies.

A credit card normally costs around €20 to €50 per year, depending on the type of card and the level of service you choose (gold, platinum, etc.). With some cards, travel or other forms of insurance are included in your annual fee. When you register for a card, you're required to indicate the bank account you wish to use to pay your monthly balance, and the contract includes a standing order authorisation to permit the card company to debit payments automatically from your account. You'll receive a monthly statement around ten days before the date that the amount due is to be debited from your account, so you have an opportunity to dispute any incorrect charges.

Before obtaining a credit or charge card, compare the costs and benefits. Like your bank account and other forms of subscription and contract, a credit card requires you to give written notification at least a month or two in advance of the expiry date if you wish to cancel it and avoid paying the next annual fee.

If you maintain a bank account abroad, it's wise to retain your foreign credit cards. One of the advantages of using a credit card issued abroad is that your bill is usually payable up to six weeks after a transaction, thereby giving you interest-free credit – except when cards are used to obtain cash, when interest starts immediately. You may, however, find it more convenient and cheaper to be billed in euros rather than a foreign currency, e.g. US$ or sterling, when payments may vary with the exchange rate. Some banks charge a foreign transaction fee of from 1 to 2 per cent on all credit card transactions originating outside the country, irrespective of whether there was a currency exchange involved.

If you lose a credit card (or other type of bank card) or discover that someone is making fraudulent purchases with it, you should report the situation immediately to the card company, as you can be held responsible for all charges made on the card until you report the loss. Your bank will give you a 24-hour telephone number for reporting losses. Some card issuers charge the card holder for a loss (€10 to €20) not involving theft or fraud, although it may be possible to insure against losing a credit card or to pay a fee to the card company, relieving you of any liability. You should also file a formal police report about the incident.

Even if you don't like plastic money and shun any form of credit, credit cards do have their uses, for example, no deposits on hire cars and no pre-paying hotel and other bills. Cards also provide greater safety and security than cash, as well as convenience and flexibility. They're particularly useful when travelling abroad and essential if you wish to make purchases over the Internet.

Loans & Overdrafts

All banks in Belgium, Holland and Luxembourg provide loans and overdrafts, although they aren't always as free with their money as banks in some other European countries, particularly regarding business loans to foreigners. Your eligibility for a loan is dependent on your income, your personal savings and assets, and the amount of debt you already have. The old maxim still applies: the surest way to qualify for a loan is to convince your banker that you don't really need one! Most banks automatically allow current account holders to overdraw their accounts by a certain amount, but make sure you request this facility when you first set up your account. Often there's a small extra service fee (normally less than €10 per year) for an overdraft facility, and some banks are particularly vindictive to customers who exceed their balances without making prior arrangements, charging high fees for even a small excess.

It pays to shop around for a loan, as interest rates vary considerably with the bank, the amount, the purpose and the period of the loan. Benelux bankers are notoriously averse to taking risks and tend to prefer making loans where there's adequate collateral or where the borrower is also making a sizeable investment from savings or other personal resources. Borrowing from private loan companies, as advertised in newspapers, is expensive (i.e. interest rates are generally high). Use them only as a last resort, when all other possibilities have been exhausted. Even then, as a foreigner, you may find that the term of your loan is limited to the length of your residence or work permit, or that you're required by the terms of the agreement to repay the loan in full if you move abroad. In general, the more desperate your financial situation, the more suspicious you should be of anyone willing to lend you money (unless it's your mum and you're on good terms with her).

Mortgages

Mortgages (home loans) are available from all major banks in Benelux, but generally banks will only lend on property located in the country where they're based. Lending criteria and terms may be rather different from what you're used to, particularly if you're from Britain or the USA. The types of mortgage available also vary from country to country, but bankers generally evaluate potential borrowers using the same criteria: the value of the property (most banks limit their mortgage lending to 80 per cent of the purchase price), the borrower's income and the amount requested. There's a variety of options regarding interest rates, whether fixed (for the full period of the loan), semi-fixed (i.e. fixed for a period of five to ten years, after which the interest rate must be renegotiated), or variable (with rates re-assessed once or twice a year), and it's possible to arrange repayment of both the interest and the capital in a variety of ways. As in other countries, lenders often require a mortgagee to have life assurance.

Belgium: In Belgium it's possible to take out a mortgage for more than the purchase price of a property, but you'll have to pay a very high interest rate. Interest rates climb steeply on loans above 80 per cent of the purchase price, and if you're paying Belgian income tax as a resident you should make sure that your interest payments don't exceed the amount you can deduct (see page 267). Loans in Belgium are usually made for a term of 10 to 25 years.

Holland: There are a number of different types of mortgage loans available in Holland, including several that are linked to a life assurance policy. These may be offered by insurance companies rather than by banks and are especially popular in Holland, as they allow you to deduct mortgage interest from your taxable income as well as avoiding tax on the interest paid by the life assurance investment. As with an endowment mortgage, you can pay a monthly life assurance premium during the term of the loan and dividends on the life assurance policy are used to pay off the loan at the end of the term. If you should die before the mortgage is repaid, the life assurance element pays the outstanding balance and may also make a payment to your family (if there's any money left over). It's also possible to arrange a combination mortgage-life assurance policy where you pay an initial (large) sum, which is invested by the life assurance company. Proceeds from the investment are used to make the mortgage payments automatically, and any surplus is re-invested to generate a lump sum at the end of the term. Most mortgages are limited to 30 years, as this is the maximum period of time a homeowner may deduct interest payments from Dutch income tax.

Luxembourg: With all the banking and insurance companies located in Luxembourg, there's no shortage of mortgage loan options, from standard bank mortgages to some of the life assurance investment options popular in Holland. It's possible to finance a home mortgage over a period of 40 years, but the loan must be repaid before you reach normal retirement age.

VALUE ADDED TAX

Value added tax (VAT) is charged on every sale or transfer of goods and services, based on the selling price. Merchants, wholesalers and manufacturers are allowed to reclaim the VAT they pay in purchasing supplies, which results in their paying tax only on the value they have added to the product. Consumers pay VAT on the final selling price and aren't able to reclaim it, so usually VAT is included in the advertised price of articles in stores and shops. Prices on certain expensive items, including cars and most property, are usually quoted excluding VAT; if in doubt, you should ask.

The three national governments of Benelux generally make as much or more of their total revenue from VAT as from income taxes and corporate taxes. There has been talk of 'harmonising' taxes, especially VAT, throughout the EU in order to avoid tax competition among member states. It has been proposed that all EU countries minimise the number of VAT rates and eliminate the zero-rated and exempt categories, but for the time being each country has its own VAT rates, exceptions and special cases.

Certain goods and services are exempt from VAT – generally food, medicines and certain insurance and banking services, which are taxed separately. VAT is payable on goods purchased outside the EU, but not on goods purchased in another EU country where VAT has already been paid. In most cases, you pay the VAT in the country where you make your purchase. However, VAT on vehicles is assessed according to the residence of the buyer, irrespective of where a vehicle is purchased.

All businesses must register for VAT, and most companies are required to file a VAT return and make payments (if appropriate) every month. Small businesses may be able to make quarterly declarations and payments or make prepayments during the year in relation to the company's annual turnover.

Belgium: Value added tax is called *taxe sur la valeur ajoutée* (TVA) in French and *belasting toegevoegde waarde* (BTW) in Flemish. In Belgium there are four different rates, based loosely on the 'necessity' of the goods or services.

Rate	Goods/Services
1%	Gold
6%	Basic foods, publications, travel costs and soap
12%	Pay television and public housing
21% (standard rate)	All other goods and services, including new buildings, vehicles, petrol, clothes, beer and wine

(Clearly, cleanliness is next to godliness in Belgium, but wealth is prized above all else!)

Holland: There are only two rates of Dutch value added tax (BTW or *belasting toegevoegde waarde*). The standard rate was raised in 2001 from 17 to 19 per cent as part of an overall reform of the Dutch tax system. There's a reduced rate of 6 per cent that applies to certain 'necessary' goods: food, medicines, water, art, books, newspapers and magazines, materials required by the visually handicapped, artificial limbs, certain goods and services for agricultural use, passenger transport, hotel accommodation and entrance fees to museums, cinemas and other tourist attractions, as well as some labour-intensive services. No VAT is charged on exports or vessels used for international transport, and gold destined for central banks is exempt from VAT.

Luxembourg: In Luxembourg, value added tax is generally referred to as TVA, for the French *taxe sur la valeur ajoutée*, according to the general rule that government and administrative matters are handled in French. As in Belgium, there are four VAT rates:

Rate	Goods/Services
3%	Butter, milk, medications, water, public transport and publications
6%	Gas and electricity
12%	Tobacco, lead-free fuel and most professional services
15% (standard rate)	Everything else, except exempt goods and services (see below)

A few items are exempt from VAT, namely banking, insurance, and postal services and some social and cultural activities. (It's easy to see what Luxembourgers consider 'essential' services!)

INCOME TAX

Although both Belgium and Luxembourg enjoy a reputation for being tax havens for the idle rich, ordinary working people in Benelux suffer some of the highest tax rates in the world (except EU staff, who are eligible for reduced tax rates). Between income tax and social security charges, some Belgians 'contribute' up to 65 per cent of their gross pay each month to the government, and the top income tax rate in Belgium is a massive 55 per cent. The Dutch have recently reduced their top rate to 52 per cent (from 60 per cent), making Luxembourg seem a haven, with an upper bracket of 'only' 46 per cent. There have been a variety of proposals both to cut the level of income tax and to simplify the taxation systems in all three countries, and the Dutch have recently made sweeping changes to their income tax system, the first phase of which takes effect in the 2001 tax year. (The tax year in Belgium, Holland, and Luxembourg is the same as the calendar year – 1st January to 31st December). There are also changes and reductions planned in Luxembourg for the 2002 tax year, but few details are currently available. Elections are scheduled in Belgium, Holland and Luxembourg for 2002, which makes it likely that there will be further changes (reductions) in the near future.

As in many other countries, employees' income tax (often referred to as salary tax) is deducted at source by their employers, i.e. on a 'pay as you earn' (PAYE) basis, and if most or all of your income is from your job, you may not even need to file a tax return, provided the tax paid on your salary is adequate to cover your tax obligations and you aren't entitled to a refund or any special allowances or tax credits. On the other hand, if you have various sources of income, it's prudent to employ an accountant or professional tax adviser to complete your tax returns and ensure that you're properly assessed, as the tax systems in Benelux are inordinately complicated. The information below applies only to personal income tax (*impôt sur les personnes physiques/belasting natuurlijke personen*) and not to companies and was current in mid-2001.

Many books are published in the local languages designed to help you understand and save taxes, and income tax guides are published each year as special editions of many of the consumer and financial magazines and journals. Many income tax guides now come with CD-ROMs containing software to help you complete your tax forms and calculate your tax liability. The Ministries of Finance in each country also publish extensive information on income taxes on their websites, often in English as well as the local languages. On the Belgian website (🖳 www.minfin.fgov.be) there's a link to a tax survey, which is updated as the laws change. The Dutch Ministry of Finance publishes a booklet in English called *Taxation in Holland*, which you can obtain from the Central Information Department, Ministry of Finance, PO Box 20201, 2500 EE The Hague (☎ 070-342 7542) or you can download it from their website (🖳 www. minfin.nl). There are local tax offices in both Belgium and Luxembourg (contact your town hall or local government for the address) where you can obtain brochures or have questions answered.

Belgium: All Belgian employers (which includes the Belgian offices of all foreign based employers) must withhold salary taxes according to the personal situation and tax status of the employee. In most cases, the taxes withheld will cover the income taxes due on your salary, and in theory if you have no other tax liability you won't have to file a tax return. However, if you have investment income, are expecting a refund, wish to claim any tax allowances, or are liable for municipal or community taxes, you must file a tax return. Self-employed individuals must make quarterly pre-payments of estimated income tax based on the amount of tax paid the previous year;

there are stiff penalties for failing to make these prepayments as well as a surcharge for 'late' payment.

Holland: As in Belgium, employers must withhold and pay taxes on their employees' salary (in many cases making adjustments for allowances and deductions). The amounts withheld should satisfy your tax obligation unless you have income from other sources or were expecting a refund; if neither applies, you don't need to file a tax return.

Luxembourg: In Luxembourg, income tax is withheld from your salary according to the information supplied on your official tax card (*fiche de retenue d'impôt*). When you first register at your town hall or at the beginning of each tax year, you're sent a tax card listing your name, address, marital status and the number of children in your household for whom you're entitled to deductions or allowances. The tax card will also indicate the tax category to which you belong:

- **Class 2** – married couples assessed jointly;
- **Class 1a** – single or widowed people over the age of 65 and single, separated, widowed or divorced people with dependants living in the household;
- **Class 1** – everyone not eligible for class 1a or class 2, i.e. all single people under the age of 65 with no children or other dependants living in the household.

The number of dependants for which you're entitled to claim tax relief is indicated by a figure following the tax class: e.g. a married couple with two children would be classified as 2.2, while a single mother with one child would be 1a.1. A married person who is widowed, divorced or separated remains in class 2 for three years following the bereavement or separation.

You must verify the information on the card you receive and then give the card to your employer, who uses it to record payroll information, including the income tax deducted from your salary and paid to the tax authorities. If any of the information on your tax card is incorrect when you receive it or if your situation changes during the tax year (e.g. if you marry or a child is born or leaves home), you must notify the tax authorities and your employer immediately. It isn't as important to notify them of the death of your spouse or of a divorce or legal separation, as your tax class won't change for another three years. The tax card includes an official form for notifying the tax office of any changes, which also lists the address where it should be sent. If both spouses work, the person receiving the 'second income' receives a special tax card, called a *fiche de retenue d'impôt additionnelle*, which tells his employer to calculate his income tax accordingly.

The employer is responsible for tracking and recording your travel and commuting deductions (based on the address at which you're officially registered) as well as any additional deductions, expenses or extraordinary charges which affect your taxes. To update your tax card for such items, you must complete Form 161 and send it to the tax office. In theory, you don't need to file a tax return at the end of the year if your only income is from employment and you've properly notified both the tax office and your employer of any special circumstances. However, there are a number of tax advantages (mostly related to investments and investment income) which cannot be claimed unless you file an income tax return.

Liability

Your liability for income taxes (and any other sort of taxes, for that matter) depends on where you're domiciled, which is usually the country you regard as your permanent home and where you live most of the year. A foreigner working in Belgium, Holland or Luxembourg who has taken up residence there is usually considered to be domiciled there. A person can be resident in more than one country at any given time, but can only be domiciled for tax purposes in one country. As far as the Benelux countries are concerned, if you're entered in the local population register, you're considered domiciled there for tax purposes unless you qualify for some form of special treatment. The tax systems in Belgium, Holland and Luxembourg distinguish between resident and non-resident taxpayers when it comes to determining what income is subject to taxation. As a rule, residents are taxed on their world-wide income, while non-residents are taxed only on income originating in the local country. There are, however, a number of situations where resident foreigners may be granted a special status, allowing them to be taxed as non-residents on certain categories of income.

There are double taxation treaties between Belgium, Holland and Luxembourg and 30 or more countries, designed to ensure that income that has already been taxed in one country isn't taxed again in another. (Most tax treaties also call for the exchange of tax return information between the two countries' tax authorities, so they can check that you're being taxed somewhere on everything you earn.) If you're in doubt about your tax liability in your home country, contact your nearest embassy or consulate in your adopted country. Americans living in Benelux (or anywhere outside the USA) should be aware that, although US tax treaties allow for exemption of various sorts of earned income and credit you for income taxes paid abroad, you must file a US income tax return even if all your income is exempt from taxation. (Note that renouncing your citizenship is not only extremely difficult but can also result in your being barred from returning to the US even as a visitor.) US citizens can obtain information on tax filing requirements from an American embassy or consulate or via the Internet at the IRS website (⌨ www.irs.gov). British nationals should consult the Inland Revenue website (⌨ www.inlandrevenue.gov.uk) for further information.

Belgium: You're considered to be a resident of Belgium if you're registered with the local commune. Temporary residents of Belgium are generally taxed as residents, but there's a loophole for foreign executives, directors, high-level specialists and research experts appointed by a foreign employer to work 'temporarily' in Belgium, who are allowed to exclude part of their salary and other income from Belgian tax if the payments relate to professional or private interests outside Belgium. Such payments include salary received for work performed abroad, cost of living and housing allowances, school fees for children attending primary or secondary school, and home leave and tax equalisation payments. The total annual exclusion is limited to €11,250 per employee, excluding school fees and removal costs related to your relocation, if these were directly paid by your employer. The exclusion limit rises to €30,000 where you work for a company qualified as a 'co-ordination or research centre' under Belgian law.

Application for this special status must be made by your employer when you're first hired to work in Belgium and he must be able to show that your 'primary economic interests' lie in your home country (or at least outside Belgium), even while you're living and working in Belgium. Other factors that are taken into consideration when the application is processed include:

- whether you were recruited for the job outside Belgium;
- the length of your assignment (and whether it's for a limited period);
- the possibility of your being transferred elsewhere;
- whether you maintain a home or own property abroad;
- whether you have children enrolled in an international school, either in Belgium or abroad;
- whether you're maintaining your contributions or eligibility for social security, bonus or private insurance plans in your home country;
- whether there's a 'diplomatic clause' in your rental agreement in Belgium (see page 89).

Holland: As in Belgium, inclusion in a Dutch municipal register is generally considered to constitute residence for tax purposes. Non-residents are restricted in terms of the tax deductions they may make against earned income and may elect to be taxed as residents under certain circumstances.

For foreigners working in Holland there's a special provision, called the '30 per cent rule', which entitles you to a tax-free allowance of up to 30 per cent of your base salary for the first 120 months you're working in Holland. You and your employer must make a joint application for this status to the tax authority in Heerlan within four months of your arrival in Holland. You must have been recruited abroad by a Dutch employer, i.e. a company registered as a withholding agent for the Dutch tax authority, and your employer must verify that you possess an expertise that isn't available in the Dutch labour market. There are some exceptions to these requirements: for example, you may qualify if you're the first employee of a new branch being opened in Holland (i.e. your employer isn't yet registered as a Dutch tax withholding agent) or if you change jobs after you arrive and previously qualified.

Once you've qualified under the 30 per cent rule, you can decide from year to year if you want to claim a further allowance, under the 'deemed non-resident' rule, which permits you to exclude certain overseas income from your tax declaration. However, you must choose this option in the course of the tax year to which it will apply, meaning that you can't wait until you file your tax return to decide whether or not you want to be treated as a 'deemed non-resident'. The latest tax information can be obtained from the Ministry of Finance website (⌨ www.minfin.nl) and the Personal Finance section of the Expatica website for Holland (⌨ www.expatica.com).

Luxembourg: In Luxembourg, tax domicile (*domicile fiscale/Wohnsitzung*) is determined by your 'place of usual abode' (*lieu de séjour habituel/gewöhnlicher Aufenthalt*), and generally you will be taxed as a resident if you're physically present in Luxembourg for at least six months or 183 days during the tax year, or if your family is living there while you travel for your work. As in Holland, non-residents are denied most personal allowances, many deductions and some other tax-reduction opportunities, but in any case most of your earned income is taxed in your country of residence, thanks to numerous agreements regarding 'border hoppers'

(*Grenzenspringer*). If you're living in a neighbouring country and working in Luxembourg, it's usually possible to have your Luxembourg employer withhold income tax and social security payments and remit them to your country of residence.

Taxable Income

The tax systems in Belgium, Holland and Luxembourg each define various categories of income, all of which you're required to declare. Net taxable income in each category consists of your gross income or payments received, reduced by expenses directly related to the generation of that income. Net losses in one category generally can't be used to offset income in another category but in most cases can be carried over to subsequent tax years (or used to offset a debt from a previous year). After the net taxable income in each category has been determined, either the tax due is calculated separately for each category (in Holland) or a single calculation is applied to the aggregate income (in Belgium and Luxembourg). In all three countries, children's income is normally included on their parents' tax return.

A feature peculiar to the Benelux countries is the idea that home ownership constitutes taxable 'income' on the basis that it saves you having to pay rent – never mind your mortgage repayments, property taxes, utility bills, maintenance costs, etc! If you own your primary residence, you must declare a hypothetical income based on the assumed rental value of your home. You must also declare a notional income on a second or holiday home, although the calculations and allowable expenses are considerably different from those for your primary residence.

Belgium: Taxable income in Belgium is divided into four categories: earned income, property income, income from movable assets, and miscellaneous income. Each category is strictly defined, both in terms of how the income is to be calculated and in terms of the expenses and other deductions that are allowed against gross income to arrive at net income. Married couples (including registered couples or cohabiting couples who qualify to file jointly) must determine their incomes separately for each category, applying a number of complex allocation rules to any joint income.

● **Earned income** includes salaries and wages as well as profits from self-employment or any business enterprise. You don't need to declare most forms of employer reimbursement for expenses, e.g. travel costs for business trips, but you must include the value of any benefits-in-kind, such as housing allowances, personal use of a company car or other perks, unless you qualify as a temporary resident under the special programme for executives and expert researchers (see **Liability** on page 261). The earned income category also includes profits and proceeds from former professional activities and 'replacement income', i.e. all redundancy or severance benefit payments, employer pensions and most forms of sick pay, all of which you must declare for tax purposes. The Belgians have recently started taxing stock options, and these must also be included on your income tax declaration in the year they're granted (although you aren't taxed on any gains you make when exercising them.). A few forms of 'social transfer' are tax exempt, primarily child benefit payments, maternity allowances and certain disability allowances paid through the Belgian social insurance system.

Earned income can be reduced by certain expenses, including most (but not all) social security contributions. Professional expenses not reimbursed by your employer are deductible against all categories of earned income, including an allowance for commuting to and from work (based on the number of kilometres travelled from your registered residence), certain insurance premiums, and most expenses related to a business or professional practice. Each category of allowable expenses is subject to a range of thresholds, limitations and burdens of proof. If this is too complicated, you can simply take a flat-rate deduction for professional expenses, based on the total income declared in this category. For the 2000 tax year there was a sliding scale for this deduction whereby taxpayers with earned income above €13,906.83 were allowed to deduct €1,529.50 plus 3 per cent of any income over €13,906.83.

● **Property income** is either actual rental income or 'cadastral income' assigned by the local property register (*cadastre/kadaster*). Cadastral income is a hypothetical rent based on the property description and valuation listed in the property register. Property is revalued every 15 years, and an annual index is applied to the last official valuation in order to arrive at the current hypothetical rental income from the property. If you own your own home and are currently living in it, you must declare property income at a rate of 100 per cent of your home's indexed cadastral valuation, which should be notified to you by the local property authority. Income from other types of property is declared either as the actual net rent received (after deduction of relevant expenses) or as 140 per cent of the property's cadastral value – whichever figure is higher. Therefore, if you own a second home which you don't rent (e.g. a holiday home), you must declare property income at 140 per cent of its cadastral value.

In the case of your own home, you're allowed to deduct from your assumed property income your mortgage interest and a lump sum for you and each family member. For the year 2000, this lump sum deduction was €3,730.80 for you and €309.87 for each family member. You may not deduct anything from the property income for a second home. Any property you use in a trade or business generating professional income is reported on a business tax return, rather than as property income on your personal tax declaration.

● **Income from movable assets** refers primarily to dividends and interest income from various types of savings account and investment. Most Belgian securities are subject to withholding, and payments received from them in the form of interest or dividends don't usually need to be declared as taxable income. You must, however, declare all income earned abroad, including foreign income subject to double taxation treaty provisions (for which you will be entitled to a tax credit at a later stage – see page 266), income from ordinary savings accounts and investments not subject to withholding, annuities and rental income (other than property rental). Savings account interest is subject to an exemption for the first €1,388.30 per household and there are a few other exemptions, which change from year to year, based on various investment incentive programmes established by the government.

● **Miscellaneous income** is comprised of all income not earned by performing a professional activity. This category includes 80 per cent of maintenance payments received (most types of alimony, child support and other court ordered maintenance payments), prizes and subsidies (including scholarships and royalties), capital gains subject to taxation (see **Capital Gains Tax** on page 275) and even gambling and lottery winnings. (You cannot even have a flutter in Belgium without the tax man breathing down your neck!)

Holland: Under the new tax system, introduced in 2001, taxable income is categorised into three 'boxes'. (Prior to the 2001 tax year, there were five categories, so the Dutch are clearly making progress.)

- **Box 1** consists of income from work and home, including:
  - income from employment (both current and previous), including wages and salaries and the value of all benefits-in-kind (such as housing or private use of a company car), as well as most social security payments, old age pensions and unemployment benefits or redundancy payments;
  - profits from business or professional activity;
  - income from other activities (such as taking in lodgers) and copyrights;
  - income from periodic payments, including scholarships and subsidies from the state, most court-mandated maintenance payments (alimony or child support), and annuities received from programmes where premiums were tax deductible;
  - certain annuities and life assurance policies;
  - tax refunds;
  - 'income' from home ownership. As in Belgium, you must declare a hypothetical income from owning your own home, which is calculated by the tax authority and available as a set of tables at the local office of the tax authority and your town hall. The notional income from owning your home is supposed to take into account all the usual expenses of home ownership, so you may deduct from this 'income' only your mortgage interest and any ground rent.

- **Box 2** is for income from holdings constituting a substantial interest in a company or other business venture. To be considered as having a substantial interest in a company, you must hold at least 5 per cent of the issued capital or 5 per cent of a particular class of shares in a company, either alone or with a partner. Residents must declare all substantial interests in all companies, whether or not they're based in Holland. Non-resident taxpayers are subject to tax only on substantial interests held in Dutch companies. Taxable income in this category consists of dividends and interest paid by the companies in which you hold a substantial interest and any capital gains on the sale or other disposal of such shares.

- **Box 3** consists of income from savings and investments. Under Dutch tax law, it's assumed that you receive a return of 4 per cent on all types of savings and investments, irrespective of the amount of dividends or interest you actually receive during the year. To calculate your taxable income, you average the net capital (asset value minus any related liabilities) invested for the year by adding its value on 1st January to its value on 31st December and dividing the result by two. 'Investments' that must be included in this category include holdings in bank and savings accounts and the value of a second home, stocks and other shares and endowment insurance policies not linked to an owner-occupied dwelling. Household assets, art objects and certain investments (such as 'environmentally friendly' investments approved by the government) are exempt. Non-residents are taxed only on property located in Holland and on profit-sharing rights (other than employee programmes) based on the net profits of companies having their seat of management in Holland.

Luxembourg: There are five categories of taxable income in Luxembourg:

- **Income from trades or businesses**, including net profits from a trade or business, including agriculture and forestry income;
- **Employment income**, including salary and all benefits-in-kind (e.g. housing or the use of a company car), as well as all sick pay, maternity benefits or other disability payments made in lieu of salary. Exempt from income tax are certain bonuses paid for night or overtime work (up to specified limits), severance pay (again, up to limits) and seniority bonuses, such as those paid to employees completing 5, 10 or 20 years of service in a company.
- **Pensions and annuities**, on which residents must normally pay tax as they're received, except in the case of pensions paid by a foreign government with which Luxembourg has a double taxation treaty. All forms of private pension are included in taxable income even when paid from abroad.
- **Investment income**, including most types of interest and dividend (so-called passive investment income) and net income from rented property, as well as 'income' from home ownership (see below);
- **Other income**, including any payments for jobs or services in excess of €250 and taxable capital gains (see **Capital Gains** on page 275).

Like Belgium and Holland, Luxembourg also requires taxpayers to pay for the benefits of home ownership by adding a nominal amount to their investment income. The value of home ownership is calculated by reference to a property's 'unitary value' (see also **Residential & Property Taxes** on page 273 and **Wealth Tax** on page 274), which is usually no more than 2 per cent of the actual market value of the property. Your taxable 'income' is calculated as 4 to 6 per cent of the unitary value, so the amount added to your taxable income for owning your home is much smaller than in Belgium and Holland.

The good news about taxation in Luxembourg, unlike Belgium, is that fortuitous receipts such as gambling winnings, gifts, rewards and prizes are exempt from tax.

Allowances, Deductions & Credits

Once you've determined your net taxable income in each tax category, you may apply certain allowances, either against specific categories of taxable income or, in some cases, against your total net taxable income. This is where things become even more complicated, particularly in Belgium. The information given below applied in mid-2001, but all three countries index most or all of their allowances each year. Revised figures are normally announced at the end or beginning of the year, when tax declaration forms are printed.

Belgium: In Belgium, there's a long list of tax allowances, referred to as 'expenses entitling to a tax relief' in the official English translation of the tax laws. Allowances are usually applied to your aggregate taxable income, either as deductions from taxable income or as tax credits. Most allowances in Belgium, however, are applied from the bottom up rather than from the top down, which means that you deduct income from or apply tax credits to the lowest tax bracket first, not from the highest bracket (see **Tax Calculation** below for an example). Note also that couples filing a joint return must calculate all their taxable income and most of their allowances separately. There are a number of rules that apply to the allocation of allowances, usually granting them to the partner with the higher income.

The principal allowances are:

- a personal exemption of €5,205.76 for a single person and €4,139.82 for a spouse;
- an exemption for dependent children of €1,115.52 for the first child, €1,735.26 for the second child, €3,544.87 for the third, and €3,941.51 for the fourth plus each additional child – suggesting that the Belgian government is keen to increase the population;
- exemptions for other dependent persons in the household, a disabled spouse, a single parent family and certain other family situations.

Some allowances (principally relating to investments or state-sponsored benefit programmes) are granted as a tax credit that may be calculated using either an average tax rate or your marginal rate (see **Tax Calculation** below). The rules relating to this type of allowance are complex and subject to a variety of limits. You're also allowed a tax credit on foreign income (from all sources) based on your average tax rate. This essentially amounts to a proportion of your final tax bill relative to the amount of your declared taxable income that came from abroad. If, for example, a quarter of your taxable income came from a foreign country with a tax treaty with Belgium, your tax credit would be 25 per cent of your total tax bill.

Holland: In its recent tax reform the Dutch government has moved towards the use of tax credits rather than personal deductions and allowances. There's a personal tax credit available to all taxpayers of €1,576, which is increased by up to €920 if you're currently employed and earning over a certain amount. For each child under the age of 27 living in your household you receive a tax credit of €1,261. Under certain circumstances, the personal tax credit for single parents in paid employment can be increased by up to €1,261. There's also a tax credit for taxpayers over the age of 65 if their total income (the sum of all three boxes) is less than €27,704.

Most tax deductions must be taken directly against the related income and within the appropriate 'box' or category of taxable income (see above), as each box is separately taxed. Those that aren't directly related to the acquisition of income are considered to be allowances. These include alimony payments, certain company start-up loans, living expenses for children up to the age of 27, medical and other extraordinary expenses, educational expenses, certain costs related to the preservation of historic buildings, and donations to charitable or cultural organisations approved by the Ministry of Finance. These allowances must be taken against box 1 income first, but if they reduce box one income to zero any excess must be applied first against box 3 income and finally against box 2 income. Only resident taxpayers are entitled to allowances, some of which are subject to thresholds or fixed amounts.

Luxembourg: There's a variety of deductions and allowances against the combined total of all five kinds of taxable income in Luxembourg. There's a standard personal allowance of €600 for single people and €1,200 for a couple, plus an additional €4,500 if both spouses work and earn at least a certain amount. Child benefits (see page 231) must be declared as taxable income, but you can claim an allowance for each child living in your household, and there's an additional allowance for children living at home who don't qualify for child benefit (up to the age of 21 or older under some circumstances). Certain gifts or donations to recognised charitable organisations may be deducted from taxable income, and there's an allowance available to households with 'extraordinary expenses', i.e. which exceed a certain percentage of the total taxable income of the household.

You're allowed to deduct up to €4,800 if you're supporting relatives, and there are a number of other deductions and allowances available for child care, children's educational expenses, household members with physical or mental handicaps or who are over 65. Certain contributions to voluntary insurance and pension programmes qualify for a tax allowance, as well as a number of investment programmes sponsored by the government to encourage people to invest and buy their homes.

Tax Calculation

Each country has its own rules regarding whether or not married couples can be taxed as a single entity and how various kinds of income and deductions or tax credits are allocated between partners or joint owners of property. In all three countries, most thresholds, limits and standard deductions and allowances are increased each year in line with inflation. Most of the examples given below are taken from information relating to the 2000 tax year. Information about Holland reflects the changes to the Dutch tax system made in 2001.

Belgium: You must combine your net taxable income from each of the four categories (see above) before any allowances or credits are applied. Tax rates are then applied to the total figure as shown in the table below:

Taxable Income (€)	Tax rate (%)
0–6,395.65	25
6,395.66–8,477.96	30
8,477.97–12,097.20	40
12,097.21–27,838.44	45
27,838.45–41,745.27	50
41,745.28–61,229.79	52.5
Over 61,229.70	55

The personal exemption and allowances for children, other dependants and special family situations are deducted from the lowest tax bracket first, as are the allowances for life assurance premiums and certain types of investment and pension fund and replacement income (subject, of course, to various thresholds and complex conditions). In the case of a couple filing together, the total taxable income and tax rate must be determined for each partner separately before any deductions or allowances are allocated; in general, the parent with the higher income deducts the allowance for all the children. The resulting total is the 'principal tax', from which you may deduct withheld taxes, tax credits and advance payments, resulting in the final amount due to the state – almost! There's still a 'crisis' surcharge to be applied and possibly a municipal income tax, depending on where you live.

The so-called crisis surcharge is levied against your principal tax figure. The surcharge, which was introduced in 1963 and is gradually being phased out, was originally a flat 3 per cent, but from the 2000 tax year varies from 1 to 3 per cent; further reductions are promised in the coming years. The communes and municipalities throughout Belgium assess local income taxes by means of a surcharge on the amount of income tax you're liable for[again. The rate varies from 0 to 10 per cent.

The following is a simplified example to illustrate how this method of deducting allowances from the lowest tax bracket first works:

A couple with three children have total taxable income of €22,500 divided as follows:

- **Wife:** €15,000
    - The wife is entitled to a personal exemption of €4,139.82 and an allowance of €6,395.65 for the three children. The total amount (€10,535.47) must be subtracted from the bottom up, reducing the amount payable in the lowest bracket first, with the result that she pays no tax at 25 per cent (the first €6,395.65 of her taxable income), no tax at 30 per cent (the next €2,082.31) and is 'disallowed' tax at 40 per cent on €2,057.71. The remaining taxable income of 4,464.53 is therefore taxed as follows: €1,561.73 at 40 per cent (= €624.69) and €2,902.80 at 45 per cent (= €1,306.26, making a total tax liability of €1,930.95).

- **Husband:** €7,500
    - The husband takes a spousal allowance of €4,139.83, leaving €3,360.17, of which €2,255.82 is subject to tax at 25 per cent (= €563.95) and the remaining €1,104.35 at 30 per cent (= €331.30) for a total of €895.25.

    - Together, the family's 'principal tax' liability is now €2,826.20, which is subject to a crisis surcharge and the addition of any applicable municipal taxes (see above), as well as any adjustment applicable for under or over-withholding or pre-payment of taxes during the year. (You may even be eligible for a tax credit if you've had too much tax withheld!)

Holland: Taxpayers in Holland are assessed separately, even married or registered couples. Income, deductions and allowances for children or other jointly 'owned' assets or benefits may be split between the partners on whatever basis they choose, as long as the entire amount is accounted for between the two tax returns. Tax is calculated according to the net taxable income (after deductions and allowances) in each box.

Box 1 tax rates are as follows:

Taxable Income (€)	Tax rate (%)
0–14,870	2.95
14,871–27,009	8.2
27,010–46,309	42
Over 46,309	52

Net income in boxes 2 and 3 is taxed at flat rates of 25 and 30 per cent respectively. Tax credits are then applied against your total tax liability (see **Allowances** on page 266). Note that social security contributions are automatically deducted from all taxable income up to €27,009 at 29.4 per cent (see page 228).

Luxembourg: In Luxembourg, families and married couples are usually taxed as a single entity, although separated, widowed and divorced taxpayers remain in tax class 2 for three years after their change in status. Children under the age of 18 are included on their parents' (or a parent's) tax return. Children over the age of 18 can be included on their parents' tax return if they're enrolled in school or a vocational programme, live at home and are receiving financial support from their parents. Earnings for the school year from part-time jobs or training schemes must be declared on the family's tax return if they exceed certain limits.

Your taxable income is the total of all five categories of income (see **Taxable Income** on page 263), minus deductions and allowances. The net figure is taxed at various rates each covering a €25 income bracket. The tax authority publishes tables showing the amount of tax due for every taxable income bracket in each tax class and for every size of family up to eight children! The tables below give a simplified picture of tax burdens for single and married taxpayers with various incomes, in which the 'effective rate' is the average tax rate for each sample income shown:

Single Taxpayer (Class 1)

Taxable Income (€)	Effective Tax Rate (%)	Tax (€)
12,500	6.02	753
25,000	16.26	4,065
37,500	24.29	9,110
50,000	39.22	14,610
62,500	32.18	20,110
75,000	34.39	25,790
125,000	39.03	48,790

Married Couple With One Child (Class 2.1)

Taxable Income (€)	Effective Tax Rate (%)	Tax (€)
12,500	0	0
25,000	1.22	305
37,500	8.44	3,165
50,000	13.86	6,929
62,500	18.54	11,590
75,000	22.69	17,019
125,000	31.22	39,019

Note that the taxes shown above don't include a solidarity tax surcharge of 2.5 per cent, which is put towards Luxembourg's unemployment benefit system.

Note also that the Luxembourg tax system is to be reformed in 2002, when personal exemption limits will be almost doubled to around €9,800 for single taxpayers and around €19,500 for married couples. Under the new system, tax rates will start at 8 per cent and rise to 38 per cent (compared with the current top rate of 46 per cent), although it's likely that the 2.5 per cent surcharge for unemployment contributions will be retained.

Income Tax Returns

Although it's claimed that you don't have to file a tax return (*déclaration/aangifte*) if your income tax obligation is satisfied by the salary taxes withheld by your employer, there are so many credits and allowances available that most taxpayers need or choose to file a return. Tax returns in all three Benelux countries are actually tax declarations: you declare your income and all other items that affect the calculation of your taxes but you don't actually make the calculation yourself (thank goodness). This is left to the tax authorities, who use the information you submit to prepare your tax assessment.

Belgium: Even if your only income is from employment, you may need to file a tax return in order to declare your liability to municipal or communal taxes. Tax declaration forms are sent out soon after the end of the tax year to which they apply. You will receive a form in French if you're living in Wallonia or in one of the French communities in or around Brussels. Taxpayers in Flanders receive forms in Flemish. There are differences in some of the allowances, particularly involving the municipal tax surcharge, depending on whether you live in a French or a Flemish area, so you must use the form you're sent. If you don't receive a tax form and you need or want to file a return, you must contact the local tax inspector's office (usually located in or near the town hall for the community in which you live). Those filing on a non-resident basis (including those on the special programme for executives and expert researchers) must obtain tax forms from the Tax Inspector for Non-residents (*Contrôle des Contributions de Bruxelles Etranger/Inspecties Buitenland*, Place Jean Jacobs 10, 1000 Brussels, ☎ 02-548 5788 or 02-548 5768).

Your tax form indicates the date by which it must be returned, which changes each year but usually falls around the end of June. If you won't be able to complete the form by the due date, you must make a request for an extension before 1st June. In fact, the government often adds a few extra days or even weeks to the deadline, particularly when there have been last-minute changes to the tax regulations or problems in printing or distributing tax forms. These extensions are publicised in the news media and are also available via the Internet from the current news (*actualités/nieuws*) pages of the Ministry of Finance website (🖳 www.minfin. fgov.be).

Your employer provides a summary of tax paid and withheld, as do most banks, insurance companies and government agencies where you have accounts or deposits. These documents must be included with your return in order to verify your claims for allowances and deductions. Married couples must state which partner is responsible for each element of income or expense and the basis for allocation of any jointly held property. Cohabiting partners may file a joint return, provided they're registered at the same address according to the local population register and meet certain other requirements.

The completed tax return and all supporting documents must be sent to the address on your tax form (usually the office of the tax inspector for the local district). If you're making a declaration under non-resident tax status, you must send your form to the Tax Inspector for Non-residents in Brussels (see above).

Holland: Income tax declarations are sent to taxpayers early in January for the tax year ended 31st December. It isn't necessary to file a return if you don't require a tax assessment, i.e. if the tax due after taking into account your salary and investment tax withholdings is less than €196. You need to file, however, if you've overpaid and need to claim a refund or allowances. Tax returns must be filed by 31st March of the year following the tax year, e.g. by 31st March 2002 for the 2001 tax year.

Luxembourg: You must file a tax return if you meet any of the following conditions:

- You have income from self-employment or any form of business income not subject to withholding.

- You taxable income includes more than €1,500 of passive investment income (interest and dividends) subject to withholding.

- Your total taxable income exceeds €45,000 if single, €25,000 if making a joint return or €21,250 if you're in tax class 1a.

The main tax return form is called Form 100 and is available in French (Form 100a) or German (Form 100b). There are three annexes to this form: annexe CI is used to report income and expenses from a trade or business; annexe SP is for reporting employment and pension income and related deductions; and annexe LD is for rental income. Separate forms are required for reporting income from other kinds of business enterprise. Forms can be obtained at the local tax office or from the *Administration des Contributions Directes, Service Imprimés*, 23 rue Mercier, 2982 Luxembourg.

Your completed tax forms, along with all supporting documents and a copy of your tax card, must be filed by 31st March of the year following the relevant tax year.

If you leave Luxembourg during the year or cease to be subject to Luxembourg income taxes for any reason, you're required to file a mid-year tax return, usually due within two months of your change of status.

If you aren't required to file a tax declaration but are entitled to a refund, you may file a form called a *décompte annuel* in order to claim your refund and adjust your tax card to correct your withholding for the coming tax year.

Tax Bills

A few months after filing your tax return, you should receive a notice of assessment from your assigned tax inspector. The assessment will summarise the basis for calculating your taxes and indicate the total amount of tax due for the year, reduced by the total of pre-payments and withholding credited to your account. Any amount due to the tax authorities must be paid within two months of the date of the assessment. (The tax authorities usually enclose a bank transfer form for you to complete.) Amounts due to you in respect of overpayments are generally credited directly to your bank account within a few weeks of the assessment (and can be used to buy Champagne to celebrate the occasion). If you're self-employed and making quarterly advance tax payments, you usually have the option to use a refund as a credit against your next pre-payment (but the Champagne method is more enjoyable).

It may take as long as six months (sometimes more, especially in Belgium) to receive your tax assessment and bill. If you don't receive an assessment by the end of the year in which you filed your tax return (or by May of the following year in Belgium, owing to the later filing date and the extra level of complication), you should contact the office to which you sent your return.

If you disagree with your assessment, you should contact the local tax inspection office as soon as possible after receiving it. (The address and phone number is indicated on the notice you receive.) The onus will be on you to explain and prove any error you claim has been made in calculating your tax bill. (You can't dispute the assessment simply because your tax computation software gave you a different figure.) Tax inspectors can be surprisingly willing to admit and correct errors, provided you approach them politely and with a carefully documented explanation of what you think is wrong. If you cannot afford to pay your tax bill as a result of circumstances beyond your control (e.g. emergency medical bills or a personal or family crisis you can document), it's possible to have the bill reduced or even waived altogether – sometimes!

RESIDENTIAL & PROPERTY TAXES

As if paying tax on the assumed rental value of your home weren't bad enough (see **Taxable Income** on page 263), in most communities you're assessed for at least one kind of property or residential tax.

Belgium: In Belgium, property tax (*précompte immobilier/onroerende voorheffing*) is levied by the municipality against all property owners as a percentage of 'cadastral income' (see page 264), re-assessed every 15 years and indexed annually for inflation. Each municipality sets its own standards for charging property tax, but rates generally range from 20 to 45 per cent of the indexed cadastral value. There are various allowances you can claim against the cadastral value according to the use and occupancy of the property. These are more generous for residential property than for business property.

There's also a municipal income tax, levied as a surcharge on your national income tax (see above). Rates for this surcharge range from 0 to 10 per cent but are around 6 to 7 per cent in most areas.

Holland: There are two property taxes levied against residential property in Holland, both of which are based on the market value of a property. One is charged to the person residing in the home and the other is charged to the owner. An owner-occupier must therefore pay both taxes. On a home valued at €400,000, the combined taxes would be around €650, although the exact rate varies by community.

The municipality also levies a variety of taxes related to garbage collection, sewage, an environmental tax, and for those living north of Amsterdam, a 'water control' tax, which is put towards the maintenance of the all-important network of dykes protecting land reclaimed from the sea. (The levy is known locally as 'the tax we pay to keep our feet dry'.) Most municipal taxes are added to water and electricity bills, and can add up to as much as €200 per month for an average home.

Luxembourg: Municipalities in Luxembourg levy a property tax (*impôt foncier*) on all forms of property based on its 'unitary value' (see page 266 and **Wealth Tax** below). Rates vary from 0.8 to 8 per cent depending on the type of property and what it's used for.

WEALTH TAX

Until 2001, Belgium was the only Benelux country not to impose a wealth tax on its residents; as a result, there were estimated to be 100,000 tax refugees living in Belgium, including 60,000 Dutch and 10,000 French nationals. However, recent changes in the Dutch tax system leave Luxembourg the only Benelux country to impose a wealth tax. (It's too early to tell if the Dutch tax refugees are planning to move back home now that their own wealth tax has been abolished.)

Wealth tax (*impôt sur la fortune*) in Luxembourg is assessed on the net value of your assets on the 1st January each year. There are four categories of assets subject to the tax: property, agricultural and forestry business, and other assets. Each category is assessed separately, and any debts can be claimed against the asset category to which they apply. What keeps the wealth tax from driving wealthy Luxembourgers out of the country is the fact that property is still valued according to estimates made by the Germans after they invaded the Duchy in 1940. The 'unitary value' (*valeur unitaire/Einheitswert*) of residential property is based on the estimated rental income it generated in August 1939, adjusted by a coefficient reflecting its use and condition. All other property is assessed on the basis of its estimated rental value in 1941. Even foreign property is assigned a unitary value based on these old records, and in most cases its unitary value is no more than 2 per cent of its current market value.

Items such as household goods, furniture and clothing are exempt from wealth tax, and assets such as cash, shares, jewellery and art collections are subject to various thresholds. For example, the first €35,000 of shares held by a single taxpayer aren't taxed, the first €70,000 held by a married couple. Taxpayers receive a general allowance of €2,500 for themselves and their spouse, plus an additional allowance if you're aged over 60 and an allowance for each child living in the household.

Once your net asset value has been determined and all exemptions and allowances subtracted, tax is assessed at the rate of 0.5 per cent. Wealth tax is paid quarterly, in February, May, August and November. Asset values are re-assessed every three years, or when your net worth changes by more than €75,000 or over 20 per cent, or if there's a change in your circumstances that affects the allowances or deductions you can claim for wealth tax purposes, which generally means if you marry or divorce or when one of your children leaves home.

Residents of Luxembourg are subject to wealth tax on their world-wide assets, while non-residents pay tax only on assets located in the Duchy, although they aren't normally eligible for allowances or deductions. There are several wealth tax treaties with other countries, designed to avoid double taxation of assets.

There's also a transfer tax of 6 per cent on all sales or transfers of property (based on the selling price) in Luxembourg – 9 per cent on property sold within the boundaries of Luxembourg city. This isn't to be confused with capital gains tax (see below).

CAPITAL GAINS TAX

Capital gains tax (CGT) is generally payable only on profits from sales that are considered 'speculative' or where a taxpayer holds a 'substantial interest' in a business. Naturally, each of the three national tax authorities has its own definition of what constitutes a 'speculative' investment and 'substantial interest'. Although most capital gains taxes are withheld at source, you're required to declare them on your income tax return if they exceed certain limits.

Belgium: Most typical forms of capital gain aren't taxed at all in Belgium. The two main exceptions are profits on the sale of property (land and/or buildings) other than your principal home that you've owned for less than a certain period and profits on the transfer of a 'significant holding' of shares in a company to a non-Belgian entity. The sale of your principal home is exempt from CGT (which is only fair, as you've been paying tax on its rental value every year). For all other buildings located in Belgium, you must pay CGT if you sell the property within five years of purchase. In the case of land, you must have owned it for at least eight years to be exempt from CGT. If you sell a property within these time limits, the capital gain resulting from the sale must be reported as miscellaneous income (see page 264) on your income tax return for the year in which the sale occurs. Note, however, that you may reduce the capital gain by 5 per cent of the property's purchase price for each full year that you've owned it. Note also that capital gains are subject to income tax at flat rates: capital gains on land sold less than five years after it was acquired are taxed at 33 per cent; other capital gains attract 16 per cent tax. Capital gains taxes are included in the calculation of the crisis surcharge (see page 269) but aren't included in that of regional and municipal tax surcharges.

Holland: In Holland you're allowed to pocket 100 per cent of any profit made from the sale of property, whether or not it's your principal home, and shares held for investment purposes. The only form of capital gain subject to tax is one resulting from selling part or all of a 'substantial interest' in a business or company, defined as at least 5 per cent of all shares or of any single class of stock or other ownership investment. In the case of married couples, the holdings of both partners are taken into account when determining the percentage of ownership. Capital gains are included with box 2 income, which is taxed at a flat rate of 25 per cent. Any capital losses are deducted from capital gains realised in the same tax year, and net losses may be carried forward indefinitely but may not be used to offset any other type of income.

Luxembourg: There are three types of capital gain subject to tax in Luxembourg. The first is any gain on 'movable assets' sold within six months of their acquisition. Movable assets include shares, artwork, jewellery, and virtually everything else you might buy except property (land and buildings). Profits on movable assets held for less than six months must be declared on your tax return and are taxed as ordinary income.

The second kind of taxable capital gain is any profit on the sale of shares, where your constructive ownership in the company (including that of your spouse and other members of your household) exceeds 25 per cent of the total ownership interest or of a particular category of shares (e.g. preferred shares or non-voting shares).

Thirdly, CGT is payable on the sale of property or immovable assets except in the case of your principal residence, provided you've lived there for at least five years. It's possible to be exempted from CGT on the sale of your home within this period if you had to sell it because of a job-related relocation. Otherwise (and for all other types of land or buildings), gains are subject to ordinary income tax. Where you've owned a property for more than two years, you're permitted to adjust the purchase price for inflation. You can also claim a €50,000 exemption for each ten-year period that you've owned a property and an exemption of €75,000 if you're selling a house or apartment that you've inherited from your parents or your spouse's parents, provided the property was the principal residence of the deceased for at least five years prior to his death.

Capital gains are taxed at 50 per cent of your average tax rate, to which the solidarity surcharge of 2.5 per cent (see page 271) is then applied. The maximum rate for capital gains is currently 23.575 per cent (50 per cent of the top income tax rate, surcharged by 2.5 per cent), but will fall to 19.475 per cent in 2002.

INHERITANCE & GIFT TAX

As in most other western countries, dying doesn't free you from the clutches of the tax man. Belgium, Holland and Luxembourg all levy both inheritance tax (*droits de succession/recht van successie*) and gift tax (*droits de donations/recht van schenking*) on their inhabitants. Inheritance tax, called estate tax or death duty in some countries, is levied on the estate of a deceased person. The country where you pay inheritance tax is decided by your tax domicile or residence, using more or less the same rules that apply to your liability for income taxes. If you're living permanently in Benelux and have been paying income tax as a resident, inheritance tax will normally apply to your world-wide estate. There's a general exception, however, for property situated abroad, which is normally subject to local inheritance tax.

When a person resident in Benelux dies, an inheritance tax return must be filed, usually within five to seven months of the date of death, depending upon whether the person died in his country of residence, elsewhere in Europe or outside Europe. The return is generally prepared by a notary (*notaire/notaris*). Estates are assessed at the market value of the property on the date of death less certain debts and liabilities of the deceased, including funeral expenses. If the estate is small (different limits apply in each country), no return is necessary. Any inheritance tax due is paid by the beneficiaries, irrespective of where they're domiciled, and not by the estate. The rate of tax and the allowances that can be claimed vary (greatly) according to the relationship between the beneficiaries and the deceased, as well as the amount being transferred by the inheritance.

Gift tax is calculated in the same way as inheritance tax, according to the relationship between the donor and the recipient and the size of the gift. Gifts made shortly before death are considered to have been advance distributions of the estate and will normally be included in the inheritance tax calculations. (Each country's definition of 'shortly' varies, however, from a couple of months to five years!) Any gift tax paid at the time of the gift will be credited against the inheritance tax due.

Inheritance law is an extremely complicated subject (especially in Benelux) and professional advice should be sought from an experienced lawyer or notary who understands the law in all the countries involved. Your will (see below) is also a vital component in reducing inheritance and gift tax to the minimum or delaying its payment.

Belgium: There are two separate tax regimes for inheritance tax, one covering residents of the Walloon region (which for this purpose includes the Brussels Capital Region), and the other for residents of Flanders (except those living in the Brussels Capital Region). The rules for calculating inheritance tax are every bit as complicated as those for income tax (which is saying something) and in the event of a death, you should consult a notary as soon as possible to start the process of evaluating the estate and completing the necessary tax returns. The value of an estate is assessed as the market values of the assets and property at the date of death, and not the cadastral value used for income and other tax calculations.

In Wallonia (and the Brussels Capital Region) the gross amount of an inheritance passing to a surviving spouse and lineal heirs is taxed at various rates, from 3 per cent on assets valued at up to €12,400 to 30 per cent on assets worth €500,000. There's no tax on estates worth less than €620. A surviving spouse and lineal heirs are each entitled to exemptions but, as with income tax, they must be subtracted from the lowest tax bracket first. Higher tax rates (from 20 to 80 per cent) apply where the beneficiaries are more distant relatives or unrelated to the deceased, and there's no exemption for these categories of heirs.

In Flanders (excluding the Brussels Capital Region) surviving spouses, cohabitants (under certain conditions) and lineal relatives of the deceased are taxed at between 3 per cent (on assets worth up to €50,000) to 27 per cent (on assets valued at over €250,000). To complicate matters further, inheritance taxes are applied separately to real estate and movable property. There's no general or personal exemption from taxation, but a small tax credit of up to €500 is granted on all inheritances valued at less than €49,500. The credit is increased for a surviving spouse and children under 21. Rates for inheritances passed to siblings range from 30 to 65 per cent, and inheritances to all others from 45 to 65 per cent. The best advice would be simply not to die while resident in Belgium if you can possibly avoid it!

Non-residents are liable for Belgian transfer tax (*droits de mutation par décès/recht van overgang bij overlijden*) on property located in Belgium. Transfer tax is calculated in much the same way as inheritance or gift taxes.

Holland: In Holland there are three categories of beneficiary: category 1 includes the spouse, direct descendants (children, grandchildren, etc.) and indirect descendants to the second degree (primarily nieces and nephews); category 2 is for siblings and direct ascendants (i.e. parents and grandparents, if still alive); category 3 covers everyone else. Category 1 beneficiaries are taxed at between 5 per cent (on assets worth less than €18,750) and 27 per cent (on assets worth over €750,000). Category 2 beneficiaries are taxed at between 25 and 53 per cent and category 3 recipients at between 41 and 68 per cent respectively.

A surviving spouse (including registered partner) receives an exemption of €262,614. Non-registered partners may receive all or part of this exemption, depending on the exact nature and duration of the relationship, and on whether or not they had any children with the deceased. The exemption for the deceased's children varies from €6,959 to €86,292 depending primarily on the age of the child at the date of the parent's death. Parents receive an exemption only if they weren't living with the deceased at the time of death. Certain bequests to religious, charitable, cultural and scientific institutions are taxed at a flat rate of 11 per cent, whatever the amounts involved.

In the case of gift tax, the rates are the same, but the exemptions differ. The first €3,752 of any transfer made to a donor's children is exempt from tax, and there's a one-time exemption of €18,759 for gifts made to children between the ages of 18 and 35. Gifts to certain public entities are also exempt.

Luxembourg: Estates of Luxembourg residents are subject to inheritance tax on the value of all movable property, but on immovable property located only in the Duchy. Foreign property is exempt from inheritance tax provided local death duty or other transfer tax is paid (which is normally the case). There's no gift tax in Luxembourg, but there's a transfer tax on donations of certain types of asset that require a notary's intervention, e.g. property and certain transfers of shares (see **Wealth Tax** on page 274).

Assets of a deceased person are assessed at their market value on the date of death, not at the unitary value used for calculating wealth tax (see page 274). Only certain types of debt, e.g. funeral costs, may be deducted from the value of the estate. Inheritance tax is then calculated using a two-step process. First, the inheritance is taxed according to the relationship of the beneficiary to the deceased at betweem 2.5 per cent for direct descendants and ascendants and 15 per cent for distant relations and those unrelated to the deceased. All bequests over €10,000 are subject to an additional tax payment based on the value of the estate. The rate is the same as for the basic tax but it's adjusted by a multiplier, which varies from 0.1 for estates worth between €10,000 and €20,000 to 2.2 on estates valued at more than €1,760,000. This means that the top rate of inheritance tax is effectively 48 per cent for a transfer exceeding €1,760,000 to an unrelated person (15 per cent + 15 per cent x 2.2 = 48 per cent).

Heirs in the direct line (children, grandchildren or parents) are exempt from taxes on inheritances that don't exceed the intestate share (see **Wills** Below) and those that are made under the forced inheritance rules. Bequests made to your spouse are tax-free only if you've had children together (adopted children don't count), and a surviving spouse is entitled to an exemption of €37,500 if there were no children from the marriage. The rules relating to inheritance are complex, and if you own any significant amount of property or have concerns about how your property will be distributed after your death, it's important to consult a lawyer or notary as soon as you've established your residence in Luxembourg.

WILLS

It's an unfortunate fact of life that you're unable to take your hard-earned assets with you when you take your final bow. All adults should make a will (*testament/ wilbeschikkingen*) regardless of how large or small their assets, particularly where there are assets or heirs located in several different countries. The disposal of your assets will depend on your country of domicile and, if you own property, may also depend on where the property is located.

The inheritance laws of Belgium, Holland and Luxembourg retain certain elements of the Napoleonic code, mainly those giving priority to children and parents (the so-called lineal heirs) of the deceased, in many cases ahead of the surviving spouse. There are, however, many legal ways to protect the interests of a surviving spouse, at least in Belgium and Holland, where it's also possible to extend spousal protection to partners, whether they're officially registered or simply cohabiting. Inheritance laws in Luxembourg, on the other hand, recognise only legally married spouses.

Luxembourg still enforces 'forced' inheritance laws, meaning that the bulk of your estate must be divided according to the law, and that provisions in your will pertain only to the portion left over after the legal requirements have been met (the so-called *quotité disponible*). You cannot disinherit your children entirely in any of the Benelux countries. They have the right to inherit a set portion of your estate, generally at least half, depending on how many children you have and their ages and status at the time of your death. (Under certain circumstances, handicapped children, for example, are entitled to special consideration.) In most cases, a surviving spouse or partner has the right to remain in the family residence, although he may not receive the ownership rights to the home.

There are several types of will that are valid in Benelux, but as with all official documents there are strict rules and specific forms must be completed when writing a will. In all Benelux countries you must use of a notary, if only to register the existence of your will with the appropriate authorities. Even a holographic (hand-written) will should be registered to ensure that your wishes are taken into account. Although it's possible to draw up your own will, it's recommended to have it drawn up by a notary to ensure that you don't trip over any local regulations. If your will doesn't conform to the requirements of your country of residence at the time of your death, it could be ruled invalid or your heirs may have to spend their inheritance fighting for their share in a Benelux court. If you've already made a will in your home country, it's usually possible to incorporate it into one that's valid in your adopted country.

COST OF LIVING

No doubt you would like to know how far your euros will stretch and how much money (if any) you will have left after paying your bills. The cost of living is generally high in Benelux. Wages are similar to or slightly higher than those in the UK, and inflation has been under 2 per cent for the last few years. Taxes, on the other hand, are generally high throughout the region, and Belgians pay the highest income taxes in Europe according to several recent comparisons.

It's difficult to calculate an average cost of living in Belgium, Holland or Luxembourg, as it depends largely on your circumstances and lifestyle. There can also be considerable differences in prices (particularly of property) between urban and rural areas. Food prices are slightly lower overall that those in some neighbouring countries. (The Germans, in particular, flock to Dutch shopping centres at weekends to stock up on groceries and take advantage of the longer shopping hours.) However, Americans will find food prices higher than at home, although that's the case in most of Europe. The difference in your food bill will obviously depend on what you eat and where you lived before arriving in Benelux, not to mention how often you dine in restaurants. Around €200 to €250 per month should feed two adults in most areas, excluding fillet steak, caviar and alcohol.

Shopping around for 'luxury' items such as hi-fi and photographic equipment, electronic goods and computers at discount centres and bargain stores can result in huge savings. Petrol is considerably cheaper than in the UK (although Americans will still groan), but in many areas it's possible (and often even desirable) to get by without owning a car. It's also possible to save money by shopping overseas (e.g. in the USA) by mail order and via the Internet. Even in the most expensive cities, the cost of living needn't be astronomical, and if you shop wisely, compare prices and services before buying and don't live too extravagantly, you may be pleasantly surprised at how little you can live on.

Approximate *minimum* monthly expenses for an average single person, couple and family of four are shown in the table below (the numbers after some items refer to the notes below). Most people will consider the figures either too high or too low! When calculating your cost of living, don't forget to deduct the appropriate percentage for income tax and obligatory insurance from your gross salary.

ITEM	MONTHLY COSTS (€)		
	Single	Couple	Couple With Two Children
Housing (1)	500	1,000	1,500
Food (2)	150	250	400
Utilities (3)	150	200	250
Leisure (4)	200	250	300
Car (5)	150	150	150
Travel	50	75	100
Insurance (6)	100	150	200
Clothing	50	100	200
Total	**1,350**	**2,175**	**3,100**

1. Rent for a modern or modernised apartment or house in an average small town or suburb. The properties envisaged are a studio or one-bedroom apartment for a single person, a two-bedroom property for a couple and a three-bedroom property for a couple with two children.

2. Doesn't include luxuries or alcohol.

3. Includes electricity, gas, water, telephone, cable or satellite TV and heating costs.

4. Includes all entertainment, dining out, sports and holiday expenses, plus newspapers and magazines.

5. Includes running costs for an average family car plus third party insurance, annual taxes, petrol, servicing and repairs, but excludes 'entry into service' tax, depreciation and credit purchase costs.

6. Includes 'voluntary' insurance such as household (building and home contents) third party liability, travel and car breakdown insurance, and life assurance.

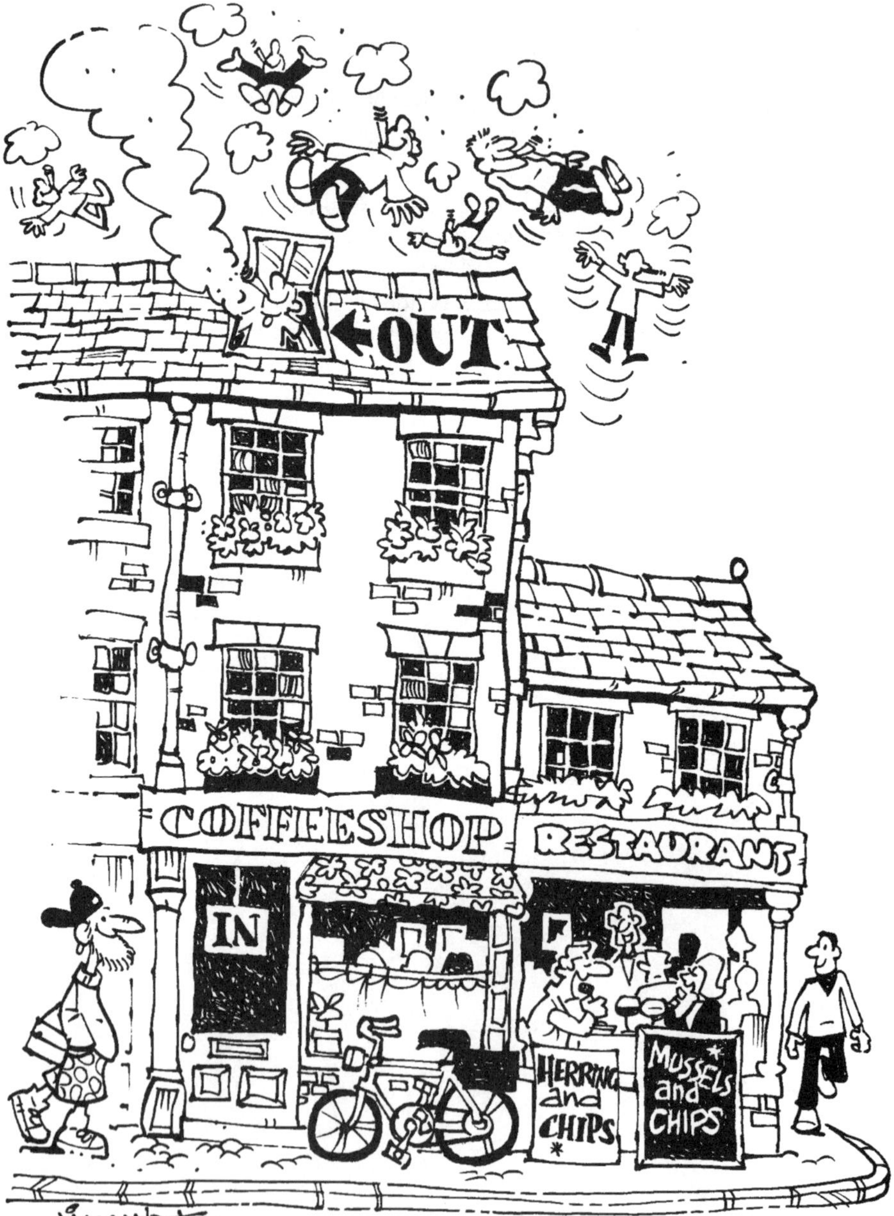
OUT
COFFEESHOP
RESTAURANT
IN
HERRING and CHIPS
MUSSELS and CHIPS
Jim Watson

15.

LEISURE

The fact that Benelux is a relatively small, densely populated area is a distinct advantage when it comes to finding things to do in your spare time. No matter where you live and work in Belgium, Holland or Luxembourg, you aren't far from a range of leisure and entertainment facilities, including literally thousands of museums (over 1,000 in Holland alone!) and a multitude of festivals and fairs, restaurants and bars, theatres, concert halls and other performing arts venues, cinemas and night life, whether you like it tame or on the wild side. The major cities in the region (Brussels, Antwerp, Amsterdam, Rotterdam, and The Hague) host internationally recognised opera and ballet companies and musical groups, and for those who want to escape city life there are the forests and countryside of the Ardennes where you can disappear for a quiet holiday amid forests and wildlife. You can also take advantage of your proximity to France, Germany and the rest of Europe, but it isn't necessary to leave Benelux (no matter what the natives may tell you) to find plenty to keep you entertained.

Leisure information is available from the three national tourist offices and from countless local and regional information centres, many of which can provide tickets to regional attractions. There's also a wealth of city and regional entertainment publications in English, principally *The Bulletin* in Brussels, *The Roundabout* in Holland and *The Luxembourg News*, plus many expatriate clubs include previews of local events in their newsletters. National and local newspapers naturally carry information about forthcoming events (in the local language), and an increasing amount of information is available via the Internet, which often offers the facility to book tickets. A useful website guide is Expatica (🖳 www.expatica.com), which contains magazine-style features, including reviews of current shows, films and many other leisure activities in Belgium and Holland.

GUIDE BOOKS

The main aim of this chapter, and indeed the purpose of the whole book, is to provide information that isn't found in standard guide books. General tourist information is available in numerous Belgian, Dutch and Luxembourg publications, as well as in the classic tourist guides. e.g. Michelin, Lonely Planet, Rough Guide, Fodors and Frommers (see **Appendix A** for a list). In each series, there's a variety of publications covering the Benelux region as a whole, individual countries and even cities. In many cases, Luxembourg is included in guides to Belgium, but you should be careful not to confuse the Belgian province of Luxembourg with the Grand Duchy of Luxembourg!

Expatriate clubs also publish a number of excellent guides to the area, aimed at both the short-term visitor and those settling in the region for the longer term. In Belgium, the American Women's Club of Brussels publishes *Hints for Living in Belgium*, which includes information about things to do and see throughout the country. The American Women's Club of Luxembourg produces a *Living in Luxembourg* guide, updated every few years, and other clubs in Antwerp, The Hague and Amsterdam produce books or booklets on specific aspects of living and working in their areas. Information on these and other publications can be obtained through the website of the Federation of American Women's Clubs Overseas (🖳 www.fawco.org) by checking the local club profile pages.

TOURIST INFORMATION

All three countries have active networks of national and regional tourist offices, including overseas branches you may want to consult before leaving home. Tourist offices publish a wide range of material, including maps, hotel and restaurant lists, and guides to sports, hobbies and activities available in their respective territories. The national tourist offices and most of the regional offices have websites on which you can either order copies of their publications for a small fee or download information free.

Belgium: The main tourist offices for Belgium are maintained by the provinces, and it's at provincial tourist offices that you'll find the most information about events, attractions and things to do in the area. Information about Flanders (including Brussels) is provided by the Tourist Office for Flanders (*Toerisme Vlaanderen*), Grasmarkt 63, 1000 Brussels (☎ 02-504 0390), whose website (🖳 www.toervl.be) offers links to the sites of the tourist offices for each province in Flanders, as well as the city tourist offices for Bruges, Brussels, Antwerp and Ostend. All these offices have information in French, Dutch, German, English, Spanish and Italian.

The tourist office for Wallonia (*Office de Promotion du Tourisme Wallonie-Bruxelles*, rue du Marché aux Herbes 61, 1000 Brussels ☎ 02-504 0390, 🖳 www. belgium-tourism.net) is next door to the Flanders Tourist Office and shares a switchboard. (Who says Flemish-speakers and French-speakers don't get on?). Its website, called BelSud, has links to the various regional tourist offices throughout the French-speaking region of Belgium, and information is available in the same languages as on the Flemish site. Note that both Flanders and Wallonia include Brussels in their territory! The Belgian national tourist office, which for some reason calls itself the Belgian Tourist Office of the Americas, also has a website (🖳 www. visitbelgium.com) that is a useful starting point for finding information about Belgian leisure activities.

Holland: Dutch tourist offices (*Vereniging Vreemdelingen Verkeer*) are identified in most towns by a blue and white sign carrying the VVV logo. There are at least 350 VVV offices in Holland and most of them are open Mondays to Fridays from 9am to 5pm and on Saturdays from 10am to noon, with extended hours during the relevant high season. VVV offices can provide maps, brochures and information about virtually every leisure activity in Holland. They also sell tickets to concerts and museums, and can take bookings for hotels and package tours, including a variety of cycling and hiking tours. The VVV's website (🖳 www.vvv.nl) is in Dutch only.

Holland Board of Tourism maintains offices in cities outside the country, including London, New York and Copenhagen. It has two websites, both claiming to be the 'official' one: 🖳 www.holland.com is run by the US branch of the Board of Tourism and is all in English, but can direct you to local sites in Holland, according to your language; 🖳 www.visitholland.com is a more generalised site and also directs you to information pages in your language. Both sites have search engines for hotel accommodation and local tourist offices.

Luxembourg: Luxembourg has a National Tourist Office (*Office National de Tourisme*) in Brussels, Paris, The Hague, Mönchengladbach (Germany), London, Copenhagen, New York and Berlin, as well as in Luxembourg city. This is the *Syndicat d'Initiative et de Tourisme de la Ville de Luxembourg*, BP 181, 2011

Luxembourg, located on the Place d'Armes and open Mondays to Saturdays from 9am to 6pm (☎ 22-2809 or 22-7565 for general information). There's also a branch of the *Office National du Tourisme* at the central train station in Luxembourg city (☎ 48-1199). The main website for the National Tourist Office (💻 www.ont.lu) offers information about events throughout Luxembourg and contact details of local tourist offices.

HOTELS

Hotel accommodation in Belgium, Holland and Luxembourg ranges from simple *pensions* and inns to luxury hotels, including a number of castles. While there are plenty of hotels in and around most cities and tourist attractions, it's generally wise to reserve rooms well in advance, in case your plans coincide with a major exhibition or trade show, when hotels may be fully booked for miles around. This can be a problem in and around Brussels and Antwerp and in the Randstad area in Holland.

As in many other countries, hotels are classified on a scale of one to five stars, according to their facilities and the type of hotel. Although this system gives an indication of standards and prices, stars are awarded on the basis of facilities, e.g. the ratio of bathrooms to guests, rather than quality and you can often find excellent ungraded and one-star hotels. For example, two-star hotels are usually small and friendly, family-run hotels, offering good value and comfortable accommodation, if not luxuries such as room service and a swimming pool.

Room rates vary not only according to the hotel classification, but also by location, day of the week and time of year. Most hotels raise their rates significantly during important exhibitions and in high season, e.g. during the tulip season in Holland, or in the summer months in beach towns such as Ostend. On the other hand, many hotels and resorts offer discounts during holiday weekends (e.g. Easter, Christmas) or in the summer months (mostly hotels that cater to business travellers). You can find a clean, pleasant double room off-season in a one or two-star hotel for as little as €25 to €45.

Five-star accommodation generally starts at €150 per night for a single room. The practice of including breakfast in the room is becoming less common, but many tourist hotels still include at least a continental breakfast (coffee, tea or hot chocolate and rolls or even croissants) or offer a full breakfast in the hotel dining room for a small extra charge (€5 to €10). Room rates must be displayed at the registration desk and in detail, along with all 'house rules' (primarily check-out times and directions to fire exits) in each room. Note, however, that the rate shown in your room may be the maximum charge for the room rather than the amount you're being charged.

You can book hotel accommodation through travel agencies or make direct reservations, either by phone or via the Internet. Many online travel services allow you to search their databases for hotels in specific cities or regions or those belonging to particular chains or having certain types of facilities (e.g. a swimming pool) or rules (e.g. permitting pets). An advantage of booking online yourself is that you can often preview the hotel and its facilities and obtain directions and other information. The three national tourist offices (see above) have their own online search and reservation services, and most city tourist offices will make bookings for you for a small fee (usually €2 to €4). If you plan to use a local tourist office for finding a hotel room, go there as early as possible. Rooms at reasonable prices can be difficult to find late in the day, particularly during holiday periods.

Belgium: The Belgian Tourist Office (see above) publishes an annual guide to hotels and restaurants, which is available from their offices and via their website (⌨ www.visitbelgium.com), where you can sign up to receive e-mail notification of special weekend and holiday packages as they become available. The website also includes lists of hotels, including descriptions of their facilities and current rates, and links for making reservations. If you'd like to stay in a Belgian castle, contact Castles Information Service (59, avenue Monseigneur, 1330 Rixensart, ☎ 02-652 0533, ✉ castles@euronet.be). The appropriately named CIS website (⌨ www.dreamit.be/castles) contains information about castles open to the public, plus links to those with their own websites.

Holland: Holland Board of Tourism and VVV offices (see above) all handle hotel bookings and can advise you about forthcoming trade shows or fairs that may make finding accommodation difficult in certain areas. The Tourist Board website (⌨ www.holland.com) allows you to search for suitable accommodation by location, facilities or special requirements, and then links you directly to the appropriate booking office.

Luxembourg: The main tourist office in Luxembourg city (see above) can make hotel bookings or provide you with a list of hotels, restaurants and other accommodation throughout the Duchy. The website (⌨ www.ont.lu) includes a list of hotels, complete with ratings and contact information. There are a large number of three and four-star hotels throughout Luxembourg, including several *châteaux* in the wine-producing region.

BED & BREAKFAST AND SELF-CATERING

Bed and breakfast accommodation is popular throughout Belgium, Holland and Luxembourg, where families let their spare rooms to visitors – including the owners of castles who are descendants of the noble families that originally built them! All three countries also offer self-catering accommodation in private residences (from farms to castles).

There are many sources for information about bed and breakfast and other private accommodation, including a vast range of guide books, but often the best place to start a search is the local or national tourist office.

Belgium: Tourist offices can provide lists of private accommodation, and there are many options on the Belgium Tourist Office website (⌨ www.visitbelgium.com), which includes booking information and, in some cases, direct Internet or e-mail links. The Castles Information Service (see above for details) lists around 25 castles in Belgium offering bed and breakfast accommodation.

Holland: Holland Board of Tourism is the main source of information about bed and breakfast accommodation in Holland, including rooms on farms (including tulip farms) and other rural private residences. Its website (⌨ www.holland.com) has a search facility linked to an organisation called Bed & Breakfast Holland (Theophile de Bockstraat 3, 1058 TV Amsterdam, ☎ 020-615 7527). Many weekend and holiday tour packages promoted by the VVV (see above) include accommodation in B&Bs or on farms; information is available from local VVV offices or on their websites.

Luxembourg: The Luxembourg Tourist Office promotes a programme of 'rural tourism', which includes all forms of private accommodation, from traditional guesthouses and B&Bs to country residences, farm lodgings and self-catering accommodation in privately owned flats, studios or chalets. It can also arrange dormitory accommodation for groups of 10 to 30 people as part of a hiking trip, bicycle tour or cross-country skiing weekend. Facilities are rated on a scale of one to four ears of corn (*épis*) that indicate the level of facilities and the appropriateness and authenticity of the accommodation. The tourist office advises that it's best to make your own reservations (meaning they don't have a centralised booking system!). For more information about the rural tourism programme, contact the *Association pour la Promotion du Tourisme rural au Grand-Duché de Luxembourg*, Château de Wiltz, 9516 Wiltz (☎ 095-7184).

HOSTELS

For those on a limited budget, hostels have long been one of the best ways to stretch your euros when it comes to accommodation. Hostels are privately run, usually non-profit establishments, which were originally intended to provide inexpensive (and usually basic) overnight accommodation for students or other young people. Times have changed and so have hostels, or most of them. As well as the traditional dormitories, with up to six beds per room, accommodation now includes private rooms, sleeping two people or a family. You no longer need to be under 27, and most hostels cater for family groups. Nor is it always necessary to be a member of one of the national hostelling associations. Having a Hostelling International card, however, generally entitles you to a discount, not only on your accommodation, but also on a number of local attractions. Although some hostels still lock the front door at night, most will provide you with a key or pass code if you're returning late. Hostels in or near city centres are more like small, basic hotels, although at much more reasonable rates (which often include breakfast). Bed rates vary from as little as €4 per night for the most basic facilities to €25 or €30 per person for a private room according to the location, the type of hostel and in some cases the season.

The main international hostelling organisation is the International Youth Hostel Association (IYHA), which issues Hostelling International cards and sets standards for both the national hostelling associations and individual hostels. There's also a European Union Federation of Youth Hostel Associations (EUFED), which works with national hostelling associations and various European governments to safeguard, monitor and promote hostelling. EUFED's website (🖳 www.eufed.org) contains information about hostelling throughout Europe. Because EUFED is an association of associations, it doesn't offer assistance directly to individuals, but its Frequently Asked Questions (FAQ) page contains essential information on hostelling.

There are four main hostelling associations in the Benelux region. (EUFED normally permits only one association per country, but made an exception in the case of Belgium, with its Flemish and French-speaking regions.) Membership of the national hostelling associations costs between €10 and €20 per year, entitling you to a 5 to 10 per cent discount on non-member prices at most hostels as well as discounts on admission to various sites and attractions. The national associations all publish some form of newsletter or magazine available only to members, and offer discounts on association publications, such as lists and ratings of hostels in Europe and the rest of the world. The national tourist offices carry lists of hostels, and there's an online booking service (🖳 www.hostelbookings.com) that covers all IYHA-affiliated youth hostels in Belgium, Holland and Luxembourg, as well as most member hostels in the rest of the world. The national associations are:

Belgium: For French-speaking Belgium and Brussels: Youth Hostels of Wallonia and Brussels (LAJ), rue de la Sablonnière 28, 1000 Brussels (☎ 02-219 5676, 🖳 www.laj.be).

For Flanders: *Vlaamse JeugdHerbergen* (*VJH*), Van Stralenstraat 40, 2060 Antwerp (☎ 03-232 7218, 🖳 www.vjh.be).

Holland: Dutch Youth Hostel Association (*Nederlandse Jeugdherberg Centrale* or *NJHC*), PO Box 9191, 1006 AD Amsterdam (☎ 010-264 6064, 🖳 www.njhc.org).

Luxembourg: *Centrale des Auberges de Jeunesse Luxembourgeoises* (CAJL), 24–26 Place de la Gare, 1616 Luxembourg (☎ 026-293 500, 🖳 www.youth hostels.lu).

CAMPING & CARAVANNING

Camping and caravanning are extremely popular in Benelux. Not only are the campsites of Europe filled with Belgians, Dutch and Luxembourgers, but there's a large number of campsites throughout the region. Caravans and motor homes can be purchased new or second-hand. Most dealers also rent them if you just want to use one for a holiday. (Note that rental units must normally meet stricter standards than used vehicles for sale.) Manoeuvring a 3.5 tonne motor home through narrow city streets or learning to back a caravan into a campsite space can take a bit of practice and there's even a knack to stowing all your gear before you set off, but camping and caravanning can be an enjoyable way to see the sights of Europe.

There are campsites in most popular coastal areas of Belgium and Holland and throughout the Ardennes. The Belgian coastal region is particularly popular with campers from the French-speaking part of Belgium (not to mention the French themselves) and in the summer it can be almost impossible to find space in a campsite near the coast if you haven't made a booking well in advance. The forests of the Ardennes have some of the quietest and most peaceful campsites for nature lovers, including a few for naturists if that's your penchant. There are even campsites in and around the major cities, offering easy access to public transport into town.

Campsites vary considerably, from those offering only basic facilities (generally toilets and washing-up areas) to 'holiday camps', complete with restaurants, swimming pools, tennis courts and even permanently installed chalets for rent. The Dutch seem particularly fond of full-service sites, which offer features such as cable television hook-up and full utility services for those who wish to convert their caravan into a semi-permanent holiday home.

There are rating systems for campsites – a different one in each of the Benelux countries! In Belgium, services are rated from one to four stars, with one star the most basic and four stars the most luxurious. The classification is determined by a complicated (what else, in Belgium?) points system, where points are awarded for such things as the proportion of camping spaces with electrical or water hook-ups, the number of toilets, showers or other sanitary facilities per campsite, the size and means of designating or separating individual pitches and whether or not the site office is staffed around the clock. In Holland, there are two rating systems, one (indicated by a number of flags) primarily for the recreational facilities and the other (one to five stars) based on overall comfort, access to water and electrical hook-ups, etc. In Luxembourg, campgrounds are rated numerically, from one to three, 1 indicating the best sites. In all cases, it can be difficult to predict exactly what facilities you'll find at any given rating level. Many one-star campsites are every bit as comfortable and clean as four or five-star sites offering a swimming pool, mini-golf and a snack bar.

Prices at campsites vary according to the rating of the site, the type of space you require, e.g. with or without electrical and/or water hook-ups, and the length of your stay. Most sites offer discounts on the daily rate for stays of a week or more and there are special rates (and fees) for those wishing to install a mobile home permanently. There's normally a pitch fee of €2 to €40 per night (averaging around €10) plus another €1 to €5 per person. Most campsites offer a 5 to10 per cent discount for holders of a Camping Carnet International (CCI), a standard identification card issued by most camping clubs and associations. If you don't have a CCI, you may be required to produce a passport, driving licence and/or other forms of identification when you check in. Membership of a camping association also has other benefits, including access to some 'restricted' camping areas and campsites (particularly in Belgium, where the camping associations own a number of sites), discounts on insurance, camping fees, and subscriptions to camping magazines and guides. There are specialised camping associations, too, from the naturist/nudist variety to clubs entitling members to camp free in the grounds of member vineyards, *châteaux* or working farms.

Naturally, in the land of bureaucracy and regulations, there are restrictions on where you can pitch your tent or park a motor home or caravan overnight. In Holland, all 'wilderness' camping is forbidden (not that there's much Dutch wilderness left), and in Luxembourg mobile homes aren't allowed to park overnight at the side of the road or anywhere outside an established campsite. The communes and towns in Belgium each have their own regulations about motor homes and caravans and where they may be parked, particularly if the municipality runs a campsite! These are usually indicated at the entrance to the town or on a notice board outside the town hall. If you plan to camp on private property, you should obtain the permission of the owner in advance. In some rural areas, farmers are likely to shoot first and ask questions later!

Campsites are signposted on the outskirts of most cities and towns where there are camping facilities. Look for a square white sign bearing the silhouette of a tent or a motor home (and usually indicating the distance to the site).

The national and regional tourist offices in Belgium, Holland and Luxembourg all have information about camping, campsites and national and regional camping clubs and associations, both in their many offices and on their websites (see page 285). Most automobile associations have similar information (see page 205). There's a variety of camping and caravanning magazines available at most news stands (in the local languages), where you can also find current campsite guides, whether local, national, regional or European. Michelin publishes guides to campsites that are cross-referenced to the appropriate red guide series (and particularly useful if you're looking for good restaurants close to your campsite or campsites close to good restaurants).

Belgium: For information on camping, contact the *Royal Camping Caravanning Club de Belgique* (known as R3CB), Avenue de Villas 5, 1060 Brussels (☎ 02-537 3681, ✉ r3cb@ping.be).

Holland: The ANWB automobile association provides CCI cards free to its members, and the ANWB City website (🖳 www.anwb.nl/city) includes a section devoted to camping, complete with a list of ANWB-rated campsites. Many Dutch campsites have their own websites, usually with most of their information in English as well as Dutch, French and other languages, and you're often able to make bookings online.

Luxembourg: In Luxembourg contact the *Fédération Luxembourgeoise de Campings et Caravanings* (FLCC), 18 rue de la Gare, 4571 Oberkorn (☎ 058-3534). The National Tourist Office website (🖳 www.ont.lu) also contains a list of campsites in Luxembourg.

THEME PARKS

There's no shortage of theme parks, either within the Benelux countries or within easy driving distance in France and Germany. There are direct high-speed train (TGV) connections from Brussels at least a couple of times a day during the summer season to Europe's largest and best known theme park, Disneyland Paris. Also near Paris is Parc Astérix, where rides and shows feature Astérix, Obélix and other characters from the popular cartoon series. More accessible from Holland and Luxembourg are the German theme parks Phantasialand (in Brühl, near Cologne) and Warner Brothers Movie World (in Bottrop, north of Essen). Fans of the little blue Smurf cartoon characters (called *Schtroumpfs* in French) can visit Walibi Schtroumpf in Maizières-les-Metz, France, just over the border from Luxembourg.

But it isn't necessary to leave either Belgium or Holland to find a theme park for a family outing. (Luxembourg has so far avoided creating any theme parks within its borders.) The following is a selection of the major theme parks in Belgium and Holland:

- **Six Flags Belgium** (formerly Walibi/Wavre) includes a water park called Aqualibi, complete with water slides, swimming pools and other water-based amusements, in addition to the usual rides and shows.

- **Bobbejaanland** in Lichtaart (Belgium), started by Bobbejaan Schoepen, a well known Belgian entertainer, features stage shows, music, rides and a roller coaster, not to mention regular appearances by Bobbejaan himself, riding a horse in Wild West shows.

- **Bellewaerde** in Ieper (Belgium) is a nature reserve and theme park.

- **The Dolfinarium** at Boudewijnpark in Bruges/Brugge in Belgium features dolphin shows.

- **The Efteling Fairy Tale Park** in Kaatsheuvel in Holland (🖳 www.efteling.nl) is rated one of the top five theme parks in northern Europe.

- **Six Flags Holland**, in Biddinghuizen, west of Amsterdam, is owned by the company that runs Warner Brothers Movie World and features material based on the Warner Brothers' cartoon characters.

● **The Duinrell Attraktiepark** in Wassenaar in Holland boasts a ski valley and ski school, open during the winter when weather permits, i.e. when temperatures are below 5°C throughout the day and it isn't raining!

Most theme parks in and around the Benelux region are open from mid-April to late October, often only at weekends until June or early July and at the end of the season after the school year starts. During the summer months, parks are open seven days a week, usually until 8pm or later. Those with indoor facilities or winter sports remain open at weekends and during school holidays year round. Entrance to most theme parks costs from €10 to €25 or more per person per day, but include all rides and shows in the general admission price. Disneyland Paris can be considerably more expensive, particularly at the height of the summer season, although discounts are available as part of travel or holiday packages. Most theme parks offer multiple day or season passes that can be good value if you're likely to visit often.

All parks offer a variety of catering and other services, although quality is variable and food prices in the parks tend to be high: a plain hamburger can cost up to €7 and a fizzy drink or bottled water €2. A few parks have full-service restaurants with good food and alcoholic drinks (for adults). Many people prefer to take a picnic and a number of parks have picnic areas. Many parks have extensive shopping facilities where you can buy T-shirts, toys, books, CDs, clothing and craft articles.

Tourist offices, travel agencies and automobile clubs have brochures and information about most theme parks and offer travel packages including admission, nearby hotel accommodation and car rental, as well as discounts on other attractions and tourist sites in the area. Most theme parks have websites, which not only provide information but also indicate the languages in use at the park. Not all parks are multi-lingual, but most theme park staff can speak and understand English if you have a question or problem, even if signs are limited to the local language(s). The Six Flags organisation has a website (🖳 www.sixflagseurope.com) that offers information about and links to all their theme parks in Europe, including Six Flags Belgium and Six Flags Holland, the Aqualibi parks in Belgium and France, the Bellewaerde park in Belgium and the WB Movie World attractions in Germany and Spain.

MUSEUMS & GALLERIES

There are literally thousands of museums and galleries in Belgium, Holland and Luxembourg, housing treasures from the region's rich artistic and cultural heritage. (Belgium claims to have the highest number of museums per capita in the world!) Many of them are world famous, e.g. the *Rijksmuseum*, the Van Gogh Museum and the Rembrandt House in Amsterdam, the Rubens House in Antwerp, and the *Musée d'Art Ancien* in Brussels, with its unique collection of 14th to 19th century paintings and drawings. Other museums are small and often specialised. Stamp collecting is a popular theme, e.g. the *Musée Postal* on the Place du Grand Sablon in Brussels and the *Musée des Postes et Télécommunications*, 4 rue d'Epernay in Luxembourg city. Charleroi in Belgium is home to the *Musée de la Photographie* (11 avenue P. Pastur, 6032 Charleroi, ☎ 07-435 810), commemorating the history of photography with over 60,000 images and at least 2,500 cameras. In Luxembourg city, there's the *Photothèque de la Ville de Luxembourg* (10, rue E. Ruppert, Zone d'Activités Cloche d'Or, ☎ 047-962 839), with 800,000 photographs dating from 1855 to the present day.

Virtually every town in Benelux has a historical museum; some have several. These range from the famous Brussels History Museum (*Musée Communal de la Ville de Bruxelles*) and the Anne Frank House in Amsterdam to the hundreds of small museums dedicated to agriculture, the arts and crafts of an area or to rural life in general (*Musée de la Vie Locale*), of which there are many in smaller towns in Wallonia. In Arnhem (Holland) there's an outdoor history museum, the *Nederlands Openluchtmuseum*, open only during the summer. Original historic buildings have been moved to the site, including a church, a windmill and an entire farm. There are exhibits and demonstrations of antique farm equipment and how cheese and butter are made, along with special events featuring various aspects of life in rural Holland. Many towns along the coastline have shipyard and maritime museums, commemorating the role that sailing and trade have played in the region's history, and Luxembourg boasts a Bus and Tram Museum (*Musée des Tramways et des Bus*), a natural history museum and at least two municipal art museums.

Not surprisingly, both Belgium and Holland have several museums devoted to beer and beer making. The old Heineken brewery in the heart of Amsterdam (Stadhouderskade 78, ☎ 020-523 9666) was de-commissioned a few years ago when the main brewery was relocated to the suburbs and has recently re-opened as a museum recounting the history of the Heineken company (although you can still sample the beer at the end of the tour). In the Grand-Place in Brussels is the Belgian Beer History Museum (*Musée de la Brasserie* – Grand-Place 10, 1000 Brussels, ☎ 02-511 4987, 🖳 www.beerparadise.be) and there's even a museum dedicated to gueuze and lambic (*Musée Bruxellois de la Gueuze*, rue Gheude 56, 1070 Brussels, ☎ 02-520 2891 – see page 328 for an explanation of gueuze and lambic beers).

All the standard guide books include lists of museums. (Both the Lonely Planet and Rough Guide series are particularly good sources of information about smaller, unusual and specialist museums.) Tourist offices are also an excellent source of brochures and information on current exhibitions, travelling shows or themed events at museums and galleries in an area. You can often purchase admission tickets in advance, either at a tourist office or through the museum or gallery ticket office. The Expatica websites for Belgium and Holland (🖳 www.expatica.com/belgium.asp and /index.asp respectively) have lists and reviews of many of the most popular museums in the area, all in English, including links to their websites and current information about special shows or exhibitions. An increasing number of museums have their own websites, providing details of opening hours, entry fees and access by public transport, and allowing you to preview exhibits and obtain information on forthcoming events or exhibitions.

Entry fees to museums and galleries vary from nothing to around €10, the average adult charge being around €4 or €5, with discounts for children, students and senior citizens. Many museums are closed on Mondays, particularly if they're open throughout the weekend. Smaller museums often close for a couple of hours at lunchtime, and many museums stop selling entry tickets around an hour before closing to allow visitors adequate time to view the exhibits; a few discount tickets (by up to 50 per cent) during the last hour before closing. Tourist offices generally have information about the various types of passes available.

It's usually possible to buy a single pass granting admission to all museums and galleries in an area during a period of one to several days. The Dutch tourist office offers an annual pass (*museumjaarkaart*), valid for most of the major museums throughout Holland. The *museumjaarkaart* costs less than €30 for adults (and there are discounts for those under 25 and over 55) and can be used in over 400 museums throughout Holland. Residents of Antwerp can visit the city's museums free of charge at any time simply by presenting their national identity card. Most museums also offer some form of membership or annual pass, and some public transport passes and other travel cards ,e.g. Youth Hostel Association, can be used to obtain discounts on museum entrance fees (see page 169).

CINEMAS

Film was embraced as an art form in Belgium and Holland almost as soon as it was invented. The Dutch government still heavily subsidises its indigenous film industry, although at most Benelux cinemas, as elsewhere in the world, Hollywood movies are the biggest draw.

The trend, as in most countries, is towards building ever larger multi-screen cinemas. In fact, Belgium is home to one of the largest movie complexes in Europe, the 25-screen Kinepolis (located in Brupark, just outside Brussels). Both Pathé and UGC operate many of the largest multiplexes, found primarily in city centres and shopping malls. In Dutch-speaking areas, films are always shown in the original language with Dutch subtitles (if necessary). In the French region of Belgium and in Luxembourg, films may be shown in the original language with French subtitles or dubbed into French (see below). 'Art cinemas' are also alive and well in many areas, featuring European-produced films in their original language, often with English subtitles. (The Dutch have few illusions about how many people outside their country speak their language and automatically subtitle many Dutch-language films in English.)

Belgium: In addition to the multiplexes, most cities have a selection of art cinemas featuring European and other 'small' films not aimed at a mass audience (and without multi-million dollar advertising budgets). The Film Museum in Brussels, which was set up in the late 1930s to preserve and protect important films as well as to study and document the art form, offers a regular programme of classic films at bargain prices (around €1.50 if booked in advance or €2.50 at the door). During the summer, there's a drive-in cinema in Brussels' *Parc Cinquantenaire* for those who prefer seeing their films under the stars (or the rain). Open-air seating is also provided if you don't want to drive to the park. Antwerp has its own Film Museum at the *Centrum voor Beeldcultuur*, where you can see silent movies with live piano accompaniment. Brussels, Ghent and Namur all host film festivals at various times of the year, featuring a range of cinematic genres.

Film listings and reviews can be found in newspapers and magazines published throughout Belgium. The 'What's On' section of *The Bulletin* is generally recommended as the best English-language source of cinema information. Note that films usually start at least half an hour later than the time listed, as most cinemas run advertisements, trailers and 'shorts' before the feature film. Ticket prices vary according to the day of the week, from about €5 to €10, Friday and Saturday evenings being the most expensive. Some cinemas offer a ten-film pass (priced around the same as six single admissions), which is excellent value if you're a film fan. Pass holders may be limited to mid-week screenings or excluded from certain showings, particularly during the first few days of a new release. Previews and Sunday morning screenings are also inexpensive ways to see popular new films and these are normally advertised in local newspapers or at cinemas.

The following abbreviations appear in cinema listings in Belgium:

- *VO* (*version originale*) – the film is in the original language, subtitled into either French or Dutch. A film labelled *VO st-bil* indicates that subtitles are in both French and Dutch. (Because foreign films are never dubbed into Dutch, these abbreviations don't appear in Flemish-language listings.)

- *ENA (enfants non admis)/KNT* (*kinderen niet toegestaan*) – children under 16 not admitted;

- *EA (enfants admis)/AL (alle leeftijden)* – children (of all ages) admitted;

- *PF (parlant français)* – the film has been dubbed into French. (Again, there's no Flemish equivalent, as films aren't dubbed into Dutch.)

- *S (séance)* – indicates the time that the screening starts (including the preliminary advertisements, trailers and shorts, normally taking at least 30 minutes).

Holland: The Dutch have long been fans of the cinema (*bioscopen*) and you should have no trouble finding cinemas in and around most larger cities and towns. There are both large multi-screen cinemas, showing the latest Hollywood films, and a choice of small, art cinemas specialising in cult films (complete with midnight screenings of the *Rocky Horror Picture Show*) or special genres, which are usually tucked away in city and town centres. In Amsterdam, for example, there's the *Ketelhuis* (Haarlemmerweg 8–10, Amsterdam, ☎ 020-680 090, 🖥 www.ketelhuis.nl), which shows only Dutch films in its 140-seat theatre. In November, there's the two-week IDFA (International Documentary Festival Amsterdam), during which new documentary films are shown at various cinemas throughout the city; look out for posters in participating theatres or advertisements in local newspapers and event publications.

Foreign films are invariably subtitled in Dutch, but many Dutch films are subtitled in English, even for screening in Holland! (Abbreviations used to indicate whether or not children are admitted to films are the same as in the Flemish-speaking areas of Belgium – see above.) Some smaller theatres still interrupt the main film for a 15-minute intermission in order to encourage you to purchase drinks and food, although most of the multiplexes have done away with this custom. Ticket prices average from €4.50 to €8 during the week, with higher prices (up to around €10) for weekend showings. Film listings are included in most newspapers (usually in Wednesday evening or Thursday morning editions) as well as in weekly and monthly entertainment magazines available from news stands, hotels and tourist offices. Current film listings for cinemas throughout Holland can also be found via the Internet (e.g. 🖥 www.veronica.nl/bioscoopagenda).

Luxembourg: Despite its size, Luxembourg has no shortage of cinemas, including a good selection of multi-screen complexes, generally located in or near the larger shopping centres. There are three main cinemas (*cinés*) in Luxembourg city, plus the Utopolis multiplex in nearby Kirchberg. The Thursday edition of the *Luxemburger Wort/Voix du Luxembourg* contains listings for all Luxembourg cinemas in a typical mixture of French and German. French films tend to be listed and summarised in French, all other films in German. New releases are reviewed in French, German and English in the 'Film & Kino' section. Films may be shown in the original language or in a German dubbed version (indicated in listings as *deutsche Fassung*). Subtitled films are indicated by the suffix *v.o.* or *Orig.*, followed by an abbreviation of the language or languages of the subtitles, generally F (French) and either NL (Dutch) or D (German). English language films may be shown in both German and original versions at different times. The *Tageblatt* also carries film listings on its website (🖳 www.tageblatt.lu). Cinema tickets cost between €4 and €8.50, depending upon the film, the theatre and the day of the week.

Luxembourg city is also home to the *Cinémathèque municipale*, one of the largest collections of films in Europe. The *Cinémathèque* is located at 17 place du Théâtre in Luxembourg city and offers two showings each evening (only one in July and August) and a matinee on Saturdays. The *Luxembourger Wort* contains a listing of what's on at the *Cinémathèque* each Thursday, along with the regular film listings. In the spring, the Symphony Orchestra of Luxembourg presents what it calls 'live cinema' at the *Conservatoire* (33, rue Charles Martel) with showings of silent movies complete with full orchestral accompaniment. Details of forthcoming films and performance times are published in local newspapers and available at tourist offices.

THEATRE, OPERA & BALLET

Lovers of theatre, opera and dance are spoilt for choice in Benelux. Not only are a number of world class opera and dance companies resident in the region, but the concert halls and auditoria of the Benelux countries are popular venues for touring companies from around the world. Most theatre performances are staged in the local languages, but there are also English-language productions, normally part of touring shows from the UK or America. If you prefer participating to watching, there are a number of amateur theatre groups and light opera societies that regularly hold auditions for new members. Check with local expatriate organisations or in entertainment publications for information.

Belgium: In Brussels, the primary venue for ballet and opera is the *Théâtre Royal de la Monnaie/Koninklijke Muntschouwburg*, usually referred to as *La Monnaie/de Munt*. *La Monnaie* is well known for attracting some of the biggest opera stars in the world, as well as for its extraordinary productions. Ballets are performed at the *Forêt National/Vorst Nationaal*, the *Cirque Royale/Koninklijke Circus* and at the *Koninkijke Vlaamse Schouwburg* (*KVS*), all in or near Brussels. The Royal Flanders Ballet is based at the *'t Eilandje* in Antwerp, a facility built specifically for the use of the ballet corps. Modern dance is on offer at the *Kaarttheater* (home to the *Roses* troupe, associated with Brussels Opera and founded by Anne Teresa de Keersmaeker, a major name in Belgian dance), at *DeSingel* in Antwerp and at the *Charleroi/Danses* in Charleroi, as well as at the *Palais des Beaux Arts/Paleis voor Schone Kunsten* in Brussels. Brussels is also home to a puppet theatre, the *Théâtre de Toone*, located in the Petite Rue des Bouchers. Ostend holds a summer theatre festival, called Theater on the Sea, and Leuven hosts a biennial dance festival called *Klapstuk*.

Tickets for opera, theatre and dance performances can be booked through tourist offices using a freephone number (☎ 0800-21221) available Mondays to Fridays from 9am to 7pm and Saturdays from 10am to midday. Many branches of FNAC also have a premium rate ticket line (☎ 0900-00600).

Holland: Amsterdam, Rotterdam and The Hague are the major Dutch centres for the performing arts. In Amsterdam, *Het Muziektheater* (Amstel 3, ☎ 06-255 455) is home to both Netherlands Opera and the Dutch National Ballet, both of which perform regularly there. The *Theater Carré* was originally built for the circus but now presents a varied programme of shows, including operas, musical comedies and theatre in the round. In The Hague major touring companies often perform at the *Nederlands Congres Centrum*, while the *Koninklijke Schouwburg* is host to plays, cabarets, puppet shows and other sorts of performance. There's also the *VSB Circus Theater*, another facility built originally for the circus, but which now hosts a variety of performing arts. In Rotterdam the *Rotterdamse Schouwburg* and the *Theater Zuidplein* both host opera and theatre performances, the *Schouwburg* mostly in Dutch, while the *Zuidplein* often presents productions by touring English-speaking companies.

In Amsterdam there are a number of small theatres and cabarets located on or around the Leidseplein, including the Boom Chicago Theatre, where you can see improvisational comedy in English. Founded by a Chicagoan in the early '90s, the show has become something of an institution in Amsterdam, with local people joining the tourists and expatriates to laugh at the vagaries of Dutch life.

Tickets for opera, theatre and dance are available through VVV offices or from the venues' own box offices or websites. In Amsterdam tickets are available at AUB (*Amsterdam Uit Buro*) on the Leidseplein (☎ 0900-0191, a premium rate line). In The Hague you can purchase tickets through the Nederlands Theaterbureau, Zeekant 102 (☎ 070-354 3411).

Luxembourg: Luxembourg doesn't have its own opera company or a national ballet corps, but the main theatre venues in Luxembourg city each offer a season of opera and ballet performances as well as plays. Both the *Théâtre des Capucins* and the *Théâtre Municipal de la Ville de Luxembourg* host performances by touring companies, usually in French or German, and both theatres offer season subscription packages, which are popular and sometimes sell out early. Single performance tickets can be difficult or impossible to obtain and it pays to join the mailing list of either or both theatres. During July, the town of Wiltz hosts the European Festival of Outdoor Theatre and Music, which includes opera, drama and comedy as well as a variety of music.

MUSIC

Although Belgium, Holland and Luxembourg may not be the first countries that come to mind when you think of music, there's no shortage of concerts, clubs and music-making of all kinds. The region has a number of major concert halls, auditoriums and arenas that are popular venues for touring orchestras, groups and individual artists. Jazz is especially popular and there are many small clubs featuring live performances by local artists and groups. Music also plays a big part in the many festivals that take place throughout the Benelux region, particularly (but not exclusively) during the summer months, and there are frequent outdoor concerts whenever weather permits.

Belgium: The Belgian National Orchestra performs regularly at the *Palais des Beaux-Arts/Paleis voor Schone Kunsten* (Rue Ravenstein 23, 1000 Brussels), where there's also a season of symphony and chamber music concerts. There are midday concerts in the *Musée d'Art Ancien/Museum van Oude Kunst* and outdoor music performances in summer in the Grand-Place, in Place de la Monnaie and on Sundays in the Bois de la Cambre. The city also plays host to the *Concours Reine Elisabeth* (named after a Belgian queen), an international classical music competition which focuses on piano, voice and violin in successive years, with an off-year every fourth year. The cycle recommences in 2003 with the piano competition. A traditional form of musical entertainment in Belgium is provided by the *carillon*, or bell tower. Antwerp, Bruges, Brussels, Ghent, Liege, Lier, Mechelen and Tournai all have bell towers that chime the hour and half-hour, and there are frequent *carillon* concerts at Bruges, Ghent and Mechelen.

The Flanders Festival is one of the largest festivals devoted entirely to classical music and every year it attracts major performers from around the world. The festival is in fact a series of festivals held successively in the eight largest cities in Flanders throughout the three months of the summer season. In total, there are more than 350 concerts in over 80 venues, including churches, concert halls and outdoor parks and gardens.

There are numerous small clubs for jazz lovers offering live music throughout the country, and several jazz festivals during the summer, including Jazz Middelheim, held in Antwerp, the Audi Jazz Festival, held in various venues throughout Belgium, both in Flanders and in Wallonia, and the Brussels Jazz Marathon, staged during the last weekend in May.

Jacques Brel is one of the best known Belgian musicians of the 20th century. Although his songs are considered part of the French *chanson* tradition, Brel was Belgian, born in Flanders but into a French-speaking family. Most Brel songs are in French, including his ode to the port of Amsterdam, but he also pays tribute to Flanders in the Flemish language in songs such as 'The Flat Country' ('Le Plat Pays') and 'Marieke', with their choruses sung in Flemish. Brel died in 1978 in the Marquesas Islands in the Pacific, where he is buried next to the French artist, Paul Gaugin, but his music is still immensely popular in Belgium and throughout most of the French-speaking world. There are schools and parks named after him in many parts of Benelux (as well as in France), and most music radio stations still play his songs on a regular basis, whatever their usual programming content.

Concert schedules, performances and other musical events are publicised in newspapers, magazines and in the cultural calendars published by tourist offices. The Belgian Tourist Office offers a telephone reservation service for Brussels and many other cities in Belgium (☎ 0800-21221 Mondays to Fridays from 9am to 7pm and Saturdays from 10am to noon). FNAC and other large music stores also offer a concert and event booking service.

Holland: Amsterdam's *Concertgebouw*, famous for its superb acoustics, is the main venue for musical concerts, including performances by orchestras, chamber music ensembles and individual performers in a variety of styles. The *Concertgebouw* hosts up to 650 concerts every year and is 'home' to both the Dutch Philharmonic

Orchestra (*Nederlands Philharmonisch Orkest*) and the Royal Concertgebouw Orchestra (*Koninklijk Concertgebouworkest*). The *Concertgebouw*'s website (💻 www.concertgebouw.nl) contains the current concert schedule and allows you to order tickets online. Rotterdam has its own Philharmonic Orchestra, which often performs at *De Doelen*, the main concert hall in Rotterdam, also renowned for its excellent acoustics. In The Hague you can hear the *Residentie-Orkest* performing in the *Anton Philipszaal*, and there's a Netherlands Chamber Orchestra (*Nederlands Kamerorkest*), which performs throughout the country. Many churches also host concerts featuring chamber music ensembles or individual performers, often free. Look out for posters or flyers or check with the local tourist office for information.

The Dutch are jazz enthusiasts, and both Amsterdam and Rotterdam are riddled with small jazz clubs and other jazz performance venues. There are also plenty of rock concerts on offer, all the usual big name bands making stops in Amsterdam, Rotterdam, Utrecht and other Dutch cities. Although you may not hear much of them outside Holland, local bands are often featured both in record shops and on local radio stations, and many are worth hearing.

During the summer, there are numerous musical festivals and outdoor concerts in Holland. Jazz festivals are popular and often draw international artists and jazz enthusiasts from around the world. In Amsterdam, there's the Canal Festival (*Grachtenfestival*), held in August, with a variety of concerts (some free) throughout the city, many on pontoons or barges moored in the canals.

VVV tourist offices and most commercial ticket agencies are the best sources of information about musical performances and events, as well as the Expatica website (💻 www.expatica.com). In Amsterdam, the AUB (*Amsterdam Uit Buro*) on the Leidseplein is a popular place to book tickets to all sorts of performances.

Luxembourg: Even Luxembourg has its own orchestra, *l'Orchestre Philharmonique du Luxembourg* (OPL), originally known as the RTL Orchestra on account of its affiliation with the national radio and television service. The main concert venues are the *Théâtre Municipal* (2 Rond-Point Schuman) and the *Conservatoire de Musique de la Ville de Luxembourg* (33 rue Charles Martel). Tickets for individual concerts are sometimes difficult to obtain, as season subscriptions are popular. Contact the *Théâtre Municipal* and the *Conservatoire* to be added to their mailing lists.

There are also open air concerts during the summer, both in Luxembourg city (usually at the Place d'Armes) and other town centres, as well as at country *châteaux*. The castles of Vianden and Bourglinster hold concerts from April to September each year, and in Echternach there's an annual festival of classical music, beginning in May. One evening every July, Luxembourg city opens the Place Guillaume to rock bands for an event known as *Rock um Kneudler*. Further information is available from the tourist office or its website.

SOCIAL CLUBS

There are a large number of social clubs of all types available to both foreigners and local residents in Benelux. Some are based on nationality or language, others on interests, and joining a club is one of the easiest ways to meet people and make friends. Clubs include British and American women's and men's Clubs, business clubs, international men's and women's clubs, Kiwani Clubs, Lion and Lioness Clubs, and Rotary International and Friendship Societies. Expatriates from many countries have their own clubs in and around major cities and it's usually possible to obtain a list from your embassy or consulate. A large number of clubs are organised around hobbies or other pastimes, such as photography, amateur radio, sporting activities, arts and crafts, chess, bridge, music and local history. Many local clubs organise activities such as trips and tours. You can often find information about clubs in your area from your town hall, signs in shop windows or on supermarket or company notice boards, and listings in expatriate publications.

NIGHTLIFE

The extent and variety of nightlife you can expect to find vary considerably according to your location. The larger cities, particularly the port towns of Amsterdam, Rotterdam and Antwerp are the major centres for discos, bars, dance halls and many other forms of nightlife, as well as the famous (or infamous) live sex shows. Luxembourg city, on the other hand, prides itself on being a quiet family town, where the pavements are virtually deserted by 10pm. There are, however, a few discos open late at weekends if you know where to look. An increasing number of Benelux cities are offering alcohol-free dance clubs and parties for young people.

The sex shows in Amsterdam and Rotterdam are aimed primarily at the tourist market, and many are more comic than pornographic (with the same couple performing 'live sex' every hour on the hour). Nevertheless, some performances are cleverly staged, audience members being coaxed onto the stage to 'assist' in the sillier parts of the show (no, not in the live sex). Entrance fees are steep – normally at least €20 or €35 if drinks (two, usually watered down) are included – and it's unlikely you'll want to stay all night, given that the performance is repeated every hour.

The famous 'red light' district of Amsterdam, where ladies of the night display their wares in their 'shop' windows, is concentrated around the Oudezijds Voorburgwal and Oudezijds Achterburgwal. The 'industry' is strictly regulated by the government, including regular health inspections, and the women even have their own union. There are, however, unlicensed foreigners also working the district. While 'window shopping' can be an interesting and even informative experience, wandering through the area alone, particularly late at night, isn't recommended and 'trading' in the district can be downright dangerous. Note also that the red light district attracts pickpockets, thieves and other criminals. Unaccompanied women are often pestered (or worse) and there are occasional muggings, knifings and other serious crimes, not all of which are reported to the police.

GAMBLING

As in most countries, gambling in Benelux is strictly controlled by the state (primarily because of the huge tax revenue earned from it) and casinos are both popular and plentiful throughout Belgium, Holland and Luxembourg. Most casinos are located in or near the major resort towns and are open from early afternoon until after midnight (opening hours of 2pm to 2am are common). The most popular games include American and French roulette, blackjack and slot machines (otherwise known as one-armed bandits). Some casinos offer baccarat, craps tables and other 'exotic' ways to part you from your money. You must be 18 to enter and are usually required to show identification and be 'properly' (i.e. smartly) dressed. Casinos offer much more than gambling, however. Many have fine restaurants and present shows or other forms of entertainment. All casinos advertise heavily in local newspapers and tourist publications, and you'll also find posters in most seaside or resort communities. There are casinos in the following towns:

Belgium: Blankenberge, Chaudfontaine, Dinant, Knokke, Middelkerke, Namur, Ostend, and Spa.

Holland: Amsterdam, Breda, Eindhoven, Groningen, Nijmegen, Rotterdam, Scheveningen, Schiphol Airport (Amsterdam), Valkenburg and Zandvoort.

Luxembourg: Mondorf les Bains.

BARS & CAFES

The sheer range of bars and cafés in the cities and towns of Benelux would fill many books (and actually does). Suffice it to say that you should be able to find some sort of bar, café or coffee house to meet your needs in just about any town, whether you're looking for a quick beer, a glass of wine, a cool drink on a warm day or a quick bite to eat and a cup of coffee.

There are bars on almost every street corner, from the rough and tumble fishermen's hangouts immortalised in Brel's song about Amsterdam to English and Irish pubs and upmarket 'yuppie bars' with tasteful New Age décor. It's possible to sample any number of varieties of genever (the Dutch drink from which gin was developed), and in Belgium you can work your way through the hundreds of Belgian beers in almost any pub or bar. (Most brewers, however, are now part of a single conglomerate.) In the larger cities, particularly in Amsterdam, you can find a variety of gay and lesbian bars.

Holland is famous for its coffee shops. The Dutch take their coffee seriously, and coffee shops have always had a significant place in the social scene in Holland (not unlike pubs in Britain). In a traditional coffee shop, you can order a sandwich or a light snack along with a cup of coffee or tea. This kind of coffee shop is sometimes referred to as a 'non-smoking' coffee shop, even though you can normally smoke an ordinary cigarette (i.e. containing only tobacco) in most of them. The 'other' sort of coffee shop, a 'smoking' one, is the kind where you can buy up to five grammes of pot (marijuana or hashish) for personal consumption, although technically not on the premises. Smoking coffee shops developed from a sort of gentlemen's agreement, based on the Dutch laws that ignore the casual use of marijuana by individuals. Regulations governing smoking coffee shops have now been more clearly defined in law: smoking coffee shops may not sell alcohol or any other sort of drugs, and local authorities can close them if they cause a public nuisance. There are estimated to be as many as 900 of this sort of coffee shop, although local opposition to them has been growing in recent years and a number have been closed under the provisions of the new law. Given the notoriety of smoking coffee shops, many traditional coffee shops have recently changed their names to 'tea shop'.

RESTAURANTS

Eating is a major recreational activity in Belgium, Holland and Luxembourg. In fact, many locals consider a meal out to be an evening's entertainment in itself, not something to be hurried through en route to the theatre or other diversion. If you're invited to a restaurant, be prepared to spend the entire evening eating, drinking and talking at the table.

Restaurants exist in all styles, sizes, shapes and price ranges, and both Belgium and Holland are well-known for their pavement snack stands and a variety of 'hole in the wall' eateries offering local varieties of fast food for under €5. In the cities, there are elegant restaurants serving gourmet French and other European cuisine and a selection of fine wines, for those willing to spend €100 or more (per person). Between these extremes you can find a satisfying selection of moderately priced restaurants offering local, exotic or one of various 'fusion' food (blending elements of local or European cuisine with the flavours and spices of the Far East, North Africa or the Middle East). In rural areas there are numerous small auberges, roadside inns and even 'truckers' restaurants offering excellent food.

Belgium: Although overshadowed by the French when it comes to matters of food, the Belgians can be counted among the world's great gourmets. Belgians know and appreciate good food, no matter where it comes from, and in recent years the influx of foreigners has led to a proliferation of ethnic restaurants, particularly in and around the Brussels area. Restaurant openings create as much excitement and discussion as theatre and opera premieres in some circles.

Belgium's most famous contribution to the art of cuisine is the humble chip (although Americans know it as the *French* fried potato). The Belgian *frite* (short for *pomme frite*, which in turn is short for *pomme de terre frite*) is what all other fried potatoes aspire to, including, if rumours are to be believed, the mass-produced fries sold at McDonald's restaurants. The secret of perfect chips is variously alleged to lie in the variety of potato used, the manner in which the potato is cut, the type of oil used for frying, a two-stage cooking process and a number of other steps in the process. True Belgians eat their *frites* with mayonnaise rather than with salt and vinegar or ketchup, so be sure to specify when ordering if you want them 'without mayo'.

The most typical accompaniment to *frites* (or is it the other way round?) is a steaming kettle full of mussels (*moules*) cooked in white wine, with some chopped onion, celery, perhaps some tomatoes and peppers or a spoonful of *crème fraîche* stirred in at the last moment. *Moules et frites* can be found almost everywhere in Belgium, but it's particularly common in the resort towns along the coast, such as Ostend. Connoisseurs use an empty shell as a pincher to extract the next mussel from its shell – finger food at its best, which also explains the popularity of *moules et frites* among children.

Typical Belgian cuisine doesn't end with *moules et frites*, however. Try *waterzooi* (chicken in rich cream sauce) or *hochepot* (a stew combining oxtail with pig's trotters, ears and snout). Other Belgian dishes include *carbonnade Flamandes* (beef simmered in dark beer), *anguille au vert* (eel prepared in a green sauce made with fresh herbs) and Belgian endive (*chicons/witloof*), often wrapped in a slice of ham and baked in a cream sauce. The Belgians also have their own distinct sorts of *charcuterie* (cold meats, sausages and hams) and cheeses (including several made by the same abbeys that produce beers) – all, of course, washed down with Belgian beer (or French wine, which is readily available throughout Belgium). For dessert, there are waffles (*gaufres/wafels*), sprinkled with sugar or filled with ice cream, or *speculoos*, spicy biscuits sometimes shaped like windmills.

Holland: Dutch food has the reputation for being heavy, filling and somewhat dull, although after a cold winter's day spent ice skating on frozen canals, a bowl of hot split pea soup (*erwtensoep* – easier to eat than to pronounce) with thick slices of sausage floating in it, accompanied by a chunk of brown bread, has amazing restorative powers! You'll also find smoked eel, *fricandel* (a sort of fried sausage) and *pannenkoeken* (pancakes, usually filled with fruit compote, honey or nuts) and *oliebollen*, a sort of doughnut (without a hole) made with raisins and dipped in powdered sugar that's popular at Christmas and New Year.

Herring is a traditional and much loved part of the Dutch diet, and there are herring stands on most street corners and in virtually all village markets. There's even a national herring test conducted each year and the results (including where to find the best herring) are published in the *Algemeen Dagblad*. For herring lovers, a particular treat is *nieuwe haring*, the first catch of the season, available only for a few weeks from the end of May. *Nieuwe* is properly eaten raw, with no onions or pickles on the side. Save those for the later, more mature herring, called *maatjesharing*, that comes onto the market in July. That comes pickled, salted, smoked, cured and embellished in all sorts of other ways. It's often served with onions on a roll or bun, although connoisseurs generally eat theirs straight.

If you're not keen on herring and other local dishes don't appeal to you, there's no shortage of ethnic restaurants. Like the Belgians, the Dutch love dining out and have adopted many of the standard dishes of their various immigrant populations. Almost every town has its Indonesian, Surinamese and Chinese or Turkish restaurants, which are particular favourites of the Dutch. There are also French, Italian and Mexican restaurants, as well as any number of the currently fashionable 'fusion' restaurants, combining two or more cuisines.

Even before the current influx of immigrants, Amsterdam was famous for the *rijstafel*, a dining ritual brought to Holland from Indonesia, when it was still a Dutch colony. *Rijstafel* consists of bowls of rice, served with little dishes of assorted 'toppings' – meat and vegetables prepared in a variety of sauces, from hot and spicy to sweet and sour, many of them peanut-based, and various fried and steamed delicacies. Although it's possible to order a *rijstafel* for just two or three people, it's normally more fun with a large group because you then have a much wider selection of dishes to share. Watch out for the smallest dishes, which often contain excruciatingly hot condiments!

Booking is recommended in most cities, particularly at weekends. Sunday is a big eating-out day for Dutch families, and restaurants are often especially crowded at Sunday lunchtime. If you're driving, make sure you watch your alcohol intake at dinner; the police often set up roadblocks on Friday and Saturday nights to catch those who should have taken a taxi home!

Luxembourg: As in the rest of the Benelux region, dining out can be a full evening's entertainment in Luxembourg. Restaurants tend to be expensive, but the Duchy also boasts the highest proportion of one and two-star restaurants per inhabitant of any country in Europe. In Luxembourg city, many restaurants have only a single sitting for the evening and you should expect to spend two to three hours enjoying both the food and the company. Many of the better restaurants (at least according to a certain well known guide book) tend to be French, but Luxembourg also has its own cuisine, which draws heavily on both German and Dutch influences. Typical Luxembourg dishes include *kuddelfleck mat tomatenzooss* (tripe in tomato sauce), *judd mat gaardebounen* (smoked collete of pork cooked with runner beans), and *brennesselszopp* (nettle soup). Many restaurants proudly offer local beers and wines, although French wines and Belgian beers are readily available.

LIBRARIES

Many towns in Benelux have community lending libraries, but most of them are small and stock only books in the local languages. Check with your town hall for the location and opening hours of the community library. Some of the public or state libraries in the larger cities have English language sections, although not all state libraries permit you to take books home. The Royal Library (*Bibliothèque Royale Albert I/Koninklijke Biliotheek Albert I*) in Brussels has a Center for American Studies, containing a wide selection of books on history, social sciences, politics and other subjects, but these are available only for use in the library. In Holland, the Central Public Libraries in Amsterdam, The Hague and Rotterdam have a particularly good selection of children's books in foreign languages (i.e. English, French and German). The *Bibliothèque Nationale* in Luxembourg city has a good reference section with many English-language titles.

Apart from these, expatriate clubs and other organisations often have lending libraries (sometimes including video and audio tapes) for the use of members. If you have connections with a university or international organisation, you can often make use of their libraries.

DAY & EVENING CLASSES

Adult day and evening classes are run by various organisations in all cities and large towns in Belgium, Holland and Luxembourg. In addition to formal further education courses (see page 159), day and evening classes offer classes and lectures in everything from astrology to zoology. The range and variety of subjects offered are vast and include local and foreign languages, handicrafts, hobbies and sports, and business-related topics. Many expatriate clubs and organisations also organise day and evening classes in a variety of subjects, including tours and field trips to nearby historical and cultural sites. Museums often offer evening classes for adults and sometimes also for children during the summer and other school holidays. It's also possible to find Internet classes, offering courses in a wide range of subjects, from creative writing to computer studies.

Adult education programmes are published in many cities and regions, and local newspapers also contain details of evening and day courses. See also **Further Education** on page 159 and **Language Schools** on page 160.

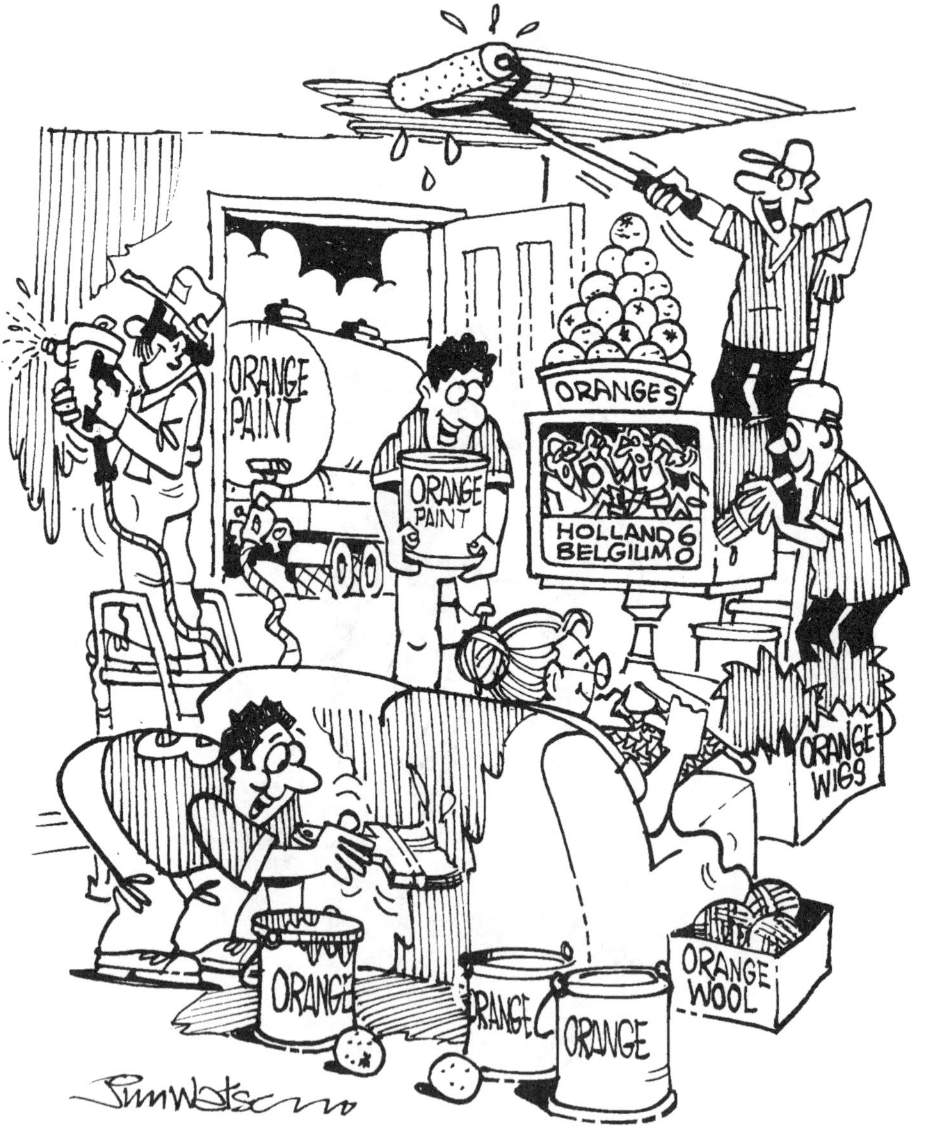
ORANGE PAINT
ORANGE PAINT
ORANGES
HOLLAND 6
BELGIUM 0
ORANGE WIGS
ORANGE WOOL
ORANGE
ORANGE
ORANGE

16.

SPORTS

There's no lack of sporting and recreational facilities, both indoor and outdoor, in the Benelux countries. At the Sydney Olympics in 2000, Holland finished in eighth place in the medals table with a total of 25, 12 of them gold, their strongest events being swimming and sailing. The Dutch are also strong competitors in the winter Olympics, especially in speed skating, a sport they claim to have invented and often dominate. The Belgians are particularly fond of hiking, caving (also known as spelunking) and aerial sports, from flying to hang gliding and parachuting (not to mention pigeon racing). Other popular participant sports in the Benelux region include athletics, football, handball, horse riding, skiing, table tennis and tennis, but there are clubs devoted to everything from basketball to pigeon racing. Spectator sports with large following include football, formula one motor racing, tennis, skiing and equestrian competitions, all of which are broadcast on television sports channels and have websites devoted to both the sport in general and individual teams. The following sections cover some of the popular sports in Benelux.

All three countries have a ministry or other governmental office devoted to sport. These are usually responsible for administering the municipal and regional sports centres found in many cities and towns. Private sports clubs and facilities are widespread, particularly in tourist areas, where they're often affiliated to a resort or hotel. Almost every sport imaginable has a national or regional federation, including rock climbing, caving, several forms of martial arts, parachuting and scuba diving. Local and national tourist offices are excellent sources of information about sports and outdoor activities.

FOOTBALL

Football (soccer – *voetbal* in Dutch) is at least as close to being the 'national sport' in Benelux countries as it is in much of the rest of Europe. Both Belgium (Red Devils) and Holland (*Oranje*) normally field impressive national teams in the World Cup and usually progress to the final round, although the Dutch have an unfortunate reputation for having produced some of the best teams NOT to have won the World Cup. Many *Oranje* team veterans have also become successful coaches throughout the world. Belgium and Holland were among the seven original members of FIFA (*Fédération Internationale de Football Association*), which sets the rules for international competition and organises the World Cup tournament. The leading professional football teams in Belgium include RSC Anderlecht and Club Bruges, while in Holland the fortunes of Ajax, Feyenoord and PSV Eindhoven are followed religiously by all the local sports media.

Throughout the Benelux region, there are organised leagues and teams for amateur footballers, including youth and women's teams. If you don't fancy getting wet and muddy, the national football organisations are now also supporting the sport of *Futsal*, or indoor five-a-side soccer, which has its own leagues, teams and season.

Belgium: Belgium has four national divisions, headed by the 'Jupiler League'. The Royal Belgian Football Association maintains an extensive website (🖳 www.footbel.com) with statistics dating back to the 19th century and lists of member teams and leagues so that you can find a club to support – from your armchair or the sidelines. Football is also a popular component of the *Association royale Belge des*

Sports du Samedi (Royal Association of Saturday Sports), which boasts 300 football teams in Brabant alone!

Holland: The *Koninklijke Nederlandse Voetbalbond* (Royal Netherlands Football Association, Postbus 420, 3700 AK te Zeist) has over a million members and is by far the largest sporting organisation in Holland. Its website (www.knvb.nl) has an English-language section, mostly related to the national team. The Dutch portion of the site also carries information about affiliated teams, both professional and amateur.

Luxembourg: While Luxembourg's national team may be rather lower in the FIFA world rankings than those of its neighbours (138th in early 2001), enthusiasm for the sport is equally strong. The *Fédération Luxembourgoise de Football* (50 rue de Strasbourg, (☎ 48-86 65, www.f-l-f.lu) estimates that there are over 700 teams active in the Duchy, playing in two senior divisions, with separate leagues for juniors, students and women.

CYCLING

Cycling is extremely popular throughout the Benelux region, not only as a sport, but also as an everyday mode of transport. In the flatter parts of Belgium and Holland, many people use sturdy bikes with wide tyres for commuting to and from work as well as for doing the shopping. Equipped with panniers, baskets or racks, these bikes can transport a surprisingly heavy load of groceries, building supplies or office work. Thin wheeled bikes are mainly used for racing, while mountain bikes are popular in hillier areas and for off-road riding. According to the Dutch tourist office, you can rent bicycles 'everywhere' in Holland. In Belgium, you can often find bicycles for hire at railway stations.

Cycle paths are common throughout the region, especially in Holland, which has over 17,000km (10,563mi) of off-road cycle paths, as well as 40,000km (24,855mi) of official cycling routes designed to keep cyclists off busy roads. Luxembourg has recently doubled its network of cycle paths to 600km (372mi). Cycle paths are usually well maintained and cycle routes are clearly signposted. One of the longest routes is the 470km (293mi) *Noordseeroute*, designated the LF1. which starts in Boulogne in France, winds through Belgium and takes you up the Dutch coast as far as the city of Den Helder in the north. You can buy cycling maps in all national and regional tourist offices, as well as in cycle shops and many bookshops and news stands.

Drivers in all three countries are used to co-existing with cyclists, but it pays to know and understand the traffic laws, which apply equally to all road users. Cyclists must use cycle lanes where provided and must not cycle in bus lanes or on footpaths or pavements. If you cycle in cities, you should wear reflective clothing, protective head gear, a smog mask and carry a crucifix (and be careful not to get your wheels stuck in tram lines). A crash helmet is recommended even when cycling in the country, particularly for children, and is much cheaper than brain surgery. Head injuries are the main cause of death in bicycle accidents, most of which don't involve collisions with cars but result from hitting fixed objects. Always buy a quality helmet that has been approved and subjected to rigorous testing. Note that bicycles must be roadworthy and be fitted with a horn or bell and front and rear lights. You should also carry an anti-theft device such as a steel cable lock (the only police-approved bike lock), although they're far from thief-proof. Bicycle theft is a big problem in Benelux, particularly in the cities, where many commuters prefer to use an old, tatty bike in order to discourage theft, while saving a newer model for the weekends. (Many locals own more than one bicycle.) If your bicycle is stolen, you should report the theft to the local police – but don't expect them to find it! Some insurance companies cover bicycle theft.

Bicycle racing is a popular sport throughout the Benelux region. Many larger cities have a velodrome and hold regular indoor races for local teams and riders. Benelux riders often enter the famous Tour de France – Belgian rider Eddy Mercxx won it five times in the '70s – and the world's most famous cycling event occasionally begins in Belgium. Not to be outdone, the Flemish have their own Tour of Flanders race, and the cycle racing season in Luxembourg runs from March to October. Luxembourg's answer to Le Mans is the town of Wiltz, where at the beginning of July there's a 24-hour cycle race called the *24 Stonne Velo Wolz*. The Dutch are also strong cycling competitors and there are several Dutch websites devoted to professional and amateur cycle racing (mostly in Dutch).

There are numerous bicycle clubs and associations, many of which are affiliated to the national cycling organisations, which can be contacted for information about local clubs:

Belgium: *Royale Ligue Velocipedique Belge/Koninklijke Belgische Wielrijdersbond* (🖥 www.kbwb-rlvb.be).

Holland: *Koninklijke Nederlandsche Wielren Unie*, Postbus 136/Polanerbaan 15, 3447 GN Woerden.

Luxembourg: *Fédération du Sport cycliste Luxembourgeoise,* 14 avenue de la Gare, 1610 Luxembourg.

TENNIS & OTHER RACQUET SPORTS

Tennis, squash and racquetball courts are available at both private clubs and public or community sports centres. Some schools (particularly international schools) make their courts available to the public during off-peak hours and at weekends. Even at public outdoor tennis courts, you must usually pay at least a small hourly fee and often you need to book court time well in advance or make a seasonal booking for a particular time each week. It can be difficult to find a court at short notice in and around the larger cities, particularly Brussels. Some hotels and resorts have their own tennis and squash courts, and organise coaching holidays throughout the year. Information is available from racquet clubs, travel agents and tourist offices.

There are also private tennis clubs, which are usually exclusive and rarely admit unaccompanied visitors. Membership can be extremely expensive (particularly at clubs frequented by high level diplomats and executives) and most private clubs have long waiting lists. Many tennis clubs have saunas, Jacuzzis, solariums and swimming pools and most have a restaurant – usually a good one. There are squash clubs in many larger towns, although some have only one or two courts. There are also many combined tennis and squash clubs. Racquetball equipment can be hired at most squash clubs. Some tennis centres have badminton courts and there are badminton clubs in many areas. Table tennis is also gaining in popularity, and most sports clubs and centres have tables and equipment. Luxembourg alone boasts over 100 table tennis clubs!

SKIING & WINTER SPORTS

Ski enthusiasts in Belgium, Holland and Luxembourg generally head for the mountains of France, Switzerland, Austria and northern Italy during the winter months. Downhill skiing is surprisingly popular in such a flat region – so much so that entrepreneurs have established indoor artificial ski slopes in Belgium and Holland where you can learn the basics or practise your technique between skiing holidays. Indoor ski slopes range in length from around 100 to 200 meters, offering a skiing area of 2,500 to 5,000m². Although good skiers will find these indoor facilities rather tame, they can be a great place to try out the sport if you've never skied, as you can rent all the equipment you need and most offer lessons for all ages and abilities. There's usually an hourly charge, plus a small additional fee if you rent skis, boots or other equipment. In Belgium there are indoor ski slopes near Brussels and Antwerp, and in Holland facilities are available near Ijmuiden and in Zoetermeer.

The Ardennes don't always have a great deal of snow, but when they do it's a popular area for cross-country skiing. The Duchy of Luxembourg boasts a number of maintained cross-country trails and you can call a special 'snow line' (☎ 42-828 220) for reports on the condition of trails. In Belgium, the ski areas of the Ardennes and the Hautes Fagnes are easily accessible by rail and road. Skis and boots can be rented in many of the towns in the area. In neighbouring France and Germany, the Juras and the Black Forest aren't far away and have a wealth of cross-country ski trails and some downhill ski runs. Note, however, that during school holiday periods, particularly in France, ski areas can be overcrowded and you will need to book well in advance.

Another popular winter sport is ice skating, on both indoor and outdoor rinks. Speed skating is said to have been developed in Holland in the 13th century, and the Dutch continue to be masters of the art. There are permanent ice rinks in many cities and larger towns, usually including separate areas for ice hockey, figure skating, and both long and short-track speed skating, all of which are popular spectator sports. Portable outdoor ice rinks are set up in Brussels (in the Grand-Place), The Hague (at the Spuiplein) and at the Place Guillaume in Luxembourg city; these are often open until 9pm or later and offer a pleasant evening's entertainment during winter.

It's usually possible to rent skates nearby, except in Holland, where everyone seems to own at least one pair of ice skates. Skating is taken seriously and new skates can be surprisingly expensive, so you should look in newspapers and expatriate publications for information about where to purchase used skates, particularly for children. When the weather is cold enough for rivers and canals to freeze, the Dutch organise ice skating races and long distance tours, such as the *Elfstedentocht*, a 200km (124mi) event taking in 11 towns in Holland. This is supposed to be an annual event, but is held only in years when conditions are suitable (i.e. the canals are frozen!). In Luxembourg, information about skating can be obtained from the *Fédération Luxembourgeoise des Sports de Glace* (Federation of Ice Sports, PO Box 2087, 1020 Luxembourg).

SWIMMING

There are public indoor and outdoor swimming pools (*piscines publiques/ zwembaden*) in most towns and resort areas, many open all year. Bathing caps are required at most pools, and men and boys must wear racing-style swimming trunks – not the baggy 'shorts' popular in the USA. Olympic-size pools are becoming the norm, although even these can be crowded at popular times, especially at weekends and during school holidays. Serious swimmers are advised to do their training early in the morning or at other off-peak times. Larger public pools may have impressive features such as wave machines and water chutes, as well as paddling pools for young children. Most public pools offer swimming lessons, either individual or group, and some run life-saving courses. There are also swimming clubs and teams that organise races and other competitions.

The main beach areas in Belgium are at Ostend and De Haan, both of which offer wide, sandy beaches and are supervised by lifeguards during the summer months. Scheveningen is the one of the largest and most popular beaches along the southern coast of Holland. The water temperature is at best cool (this is the North Sea) and the summer beach season tends to be short. There can also be problems with pollution, due to the intensive industrial activity along the coast, and signs are displayed when conditions are 'unfavourable' for bathing, although the problem has been greatly reduced in recent years. Even when swimming is only for the hardy, the North Sea beach towns offer opportunities for walking, dining, shopping and other less energetic activities. Lakes and recreation parks offer fresh water swimming in many areas throughout Belgium, Holland and Luxembourg, along with separate areas for a variety of water sports (see below).

WATER SPORTS

The Benelux region boasts many rivers, lakes and canals, as well as a long coastline, and popular water sports include sailing, windsurfing, water-skiing, jet-skiing, rowing, canoeing, kayaking, barging, rafting and scuba diving. There are clubs for most watersports in all major towns. Instruction is usually available, and members often organise group holiday trips to warmer locations. (Many of the sub aqua clubs offer bargain excursions to some of the top diving areas of the world.) Rowing and canoeing are possible on most lakes and rivers, where boats can usually be rented. Some of the best canoeing and kayaking conditions occur early in the year, when melting snow fills the rivers, but remember that the water is cold. In fact, wetsuits are recommended for most water sports, even in summer.

Be sure to observe all warning signs on lakes and rivers. Certain areas are often designated for high-speed or motorised water sports (e.g. windsurfing, waterskiing and jet-skiing) in order to avoid accidents with slower craft and swimmers, and the penalties for straying out of the designated area can be severe. Take particular care when canoeing, as even the most benign of rivers have patches of white water that can be dangerous for the inexperienced. It's wise to wear a life-jacket or at least a buoyancy aid, even if you're a strong swimmer. On some rivers and canals there are quicksand-like banks of silt and shingle which are dangerous.

The Dutch, in particular, are devotees of fast sailing and power boats and hold many yacht races, both on inland waters and in the open sea. With their long history of sea-faring, it isn't surprising that there are over 280,000 boats over six metres in length moored in Dutch marinas and another million or so smaller vessels (including rowing boats and inflatable dinghies) stored in garages, back gardens and elsewhere. One problem is the depth (or rather shallowness) of waterways, and inexperienced or over-ambitious sailors can get stuck or do serious damage to their craft. The government has found it too expensive to dredge areas where silting is a constant problem and is understandably hesitant to raise usage fees to pay for this operation. In heavily used or working rivers and canals, it's necessary to know the boating regulations regarding how and when to defer to barges and larger vessels, and be prepared to wait (and pay) for the use of locks or bridges that must be opened.

AERIAL SPORTS

The Benelux region has numerous small airports and if you're interested in flying, gliding, ballooning or other aerial pursuits, you should have no trouble finding suitable facilities. While the Ardennes don't offer as spectacular an environment for gliding and hang-gliding that you'll find in the Alps or Pyrenees, the low density of air traffic and the wooded scenery make the area popular for all forms of aerial sport.

Hang-gliding and paragliding involve jumping off a mountain or cliff with a large kite or parachute strapped to your back to 'ease' your descent. Given the right warm air currents (thermals) and updrafts, you can stay aloft for quite a while and enjoy a bird's eye view of the countryside. Participants must have the proper equipment and complete an approved course of instruction, after which (if you survive) you receive a proficiency certificate and are permitted to go solo. If you're in more of a hurry to reach the ground, you could try parachuting.

Ballooning is becoming increasingly popular in Benelux. Drifting silently (except when the air in the balloon needs heating and there's a roar of gas jets) over the countryside can be a magnificent experience, particularly with a magnum of Champagne to hand. Many resorts and tourist offices can direct you to hot air balloon companies which organise excursions (depending on suitable weather conditions). Balloon trips are particularly popular in the wine-growing areas of Luxembourg. There are also international balloon events and races in various regions of Benelux and in neighbouring countries, filling the sky with brightly coloured and sometimes fancifully designed balloons.

Light aircraft and gliders (sailplanes) can be hired with an instructor or without (provided, of course, you have a pilot's licence) at many small airports in Belgium, Holland and Luxembourg. There are also flying schools and clubs at private airports in Antwerp, Ostend, Rotterdam, Groningen and other cities. There are a number of specialised airfields in Luxembourg, including a microlight field near Larochette, a gliding airfield at Op der Hoh and the Airfield Noertrange, which is a well known parachuting centre. The Luxembourg Tourist Office offers a pamphlet on flying activities, produced by the *Fédération Aéronautique Luxembourgeoise*, and both the Belgian and Dutch tourist offices can provide detailed information about aerial sports facilities.

If you prefer keeping your feet on *terra firma*, there's always kite flying, and in the spring and summer months kiting festivals and events are staged in a number of areas. Note, however, that kite flying is prohibited in certain areas, e.g. close to airports and airfields where it's a hazard to aircraft.

Before taking up aerial sports (apart, perhaps, from kite flying) you're advised to make sure that you have adequate health, accident and life insurance and that your affairs are in order. Why not try fishing instead – a nice safe sport (unless, of course, you're a fish)?

GOLF

Interest in golf has been steadily growing over the last few decades in Benelux. Although most golf courses are controlled by private clubs, many extend guest privileges to members of foreign golf clubs and to those accompanied by local club members. To join, however, you may need to be 'proposed' by an existing member. During the week, some clubs open their courses to the public or to members of other sports or social clubs and associations. Check with local expatriate associations for any special arrangements they may have with golf clubs, many of which advertise in expatriate publications and newsletters.

Belgium: There are over 70 golf clubs in Belgium, the majority of which are concentrated in the Brussels area. Some are both 'exclusive' and expensive to join. Most courses are members of the Royal Belgian Golf Federation (🖳 www.golf.be). Green fees vary from €30 to €57.50 according to the time of day and the day of the week. There's also considerable interest in professional golf, as the Belgian PGA has produced a number of champions. You can follow the fortunes of Belgian golfers on its website (🖳 www.pga.be).

Holland: You should have no trouble finding a golf course anywhere in Holland, as there are many nine and 18-hole courses, both public and private, including around 75 clubs. Green fees average €30.

Luxembourg: There are six golf courses in the Duchy, all of them private clubs but most allow non-members to play. Some courses insist that you have a handicap (a golf handicap, that is) and some have dress regulations.

HIKING, ROCK CLIMBING & CAVING

Walking and hiking are popular pastimes in Benelux, where there's a wide variety of terrain, from beaches to broad flat marshes, open fields and the hills and forests of the Ardennes. In Luxembourg alone there are 5,000km (3,106mi) of marked hiking paths and trails, including 171 official hiking routes and 19 national footpaths, organised by 'theme' and varying from 13 to 84km (8 to 60mi) in length. At least two major European hiking paths pass through the area: the E2, which runs from Holland to the Mediterranean; and the Atlantic-Bohemian Forest Path (E3), which runs right across Europe from west to east.

If you prefer walking on level ground, you may want to try the peculiarly Dutch sport of *wadlopen* (mud walking). In the nature reserve at Wadden Sea, the shore dries out at low tide and bands of hikers march across the salt marsh and along the exposed sea bottom to reach sand bars – not the drinking kind, but small islands normally separated from the mainland by the sea. When the tide comes back in, you're picked up and returned by boat (assuming, of course, that you reached the bar – otherwise you're in for a long swim). For safety reasons, you must be accompanied by a licensed guide from a recognised *wadlopen* organisation. There are several of these, all of which can be contacted through the Dutch Tourist Office or at the Wadden Sea National Park. Hikes take three to five hours, plus a similar time for the return journey, and you should be in reasonable condition, as there's no stopping or turning back! Starting times vary according to tides and weather conditions.

Rock climbing and caving are popular in the hillier regions of the Ardennes, which are composed largely of limestone. Both Belgium and Luxembourg are blessed with a large number of crags suitable for climbing, particularly along the rivers that traverse the region. In both countries you must have authorisation from the land owner before attempting a climb, and many landowners license climbing and caving rights to clubs, which assume responsibility for maintaining the site and ensuring that climbers and cavers are properly qualified and insured. The *Club Alpin Belge/Belgische Alpen Club* (CAB/BAC) leases climbing rights to many of the best and most popular locations in Belgium; it offers reciprocity with a number of foreign clubs and recognises the European *klimkaart* qualification. In Luxembourg most of the best natural climbing sites are under the jurisdiction of the *Ministère des Eaux et Forêts*, which issues permits from its office in Diekirch. Many public sports halls and fitness centres now offer indoor climbing walls for practice or instruction.

The various clubs and associations that are part of the *Union Belge de Spéléologie* (UBS) control access to the many caves available for exploration in Belgium. The UBS has a website (💻 www.speleo.be) where you can find details of caving clubs and sites, as well as instruction, equipment and insurance. Caving is dangerous if you don't take proper precautions; you should take particular attention to weather conditions, as a sudden shower can have fatal consequences when you're underground. Never go caving or climbing alone or without telling others where you're going and when you plan to return.

FISHING

No license is required for fishing at sea in Benelux. In harbour towns along the coast, you should have no difficulty finding fishing boats for hire, particularly during the summer, although North Sea fish stocks have been severely depleted by commercial fishing. To fish from the shore or in most inland streams, rivers, ponds or lakes, you may need a licence or permit, depending on the area and the type of fishing you wish to do. In many areas, there are private fishing lakes, where you can pay an hourly fee to cast your line without needing a license. There may be local regulations related to the type and size of fish that may be caught, and in some places even the type of bait is restricted at certain times of the year. Ask at the office where you obtain your fishing licence or at a local fishing tackle shop.

Belgium: Fishing licences are available from post offices and are limited to the local province or region. No night fishing is permitted and you may not sell your catch.

Holland: You need two permits for fishing in Holland. The first is a *sporvisakte*, which you can obtain at any post office, most tourist offices or at local tackle shops or fishing clubs. In addition, you must have a permit from the owner or leaseholder of the property where you're fishing (*vergunning*). Fishing rights are usually sold or rented to angling clubs but sometimes belong to the local municipality. If you belong to an angling club, your membership gives you a *vergunning* for the club's waters; otherwise day passes are usually available from local tackle shops.

Luxembourg: Luxembourg is a paradise for sport fishermen, with its network of lakes, ponds and rivers well stocked with trout, pike, pike-perch, eel and carp. Fees for fishing licences vary, according to whether you plan to fish from the bank or from a boat and whether you're on inland or boundary rivers or on private waters. Licences are available at tackle shops and apply to specific fishing locations. Contact the *Fédération Luxembourgeoise de Pêcheurs sportifs,* 47 rue de la Libération, 5969 Itzig for more information.

HUNTING

Hunting is a popular sport in Benelux, although it's strictly regulated regarding both what and where you may hunt. Importing a hunting weapon into any of the Benelux countries requires a European Firearms Pass and you must qualify for a hunting licence in order to keep your gun at home, as hunting and gun licences are normally combined in the same permit. To obtain a hunting licence, you must be aged at least 18, show proof of adequate third party insurance (in case you shoot something or someone you weren't intending to shoot) and demonstrate that you have access to a licensed hunting ground (e.g. by invitation of the landowner or by membership of a recognised club). It's also necessary to pass an exam covering both the theoretical and practical side of the sport, although the results of other European national hunting examinations are often transferable. There are no public areas open to hunting, so you must either be invited by a property owner or be part of a club or organisation that has hunting rights for a particular area (usually leased from the property owner). Non-residents can purchase a short-term licence (usually valid for a few days or a week), provided they're authorised to hunt by a landowner or licensed hunter.

Belgium: Hunting licenses are issued by the regional Division of Nature and Forests (*Ressources Naturelles et de l'Environnement, Division de la Nature et des Forêts/Administratie Milier-, Natuur-, Land- en Waterbeheer*). Information about hunting is also available from the *Société Royale St.-Hubert/Royal St.-Hubert Club* in Brussels (☎ 02-245 6851).

Holland: Holland issues around 33,000 hunting licences a year. There are defined seasons but no bag limits, as hunters are expected to respect the need to maintain game and wildlife stocks. No shooting is allowed on Sundays and there are restrictions on hunting on public holidays and in bad weather. Hunting large game (deer or wild boar) requires a special permit from the provincial government. Contact the Royal Netherlands Shooting Association (*Koninklijke Nederlandse Jagers Vereniging – KNJV*, Postbus 1165, 3800 BD Amersfoort, 💻 www.knjv.nl – the website has an English-language section).

Luxembourg: The forested areas of Luxembourg are widely known for their wild boar and deer, particularly the Goodland forest. Hunting licences and regulations are under the control of the *Direction des Eaux et Forêts, Division Chasse et Pêche*, PO Box 411, 2014 Luxembourg.

RUGBY

Perhaps because of the French influence, rugby enjoys surprising popularity throughout Benelux. The Belgian Rugby Union (Marathonlaan 135C, 1020 Brussels, (☎ 02-497.93.32) boasts a membership of some 4,000 players, over 100 trainers and around 65 referees and has separate divisions for Flemish and Walloon teams. The Dutch Rugby Union (*Nederlands Rugby Bond*, PO Box 8811, 1006 JA Amsterdam, (☎ 021-591 8145) can provide a list of organised teams, as can the Luxembourg Rugby Federation, 14 ave de la Gare, Luxembourg city (☎ 29-7598), while the Rugby Club Luxembourg holds open training on Tuesday and Thursday evenings at 7pm in Cessange. The club's website (⌨ www.rcl.lu) provides details, including dates and times of women's team training and information can also be obtained from international rubgy sites (e.g. ⌨ www.planet-rugby.com).

HEALTH CLUBS

There are gymnasiums and health and fitness clubs in most towns in Benelux, where sadists are employed and masochists go to torture themselves. Working out is becoming increasingly popular and many companies provide health and leisure centres or pay for corporate membership for staff. Most health and fitness clubs have tonnes of expensive, bone-jarring, muscle-wrenching apparatus, designed either to get you into shape or kill you in the attempt. Middle-aged 'fatties' shouldn't attempt to get fit in five minutes (after all, it took years of dedicated sloth and gluttony to put on all that weight), as over-exertion can result in serious injuries and heart attacks. Most gymnasiums and health clubs will ensure this doesn't happen by carrying out a physical assessment, including a blood pressure test, fat distribution measurements and heart rate checks, before you set foot (or hand) on any machines. In your rush to become one of the body beautiful it pays to take the long route and give the intensive care unit (or mortuary) a wide berth.

To join a club, you usually pay an initial (joining) fee and a monthly fee. The latter depends on the type of service you've chosen. You can often reduce it by opting to use the facilities only during off-peak times, e.g. during the mornings or before 5pm during the week. Many clubs also offer classes in various forms of aerobic exercise and dance and may have such 'exotic' offerings as a climbing wall, beauty salon and massage parlour, as well as a well-stocked bar and snack bar or restaurant. Top class hotels and many resorts often have health clubs and swimming pools that are open to the public at certain times or on certain days.

OTHER SPORTS

The following is a selection of other popular sports in Belgium, Holland and Luxembourg:

Athletics: Local athletics clubs offer training and competition in a variety of track and field sports as well as indoor athletic sports. Most of the larger cities hold jogging or running events, such as the annual City-Pier-City Run in The Hague, featuring an invitation half-marathon and amateur runs of 2, 5 and 10km.

Basketball: Basketball is popular throughout Benelux, both as a spectator and as a participation sport. There are amateur clubs in many larger cities and towns, and the sports channels on cable and satellite television carry matches from around the world, including US college games, particularly during the NCAA tournament season.

Bungee Jumping: If your idea of fun is jumping off a high bridge or platform with an elastic rope attached to one limb to prevent you merging with the landscape, bungee jumping may be just what you're looking for. At most bungee jumping centres in Belgium and Holland (none appears to have sprung up in Luxembourg yet) you jump from a crane rather than from a bridge or cliff (of which there are few in Benelux), although you can leap off the Scheveningen pier near The Hague. Further information about bungee jumping in Benelux can be obtained via the Internet (e.g. 🖥 www.bungeezone.com and www.bungy.nl).

Fencing: Swashing and buckling with foil, épée or sabre (the three types of weapons used in the sport of fencing) is done these days with electrical scoring equipment but still makes for a great spectacle (and plenty of exercise if you take part yourself). There are fencing clubs throughout the region offering lessons and amateur competition. Major fencing tournaments are often covered on television, complete with slow-motion instant replays.

Handball: Using an indoor pitch similar to five-a-side soccer pitch, handball players pass the ball around by hand and attempt to throw it into a small goal. (It's popular among footballers with two left feet.) Handball is taught at schools in Benelux and there are numerous clubs in all three countries. A list of national handball organisations, clubs and events is available on the European Handball Federation website (🖥 www.eurohandball.com).

Horse Riding: Horse riding is popular and pony riding is strongly promoted as a good form of exercise for children. You'll find riding schools and equestrian centres everywhere and there are bridle paths in most larger parks and forests. Most centres require a hard hat, crop and waterproof shoes or riding boots. Competitive equestrian events, such as dressage and show jumping are popular spectator sports, often broadcast on television sports channels.

Martial Arts: For those brought up on a diet of Bruce Lee, unarmed (?) combat such as Kung Fu, Judo, Karate, Aikido, Kendo and various forms of kick boxing are taught and practised at sports clubs throughout Benelux. Judo is particularly popular among schoolchildren, and many local festivals feature demonstrations by the local judo club.

Motor Racing: As in much of Europe, motor racing in Benelux usually refers to formula one, although motor cycle racing, rallying and other kinds of car races are also big attractions. In Belgium there's a track at Spa, which hosts a formula one Grand Prix each year, as does Zandvoort in Holland. Dutch driver Jos Verstappen is said to have the largest fan club in formula one racing. (He's better looking than Michael Schumacher.) If you fancy doing your own driving, there are numerous go-karting tracks, such as Mondercange in Luxembourg.

Pigeon Racing: The sport of pigeon racing was started in Belgium and remains extremely popular there. Most weekends, you'll see lorries full of pigeons being transported to starting points throughout Belgium, France and other neighbouring countries, where the birds are released and their flight back to their home lofts clocked to determine the fastest average speed. Races cover distances of several hundred kilometres and pigeons have been clocked at up to 145kph (90mph) – presumably with a hefty tail wind. Belgian radio carries flying condition reports at weekends and during all big races, including the *Concours National*, an annual event since 1881 which pits champion birds against each other in a race of 750km (470mi) from the start in Toulouse, France. The headquarters of the *Fédération Colombophile Internationale* (which is the world governing body for the sport of pigeon racing, not a Peter Falk fan club) is located in Brussels.

Skating and Skateboarding: Roller skates and inline skates have become increasingly popular but have yet to entirely replace the good old skateboard for many young people, mainly adolescent boys. Many cities and towns have established skate parks or centres to offer skaters a variety of surfaces, jumps and ramps for practice (and no doubt to keep the pavements safe for pedestrians). There's even a Skater Association in Luxembourg (🖳 www.skate.lu). Helmets and knee and elbow protection are required at all public skate parks (with good reason).

Ten-Pin Bowling: There are centres for ten-pin bowling in most major cities and towns, as well as for nine-pin skittles (*kegeln*). *Kegeln* uses smaller balls with no finger-holes, just a large opening for your hand, and is performed on a long, narrow *Kegelbahn* (bowling lane) with a warped floor – specially designed to make the ball go where you don't want it to!

Miscellaneous: Many foreign sports and pastimes have a group of expatriate fanatics in Benelux, including cricket, American football, baseball, boccia, pétanque, croquet, polo, rounders and softball. For more information enquire at community centres and tourist offices, embassies and consulates, and at local expatriate clubs and associations.

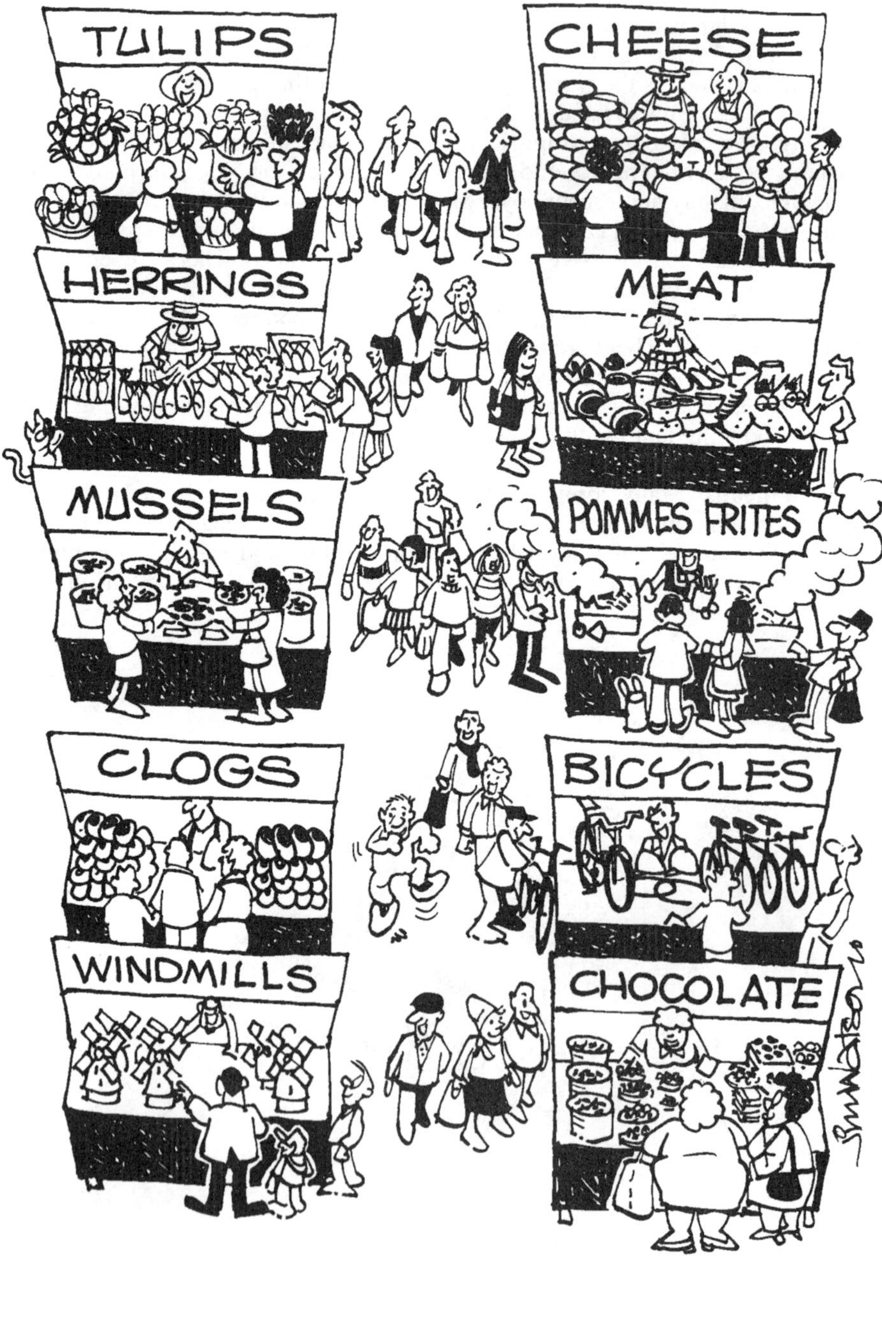
TULIPS
CHEESE
HERRINGS
MEAT
MUSSELS
POMMES FRITES
CLOGS
BICYCLES
WINDMILLS
CHOCOLATE

17.

SHOPPING

The Benelux region offers a combination of traditional local shops and branches of stores from neighbouring France and Germany. Both French and German hypermarket chains have outlets throughout Benelux, and there are branches of German electronics and furniture shops in Luxembourg. Many Parisian department stores and boutiques also have outlets in Brussels.

Shopping, and commerce in general, is subject to a plethora of rules, regulations and legal constraints, which influence when, where and how you can shop. Most of these rules relate to local labour laws (or those of the EU, which is based in Brussels) regulating employees' working hours and conditions. Shop opening hours are restricted (see below), and sale periods are limited to two per year – a winter sale, usually in January, and a summer sale in July – when shops can discount prices on all seasonal merchandise. The exact dates of sales are set by national or regional authorities and publicised in newspapers, magazines and other media well in advance. (If you miss the advertisements, simply ask a neighbour or colleague; everyone seems to know the dates almost as soon as they're announced.) Unscrupulous shopkeepers sometimes raise prices just before the sales begin in order to make their 'discounts' look bigger than they are, although this practice is illegal. The only other time shops are permitted to cut prices on all or most of their stock is before 'remodelling' or 'going out of business', which seem to occur repeatedly in some shops!

Except in antique or second-hand shops where items aren't priced, bartering or haggling over prices isn't usual, and all prices advertised or quoted to private customers should include value added tax (*taxe sur la valeur ajoutée* or TVA/*belasting toegevoegde waarde* or BTW). Prices are likely to be marked in 'old' currency as well as euros for some time after 1st January 2001. Most larger stores accept both credit and debit cards for payment, although smaller shops may not accept either or may accept only locally issued debit cards.

SHOPPING HOURS

Shopping hours are regulated throughout Benelux in accordance with labour laws applying to shopkeepers and assistants. In most city centres, shops are open from around 9.30 or 10am until 6 or 6.30pm Mondays to Saturdays, with one late evening each week (usually Thursday or Friday) when shops stay open until 8pm. Many smaller stores close at midday for a couple of hours and it isn't uncommon to find shops closed on Mondays, either in the morning or all day. In summer and during the Christmas holidays, many family-owned shops close for two weeks or more, although food shops are required to display a sign indicating when they will be closed, and some even make arrangements for bread or other 'necessities' to be made available at a nearby shop or other outlet.

Large shopping centres (where they exist) and the larger supermarkets and hypermarkets generally stay open until 8pm during the week, but often close earlier on Saturdays – sometimes as early as 4pm. Only a few shops open on Sundays, mostly small food shops and florists (in case you're going to someone else's house to eat – see **Social Customs** on page 353). If you run out of something 'essential', e.g. nappies, cat food or beer, you can often find shops open late in petrol stations (at least those on a major road), railway stations and airports, although prices tend to be high.

Belgium: The larger supermarkets in Belgium, especially those near major cities such as Brussels or Antwerp, often stay open until 9pm on Fridays and the day before a public holiday. As you might imagine, shopping at these times can be a nightmare, so plan ahead and avoid them if you can!

Holland: Large shopping centres are more common in Holland than elsewhere in Benelux, and food shops are generally open from 8am to 6pm Mondays to Saturdays. The number of stores in a town permitted to have extended opening hours is determined by its population – one for every 10,000 inhabitants. As railway stations and airports offer little in the way of 'essentials', petrol stations are the best (and sometimes the only) option late at night or on a Sunday.

Luxembourg: In Luxembourg city, Thursday is late shopping day, although this may mean only until 7 or 7.30pm. (Luxembourgers admit that they aren't really 'night owls' and this also applies to their shopping habits.) Shopping centres outside towns are generally open until 8pm every day, and some are also open on Sunday mornings.

SUPERMARKETS & HYPERMARKETS

Belgium and Luxembourg are well provided with French and German supermarkets and hypermarkets as well as having a few local 'large surface' stores (over 2,500m²/26,910ft²), usually combining food and other products. The French retailing giants Auchan, Carrefour and Cora all have a presence in both countries, as well as the smaller Cactus, Champion and Match. German stores such as Aldi, Profi and Spar are found throughout Benelux. Belgian supermarket chains include Biggs, Colruyt, Delhaize, GB Super and Maxi, some of which have vending machines you can use to buy groceries (with a cash or credit card) when stores are closed. At all these stores, you can find most food and grocery items plus a selection of household and other goods. There's often a meat counter and in some stores bread and pastries are baked daily, although they're often made with frozen dough and may not taste as good as similar products from a local bakery.

Dutch supermarkets tend to be small, as the Dutch prefer to buy their food from local shops (see below). Albert Heijn supermarkets can be found everywhere and are known for high quality (and rather expensive) food. Edah's is another Dutch favourite, primarily for basic items, detergents and drinks, and there's also Dirk van den Broek, which is more of a warehouse store offering a large selection of basic items at low prices.

You need a €1 coin (or a token the same size and shape) to unlock a shopping trolley from the car park or just outside the shop. The coin is returned when you replace the trolley. Many supermarkets charge for carrier bags, so it's worthwhile taking your own or a shopping basket. Americans may be startled to discover that they must bag their own groceries at the checkout and even, in some stores, scan the bar codes themselves! An increasing number of Benelux supermarkets have self-scanning checkouts, where you can pay for your purchases without the services of a checkout assistant. To use the self-scanning facility, you must first register for an authorisation card (actually a sort of combined debit and customer loyalty card). The first time you use it, you will be supervised by an assistant, but after that you're subject only to occasional random checks. (Honest lot, these Beneluxers!)

Supermarkets and hypermarkets in Belgium and Luxembourg generally accept cash, cheques and credit or debit cards. The Dutch (and occasionally Luxembourgers) tend to be rather more conservative and smaller stores may accept only debit cards or cash (and sometimes *only* cash). Many stores have customer loyalty cards, whereby each time you make a purchase you earn 'points', which can be redeemed for goods, discounts or (occasionally) cash.

Most larger stores have a separate section or shop near the entrance selling fruit juice, fizzy drinks, water, beer and wine, which are often sold in returnable bottles or cases. A small deposit for each bottle or case is added to your bill, and when you return empty bottles or cases you receive a voucher redeemable for cash or other purchases. Many stores now have machines that handle the bottle returning process – put your empties into the machine and out comes your voucher. Note, however, that machines accept only the types of bottles sold in that particular store. It's possible (and very popular) to have drinks delivered to your home. Ask your neighbours which delivery service they use or contact your nearest brewery or drinks distributor.

In Belgium, you can buy soft drinks and alcohol at drive-in shops. You literally drive into the store (often a converted garage in a city centre or a small warehouse on the outskirts) and load cases of water, fizzy drinks or beer into your boot. You can also buy beer in kegs and barrels or assemble your own 'metre of beer' (a selection of types and brands of beer laid end to end in a wooden case a metre long), adding a distinctive glass for each (see **Alcohol** on page 327). Drive-in shops also sell crisps, pretzels and other snack foods, and some stock a small selection of wine.

SPECIALIST FOOD SHOPS

Most town centres in Benelux have a wide variety of specialist food shops, such as butchers, bakers, cheese shops, and coffee and tea shops. Many local residents buy their food daily in small quantities rather than stocking up at a supermarket, which means that using local shops can be an excellent way to get to know people and integrate into the community, as well as discovering local delicacies you might not otherwise find out about.

Butchers (*boucheries/blagers*) often specialise in a single type of meat or meat from a particular source. There are mutton and lamb shops (*moutonneries/lam- en schapenvlees*), and shops selling mostly cooked meats and sausages (*charcuterie/ vleeswaren*) as well as pork and various local and regional specialities. In Belgium, look for Ardennes ham and *filet d'Anvers*, which is a type of smoked beef. *Tête de veau* used to be a popular delicacy but has recently fallen out of favour because of concerns over BSE, as it's a whole calf's head cooked with everything (yes, everything!) still inside. Both Dutch and Luxembourg pork butchers offer a large assortment of sausages, some based on German varieties (*Wurst*), but others unique to a particular region. 'Poultry' shops (*volaillers/wild en gevolgelte*) sell not only chicken and turkey, but also game such as wild boar, venison, rabbit and pheasant during the hunting season. You're likely to find butchers selling horsemeat (*boucherie chevaline*) – particularly in Belgium – indicated by a horse's head above the door, as many Beneluxers have turned to horse meat as a substitute for beef. If you're tempted to try horse or any other type or cut of meat you aren't familiar with, a butcher is often the best source of cooking instructions and recipes.

Bakeries are sometimes split into *boulangeries/warme bakkerij*, which specialise in breads and rolls, and *pâtisseries/banketbakkerij*, which sell home-made cakes, biscuits and pastries, although most bakers offer a selection of both. Belgium is well known for its biscuits, particularly *speculoos* or *speculaas*, which are spicy biscuits often associated with Christmas and used as decoration rather than eaten. In fact, the English word 'biscuit' is borrowed from the French *biscuit*, meaning 'twice cooked' and the American word 'cookie' comes from the Dutch *koekje*, which means 'little cake'. The Dutch also have a unique range of biscuits and pastries.

Benelux is a chocoholic's paradise and there are chocolate shops throughout the region. Belgian chocolates are famous throughout the world, especially the widely exported *Godiva*, *Corné Toison d'Or*, *Leonides* and *Neuhaus* brands. Mary's is the official purveyor of chocolates to the Belgian royal family, and there are many other less well known brands as well as master *chocolatiers*, whose products are only available locally. Belgian chocolates normally contain fillings made with fresh ingredients, including eggs, milk and butter, so if you aren't planning to eat them immediately (hard to avoid sometimes!) make sure you keep them refrigerated, especially in summer. Chocolates are normally sold by weight, and prices in Belgium are often considerably lower than elsewhere (even in neighbouring countries such as France and Germany). Most of the major brands have factory outlet shops, e.g. the Neuhaus Cash & Carry in Vlezenbeek.

Dutch chocolate has its own distinctive character and there's considerable rivalry between the Belgians and the Dutch as to who makes better chocolate. Most grocers and news stands offer a large selection of chocolate bars, which the Dutch claim to have invented as a convenient way for soldiers in the field to take their daily 'ration'. Droste is the largest and probably best known Dutch chocolate maker, but as in Belgium there are small shops in many cities and towns selling local specialities available nowhere else.

Coffee is also popular in Benelux, particularly in Holland where the average person consumes 154 litres a year – almost four cups a day! Douwe Egbert, founded in 1753, is the largest coffee maker in Europe and has a chain of shops throughout Holland. There are also numerous local coffee shops selling coffee beans, ground coffee in a variety of blends, coffee makers, cups and other coffee-related products. Coffee shops and tea rooms (*salons de thé* in both French and Dutch) are popular meeting places in most towns, where people sometimes linger for hours over one or two cups of coffee or tea and a pastry.

MARKETS

Street markets are common throughout Benelux, where most towns have an agricultural market once or twice a week, usually in the central square, as well as various specialist markets. Flea markets are also popular, as are antique markets. During December, there are countless Christmas markets, featuring hand made gifts and ornaments, regional foods, Christmas trees and plenty of spirits to keep you warm while you shop! Most street markets (except Christmas markets) start early in the morning and continue only until noon or early afternoon. Details can be found at town halls and tourist information offices. The principal markets in the three countries are as follows.

Belgium: In Brussels, the Grand-Place is where many of the largest and most impressive markets are held. The world famous Flower Market is open every day except Mondays and all year round except in winter when other markets, including a Christmas market, take its place. On Sundays, the Flower Market also includes birds and accessories such as cages and perches. The *Marché du Midi/Zuid Markt* near the Gare du Midi/Zuid Station features bicycles on Sundays, and there's an antiques market in the Place du Grand Sablon at weekends. There are weekly agricultural markets in most other cities and towns, as well as specialist markets that are advertised in local newspapers.

Holland: Amsterdam has a wide variety of street markets, including the permanent floating Flower Market, open daily on barges moored on the Singel canal. There are four other large permanent markets: the Albert Cuypmarkt, the Dappermarkt, the Westermarkt and the Noordenmarkt, each with different specialities according to the day and season, but all including factory-reject clothing at reasonable prices. On Saturday mornings, the Noordenmarkt features a *Biologische Boerenmarkt* selling organic foods, herbs and candles.

Luxembourg: In Luxembourg city, many outdoor markets are held in the Place Guillaume. On Wednesday and Saturday mornings, there's a fruit, vegetable and flower market. A Christmas market takes place at the Place d'Armes during December, while at the Foire Internationale in Kirschberg there's a variety of annual specialist markets, such as the International Bazaar (usually in late November or early December) and the Antique and Book Fair (in March).

DEPARTMENT & CHAIN STORES

Department stores offer a wide range of products, from clothes and sports equipment to household appliances, electronic equipment and furniture, whereas chain stores tend to specialise in one or a few related products. Many of Benelux's department stores (*grands magasins/warenhuisen*) are branches of multinational chains (often foreign) including C&A, Hennes & Mauritz (H&M) and Galeries Lafayette, which can be found in most larger cities.

Belgium: Several French department stores and chains have branches in Belgium, particularly in the Brussels area, including Galeries Lafayette, ProModes and Pimkie, as well as Etam (mid-price clothing), and FNAC (CDs, electronic equipment and books). Another French department store, Tati, has recently opened in Brussels, offering low prices and a rather eclectic and ever-changing selection of goods. (It's also known for its bargain wedding dresses, which are often displayed in the window.) There are large shopping centres (malls) on the outskirts of many cities and larger towns, containing a range of department and chain stores (and generally offering free parking, which isn't usually available at city centre branches of the same stores).

Holland: Probably the best known department store in Holland is Bijenkorf (which means 'bee hive'). The huge flagship store in Amsterdam has departments for everything from clothing to toys, leather goods, furniture and household appliances. There are also branches in each of the larger cities in Holland, although these have a less extensive range of products. At the other end of the scale are Hema stores, owned by the same company as Bijenkorf and equally well known, but for low budget, 'no frills' products (many of which are identical to those on offer – at higher prices – at

Bijenkorf!). Vroom & Dreesman, usually known simply as V&D, is another Dutch department store that stocks a wide range of goods and has branches throughout the Benelux region and the rest of Europe.

Luxembourg: The only large department stores in Luxembourg are on the outskirts of Luxembourg city and include C&A and H&M, although many locals prefer to travel to nearby shopping centres in Germany or France (see **Shopping Abroad** on page 335).

ALCOHOL

Although Beneluxers don't consume nearly as much beer and wine as their French and German neighbours, drinking is still an integral part of everyday life. Each country has its own specialities as well as selling wines and beers from other EU countries, including France and Germany.

Beer: Germany is widely considered to be the beer capital of the world, but to beer connoisseurs Belgium is 'Mecca'. It's said that there are over 370 different kinds of beer made in Belgium – one for each day of the year plus an extra five for special occasions. There are well over 100 breweries in the country, including the six monasteries (there's a seventh in Holland) with exclusive rights to produce Trappist beers (see below). What's more, each type of beer is only properly served in the appropriate glass, and Belgians often have elaborate collections of beer glasses – one for each of their favourite brands! Don't EVER offer a Belgian a beer in an all-purpose mug or glass or, even worse, without a glass. Belgian beer should NOT be consumed directly from the bottle or can. (Americans take note!)

Trappist beers are produced within the walls of Trappist monasteries, although no longer exclusively by monks; some monasteries need to hire workers from the local area to staff their breweries. The Belgian monasteries are Achel, Chimay, Orval, Rochefort, Westmalle, and Westvleteren, and the sole Dutch Trappist brewer is based in the monastery at De Schaapskooi. Trappist beers are made with strong malts and lots of hops and are full of flavour, as well as usually being dark. What distinguishes Trappist beer from most other beers is a second fermentation in the bottle; when the beer is bottled, sugar and extra yeast are added so that it continues to ferment. It's therefore important to store Trappist beers upright and to pour them slowly and carefully (into the appropriate glass, of course) so that the residue of the second fermentation is left in the bottle. Glasses for Trappist beers are broad-bottomed goblets designed to prevent any sediment escaping from the bottle from re-mixing with the liquid as you drink it.

There are also abbey beers, which are usually produced by commercial brewers using methods or recipes from the abbey that gives its name to the beer. Where the abbey is still in existence, the brewery usually has permission from the religious order to use the name (in exchange, one assumes, for some financial consideration). Leffe, a popular pale beer (*bière blonde/pils*), is one of the best known abbey beers. Some abbey beers are made with a second fermentation in the bottle (in the Trappist style), but aren't permitted to use the word 'Trappist' in advertising or packaging. Duvel is a distinctive pale beer produced in this manner. Other brewers simply give their beers monastic-sounding names, and there have been numerous Belgian lawsuits over the use of such names and of pictures of jovial monks on the labels of beers not formally affiliated with a religious order.

Every kind of beer you can imagine is made somewhere in Belgium (or so it's claimed), plus a few varieties you wouldn't even dream of. Cherry-flavoured beer may not sound appealing, but this is a Belgian speciality (called *kriek*) and a particular favourite of people who normally don't like beer. *Kriek* is made with a base of *lambic* or *gueuze*, types of beer made only in the valley of the Senne river, south of Brussels, by a traditional method. No yeast is added to the malt mixture, but the windows and doors of the brewery are left open to allow yeasts naturally occurring in the air to start the fermentation process. The beer must then be aged for several months before the brewer, like a Champagne maker, 'assembles' a mixture of 'vintages' to produce the desired taste. *Gueuze* requires re-bottling and re-fermentation in a corked bottle, much like Champagne. The resulting beers are light and almost lemony in their unflavoured state, and sour cherry juice (from a particular type of local cherry, of course) is added to make *kriek*. If you aren't fond of cherry, you can choose from cassis, raspberry, peach and other fruit flavours!

Other Belgian beers include Kwak, whose bespoke glass has a rounded base and must be supported by a wooden holder (designed to permit the driver of a horse-drawn carriage to enjoy a 'take-away' beer that could be hung from his seat if he was unable to leave his horses unattended at a tavern stop), Hoegaarden, a light wheat-based beer (*bière blanche*/*witbier*), and beers with names such as Forbidden Fruit, Satan and Morte Subite (Sudden Death)!

Among Dutch beers, Heineken is the most familiar and widely drunk, although Grolsch, in a distinctive bottle with a resealable stopper, has also become popular throughout the world. However, there's also a wide range of beers from smaller, less well known breweries that are well worth trying, including Amstel, Dommelsch, Jupiler, and Palm, as well as beers produced by an increasing number of tiny local breweries.

Luxembourg also has a long and distinguished history of brewing, dating back to 1083 at the abbey of Altmunster, now the site of the Mousel brewery. Diekirch is Luxembourg's most exported beer (mainly to Belgium and France), but there are many others worth sampling. The *Brasserie Nationale* in Bascharage sells beer by the keg and also hires out a variety of catering and party equipment.

Many breweries, including the Trappist monasteries, are open to visitors and an increasing number have multilingual websites where you can find out not only the history of each type and brand of beer, but also how to store and serve them.

Wine: The main wine producing region of Benelux is in Luxembourg, along the banks of the Moselle River. Not surprisingly, the wines produced here are similar to German Mosels, which are made on the other side of the river! There are numerous wine festivals in the spring and summer months, and you can buy wine directly from the *caves* (with or without a tour and tasting session beforehand) as well as from some larger supermarket chains, notably Cactus and Match. These also have wine clubs that give members advance notice of special offers and discounts on wines bought in bulk (i.e. by the case). From most parts of Benelux it's a short trip to the vineyards and cellars of Champagne, the Mosel and the Rhine, and French and German wines, as well as those from other parts of Europe, are widely available in shops throughout the region.

Genever: It's debatable whether genever (or jenever) is a type of gin or gin is a type of genever. In either case, genever was originally developed in Holland as a cheap medicine – the diuretic properties of the juniper berry were administered with a 'flavouring' of alcohol. Somehow the medicine became popular as a drink and was introduced to Britain in the 18th century, from where it was exported to India and mixed with quinine (better known as tonic), which the British used to protect themselves from malaria, to make it more palatable – hence gin and tonic, which the British have claimed as their invention ever since!

While gin is distilled until it's almost pure alcohol before being diluted to drinking strength (40 to 45 per cent proof), genever made in Holland and Flemish-speaking parts of Belgium is distilled only to around 35 per cent. The resulting spirit has a rich malty taste which varies from region to region according to the grains and flavourings used (lemon genever is particularly popular). Genever should be drunk neat or with a little water so that you can appreciate the particular taste of each variety, and *not* with tonic.

CLOTHES

Winters in Benelux are generally cool and damp, so warm, waterproof clothing (gloves, scarves, coats and boots) is essential, although light clothing can usually be worn in summer. Beneluxers aren't renowned for snappy dressing, and most people dress fairly conservatively. However, in large cities, particularly Brussels and The Hague with their multinational communities, a variety of clothing styles can be seen, and Amsterdam still has a 'hippy' element that takes pride in extreme or outrageous outfits. In rural areas, locals tend to expect their neighbours (especially foreigners or immigrants) to conform to more traditional dress codes. While jeans and tee-shirts are popular with the young and acceptable for most leisure activities, a jacket and tie is expected at more expensive restaurants, and formal attire is usual when attending the theatre or a concert.

Business wear for both men and women tends to be conservative, although less so than a few years ago. Upper management tends to dress more formally than those lower down the chain, and certain professions (notably the financial services industries in Luxembourg) call for ultra-traditional clothing. For men, a plain, dark suit is the best choice in most situations and a tasteful tie is essential (no multicoloured tulips or Van Gogh sunflowers). For women, conservatively tailored suits and dresses are considered appropriate; tight or revealing clothing should be avoided.

Department stores and clothing chains offer the best selection of clothing and sportswear at reasonable prices. C&A, H&M, Marks & Spencer and the Dutch Vroom & Dreesman are all good sources of high quality, reasonably priced clothing. Some hypermarket chains, such as Auchan and Carrefour, also offer a wide range of clothing, although not generally of designer quality, and their low prices make them attractive for 'necessities' such as underwear, socks, pyjamas and children's wear. Fashionable and high quality clothing is readily available, although it tends to be expensive. There's no shortage of designer shops in Brussels, Antwerp, Amsterdam and The Hague, and if money is no object you can pop down to Paris for a shopping spree (just an hour and 15 minutes by train from Brussels).

Clothing comes in continental sizes, which may differ from those in other countries, e.g. Britain and the USA (see **Appendix D**). Britons and Americans may also have difficulty finding shoes that fit, as most styles are short and wide (although those with large feet should have no such trouble in Holland). Shops selling Italian and Swiss footwear offer a wider range of sizes, although at significantly higher prices.

NEWSPAPERS, MAGAZINES & BOOKS

News reading habits vary widely among the three countries. While relatively few Belgians buy a daily paper, the Dutch don't seem to be able to get enough news, and in Luxembourg city there are five daily newspapers to choose from and many people read more than one. All three countries take their newspapers more seriously than some others and there's no 'tabloid press' anywhere in Benelux, where the more sensational news tends to be covered in weekly magazines. English-language newspapers are readily available at news stands in towns and cities, as well as at railway stations and airports. These include British newspapers such as *The Times*, *Guardian* and *Financial Times*, as well as the *International Herald Tribune* and *USA Today*. Many news stands also sell an assortment of daily newspapers from other European countries (e.g. Germany, France and Italy) as well as Turkish and Arabic-language newspapers. If your favourite paper is unavailable in Benelux, or a few days out of date, you may be able to find it on the Internet, where many British and American newspapers have comprehensive websites.

Weekly and monthly magazines are popular, especially those containing television listings, which include celebrity interviews and general interest articles. Each country publishes an English-language news weekly, although international weeklies such as *The Economist*, *Time* and *Newsweek*, and most major French and German weekly news journals are also widely available.

There are plenty of bookshops throughout Benelux, most of which have at least a few English-language titles. It's possible to order books from abroad, but these can be expensive and it may be cheaper to buy them from Internet bookshops such as Amazon or from mail-order services. Be careful, however, to check the conditions regarding shipping. Some American booksellers don't ship to Europe and those that do sometimes make high shipping charges that cancel any saving you thought you were making. It may be better to order from websites based in the EU (e.g. amazon.co.uk or amazon.de rather than amazon.com) if you want the lowest prices or the fastest delivery.

Most expatriate clubs and associations have libraries for members, and the public library systems have English-language sections (see **Libraries** on page 304).

Belgium: Because there are three different languages in Belgium, it has no 'national' newspaper. The Flemish daily, *Het Laatse Niews*, is the most widely read (according to its circulation figures), and there are a number of other popular Flemish-language newspapers, including *De Standaard* and *De Gazet van Antwerpen*. French speakers generally seem less interested in reading a daily newspaper, but *Le Soir*, *La Libre Belgique* and *La Dernière Heure* are the major 'independent' (i.e. liberal) publications. The lower-circulation *Le Peuple* is more left wing, as is the Flemish-language *De Morgen*. Belgium's English-language weekly news magazine is called

The Bulletin, which is a good source of information about local cultural events as well as covering general news.

There are many English-language book shops, particularly in the Brussels area and Antwerp, including branches of Waterstones. The French chain FNAC has a selection of popular English titles in its European book department and there's a variety of smaller specialist bookshops, including antiquarian dealers specialising in English-language titles. The SHAPE book shop in the SHAPE shopping complex, near Mons (75km/46mi south-west of Brussels) has a vast selection of books, magazines and newspapers in English and many other languages.

Many communes have public libraries, some of which have English-language sections or reference collections. The Royal Library in Brussels (*Bibliothèque Royale Albert I/Koninklijke Bibliotheek Albert I*) has a well stocked Center for American Studies with books on art, culture, literature and history. It isn't a lending library, so you cannot take books away, but use of the library is free once you've registered.

Holland: The major Dutch newspapers include *De Telegraaf* (right wing), the *Algemeen Dagblad* (middle-of-the-road) and *De Volkskrant* (left wing). *Parool* is a (politically) independent newspaper, which was published by the resistance movement during the Second World War. There are also local and regional dailies, such as *De Haagsche Courant* published in The Hague. Same-day delivery of *The Times* and other British newspapers is available in most of the larger cites in Holland. Contact the relevant UK subscription office for details and prices.

The Dutch also publish a wide variety of women's weekly and monthly titles, motoring and caravanning magazines, travel journals, television listings and business reviews, as well as literary, social and political journals. *Roundabout* (listing local events) and the *Dutch News Digest*, both published in Amsterdam, are generally available alongside many other English-language magazines. Amsterdam's Leidsestraat has a large number of magazine shops stocking an extensive range of foreign professional journals in English (e.g. the *Harvard Business Review* and *New Scientist*) and other languages. The department store Bijenkorf also has a good selection of English-language newspapers and magazines, although the news stands at Schiphol airport don't carry as broad an assortment of foreign publications as can be found at many other international airports.

There's no shortage of book shops anywhere in Holland and it seems that almost every book ever written in any language has been translated into Dutch. The American Book Center in Amsterdam's pedestrian shopping zone stocks both British and American books, magazines and newspapers. There's a Waterstones in the same street, as well as in most other Dutch cities. In Rotterdam, English-language titles can also be found at the Donner book shop.

Luxembourg: The most widely read newspaper in Luxembourg is the *Luxemburger Wort/La Voix du Luxembourg*, available in German or French. The English-language paper *Luxembourg News* is published every Thursday and not only summarises the news, but also lists cultural events and festivals and includes advertisements for foreign household goods and electrical appliances.

There are a number of English-language bookshops including Chapter I and Magasin Anglais (Luxembourg city), and Little Britain (Strassen), while shops such as Messageries du Livre (Gasperich) sell books in a variety of languages, including English. These shops can often arrange subscriptions to British publications or you can contact the publishers in the UK directly. You can also have British Sunday newspapers delivered to your home by Paperchase in Luxembourg city (☎ 49-1204).

FURNITURE & FURNISHINGS

Furniture in Benelux tends to be either expensive (designer originals and genuine antiques) or cheap (DIY or flea market junk) with little on offer in between. Most furniture stores, including 'warehouse' shops on the outskirts of towns, don't carry a large stock, and unless you're content to buy a display item you may have to wait 6 to 12 weeks for delivery, particularly for upholstered chairs and beds, which are made to order. If you're shipping a bed from your home country, be sure to bring plenty of bed linen with you, as Benelux sheets and pillowcases may not fit. Conversely, if you intend to buy a bed in Benelux, it may not be worthwhile taking bed linen with you.

Homes in Benelux don't usually have built-in cupboards, but wardrobes are available at various prices. If you're on a tight budget, there are modular clothing racks or shelving with an optional clothes rail. Second-hand shops and boot or jumble sales, which are often organised by expatriate organisations, are also a good place to find reasonably priced wardrobes. At the other end of the scale, it's possible to find beautiful (and expensive) wardrobes in the many antique shops and markets, but be careful not to buy anything too big if you might want to take it back home with you. Judging by the number of second-hand wardrobes for sale in Benelux, many foreigners make this mistake!

Most of the larger department stores sell furniture, and many even have interior design advisers to help you co-ordinate your furniture and furnishings. Prices tend to be high but often include delivery and installation. Stores specialising in home furnishing include Conforama, IKEA and Habitat for those on a budget, and Cuir No.1, Scandinavia and Roche Bobois for more expensive ranges. In Brussels, the US Embassy sells used office and home furnishings twice a year at reasonable prices. Sales are advertised in local newspapers, particularly the English-language press. Many expatriate organisations also organise sales or advertise used furniture and furnishings, including the American Women's Clubs in Brussels, Antwerp, The Hague, Amsterdam and Luxembourg city.

HOUSEHOLD GOODS

The number of cupboards, storage units and kitchen appliances you will need to install in a new home varies across the three Benelux countries. If you're moving to an area near the German border, your kitchen may consist of nothing but four walls with some pipes protruding from of one of them, to which a sink is to be attached! In this case, you should ask whether you can purchase fittings and appliances from the vendor or outgoing tenant, which will save you considerable time and trouble. In French-speaking areas, a sink and cooker may be installed, but you will need to fit cupboards and connect appliances such as a refrigerator.

Most furniture shops and almost all DIY stores sell kitchen units and appliances, although you should be prepared to wait at least six weeks for delivery. If the thought of being unable to use your kitchen for two months is more than you can bear, you could contact local expatriate organisations or look at advertisements in English-language publications for second-hand kitchen equipment. IKEA sells good quality products at low prices, although you need to be prepared for some DIY. Be sure to check regulations concerning connections to mains water or electricity, which must often be made or at least checked by a licensed plumber or electrician. If you don't obtain the necessary approvals and suffer a fire or flood, you risk invalidating your insurance policies. Some stores sell kitchens including installation and all can refer you to local plumbers and carpenters. Appliances and cabinets come in standard sizes, but not all kitchens (particularly in older buildings) conform to current standards. Be sure to measure your kitchen carefully and check the dimensions of items, particularly if you're buying second-hand.

Carpets and curtains can be purchased at specialist, furniture and department stores. Most cities have dozens of carpet shops where you can find everything from cheap off-cuts to expensive antique and Oriental carpets. Shop carefully and be wary of stores that have been running 'going-out-of-business' sales for months or years on end. Belgium is the place to find net (or real lace) curtains; the Dutch often don't bother with curtains at all, and you will be easily identifiable as a foreigner if you insist on hanging curtains in your windows.

If you already own small appliances, it's usually worthwhile taking them with you when moving to any Benelux country. Provided they're designed to be used with a 240/250V, 50 Hertz (cycles) electrical supply, you will need only to change the plug. If you're coming from a country with a 110/120V, 60 Hertz supply, you will also require converters or transformers (see **Electricity** on page 93). Americans will be happy to hear that US-style refrigerators (big ones, with ice and water in the door) are becoming available in Europe, already wired for the local electricity supply. The bad news is that, besides being outrageously expensive (compared with European fridges) both to buy and to run, they often don't fit into Benelux kitchens.

LAUNDRY & DRY CLEANING

All large towns in Benelux have dry cleaners (*nettoyage à sec*/*droogkuis*), most of which also do minor clothes repairs and alterations, as well as dyeing. Dry cleaning is expensive and you must pay in advance. There are two levels of service: standard and de luxe. De luxe service is supposed to involve special care with delicate buttons or trims, and may include a collection and delivery service. (Note that many dry cleaners close promptly at 6pm and aren't open at all on Saturdays.) Standard service is usually quicker, i.e. a day or two rather than a week, but there's no collection or delivery service and no guarantee that buttons and trims won't be damaged. Some shops offer an 'express' service, but this is a relative term; don't expect to find a same-day service, even in shops that do dry cleaning on site! If you aren't in a hurry and your outfit is expensive or fragile, de luxe service is usually worth the small extra charge.

Dry cleaners also clean carpets, curtains and upholstery, and they often provide a collection and delivery service, including taking down and re-hanging curtains. Most dry cleaners also offer laundry services and in larger cities (particularly Brussels) many offer a collection and delivery service from offices – if you don't mind taking your dirty washing to work!

Launderettes or laundromats (*salons lavoirs/wassersalons*) can generally be found only in larger cities, where they usually open seven days a week between around 7am and 10pm. Launderettes have large washing and drying machines, which are useful for bed linen, tablecloths and other articles that won't fit in a domestic washer or dryer. Large pressing tables and ironing boards are also usually available.

HOME SHOPPING

Home shopping includes mail-order, telephone, TV and Internet shopping, all of which are becoming increasingly popular in Benelux.

Mail-order Catalogues: The region is well served by most of the established European catalogue companies, including 3 Suisses, La Redoute, Neckermann and Quelle, all of which offer good quality products at reasonable prices and guaranteed delivery times. Home shopping catalogues can be purchased from most shops selling magazines, and the price of the catalogue is usually discounted from your first order. Goods can be ordered by telephone, post or e-mail and must normally be paid for with a credit card.

You can also order from UK catalogues and have items posted to you. Some American merchants, such as Lands End and Eddie Bauer, have European catalogue centres (usually in the UK or Ireland) with local telephone numbers in each country. Calls are normally answered in the local language, but most operators speak English or you can ask to be transferred to an English-speaker. You can of course order catalogue products from anywhere in the world, but you may incur high delivery costs and long shipment delays as well as VAT and customs duty on certain goods. Note, however, that some mail-order companies outside the EU (e.g. in the USA) can't or won't send goods abroad. If something is unavailable in Benelux, you can ask friends or family in your home country to send it, but you may still be liable for VAT or duty (and having a package marked 'GIFT' won't make any difference!).

Telephone & TV Shopping: If you have cable or satellite TV, you may have access to one or more shopping channels. Many 'ordinary' television channels also carry advertising for exclusive offers on CDs, books, health or cleaning products, etc. that can be ordered by phone. It pays to be wary of this sort of offer, as products can be disappointing or even downright shoddy. On the other hand, there are TV shopping channels such as The Wish Channel featuring luxury goods, vehicles and even properties for rent or purchase.

Internet Shopping: Shopping via the Internet is the fastest-growing form of retailing and in most cases safer than shopping by phone or mail-order. (Secure servers, with addresses beginning https:// rather than http://, are almost impossible to crack.) With Internet shopping the world is literally your oyster, and savings can be made on a wide range of goods including CDs, clothes, sports equipment, electronic equipment, jewellery, books, wine, computer software, and services such as insurance, pensions and mortgages. Huge savings are also possible on holidays and travel, and most rail and airline tickets can be booked online, with postal delivery or collection from a local travel agency. Small, high-price, high-tech items (e.g. cameras, watches and portable or hand-held computers) can usually be purchased cheaper than in shops, with delivery by courier within a few days.

You can order products online at a number of stores, although home delivery of items ordered online hasn't caught on in Benelux, where people generally prefer to do their shopping 'in person'. Belgian shops that accept orders online or by phone are listed on 🖳 www.homeshopping.be, whose home page is in English. Delhaize is the only grocery store that currently accepts Internet orders for home delivery (🖳 www.caddyhome.be). You pay the delivery person with a cheque or cash, and there's a small service charge.

Buying Overseas: When buying goods overseas, ensure that you're dealing with a bona fide company and that the goods will work in the country where you're living (if applicable). Make sure to check shipment and delivery terms before you order. If possible, pay by credit card when buying by mail-order or over the Internet. This provides you extra protection, as the credit card issuer may be jointly liable with the supplier if problems arise. When you buy expensive goods abroad, have them insured for their full value. When buying overseas, take into account shipping costs, duty and VAT (if applicable). If you purchase a small item by mail from outside the EU, you may need to pay VAT on delivery or at the post office on collection.

SHOPPING ABROAD

Shopping abroad makes a pleasant change from your daily routine and can broaden your choice of goods, as well as allowing you greater flexibility regarding shopping hours and, in many cases, saving you money. If you shop abroad, don't forget your passport or identity card, car papers, and foreign currency (if applicable) as well as your dog's vaccination certificates if you intend to take it with you. Many families, particularly those living near a border, regularly take advantage of lower prices outside the Benelux region, particularly when shopping for clothes or household appliances. Some American and British expatriate clubs organise day trips to popular shopping areas in France, Germany and even the UK.

The cities of Trier (in Germany) and Metz (in France) are especially popular with Benelux shoppers with their large out-of-town shopping centres and an abundance of unique specialist shops in the city centres. The improbably named McArthur Glen Village in Troyes (France) comprises factory outlet stores offering up to 50 per cent off branded merchandise all year round. Mettlach (Germany) is well known for its discount shops and especially for the Villery & Bosch outlet store, offering large discounts on china and porcelain. From northern Belgium and coastal parts of Holland, a trip to the Lakeside Shopping Centre in Thurrock, Essex, the largest shopping centre in southern England, is popular among (shopoholic) expatriates, especially during the January sales. (Since 1993, there have been no cross-border shopping restrictions within the European Union for goods purchased duty and tax paid, provided they're for personal consumption or use and not for resale.)

DUTY-FREE ALLOWANCES

Duty-free shopping within the EU ceased in mid-1999, although it's still available when travelling further afield. Any EU citizen aged over 17 (unless otherwise stated) is entitled to import the following goods purchased duty-free outside the EU:

- One litre of spirits (over 22 per cent proof) or two litres of fortified wine (under 22 per cent proof) or two litres of wine;
- 200 cigarettes or 100 cigarillos or 50 cigars or 250g of tobacco;
- 60ml of perfume;
- 250ml of toilet water;
- 500g of coffee (or 200g of coffee extract) and 100g of tea (or 40g of tea extract) for those aged 15 or over;
- Other goods (including gifts, souvenirs, beer and cider) to the value of around €100 (amounts are still being 'harmonised').

Since 1993, duty-free sales have been 'vendor controlled', meaning that vendors are responsible for ensuring that the amount of duty-free goods sold to individuals doesn't exceed their entitlement. Duty-free goods purchased on ships and ferries are noted on boarding cards, which must be presented with each purchase.

RECEIPTS

When shopping, always insist on a receipt and keep it with you until you've reached home. This isn't only in case you need to return or exchange goods, but also to verify that you've paid if a security alarm sounds as you're leaving a shop or any questions arise. Returning or exchanging goods is virtually impossible without the original receipt, and in many cases you must return goods within a few days of purchase. Smaller stores often won't give a refund but issue an exchange coupon (*bon d'achat/bon*) valid only in that shop for a limited period. If you buy an electronic or electrical item, don't throw away the box or packing material until you're certain that it works properly. Some shops require the return of electrical equipment in its original box complete with instruction booklets and warranty cards.

CONSUMER ASSOCIATIONS

There are strict consumer protection laws throughout Benelux, many of which are Europe-wide (in accordance with Article 153 of the Treaty of Amsterdam and the European Commission's Directorate General for Health and Consumer Protection). The Brussels-based *Bureau Européen des Unions de Consommateurs* (BEUC) is an umbrella organisation for consumer associations throughout Europe. If you have a complaint against a retailer or manufacturer that you're unable to resolve directly, you should contact your local BEUC affiliated consumer association. A list of these is available from the BEUC (36 avenue de Tervueren – bte 4, 1040 Brussels, ☎ 02-743 1590, 💻 www.beuc.org) or from the relevant national consumer association:

Belgium: ABC-Test-Achats, 13 rue de Hollande, 1060 Brussels (☎ 02-542 32 11).

Holland: CB-Consumentenbond, Enthovenplein 1, 2521 CD The Hague (☎ 070-445 4590, ✉ cbemail@euronet.nl).

Luxembourg: Union Luxembourgeoise des Consommateurs, 55 rue des Bruyères, 1274 Howard, ☎ 496-0221, ✉ ulcegc@mailsvr.pt.lu.

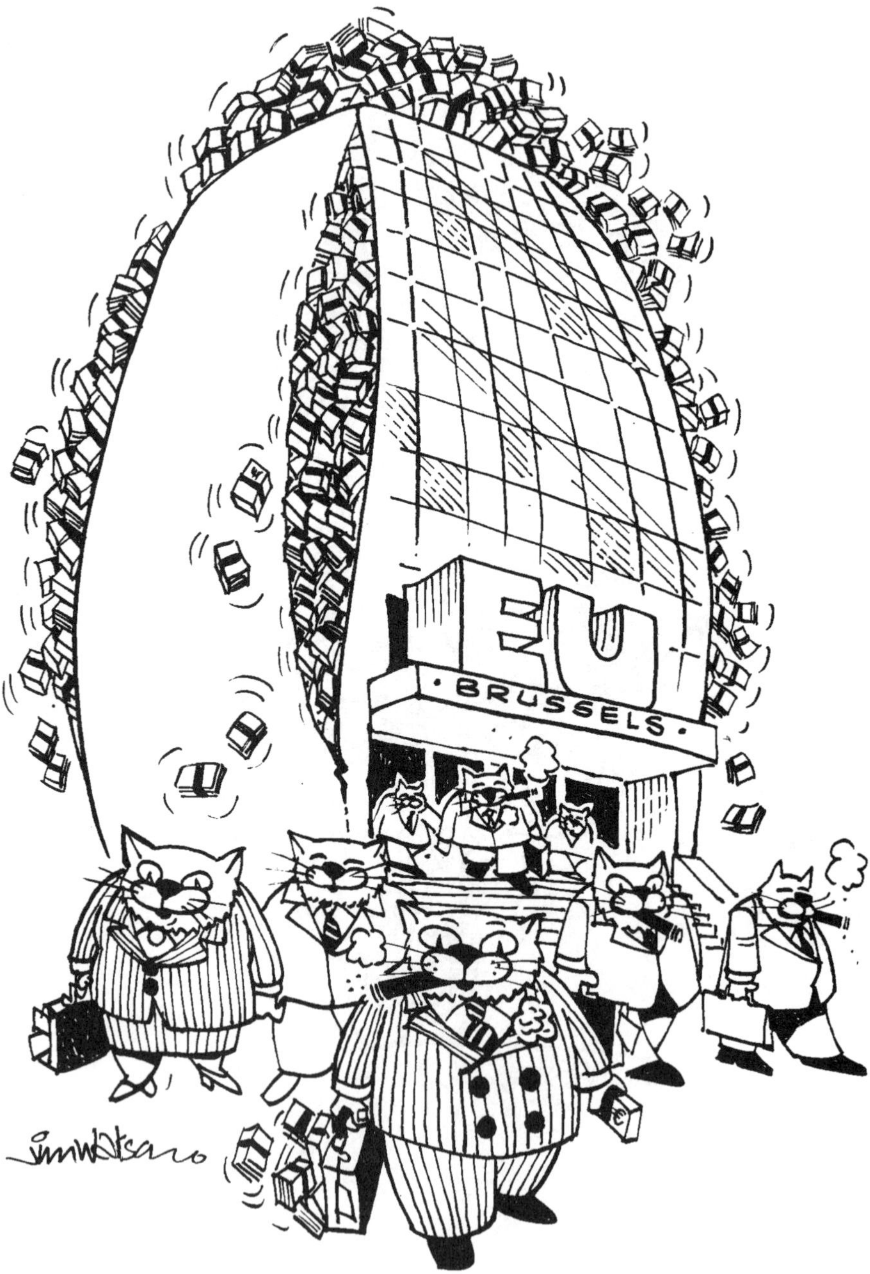
EU
BRUSSELS

18.

ODDS & ENDS

This chapter contains miscellaneous information, including everything you ever wanted to know about tipping and toilets (but were afraid to ask). Most of the topics covered are of general interest to anyone living or working in Benelux. Although admittedly not all are of vital everyday importance, you may find some of them helpful.

CITIZENSHIP

Benelux laws regarding nationality and citizenship are based on the legal principle of *jus sanguinis* (right of blood) rather than *jus soli* (right of territory). What this means is that being born in one of the Benelux countries doesn't automatically make you a citizen of the country. Nationality is considered to be something you inherit from your parents, and it's normally the father's nationality that determines a child's citizenship, although it's possible for a child to inherit the nationality of either parent. If the parents are of different nationalities, a child can have dual nationality if the laws of the relevant foreign country permits this and the birth is registered in both countries. In most cases, a child must choose one nationality or the other when he reaches the age of majority. A child born in Benelux to foreigners may be eligible for local nationality when he reaches the age of 18.

Belgium: As a foreigner, you can adopt Belgian citizenship by going through a naturalisation process. The main requirements are that you're at least 18 years of age, have had your principal residence in Belgium for the last three years, and have 'genuine attachments' to the country, such as a job, friends and family, investments and (probably most 'attaching' of all) debts. You must complete the relevant forms and produce translated and verified copies of your birth certificate, proof of residence in Belgium and any other documents supporting your case, and submit them to the administration of the commune where you live. Your dossier is processed by the *Service des Naturalisations* and your case is assessed by the national House of Representatives (*Chambre des Représentants*), who conduct further investigations if necessary. Eventually, your request for naturalisation becomes part of a legislative act which is sanctioned by the King (or more likely by one of his staff) and published in the *Moniteur belge*, the official journal of the national legislature. From the date of publication, you're officially Belgian and entitled to the same rights (and subject to the same obligations) as other Belgian citizens. Your children under the age of 18 automatically also become citizens, provided they live with you (or, as the statute reads, 'are under your authority', which may be a different matter altogether!).

If you marry a Belgian citizen or your spouse becomes naturalised while you're married, you can apply for naturalisation after you've been living together in Belgium for three years. The procedure is a simplified version of the full naturalisation process, and if you were married in Belgium you can use the same birth certificate you provided for the registration of your marriage, which saves you translation and verification fees.

Holland: When some of the restrictions on dual nationality were abolished in 1995, there was a flood of naturalisations in Holland, some 71,000 people 'going Dutch' that year. However, the Dutch government has since made several changes to the nationality laws in order to oblige new Dutch citizens to formally renounce their prior nationality, although certain categories of people are exempt from this requirement.

To become a Dutch citizen through naturalisation, you must have lived in Holland for at least five years and have an 'indefinite' residence permit. Marrying (or even cohabiting with) a Dutch citizen reduces the residence requirement to three years. You must be interviewed by a municipal official to prove that you know the Dutch language and are properly 'integrated' into Dutch society. Under the new laws, unless you fall into one of the excepted categories, you're required to renounce your former nationality once your naturalisation becomes official, at which point your children also become Dutch. The naturalisation process is handled by the Ministry of Justice and costs around €225, or €350 if you make a joint application with your spouse.

Luxembourg: Around 1,000 foreigners take Luxembourg nationality each year by one of the two available paths: 'option' or naturalisation. If you're between the ages of 18 and 25, you can 'opt' for nationality if you were born in Luxembourg (and didn't acquire nationality from one of your parents), completed most of your schooling there or are married to a Luxembourg citizen. You must have resided in Luxembourg for the past five years and agree to renounce your former nationality. To become a citizen by naturalisation, you must be over the age of 18, have lived in the Duchy for at least ten years and agree to renounce your previous nationality. Further information about becoming a citizen of Luxembourg is available from the Ministry of Justice in Luxembourg city (☎ 478-4545).

CLIMATE

The climate of the Benelux countries can be summarised as cloudy, damp and mild, which no doubt explains why so many vehicles with Benelux number plates can be seen heading south for summer holidays (and on just about every other holiday). Average annual rainfall is almost as high as in Britain at 750 to 1,000mm (30 to 40 inches), but Benelux's location – at the point where warm air masses from southern Europe collide with colder Atlantic and arctic weather systems – tends to keep the region overcast and foggy for most of the year. The Belgians estimate that rain falls on 210 days each year, and in Holland they claim there are only 25 days a year with completely clear skies.

Both summers and winters are mild. Heat waves are rare in summer, even on the coast where temperatures tend to be slightly warmer than inland, and few buildings are air-conditioned – it simply isn't necessary. In winter, temperatures don't normally remain below freezing (0°C/32°F) for long and there's usually little snow, except in higher regions. The upper slopes of the Ardennes sometimes have enough snow to allow skiing, particularly in the northern part of Luxembourg, but not every winter.

Approximate average maximum daytime temperatures in Celsius and Fahrenheit (in brackets) in the three capital cities during each season are:

City	Spring	Summer	Autumn	Winter
Brussels	13 (55)	23 (74)	14 (56)	6 (42)
Amsterdam	11 (52)	21 (69)	13 (56)	5 (41)
Luxembourg	8 (47)	17 (63)	10 (49)	1 (33)

A quick way to make a *rough* conversion from Centigrade to Fahrenheit is to multiply by two and add 30 (see also **Appendix D**). Weather forecasts are broadcast on TV and radio and published in daily newspapers, as well as being available via the Internet.

CRIME

The Benelux countries have similar crime rates to those of most other European countries, and in common with them crime has been on the increase throughout much of the last decade. Many people blame the influx of foreigners and asylum seekers, particularly those who are illegally attempting to enter the UK or America via the port cities of Benelux. Others (particularly in neighbouring countries) point the finger at liberal attitudes towards drugs and prostitution, particularly in Holland (although Belgium is also acknowledged to have a drug problem). Most crimes are against property, but there has been an increase in violent crimes over the past decade. Muggings are not unheard of, particularly in Amsterdam, Rotterdam and Antwerp, but pick-pocketing is by far the most common crime.

Pickpockets are active in most railway stations and airport terminals as well as in crowded shopping centres and wherever there are large numbers of tourists. You should therefore take the usual precautions, i.e. don't flash large sums of money around, don't carry your wallet in a back pocket, hold on tightly to your handbag or shoulder bag and make sure it's securely closed before you leave a shop or ticket counter. It's sensible to carry separate wallets for cash, credit cards and identification documents. After a pick-pocketing incident, it can take weeks to replace all your identification papers, driving licence and credit cards, when in fact most thieves are only after your cash. If someone confronts you and demands your wallet or purse, it's better to hand it over than to risk being injured or worse if you resist.

Burglaries are also becoming more common, particularly in cities. There are still a few rural areas where residents claim that they can safely leave their homes unlocked, but it's widely assumed (at least by criminals) that most foreigners have expensive furniture, electronic equipment and other items worth stealing, so it pays to err on the side of caution. In several of the larger cities (e.g. Brussels, Amsterdam and The Hague) there has been an increase in the number of police patrolling the streets, especially after dark. According to recent statistics, this seems to be having some effect, at least in one of Amsterdam's toughest districts, where the number of assaults fell by almost 40 per cent in one year. On the other hand, publicity of particularly violent or unpleasant incidents has given the impression that crime figures are still on the increase, and many locals consider it 'unsafe' to be out after dark, irrespective of statistics or risk factors. (In Amsterdam, it's legal to carry a pepper spray to 'deter' would-be attackers!)

DRUGS

Holland has long been considered a 'haven' for those with an interest in 'recreational' drugs. The Dutch aren't quite as tolerant as many think, however. Not only is the use of drugs (both hard and soft) illegal, but possession, import, export, manufacture and trafficking in drugs is severely prosecuted. The difference between Holland and many other countries is that the use of drugs is classified as a public health rather than a criminal problem in an attempt to keep young people out of the grip of organised crime. Possession of small amounts of so-called soft drugs (i.e. marijuana and cannabis) for personal use is therefore considered a minor offence and often isn't prosecuted, although police officers are required to confiscate the drugs and refer the offender to an appropriate health care or social service agency.

The (in)famous 'coffee shops', which supposedly sell soft drugs legally (see page 301), are actually committing an offence, although the authorities have agreed not to prosecute if the coffee shop owner continues to operate under strictly controlled guidelines. Coffee shops cannot sell alcohol or hard drugs and may not sell more than 5g (0.17oz) of soft drugs per person in a single transaction. They aren't allowed to advertise, sell to anyone under the age of 18 or cause a nuisance. The last stipulation is a sort of get-out clause, which can be liberally interpreted by the local mayor in order to shut down a coffee shop if it's believed to be encouraging drug use among the young, linked to criminal organisations or pandering to the 'drug tourist' trade (or local residents simply don't like the idea of a 'coffee shop' on the corner).

Possession of hard drugs or certain 'precursors' (i.e. substances used in the manufacture of hard drugs, even if they themselves aren't illegal) is prosecuted vigorously in Holland, with penalties of up to 12 years' imprisonment and fines up to €50,000. Importing and exporting are considered to be the most serious offences and thus are most heavily punished. Customs authorities in neighbouring countries (especially Germany and France) regularly stop cars with Dutch and Belgian number plates and check for drugs.

Belgium is tackling its drug problem in much the same way as Holland, by 'decriminalising' the possession of small amounts of soft drugs for personal use. Luxembourg, on the other hand, takes a more traditional approach towards the possession of drugs (i.e. it's an offence), although the country seems to be relatively drug-free.

GEOGRAPHY

Long before the term Benelux was coined, the region was known as The Low Countries (Belgium was part of the Kingdom of the United Netherlands until 1830) on account of its dominant geographical feature: low altitude. In fact, much of Belgium and Holland is at or slightly below sea level. Of the total land area of 74,640km² (28,820mi²), around 8,000km² (3,000mi²) has been reclaimed from the sea. Both the Belgians and the Dutch have built systems of sand dunes, sea walls and dykes in shallow deltas and pumped out the standing water to create new areas of land, called polders. Originally polders were intended for farming, but since the '50s some of them have been given over to residential or industrial use, and in 1986 an entire Dutch province (Flevoland) was established on reclaimed land. The lowest point in Benelux, part of the Prince Alexander Polder north of Rotterdam, is 6.7m (22ft) below sea level.

Moving eastwards from the coast, the landscape of Benelux is mostly flat and close to sea level until you reach the foothills of the Ardennes, the only 'mountains' in the region. The Ardennes are actually a wooded plateau, part of the Middle Rhine Highlands, which forms the watershed for most rivers flowing through the region. The highest point of the Ardennes (and of Benelux), at Botrange in the eastern corner of Belgium, is 694m (2,277ft) above sea level. Nestled as it is in the midst of the Ardennes, landlocked Luxembourg is the highest of the three Benelux countries, and the Oesling province in the north of the country boasts an average altitude of almost 450m (1,500ft) as well as the highest point in Luxembourg, the Buurgoplaatz at 564m (1,834ft). The highest point in Holland is the Vaalserberg in the south-east corner of the country, which rises just 310m (1,053ft) above sea level.

The Benelux region is criss-crossed by a number of rivers, the most important of which are the Schelde (Scheldt in Flemish/Escaut in French), the Meuse (Maas/Sambre) and the Rhine (Rijn in Dutch). There's also an extensive network of canals linking the rivers and making water transport an important means of transporting goods to markets throughout northern Europe.

Belgium: Belgium's total land area is 30,528km² (11,787mi²), making it the second smallest country in the EU, after Luxembourg. It shares borders with Holland (450km/270mi), Luxembourg (148km/89mi), Germany (167km/100mi) and France (620km/372mi) and has 66km (40mi) of coastline along the English Channel and the North Sea. At the closest point, Belgium is just 104km (65mi) from the UK.

Holland: The last time the land area of Holland was calculated, it covered 41,526km² (16,033mi²), but this figure is subject to change with the completion of new dykes and polder projects. Around a quarter of the country is below sea level and is protected by a system of dykes and sea walls, although flooding is possible during severe storms and high tides or when high water levels in the rivers flood the polder areas, as happened in 1995.

Holland is the largest of the Benelux countries, although still among the smaller members of the EU. It shares borders with Belgium (450km/270mi) and Germany (577km/346mi), and the Rhine flows almost directly through the centre of the country, splitting into a number of smaller rivers (the Waal, Lek, Ijssel and Neder Rijn) as it approaches the coast. The Maas (Meuse) and Scheldt (Schelde) rivers also meet the sea in Holland. It's estimated that there are over 5,000km (3,000mi) of navigable rivers and canals in Holland.

Luxembourg: At 2,586km² (1,000mi²), Luxembourg is the smallest country in the EU. It's bordered by Belgium (148km/89mi) to the north, France (73km/44mi) to the south and Germany (138km/83mi) to the east. The border with Germany is made up of three rivers, the Our, the Sûre and the Mosel/Moselle.

GOVERNMENT

The Benelux countries are constitutional and hereditary monarchies, where the monarch is the head of state and has some executive as well as legislative power, usually shared with a cabinet or council of ministers and the legislative bodies.

Belgium: Belgium officially became a federal state in 1992 with the passage of the St Michael's Agreement. Over the next few years, the Belgian constitution was re-written and legislation passed to allocate specific powers to the regions (Flanders, Wallonia and Brussels), communities (which were defined by language – Flemish, French or German), provinces and communes. The result was a five-tier system that attempts to balance the interests of the various political and cultural factions while devolving power to local authorities, wherever possible.

Belgium's current king is Albert II, who was crowned in August 1993 after the death of his brother, King Baudoin. Albert's heir is Prince Philippe. The King is head of state and appoints (and can remove) ministers, with whom he holds executive power. The King must countersign all legislative decrees issued by the national parliament, and he can also propose legislation, which must be countersigned by the appropriate minister. The King can dissolve parliament, but only under certain conditions defined in the constitution.

The national parliament is composed of two houses: the House of Representatives and the Senate. The House of Representatives is made up of 150 directly elected members of parliament, divided roughly equally between French and Flemish speakers. The Senate has 40 elected senators plus 21 members appointed by the community parliaments (ten from the Dutch, ten from the French and one from the German-speaking community) and a further ten (four French and six Flemish) 'co-opted' by the elected senators. In addition, adult members of the royal family may hold seats in the Senate if they wish. Parliament is responsible for national defence, foreign relations, general policy making and regulatory functions, and the administration of justice, social security, agriculture, the railways and other nationalised industries.

At regional, community, provincial and communal levels, there's a directly elected parliament or council, presided over by a governor or president. Regional councils are responsible for most aspects of economic policy, including public works, employment and housing, and some kinds of taxation. Communities are responsible for education, the media and other language-related matters, including health care (on the basis that you shouldn't have to struggle with a foreign language when you're ill!). The provinces and communes deal with local matters, including some taxation and public health issues.

Holland: The Dutch monarchy is currently the only one in the Benelux region that is hereditary in both the male and female lines. The current monarch is Queen Beatrix Wilhelmina Armgard, who ascended to the throne in 1980. Her son, Willem-Alexander, is the heir. The Queen is responsible for bringing together potential coalition partners after general elections (it's rare for any party to have a clear majority), and she appoints a *formateur* to establish a new government who usually becomes prime minister.

The parliament (*Staten-Generaal*) has a bicameral structure, with upper and lower houses (*eerste kamer* and *tweede kamer*). Only the *tweede kamer* can propose or amend bills; the *eerste kamer* can debate legislation and delay its passage, but otherwise has limited powers. *Tweede kamer* members are directly elected every four years, half on a country-wide basis, the other half representing specific regional districts under a system of proportional representation. There are also three councils of state, including a national ombudsman.

At local level, there are 12 provinces and 625 municipalities (*gemeente*), each with an elected council (*provinciale staten* and *gemeenteraden*). Local mayors (*burgemeester*) are appointed by the Crown to preside over the councils. Foreigners who have lived (legally) in Holland for at least five years may vote in local elections.

Luxembourg: The head of state in Luxembourg is the Grand Duke, currently Grand Duke Henri, who acquired the crown in October 2000 on the abdication (actually more a retirement) of his father, Jean II. Under the constitution, the monarch has a wide range of powers, including that of appointing ministers and assembling and dissolving the government, but many of these powers must be exercised in consultation with the relevant elected lawmakers.

The main legislative body is the Chamber of Deputies, comprising 60 delegates, directly elected for five-year terms. Voting in Luxembourg is mandatory for all citizens over the age of 18, except those imprisoned for certain criminal offences and deprived of their electoral rights. Postal votes are accepted only from those who are out of the country on election day for professional reasons and those who are too sick to go to the polls. If you don't vote, you're required to justify your abstention before a panel of judges, who can levy a fine if they aren't convinced by your reason for not voting.

The Grand Duke also appoints a council of state made up of 21 advisors, which works with the Chamber of Deputies but has no legislative authority. The council acts as a supreme court in administrative disputes as well as reviewing all draft legislation and offering general counsel to the Grand Duke.

At local level, voting districts are divided into cantons, communes and municipalities, each with an elected council and mayor. A commissioner appointed by the central government coordinates programmes and projects within each district, primarily with respect to public works and health and educational matters.

LEGAL SYSTEM

Like most of continental Europe, the Benelux countries each have a system of civil law, based on written statutes, rather than a common law system like those of the UK and USA. Court cases are decided by a judge or a panel of magistrates, who are responsible for investigating the facts and circumstances of the case. Unlike under the common law system, in some of the lower courts it isn't always necessary to have a lawyer, who has more of an administrative than a legislative function. (No adversarial 'showdowns' in Benelux courts, which could be why Europeans are fascinated by American courtroom dramas.)

Judges are appointed by the monarch for life (not bad job security!) and are prohibited from having outside interests or investments that would conflict with their judicial role. There's no jury system, and judges pronounce sentences according to the written provisions of the law.

If you need an English-speaking lawyer, you can usually obtain a list from your country's embassy or consulate. Certain legal services and advice may also be provided by embassies and consulates in Benelux, including an official witness of signatures (Commissioner for Oaths or what the Americans call a 'notary public'). **Never assume that the law in Belgium, Holland or Luxembourg is the same as in any other country, as this often isn't the case.**

Belgium: At local (cantonal) level, justices of the peace rule on civil and commercial cases, and criminal cases are tried by police tribunals. At district level there's a different tribunal for each type of case: civil, criminal, juvenile, commercial and labour. Appeals are referred to the Supreme Court of Justice in Belgium, but its three chambers can rule only on the application of the law and not on any facts or circumstances relating to particular cases.

Holland: Simple cases are tried in cantonal courts (*kantongerechten*), and more serious cases in district courts (*arrondissementsrechtbank*). Appeals are heard in five specialised appeal courts (*Gerechtshof*). The Supreme Court (*Hoge Raad*) can rule only on the application of the law to each case. Unlike supreme courts in many other countries, it cannot determine whether a law is constitutional, which can be done only by parliament. Any laws that are at variance with international agreements signed by the Dutch monarch cannot be enforced in Dutch courts. An independent state councillor acts as ombudsman in disputes between individuals and the state.

Luxembourg: Criminal cases are heard by the criminal court of assizes, which consists of six magistrates. The Superior Court of Justice is the ultimate court of appeal in the Duchy.

DEFENCE

The combined military force of the Benelux region consists of around 98,000 full-time personnel, both male and female. Holland has the largest contingent (53,000) and maintains an army, a navy and an air force. Belgium has the largest army (28,500 to Holland's 27,000) but a much smaller navy (only 2,700 compared with 13,800), making a total of 44,500 personnel, including the air force. Tiny Luxembourg maintains an army of 800 full-time soldiers. Compulsory military service ended in 1995. All three nations are members of NATO and have sent troops on a number of United Nations peace-keeping missions in recent years.

Luxembourg spends only around 0.7 per cent of its GNP on its army, slightly less than 2 per cent of total government spending. Belgium's military expenditure is around 1.7 per cent of GNP and 3.5 per cent of government spending, while Holland has the largest military budget, at 2.1 per cent of GNP and 4.4 per cent of spending, compared with 7.2 per cent in the UK.

MARRIAGE & DIVORCE

The legal age for marriage, as for concluding any other kind of contract, is 18 in all three Benelux countries, and at least one partner must be a resident of the town where the wedding is to take place. As in many other European countries, it's the civil ceremony that constitutes the legal process of marriage; a religious ceremony may take place only after the 'official' wedding at the town hall.

You must apply to your town hall at least three months in advance of the date you wish to marry. This is partly to ensure that the date is available, but also because it can take that long to complete all the necessary paperwork! Be sure to ask at your town hall for a list of the documents required, which are subject to change at short notice. All the paperwork has to be submitted and processed at least ten days before the ceremony, when the banns are posted, and you may find that it takes some time to assemble the necessary documents (which you may be able to do via your local embassy) and have them officially translated. Generally, you need birth certificates, certificates of residence and a doctor's certificate or statement verifying that you've had a physical examination (often including a chest X-ray) and are free of certain diseases (e.g. AIDS and syphilis).

If either partner has been married before, he will need to produce divorce papers or verification of the former spouse's death. True to bureaucratic tradition in Benelux, if either partner has lived abroad at any time in their adult lives, he may be required to submit proof that he wasn't married abroad (especially if he was living in a country that is less meticulous in its record-keeping as the Benelux nations, i.e. practically anywhere!). For some reason, these 'unusual' requirements tend to surface a day or two before the deadline for the submission of paperwork, and it pays to have developed a good rapport with the local bureaucrats, in which case it's often possible to make a formal written declaration that you're not engaging in international bigamy!

Women are entitled to retain their maiden names after marriage or to adopt the surname of their husbands if they prefer. Hyphenated surnames are common, although they're sometimes used only in official documents when referring to the whole family. Children in all three countries take the surname of their father, unless the identity of the father is unknown or the parents specify a different surname on the birth certificate (where this is permitted).

Divorce is legal in all three countries, where grounds for divorce include mutual consent, serious cause (normally adultery or cruelty) and legal separation for a minimum period. Support for any children and for the dependent spouse is decided by the courts, and property must be divided between the divorcing spouses according to the laws in effect at the time and place of the marriage, which can be difficult to determine if the couple was married abroad. In Belgium and Luxembourg there are restrictions as to how soon a woman can remarry after divorce (a practice supposedly designed to keep lines of parentage distinct).

Surprisingly, several human rights organisations have expressed concern about family violence in all three Benelux countries, where family structures are quite traditional and there's a strong sense of privacy in family matters.

Belgium: To marry in Belgium, foreigners must supply a formal statement from their embassy declaring that they're eligible for marriage under the laws of their home country. Divorced women are required to provide a doctor's statement that they aren't pregnant if they're remarrying within 300 days of the finalisation of their divorce. It's common for couples to prepare marriage contracts specifying the financial arrangements between them. A marriage contract (sometimes called a pre-nuptial agreement) is drawn up by a notary (*notaire/notaris*) and this should be done before the wedding in order to avoid high fees and transfer costs. Those marrying without a contract must agree that all property acquired during the marriage (except anything inherited by one partner only) will be jointly owned, while each partner retains full ownership of goods and property owned prior to the marriage.

Women in Belgium continue to use their maiden names on all official documents. When a hyphenated name is used (normally in documents referring to the family), the husband's surname appears first.

Holland: In Holland, a couple can legally be married if both are at least 16 years of age and the bride is pregnant or the couple already has one or more children together. Otherwise the legal age is 18.

People of the same sex can now marry in Holland and are entitled to almost the same legal protection as heterosexual couples. However, as Holland is one of only a handful of countries that have legalised gay marriages, the Dutch government warns that it cannot guarantee international recognition of the relationship. Dutch law also protects the rights of any children a gay couple may have (on the assumption that a third party needs to be involved in the procreation process!). The Dutch also recognise quasi-marital relationships, referred to as registered partnerships, between homosexual and heterosexual couples, who may convert their partnership into a marital agreement.

A divorced woman may remarry whenever she wishes; if she has a child after remarrying, it's legally the child (and heir) of the new husband, even if the birth occurs less than 307 days after the divorce.

Luxembourg: Divorced women aren't permitted to remarry in the Duchy for a year or so after their divorce becomes final. Luxembourg law still differentiates between legitimate and illegitimate children, mostly in the area of inheritance rights, although this may change in the next few years in accordance with EU directives.

PETS

If you plan to take a pet to Benelux, it's important to ascertain the current regulations, which are constantly changing. Make sure you have the correct papers, not only for your country of destination but for all the countries you will pass through. Particular consideration must be given before exporting a pet from a country with strict quarantine regulations, such as Britain. If you need to return prematurely, even after a few hours or days, your pet may have to go into quarantine, e.g. for six months in Britain, which apart from being very expensive is distressing for both pets and owners. Britain has recently instituted a system for admitting certain animals from certain countries without the need for quarantine whereby they must be microchipped and have a 'passport' listing their vaccinations. Animals which don't meet these criteria or are being imported from Eastern Europe, Africa, Asia and South America must be quarantined.

You can bring a pet into the Benelux region provided it has a certificate of health issued less than eight days before your arrival, including a valid rabies vaccination certificate (at least a month and no more than a year before the date of entry) in the case of dogs and cats, except those being imported from the UK. Animals other than dogs and cats require an import certificate from the ministry of agriculture of the appropriate country. Contact your vet or local consulate or the relevant ministry of agriculture for further information.

Belgium: Belgium is a country of dog-lovers and many owners take their dogs with them wherever they go, including to shops and restaurants. You may even see proud owners wheeling their dogs around supermarkets in a shopping trolley, although many stores discourage this practice! Most landlords permit pets, sometimes with an additional deposit, but make sure your pet is written into the lease.

Dogs must be registered with your commune, which involves having them tattooed or microchipped at the age of four months or when they're sold (e.g. by breeders). A unique number is tattooed onto the dog's skin or stored in a microchip inserted under the skin at the back of the neck. It used to be common to tattoo a dog in its ear, so that the tattoo was easily visible. Unfortunately, dog thieves started chopping off ears to avoid detection, so if your dog is potentially valuable to others (even with an ear missing), you may want to insist on it being tattooed inside a hind leg. The identification number and your address details are registered with the national pet registry, accessible 24 hours a day. If your pet is found lost or injured, you can be identified as its owner and contacted. The cost of registration depends on a number of factors: if your pet has been tattooed or microchipped abroad and you're simply transferring the registration to Belgium, you should pay around €50; if you have your pet tattooed or chipped at the same time as another operation (e.g. neutering), you may pay only an additional €5 or €10; if your pet requires an anaesthetic and is having no other treatment, you could pay up to €120. Cats aren't required to be registered, but it's recommended.

Some communes ban pit bull terriers and other breeds considered to be 'dangerous' or 'vicious', and all dogs must be kept on a leash whenever they're taken outside your home. If your dog escapes and is found wandering about on its own, it will be caught by the police and you must pay to retrieve it. Third party liability insurance is available to cover any damage your pets may do to other people's property (or to other people).

Dogs and cats aren't required to have an annual rabies vaccination in Belgium unless you plan to leave them in kennels or a cattery, or take them to a campsite or anywhere outside Belgium. Some communes require dogs to be vaccinated against rabies as part of the registration process. In any case, it's wise to keep your pets up to date with their immunisations.

Animal medicines are sold by chemists and veterinary surgeries, which are indicated by a blue cross. Vets (*vétérinaires/dierenartsen*) are listed in the telephone book under 'liberal professions' (*professions libérales/vrije beroepen*) – see page 119. You can find an English-speaking vet by calling the CHS helpline (☎ 02-648 4014).

Holland: In Holland you must register your dog with the local town hall and there's an annual tax on dog ownership (*hondenbelasting*). Both cats and dogs should be tattooed for identification purposes, and many owners in Holland also have their pets microchipped to verify the tattoo number.

Annual rabies vaccinations aren't mandatory for cats or dogs unless you plan to travel with them or put them in a cattery or kennels. Other vaccinations are required, however, and you should ask a vet to check that your dog or cat is properly protected and that you have the necessary documentation. Vets (*dierensarts*) are listed in the telephone book and most larger towns even have an animal ambulance (*dieren-ambulance*).

In most Dutch towns you're liable for a fine if you permit your dog to foul the pavement, especially where there are signs saying '*hond in de goot*' (dogs in the gutter). Nevertheless, you should be careful where you tread: Amsterdam in particular has long been infamous for the amount of canine waste on its pavements. There's a charge of up to €5 to take a dog on a train. For a ride on tram or bus, a dog needs a child's ticket. (Cats and birds travel free!)

Luxembourg: Dogs must be registered with your commune and there's an annual tax on dog ownership of up to €300 in some communes. Cats don't need to be registered. Rabies is a serious problem in Luxembourg, especially amongst the wild animal population, so annual rabies vaccinations are required for both cats and dogs, as well as a multi-purpose vaccination to protect them against distemper and a number of other diseases. Cats must be given an additional vaccination if they're allowed outdoors.

In Luxembourg you must clean up after your dog and you can buy 'doggie bags' from machines in public areas popular with dog owners. You should also look out for marked areas where dogs aren't allowed, as fines for canine misdemeanors can be steep and are payable on the spot if you're caught!

POLICE

The police forces in Benelux are generally organised into local and national services and all police officers are armed, usually with both a baton and a pistol. In all three countries you're expected to carry identification (national identity card, passport or residence permit) whenever you leave home. The police have the right to stop you simply to check your identification papers and you don't always have the right to contact a lawyer, nor do the police necessarily have to explain your rights to you before beginning an interrogation. If you're arrested, for lack of identification or any other reason, you should ask the police to contact your national consulate or embassy, which can arrange for a member of staff to visit you, provide you with the names of English-speaking lawyers, and contact friends or family for you.

Belgium: Traditionally, there have been three kinds of police in Belgium: communal police (*police/politie*), gendarmes or *rijkswacht*, and judicial police (JP). There are almost 600 separate communal police forces, whereas the *gendarmerie* is a national force, dealing with serious crime and inter-communal issues and patrolling main roads. The judicial police work with the justice system, also on a national level, and play a similar role to the CID in Britain or the FBI in America. However, Belgium is currently in the midst of a reorganisation of its police force, which is expected to take several years, whereby the communal police forces are to be regrouped into around 200 police 'zones' (*zones inter-police* or ZIPs), and the *gendarmerie* and judicial police combined into a single national police force.

You can be arrested and held for up to 12 hours by any police officer if you're asked to show your identity card and can't produce it. On the other hand, even with a search warrant, the police cannot disturb you at home between 9pm and 5am, and you have the right to refuse them entry if they turn up during these hours (although you can be fairly sure they'll return on the stroke of 5am!). Police investigating non-payment of radio and television tax may only visit you between 8am and 6pm.

Holland: There are around 40,000 police officers in Holland, divided between the 25 regional police forces and the Dutch National Police Agency (KLPD). Regional police are responsible for general law and order and also have specialist departments, dealing in areas such as juvenile delinquency, vice, and certain matters relating to immigrants. The KLPD is responsible for monitoring traffic on motorways and waterways and in the air, as well as for the safety and security of the royal family. It also liaises with foreign police forces and Interpol.

Dutch police, particularly in Amsterdam, have a reputation for being rather lax, especially in dealing with drug abuse and prostitution, and corruption has been a problem in recent years, with some 80 officers dismissed annually for dishonesty. Considerable efforts have been made to develop a police monitoring system, involving local mayors, regional chiefs of police and the chief public prosecutor, in an attempt to restore public confidence. In recent years, there has also been a move towards putting more police on the street, although local police forces have had difficulty recruiting sufficient officers to fulfil promises of increased street patrols. In order to cover as much ground as possible, some local police patrol their sectors by bicycle or even on roller skates (with appropriate safety equipment, of course!).

Luxembourg: Luxembourg has local police, organised by commune, and national police (*gendarmes*), who also patrol main roads. Foreigners arrested or 'detained' by the police have the right to ask their embassy to be notified (or *not* to be notified!).

POPULATION

The combined population of the Benelux region is 26,324,000 (around 15.7 million in Holland, 10.3 million in Belgium and just 413,000 in Luxembourg), which makes it one of the most densely populated regions in the world, with around 350 people per km^2 (910 per mi^2) overall and over 450 per km^2 (1,190 per mi^2) in Holland. For many years the Dutch government encouraged its citizens to emigrate in an attempt to alleviate crowding, but that policy was dropped in the early '80s, and for the past decade or more the population of Benelux has been growing by 0.5 per cent (around 130,000 people) annually, largely because of the influx of immigrants. Most people live in urban areas and half the population of Holland lives in a circle of cities called the Randstad, which includes Amsterdam, The Hague, Rotterdam and Utrecht.

Life expectancy averages 78 years across the region (81 for women and 74 to 75 for men), with Luxembourg the lowest at 77.1 years and Holland the highest at 78.3. Around 15 per cent of the population is aged 65 or older, and (as in most other European nations) the subject of pensions and how these will be financed is of considerable concern.

RELIGION

The Benelux region (and Holland in particular) has a long-standing tradition of religious tolerance, and every resident has complete freedom to choose his religion without hindrance from the state or community. The governments don't support any religion financially, although religious education is part of the national curriculum in all three countries and often at least partly state subsidised.

Christianity, particularly Roman Catholicism, is the most common religion, especially in Belgium and Luxembourg, and many of the public holidays are based on Christian holy days. Islam has become the second most common religion in all three countries, largely as a result of the influx of Moslem immigrants and refugees. In Belgium particularly, this has aroused hostile feelings toward various immigrant groups.

Belgium: Belgium's population is overwhelmingly (95 per cent) Roman Catholic, although it's estimated that less than 15 per cent regularly attend church services. The most regular church-goers are in the northern, Flemish-speaking areas and the Ardennes, while in Brussels and many industrial areas in the Walloon region, church-going is becoming less common. Nevertheless, the Church still has considerable influence over social and cultural practices. For example, most couples have a religious as well as a civil marriage service, and most children are baptised in a formal church ceremony. Many Belgian families send their children to religious education classes and First Communion is a major celebration in most Belgian households.

The Moslem religion has around 150,000 adherents in Belgium and the number is increasing as the immigrant community grows. The various Protestant religions account for another 100,000 Belgians, primarily in and around Hainaut and Brabant. There's a small Jewish community, numbering around 35,000, concentrated in Brussels and Antwerp.

Holland: The Dutch have a long history of religious tolerance, which has made the country a refuge for people fleeing religious persecution. Of the three Benelux countries, Holland has by far the most religious diversity, with around 34 per cent Catholic, 25 per cent Protestant, 4 per cent Moslem, and 2 per cent other religions (including 0.5 per cent Hindu and 0.2 per cent Jewish). The remaining 35 per cent of the population claim not to follow any organised religion.

The Catholic Church in Holland has a fairly liberal attitude, and the clergy regularly find themselves at loggerheads with the Vatican on issues such as the role of women in the Church. The Protestant Calvinist tradition, on the other hand, is strongly conservative, stressing hard work, clean living and obedience to strict moral principles.

Luxembourg: The religious make-up of Luxembourg is similar to that of Belgium with around 95 per cent of the population Roman Catholic, although church-going is rather more popular in conservative Luxembourg. In Luxembourg city, where there's a large foreign-born population, there are services for various religions, including Moslem, Anglican and other Protestant sects, often held in the chapels or meeting rooms of Catholic churches.

SOCIAL CUSTOMS

All countries have particular social customs and Belgium, Holland and Luxembourg are no exceptions. As a foreigner you will probably be excused if you accidentally insult your host (although you may not be invited again), but it's best to make yourself aware of local customs and modes of behaviour. Generally, social customs are similar in all three countries, although important differences are noted below.

- When you're introduced to people, you should always use the formal word for 'you' (*vous* in French, *u* in Dutch or *Sie* in German) and refer to them as Mr or Mrs (*Monsieur* or *Madame* in French, *Meneer* or *Mevrouw* in Dutch, or *Herr* or *Frau* in German) followed by their surname, unless you're specifically asked to use first names. Younger people, particularly in Holland, are usually quick to switch to first names and the familiar form of address (*tu/je/du*), but you should usually allow them do so first.

- Expect to shake hands with just about everyone you meet. In many offices, you shake hands with all your colleagues when you arrive in the morning and again as you leave at night. The first few minutes of many business meetings are taken up with introductions and hand-shaking all around. Friends often kiss in the French manner, alternating cheeks (normally starting with the left). Three kisses are reserved for close friends; two suffice for most acquaintances.

- People throughout the Benelux region guard their private lives closely. Someone you meet socially may resent questions about his job, and work colleagues don't openly discuss their own or anyone else's family or private life. It's generally less usual to socialise with work colleagues outside the office than in the UK or USA.

- It's generally considered rude to call on people unannounced, and you should phone in advance to make sure that they're ready to see you. If you have visitors, you're expected to offer them food and drink (at least tea and biscuits), and you'll find that most Beneluxers are generous hosts.

- Entertaining in restaurants is common, especially among business colleagues. Most invitations outside work hours (i.e. anything other than lunch) include your spouse, since this is an intrusion on your private time, but it's wise to check if there's any doubt.

- If you're invited to someone's home, bring a small gift, e.g. flowers or chocolates, but note that some flowers have a particular significance. Avoid chrysanthemums and carnations (normally used only for funerals) and red roses (which indicate romantic intentions). In Holland it isn't unusual to give a man flowers, but you may want to confer with a florist or a mutual friend first.

- When you enter a shop, say good morning or good afternoon to the shopkeeper and any customers. Make sure you also say goodbye and thank you when you leave, whether or not you've purchased anything.

- In Holland, speaking one's mind directly and openly is considered a basic right. It may seem abrupt or even rude at first, but almost any subject is open for discussion (even argument) and there will be no hard feelings after even the most heated debate. (Don't try this in Belgium or Luxembourg, however!)

- Don't make fun of or criticise the royal family of any of the Benelux countries. Unlike the inhabitants of certain countries (no names mentioned), the Belgians, Dutch and Luxembourgers hold their royalty in high esteem and respect their right to privacy (although there's nothing like a royal wedding or birth to stimulate the local media).

TIME DIFFERENCE

Times in Benelux are usually written using the 24-hour clock, e.g. 10am is written as 10.00 and 10pm as 22.00. French-speaking areas of Belgium often use French notation (e.g. 22h or 22 heures), while German speakers (in Belgium and Luxembourg) may write times in the German manner (e.g. 22U or 22 Uhr). In Dutch, 10pm is often written 22 uur. If you're making an appointment with someone in German or Dutch, remember that 'half twelve' in both languages means 11.30 and not 12.30!

Like most of continental Europe, the Benelux countries are on Central European Time (CET), which is Greenwich Mean Time (GMT) plus one hour. All three countries change to summer time in the spring (the last weekend in March), when clocks are put forward one hour, and back to CET in the autumn (the last weekend in October). Time changes are announced in local newspapers and on radio and TV, and take place at 2 or 3am on Sunday.

The time difference between Benelux at **noon** in winter and some major international cities is shown below:

LONDON	JOHANNESBURG	SYDNEY	AUCKLAND	NEW YORK
11am	1pm	10pm	midnight	6am

TIPPING

Tipping is fairly common throughout Benelux, although not as widespread as in the USA. In many restaurants, menu prices include service (*service compris/service inclusief*) or a service charge (usually around 15 per cent) is automatically added to your bill. Where this is the case, you can leave a few extra coins, or round up to the next whole euro to indicate your appreciation of particularly good service (or just to lighten your pockets), but many locals don't bother to tip at all.

Those who are usually tipped include porters, toilet and cloakroom attendant, ushers, tour guides, taxi drivers and hairdressers – with the following exceptions: taxi fares in Belgium include a surcharge to cover 'service'; many of the large film distributors (usually those with the multi-screen cinemas) no longer permit ushers to accept tips (or, more usually, simply don't hire ushers); and in smaller barber shops and hairdressers, you normally tip only the shampoo girl or apprentice. Your removal men can be tipped €10 to 20 each, particularly if they had to negotiate lots of stairs or other obstacles. For simpler moves, an offer of sandwiches and soft drinks or beer is sufficient (but only offer beer *after* the job is completed!).

At Christmas or New Year, you will usually receive calls from the postman, refuse collectors and local firemen, all offering their greetings and sometimes a calendar or address book in exchange for a 'gratuity'. (You can decline, but don't expect reliable service for the rest of the year – and make sure your house doesn't catch fire!) Also included in round of year-end gratuities are your concierge, cleaning lady, gardener and any other service provider you deal with on a regular basis. (Your cleaning lady or au pair may be entitled to an extra half month's salary or more at the end of the year, in which case a tip is superfluous.) Tips can range from a couple of euros up to €20 or €30, depending on the level and quality of the service rendered. If in doubt, check with neighbours to see what's considered appropriate, and remember the origin of the word 'tip': it's an abbreviation for 'to insure promptness', and a small annual investment often reaps rewards – although not always!

TOILETS

Toilets are referred to as the WC ('water closet') or *les toilettes* in French (the Dutch use the English words *toilet* and *closet!*) and ladies and gents are marked *Mesdames/Messieurs* in French or *Heeren/Vrouwen* or *Dames* in Dutch. Most public toilets charge a small fee, which is often paid to an attendant as you enter. In other cases, toilets have coin-operated locks. This could explain why, in some areas, it isn't uncommon for men to relieve themselves in public – more or less discreetly. (Happily this is one area where women don't insist on equal rights.) In most areas, restaurants are required to allow anyone to use their toilets, whether or not they intend to eat there.

BEWARE MINES!
I LIVE HERE
BEWARE 9,000,000,000 VOLTS

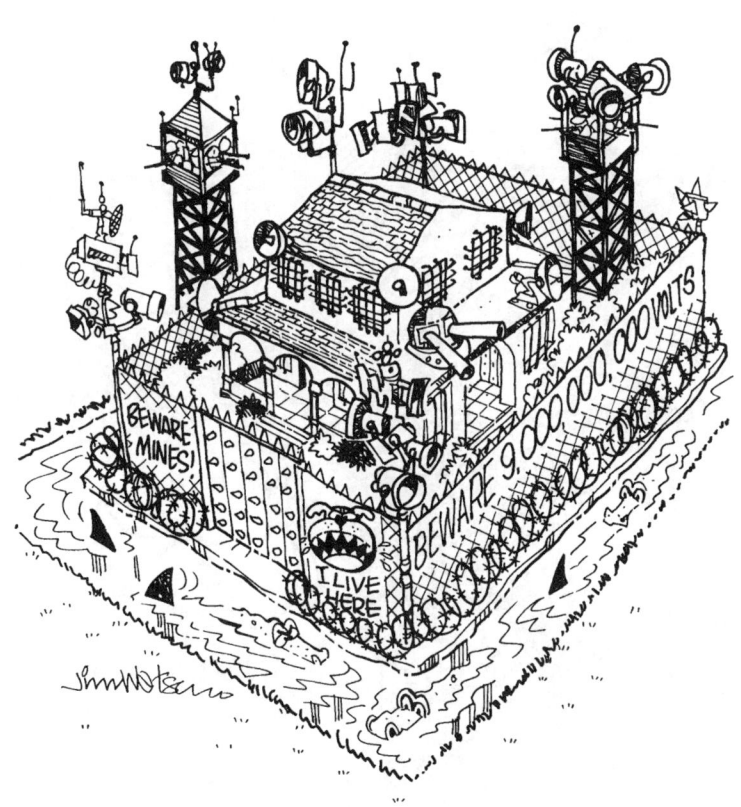

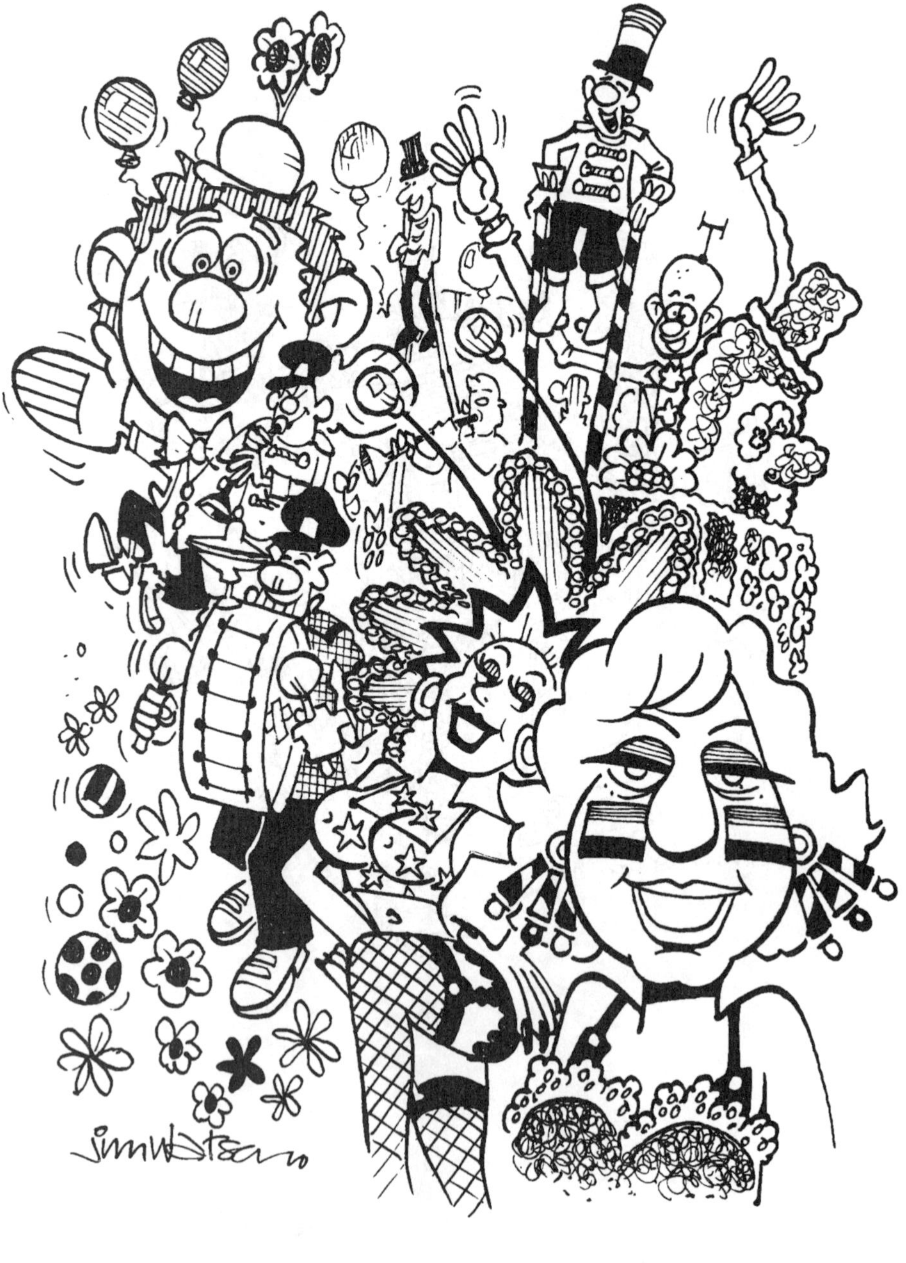

19.

THE PEOPLE

Who are the Belgians, Dutch and Luxembourgers? What are they like, both individually and collectively? Let's take a candid and totally prejudiced look at the people of Benelux, tongue firmly in cheek, and hope they forgive my flippancy or that they don't read this bit, which is why it's hidden away at the back of the book.

The typical **Belgian** is practical, a good citizen, distrustful of authority (particularly the police), Catholic, generous to a fault, adept at compromise, a conformist, a snob, well-educated, affluent, over-taxed, responsible, a car lover and a poor driver, materialistic, a Tintin fan, proud, a bureaucrat, artistic, friendly, a gourmand, individualistic, industrious, malleable, bourgeois, modest, obedient, liberal, a Royalist, orderly, a bit dull, and generally thinks of himself as either Flemish or Wallonian – or even European – anything except Belgian.

The typical **Dutchman** (or woman) is a businessman, proud, uncompromising (leaving compromise to the Belgians!), a conformist, a cyclist, extremely tolerant, a linguist, self-centred, superior, overweight, wealthy, decent, outspoken (blunt), boring, a Protestant, reasonable, pedantic, miserly, a soccer fanatic (or hooligan), an ice skater, tall, an amphibian, ambitious, classless, open-minded, an eccentric driver, egalitarian, morally superior, inventive, law-abiding, loyal, spotless, dull, hard-working, home-loving, an internationalist and impossible to understand.

The typical **Luxembourger** is a banker, affluent, Germanic with French tastes, friendly, conservative, hospitable, austere, loyal, reserved, discreet, tolerant, hypocritical, anonymous, at least trilingual (many are quadrilingual), and actually a Belgian, German or some other foreigner.

You may have noticed that the above lists contain 'a few' contradictions, which is hardly surprising, as there's no such thing as a typical Belgian, Dutchman or Luxembourger – and what's a 'Beneluxer' anyway? Apart from the numerous differences in character between the inhabitants of the three nations known collectively as Benelux, the population encompasses a hotchpotch (a Dutch word, by the way) of foreigners from all corners of the globe. However, while it's true that not all Belgians, Dutchmen or Luxembourgers are stereotypes (some are almost indistinguishable from 'normal' people), a few eccentrics shouldn't be allowed to spoil a good generalisation.

The issue of Belgian nationality is something of a minefield. Belgians are either Flemish or French and fiercely loyal to their linguistic community rather than any concept of Belgium as a country. The small German-speaking population often gets left out of these discussions entirely, although they also have their rights. (English serves as the *lingua franca* and enables the Belgians and foreigners to communicate with each other.) Every so often there's talk from one side or the other of splitting Belgium into two separate countries, but no one's quite sure what would become of Brussels (Brussels is the exception to every Belgian rule), so yet another compromise is struck and the crisis resolved. There's also the sticky problem of who exactly would claim the royal family, who are admired and respected by both sides (no small feat in Belgium!).

The Dutch are the only ones in the region without a national identity crisis – unless you count the tendency of everyone else in the world to refer to their country as 'Holland', including (our apologies) the author of this book! There are two provinces in the Netherlands called Noord-Holland and Zuid-Holland, but there are also ten other provinces, none of which have anything at all to do with the word Holland.

Being a tolerant people, however, most Dutch are resigned to having the name of their country mangled by ignorant foreigners who don't know any better.

The Dutch are also remarkably understanding of the fact that virtually no one else in the world needs or wants to learn their language, which even they describe as sounding like someone gargling. What the Flemish (or Flemings) speak in Belgium is remarkably similar to Dutch (but with numerous different accents and dialects), although the Flemish disdain many of the adopted French words in order to demonstrate their contempt for their Wallonian countrymen. The French-speaking Belgians in Wallonia (Walloons) also have their own expressions (some would say secret codes) in order to confound the scions of the *Académie française*, who tend to think they control the French language (although, paradoxically, the Walloons are more Gallic than the French). As a Walloon would no doubt be quick to remind a Fleming, in bygone days the upper classes spoke French, while Dutch was reserved for addressing servants and animals. Luxembourgers live a thoroughly schizophrenic existence when it comes to languages, speaking Lëtzebuergesh, a peculiar corruption of German, or proper German amongst themselves, while using French for most 'official' purposes. Even their national motto sounds rather defensive: 'We want to remain what we are.'

A few things unite all three Benelux nations. Beer, for one. The Belgians are said to produce several hundred different brands, kinds and qualities (many drunk from a special glass), although nowadays most Belgian brewers are owned by a single megabrewery concern. Their national football league is even named after a beer! The Dutch and Luxembourgers also have home-brewed beers and are equally fiercely loyal to them. (Not surprisingly, both claim to produce the best beer in the world.)

Driving also unites the Beneluxers, who are committed car lovers and take great pride in their cars, keeping them almost as spotless as their homes. However, it's a different matter when it comes to driving skills: Belgian drivers have long been the curse of French roads (probably because they actually drive worse than the French – some feat!), while Belgians complain incessantly about Dutch drivers (especially those towing caravans) and everyone wonders about the funny number plates with the letter L – could they be Laplanders, Latvians or Lithuanians? Benelux is also noted for its love of cycling, particularly Holland, where they even do it underground (it's true!).

Belgians are known as the great compromisers. How else can a country so small survive as a single nation with two and a half linguistically based 'communities' all doing their best to avoid any contact with one another? Compromise isn't, however, something that comes naturally to the Dutch, although tolerance is quite another thing. The Dutch social and political spectrum takes in everything from the strictest Calvinist notions that dancing and card playing are demonic temptations, to allowing personal indulgence in cannabis (and other 'recreational pharmaceuticals') and the right to euthanasia. The Red Light district in Amsterdam is world-famous for its legalised and regulated prostitution ('primarily for the tourists', as most solid citizens are quick to assure you), and the tolerant (healthy) attitude towards sex of all sorts (really, ALL sorts) extends to a mind-boggling range of associated 'merchandise' and 'services'.

In the countryside you will (again) be told that the sex industry is 'primarily for tourists', and perhaps the Dutch aversion to hanging curtains in their front windows (to compensate they hang carpets on their walls) attests to the fact that there really IS nothing out of the ordinary going on in most homes. The Dutch are a blunt and direct people and will gladly enlighten you regarding their view of the world, especially if it involves pointing out the mistakes you're making. Like most people, the Dutch aren't great listeners, particularly if you offer to point out their own shortcomings.

The Luxembourgers 'are what they are', and provided the way you are isn't too different from the way they are, everyone is happy – OK? Luxembourg, Europe's last grand-duchy, has in many ways become the Switzerland of the EU. (If the Swiss won't join, someone has to do it!) There are banks everywhere and Luxembourg bankers are the very models of discretion, to the intense displeasure of other EU governments, who watch in envy as their citizens' money disappears into Luxembourg bank vaults. Luxembourg is, however, willing to withhold taxes on foreigners' accounts and share information with European tax authorities – but only when Switzerland agrees to do the same. (No fools, these Luxembourg bankers!)

In the meantime, the Luxembourg tourist industry does well for itself, providing entertainment and accommodation for foreigners stopping off to count their money. For the Germans, Luxembourg (with the world's highest GDP) is *almost* up to their own standards of comfort, cleanliness and affluence, and what's more they even speak the same language (after a fashion)! For the French, Luxembourg is a neighbour who not only speaks French (pretty well, in fact) but who also appreciates fine wine (mostly French) and food (also often French). It also has a famous radio station that nobody listens to any more.

The Belgians, Dutch and Luxembourgers are diverse peoples who don't always see eye to eye, although nothing is guaranteed to bring them closer together than being made the butt of jokes by foreigners!

Now for the serious bit!

Beneluxers enjoy a high standard of living, excellent public services, good schools, comprehensive social security benefits, superb health services and hospitals (no waiting lists), efficient local government, exceptional working conditions and employee benefits, and a first-class transport system with modern motorways and railways. They're enthusiastic Europeans and firmly support the euro (they cannot wait to spend their own currency abroad) and closer integration, and live in harmony with their foreign guests.

The Benelux countries are famous for many things, including their beer, culture, soccer, gastronomy, historic towns, cable TV, jenever, *frites* (chips), clogs, bicycles, dykes, canals, windmills, flowers, polders, cheese, mussels, diamonds, architecture, soccer, bureaucrats, Philips, seaports, stable government, chocolate and banking, to name just a handful. They also have a rich cultural history (contrary to popular belief, the only famous Belgians aren't Hercule Poirot and Tintin) and have produced many great artists, including such world-famous names as Bosch, Brueghel, Escher, Frans Hals, Joseph Kutter (I had to include one Luxembourger!), Magritte, Mondriaan, Rembrandt, Rietveld, Rubens, Jan Steen, van Eyck, Vermeer and van Gogh.

Beneluxers have enjoyed the good life for so long that they've almost forgotten what it's like to live in the real world. However, they do share a few of the rest of the world's problems including rampant bureaucracy (Brussels is the capital of the European Union), a drug problem, unemployment, high income and social security taxes, bogus asylum seekers and refugees, pollution, housing shortages, overpopulation, corruption in high places, soccer hooligans, high labour costs and poor weather.

While doing battle with Benelux (particularly Belgian) bureaucracy is enough to discourage anybody, the Benelux people are generally welcoming and, provided you're willing to meet them half way and learn (at least a few words of) their language, you'll invariably be warmly received. The region enjoys one of the world's best lifestyles and an enviable quality of life, and although foreign residents may criticise some aspects of life in Benelux (especially the weather), most feel privileged to live there and few consider leaving once they've become acclimatised.

Long live Belgium! Long live Holland (the Netherlands)! Long live Luxembourg! Long live Benelux!

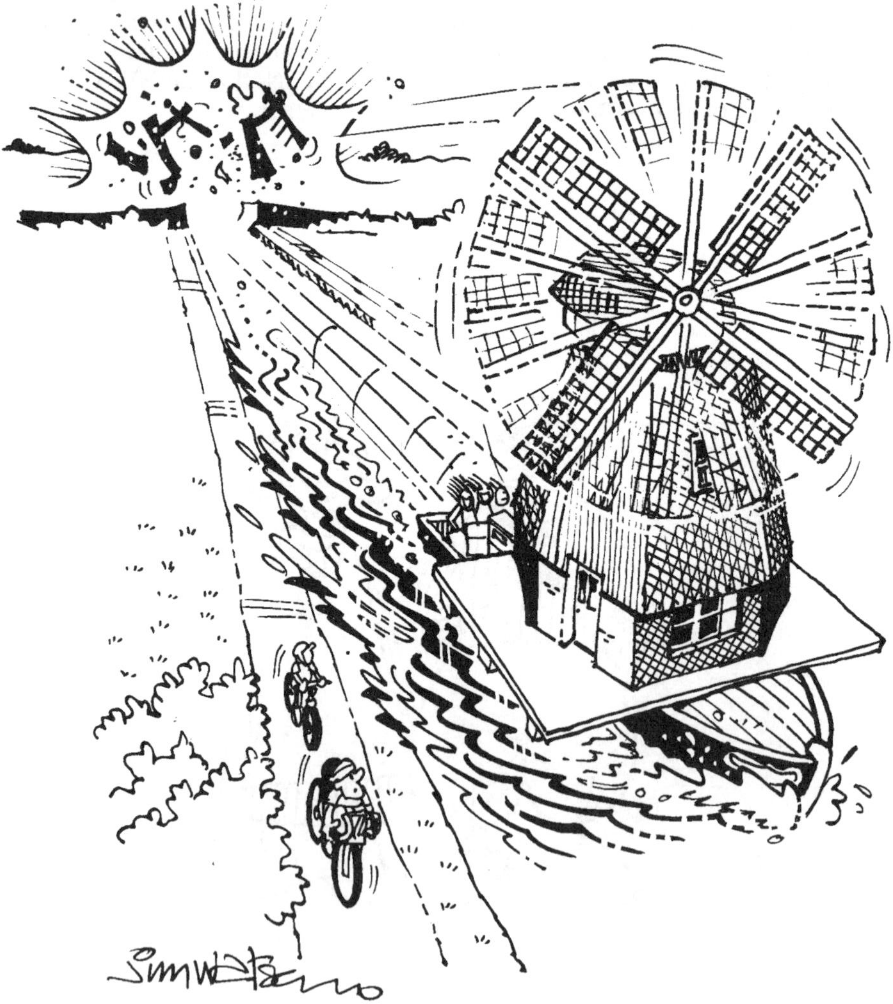

20.

MOVING HOUSE OR
LEAVING BENELUX

When moving house or leaving Belgium, Holland or Luxembourg, there are numerous things to be considered and a 'million' people to be informed. The checklists contained in this chapter are intended to make the task easier and may even help prevent an ulcer or nervous breakdown – provided of course you don't leave everything to the last minute.

MOVING HOUSE WITHIN THE COUNTRY

When moving house within the same country (or, in some cases, within the Benelux region), the following items should be considered:

- You must usually give your landlord at least three months' notice before vacating rented accommodation (refer to your rental contract). If you don't give your landlord sufficient notice and don't have a 'diplomatic clause' in your lease, you will need to find someone to take over your apartment. Normally, your termination notice must be sent by registered post in order to be valid. Be sure to check the terms of your rental contract for any redecoration or repairs that you're responsible for before you leave.

- If you're resigning from your job, note that your resignation letter must also be sent via registered post.

- Inform the following of your impending move:
  - your employer;
  - your town hall;
  - your electricity, gas, telephone and water companies;
  - your insurance companies (e.g. health, car, house contents and private liability), banks, post office, stockbroker and other financial institutions, credit card and hire purchase companies, lawyer, accountant and local businesses where you have accounts;
  - your family doctor, dentist and other health practitioners. Health records should be transferred to your new doctor and dentist, if applicable.
  - your children's schools. Try to give a term's notice and obtain a copy of any relevant school reports or records from your children's current schools. If applicable, arrange for schooling in your new community.
  - all regular correspondents, social and sports clubs, professional and trade journals, and friends and relatives. Give or send them your new address and telephone number (address cards are available free from post offices.
  - the appropriate vehicle registration and licensing authorities if you have a local driving licence or a car registered in the country;
  - your local consulate or embassy if you're registered with them.
- Return any library books or anything borrowed.
- Re-register your dog in your new community.
- Arrange shipping for your furniture and belongings (or transport, if you're doing your own move).

- Arrange for a cleaning company and/or decorating company to renovate your apartment, if necessary.
- If applicable, ensure the return of the deposit from your landlord.
- Cancel regular deliveries, e.g. newspapers and magazines.
- Arrange to have your mail redirected by the post office.
- Ask yourself (again): **"Is it really worth all this trouble?"**

LEAVING BENELUX

Before leaving any of the Benelux countries for an indefinite period, the following actions should be taken, if applicable, in addition to those listed above:

- Give notice to your employer, if applicable.
- Check that your own and your family's passports are valid.
- Check whether there are any special entry requirements for your country of destination by contacting the local embassy or consulate in Belgium, Holland or Luxembourg, e.g. visas, permits or inoculations. An exit permit or visa isn't required to leave the Benelux.
- Contact the appropriate authorities to check whether you qualify for a rebate on your income tax and pension contributions. (Note that in Luxembourg, you must file an income tax return for the current year up to the date you officially leave the Duchy.) Private company pension contributions may be repaid in full, but before a pension fund will refund you, you must provide a statement from your community stating that you have de-registered and are leaving the country.
- Arrange to sell anything you aren't taking with you (e.g. house, car and furniture) and to ship your belongings. Find out the exact procedure for shipping your belongings to the country you're moving to (check with the relevant local embassy or consulate). You may need to complete forms before you arrive there. Note that if you've been living in a Benelux country for less than a year, you're required to re-export all imported personal effects, including furniture and vehicles (if you sell them, you may be required to pay duty and VAT).
- If you plan to take a car with you, you must import and re-register it in your new country of residence within a limited period.
- Check whether your pets require inoculations or will need to be quarantined.
- Contact telephone and other utility companies to cancel your contracts, and pay the final bill when it arrives.
- Arrange health, travel and other insurance.
- Depending on your destination, you may wish to arrange health and dental check-ups before leaving. Obtain a copy of your health and dental records and a statement from your health insurance company stating your present level of cover.
- Terminate any local loan, lease or hire purchase (credit) contracts and pay all outstanding bills (allow plenty of time, as some companies are slow to respond).

- Check whether you're entitled to a rebate on your road tax, car and other insurance. Obtain a letter from your motor insurance company stating your no-claims bonus status.
- Sell or let your house, apartment or other property.
- Check whether you need an international driving licence or a translation of your local or foreign driving licence for your country of destination.
- Give friends and business associates an address (postal and e-mail) where you can be contacted.
- If you will be travelling or living abroad for an extended period, you may wish to give someone 'power of attorney' over your financial affairs in Belgium, Holland or Luxembourg so that they can act on your behalf in your absence. This can be for a fixed period or open-ended and can be limited to a specific purpose only. You should, however, take legal advice before doing this!
- Buy a copy of *Living and Working in* ******** before leaving. If we haven't written it yet, drop us a line and we'll get started on it right away!

Bon voyage! Goede reis!

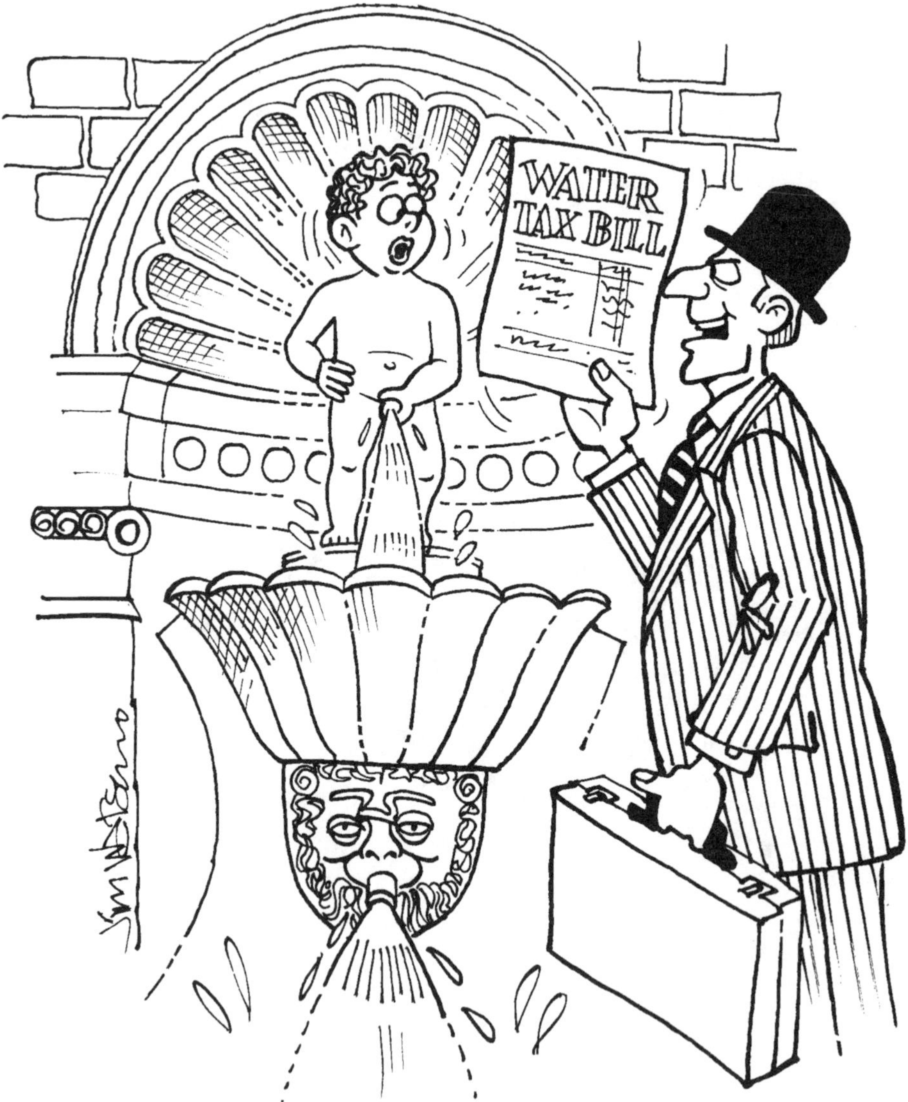
WATER
TAX BILL

APPENDICES

APPENDIX A: USEFUL ADDRESSES

Embassies & Consulates

Foreign embassies and consulates are located in Brussels (Belgium), The Hague (Holland) and Luxembourg city, and many countries also have consulates in other cities, e.g. Antwerp and Amsterdam. Embassies and consulates are listed in the Yellow Pages under 'Embassies & Consulates' (heading no. 7592 in Belgium, heading no. 3830 in Luxembourg, and under *Ambassades en Consulaten*' in the Dutch *Telefoongids*). Note that many countries have more than one office in a city, so before writing or calling you should telephone to confirm that you have the correct address.

Belgium

Australia: Rue Guimard/Guimardstraat 6-8, 1040 Brussels (☎ 02-231 0500, 💻 www.ausemb.be).

Austria: Place du champ de Mars 5, Bte 5/Marsveld plein 5, bus 5, 1050 Elsene (☎ 02-289 0710).

Canada: Ave de Tervueren/Tervurenlaan 2, 1040 Brussels (☎ 02-741 0611).

Denmark: Rue d'Arlon/Aarlenstraat 73, 1040 Brussels (☎ 02-233 0900).

Finland: Ave des Arts/Kunstlaan 58, 1000 Brussels (☎ 02-287 1212).

France: Rue Ducale/Hertogsstraat 65, 1000 Brussels (☎ 02-548 8711, 💻 www.amba france.be).

Germany: Ave de Tervueren/Tervurenlaan 190, 1150 Brussels (☎ 02-774 1911).

Greece: Ave F. D. Roosevelt/F. D. Rosseveltlaan 2, 1050 Brussels (☎ 02-648 1730).

Ireland: Rue Froissart/Froissartstraat 89–93, 1040 Brussels (☎ 02-230 5337).

Italy: Rue Emile Claus/Emile Clausstraat 28, 1050 Brussels (☎ 02-643 3850).

Luxembourg: Ave de Cortenbergh/Kortenberglaan 75, 1000 Brussels (☎ 02-737 5700).

Netherlands: Ave Hermann-Debroux/Hermann Debrouxlaan 48, 1160 Brussels (☎ 02-679 1711).

New Zealand: Square de Meeüs/Meeüssquare 1–7, 1000 Brussels (☎ 02-512 1040).

Norway: Ave Louise/Louizalaan 130a, 1050 Brussels (☎ 02-646 0780).

Portugal: Ave de la Toison d'Or/Guilden Vlieslaan 55, 1060 Brussels (☎ 02-533 0700).

South Africa: Rue de la Loi/Wetstraat 26, box 7, 1040 Brussels (☎ 02-285 4400).

Spain: Rue de la Science/Wetenschapsstraat 19, 1040 Brussels (☎ 02-230 0340).

Sweden: Ave Louise/Louizalaan 148, 1050 Brussels (☎ 02-289 5760).

Switzerland: Rue del la Loi/Wetstraat 26, box 9, 1040 Brussels (☎ 02-285 43 50).

United Kingdom: Rue d'Arlon/Aarlenstraat 85, 1040 Brussels (☎ 02-287 62 11, 🖳 www.british-embassy.be).

United States of America: Bd Du Régent/Regentlaan 27, 1000 Brussels (☎ 02-508 2111, 🖳 www.usinfo.be).

Holland

Australia: Carnegielaan 4, 2517 KH The Hague (☎ 070-310 8200, 🖳 www.australian-embassy.nl).

Austria: Van Alkemadelaan 342, 2597 AS The Hague (☎ 070-324 5470).

Belgium: Lange Vijverberg 12, 2513 AC The Hague (☎ 070-312 3456).

Canada: Sophialaan 7, 2514 JP The Hague (☎ 070-311 1600).

Denmark: Koninginnegracht 30, 2514 AB The Hague (☎ 070-302 5959).

Finland: Groot Hertoginnelaan 16, 2517 EG The Hague (☎ 070-346 9754).

France: Smidsplein 1, 2514 BT The Hague (☎ 070-312 5800).

Germany: Groot Hertoginnelaan 18–20, 2517 EG The Hague (☎ 070-342 0600).

Greece: Amaliastraat 1, 2514 JC The Hague (☎ 070-363 8700).

Ireland: Dr Kuyperstraat 9, 2514 BA The Hague (☎ 070-363 0993).

Italy: Alexanderstraat 12, 2514 JL The Hague (☎ 070-302 1030).

Luxembourg: Nassaulaan 8, 2514 JS The Hague (☎ 070-360 7516).

New Zealand: Carnegielaan 10 ET4, 2517 KH The Hague (☎ 070-346 9324).

Norway: Lange Vijverberg 11, 2513 AC The Hague (☎ 070-311 7611).

Portugal: Bazarstraat 21, 2518 AG The Hague (☎ 070-363 0217).

South Africa: Wassenaarseweg 40, 2596 CJ The Hague (☎ 070-392 4501).

Spain: Lange Voorhout 50, 2514 EG The Hague (☎ 070-302 4999).

Sweden: Burg van Karnebeeklaan 6, 2585 BB The Hague (☎ 070-412 0200).

Switzerland: Lange Voorhout 42, 2514 EE The Hague (☎ 070-364 2831).

United Kingdom: Lange Voorhout 10, 2414 ED The Hague (☎ 070-427 0427, 🖳 www.britain.nl).

United States of America: Lange Voorhout 102, 2514 EJ The Hague (☎ 070-310 9209, 🖳 www.usemb.nl).

Luxembourg

Austria: 3 rue des Bains 3, 1212 Luxembourg (☎ 47-11881).

Belgium: 4 rue des Firondins, 1626 Luxembourg (☎ 44-27461).

Denmark: 4 bd Royal, 2449 Luxembourg (☎ 22-21221).

France: 8B bd Joseph II, 1840 Luxembourg (☎ 45-72 711).

Germany: 20–22 ave Emile Reuter, 2420 Luxembourg (☎ 45-34451).

Greece: 117 Val Ste Croix, 1371 Luxembourg (☎ 44-5193).

Ireland: 28 rte d'Arlon, 1140 Luxembourg (☎ 46-0610).

Italy: 5 rue Marie-Adélaïde, 2128 Luxembourg (☎ 44-36441).

Netherlands: 5 rue C.-M. Spoo, 2546 Luxembourg (☎ 22-7570).

Spain: 4 bd Emmanuel Servais, 2535 Luxembourg (☎ 46-0255).

Switzerland: 25A bd Royal, 2449 Luxembourg (☎ 22-74741).

United Kingdom: 14 bd F.-D. Roosevelt, 2450 Luxembourg (☎ 22-9864, ✉ brit emb@pt.lu).

United States of America: 22 bd Emmanuel Servais, 2535 Luxembourg (☎ 46-0123, 💻 www.amembassy.lu).

Publications

Ackroyd Publications, Ackroyd Publications, Subscription Department, 1038 Chaussée de Waterloo, 1180 Brussels, Belgium (☎ 02-373 9909, 💻 www.ackroyd.be). Ackroyd Publications publish the following six English-language magazines in Belgium, most of which are free:

- **Amcham** – quarterly magazine of the American Chamber of Commerce in Belgium;
- **The Bulletin** – weekly Belgian news magazine;
- **Expat Directory** – annual directory containing essential information, addresses and contact names for new residents in Belgium;
- **Newcomer** – practical guide for new arrivals in Belgium published in March and in September;
- **What's On** – comprehensive arts and entertainment guide for Belgium listing cultural events, TV programmes and services.

Dutch News Digest, Roerstraat 113/2, 1078 LM Amsterdam, the Netherlands (☎ 020-664 2227).

Holland Horizon, Ministry of Foreign Affairs, Foreign Information Division (DVL/BZ/VB), Postbus 20061, 2500 EB The Hague, the Netherlands (💻 www.ifes-nederland.nl/pbs/literature.php) – free quarterly magazine containing reports on economic, cultural, historical, social and political developments in Holland, published in English and other foreign languages.

Luxembourg News, 25 rue Philippe II, 2340 Luxembourg (☎ 46-1122, 💻 www.news.lu) – monthly English-language magazine.

Roundabout, Postbus 96813, 2509 JE The Hague, the Netherlands (☎ 070-324 1611, 💻 www.roundabout.nl) – comprehensive monthly English-language magazine giving details of what's on in Holland.

X-Pat Journal, Van Essen Publishing Concepts & Services, Van Boetzelaerlaan 153, 2581 AR The Hague, the Netherlands (☎ 070-306 3310, 💻 www.xpat.nl) — quarterly English-language magazine for expatriates living in Holland. Contains practical information and tips, lists, useful addresses, telephone numbers and websites. A quarterly cultural diary gives an overview of events of interest to expatriates.

Miscellaneous

ACCESS, 2nd floor, Societeit de Witte, Plein 24, 2511 CS The Hague, the Netherlands (☎ 070-346 2525, 🖥 www.euronet.nl/users/access) – non-profit foundation which helps English speakers to settle in and make the most of life in the Netherlands.

American Citizens Abroad (ACA), PO Box 321, CH-1211 Geneva 12, Switzerland (☎ +41 022-347 68 47, 🖥 www.aca.ch).

The Centre for International Briefing, Farnham Castle, Farnham, Surrey GU9 0AG, UK (☎ 01252-721194, 🖥 www.cibfarnham.com) – organises briefing courses for people moving overseas.

Connect International, Damsterdiep 38, 9711 SM Groningen, the Netherlands (☎ 050-589 1634, ✉ connect@inn.nl) – non-profit organisation offering services and support to foreigners of all nationalities and helping to familiarise them with the social, cultural and commercial aspects of the northern Holland.

Corona Worldwide, Commonwealth Institute, Kensington High Street, London W8 6NQ, UK (☎ 020-7610 4407) – provides information for women expatriates.

Employment Conditions Abroad, Anchor House, 15 Britten Street, London SW3 3TY, UK (☎ 020-7351 5000, 🖥 www.eca@eca-international.com) – publishes information for expatriates on over 75 countries.

European Council of International Schools (ECIS), 21b Lavant Street, Petersfield, Hants GU32 3EL, UK (☎ 01730-268244, 🖥 www.ecis.org).

The Experiment in International Living, Kipling Road, PO Box 676, Brattleboro, Vermont 05302-0676, USA (☎ 802-257 7751, 🖥 www.experiment.org).

FOCUS Career Services, Rue Lesbroussart 23, 1050 Brussels, Belgium (☎ 02-646 6530).

International Living, PO Box 1598, Newburg, NY 12551-9983, USA (☎ 0800-643 2479).

APPENDIX B: FURTHER READING

The lists contained in this appendix are only a selection of the hundreds of books written about Belgium, Holland and Luxembourg. In addition to the (mostly) general guides listed below, there are numerous guides covering individual regions and cities.

The publication title is followed by the author's name and the publisher's name (in brackets). Note that some titles may be out of print but may still be obtainable from bookshops and libraries. Books prefixed with an asterisk (*) are recommended by the author.

Living & Working

*At Home in Holland (AWC, The Hague)

Brussels: The Art of Living, Piet Swimberghe & Jan Verlinde (Stewart, Tabori & Chang)

Brussels for Less (Metropolis International)

Culture Shock! Netherlands, Janin Hunt (Kuperard)

*Expat Toolkit: A Guide to the Dutch Workplace (Loyens & Leoff)

Food Shopper's Guide to Holland, Ada Henne Koene

*Here's Holland, Sheila Gazaleh-Weevers (🖳 www.heresholland.com)

*The Hints Book: Living and Working in Belgium, Nancy Kapstein (AWC, Brussels)

*The Holland Handbook (X-Pat Journal, 🖳 www.x-pat.nl)

*Introducing Antwerp (AWC, Antwerp)

The Job Booklet (Access)

Living in Amsterdam, Brigitte Forguer (Thames & Hudson)

Living in Holland, Marilyn Warman (🖳 www.nuffic.nl)

*Living in Luxembourg (AWC, Luxembourg)

Living & Working in the Netherlands, Pat Rush (How To Books)

*The Low Sky: Understanding the Dutch, Han van der Horst (Scriptum)

*The Netherlands: A Practical Guide for the Foreigner and for the Dutch (NRC Handelsblad)

Netherlands (Cultures of the World), Pat Seward (Benchmark)

Simple Guide to Holland, Customs and Etiquette, Mark T. Hooker (Simple Guides)

Tall Man in a Low Land, Harry Pearson (Abacus)

General Tourist Guides

AA/Thomas Cook Travellers Belgium, G. McDonald (Thomas Cook)

Amsterdam, Rodney Bolt (Cadogan Guides)

Blue Guide Belgium, Derek Blyth (A&C Black)

Brussels Insight Guide (Insight Guides)

Fodor's Belgium and Luxembourg (Fodors)

*Frommer's Belgium, Holland & Luxembourg, George McDonald (Frommer)

Holland, R. Bolt (Cadogan)

Holland Guide, Ron Charles (Open Road Publishing)

*Insight Guide: Belgium (Insight Guides)

*Insight Guide: The Netherlands (Insight Guides)

*Let's Go Amsterdam (St. Martins)

*Lonely Planet: Belgium & Luxembourg (Lonely Planet Publications)

*Lonely Planet: Brussels, Bruges and Antwerp, Leanne Logan (Lonely Planet Publications)

*Lonely Planet: Netherlands (Lonely Planet Publications)

Luxembourg: The Grand Duchy (Editions Guy Binsfeld)

Luxembourg and its Surroundings (Cosyn Guides)

*The Living Book of Luxembourg City (Luxembourg City Tourist Office)

*Michelin Green Guide: Belgium, Grand Duchy of Luxembourg (Michelin)

*Michelin Green Guide: Netherlands (Michelin)

*Michelin Red Guide: Benelux (Michelin)

Rick Steves' France, Belgium and the Netherlands, Rick Steves (Avalon Travel Publications)

*Rough Guide to Brussels (Rough Guides)

*Rough Guide to Amsterdam (Rough Guides)

*Rough Guide to Belgium and Luxembourg, Martin Dunford & Phil Lee (Rough Guides)

* Rough Guide to Holland (Rough Guides)

*Time Out Brussels Guide (Penguin)

*Time Out Guide to Amsterdam (Penguin)

Miscellaneous

The Art of Dutch Cooking, C. Countess can Limburg Stirum (Hippocrene)

Belgium (Cultures of the World), Robert Pateman (Benchmark)

By Pike and Dyke: A Tale of the Rise of the Dutch Republic, G. A. Henty (Preston-Speed)

*Curious Landscape: Foreign Writers on the Netherlands, Gwynne & Peter van Zonneveld (Atrium)

Daily Life in Rembrandt's Holland, Paul Zumthor (Stanford UP)

Dutch Republic, Jonathan Israel (Clarendon)

*Everybody Eats Well in Belgium Cookbook, Ruth Van Waerebeck (Workman)

*Flemish Cities Explored, Derek Blyth (Pallas Athene)

Garden Lover's Guide to the Netherlands and Belgium, Barbara Abbs (Princeton Architectural)

*The Good Beer Guide to Belgium and Holland, Tim Webb (Storey Communications)

The Great Beers of Belgium, Michael Jackson (Prion)

History of the Dutch-speaking Peoples, Pieter Geyl (Phoenix)

History of Holland, Mark T. Hooker (Greenwood)

*Holland: Living with Water, Art de Vos (Scriptum)

How to Remain What You Are, George Erasmus (Editions Le Phare)

*War Walks, Richard Homes (BBC Consumer Publishing)

*Xenophobe's Guide to the Belgians, (Oval)

*Xenophobe's Guide to the Dutch (Oval)

APPENDIX C: USEFUL WEBSITES

There are many general and specific websites for foreigners planning to live or work in the Benelux countries. Most information is useful and websites generally offer free access, although some require a subscription or payment for services. Relocation and other companies specialising in expatriate services often have websites, although these may only provide information that a company is prepared to offer free of charge, which although it can be useful may be rather biased. However, there are plenty of volunteer sites run by expatriates providing practical information and tips. A particularly useful section found on most expatriate websites is the 'message board' or 'forum', where expatriates answer questions based on their experience and knowledge.

The following list contains some of the most useful websites, but is by no means definitive. Sites are listed alphabetically within each category.

General

Direct Moving (🖥 www.directmoving.com) – the first world-wide relocation portal with lots of expatriate information, tips and advice and good links.

Escape Artist (🖥 www.escapeartist.com) – among the most comprehensive sites, packed with resources, links and directories covering most expatriate destinations. You can also subscribe to a free monthly online expatriate magazine, *Escape from America*.

ExpatAccess (🖥 www.expataccess.com) – specifically for those planning to move abroad, with free moving guides to help you through the relocation process.

ExpatBoards (🖥 www.expatboards.com) – comprehensive site for expatriates, with popular discussion boards and special areas for taxes and other important issues.

Expatica (🖥 www.expatica.com) – expatriate information for Belgium and Holland, as well as France and Germany.

Expat Exchange (🖥 www.expatexchange.com) – reportedly the largest online community for English-speaking expatriates, containing articles on relocation and a question and answer facility.

Expat Forum (🖥 www.expatforum.com) – provides cost of living comparisons as well as over 20 country-specific forums.

Expat Network (🖥 www.expatnetwork.com) – the leading expatriate website in the UK, which is essentially an employment network for expatriates, although there are also numerous support services plus a monthly online magazine, *Nexus*.

Expat World (🖥 www.expatworld.net) – contains a wealth of information for American and British expatriates, including a subscription newsletter.

Expatriate Experts (🖥 www.expatexpert.com) – run by expatriate expert Robin Pascoe, providing valuable advice and information.

Expats International (🖥 www.expats2000.com) – international job centre for expatriates and their recruiters.

Federation of American Women's Clubs Overseas (🖥 www.fawco.org) – the main website of FAWCO, which has clubs in Amsterdam, Antwerp, Brussels, The Hague, Luxembourg and Rotterdam.

Gap Year (🖥 www.gapyear.co.uk) – mainly targeted at students doing a gap year, but full of useful information and advice about countries and travelling.

Global People (🖥 www.peoplegoingglobal.com) – provides interesting country-specific information with particular emphasis on social and political aspects.

Living Abroad (🖥 www.livingabroad.com) – provides an extensive and comprehensive list of country profiles (payment required).

Outpost Information Centre (🖥 www.outpostexpat.nl) – contains extensive country-specific information and links; operated by the Shell Petroleum Company for its expatriate workers, but available to everyone.

Real Post Reports (🖥 www.realpostreports.com) – provides relocation services, recommended reading lists and 'real-life' stories containing anecdotes and impressions written by expatriates in just about every city in the world.

World Travel Guide (🖥 www.wtgonline.com) – general website for world travellers and expatriates.

Belgium

AWC Brussels (🖥 www.awcb.org) – the American Women's Club of Brussels.

Belgian Ministry of Foreign Affairs (🖥 http://diplobel.fgov.be).

Expatriate Online (🖥 www.expatriate-online.com) – one of the most extensive online resources for anyone planning to live or work in Belgium.

Belgium Today (🖥 www.europe-today.com/belgium) – provides comprehensive information for visitors, businessmen and residents.

Belgium Tourist Office (🖥 www.visitbelgium.com) – official website of the Belgian Tourist Office in the Americas, covering topics such as Introduction to Belgium, Art Cities, and Before you Go, and including a calendar of events.

Expatriate Online (🖥 www.expatriate-online.com) – a comprehensive site containing useful information for expatriates.

An Expatriate's Guide to Belgium (🖥 www.netcat.co.uk/rob/be/bel_idx.shtml) – a personal guide to living in Belgium providing useful information about language, money, housing, driving, things to do and experiences of other expatriates.

Expats in Brussels (🖥 www.expatsinbrussels.com) – dedicated to foreigners living in Brussels.

Living in Belgium (🖥 www.living-in-belgium.com) – a comprehensive guide to living in Belgium.

xPATs.com (🖥 www.xpats.com) – a useful site for expatriates planning to live or work in Belgium.

Holland

AWC Amsterdam (🖳 www.awca.org) – the American Women's Club of Amsterdam.

Cities in The Netherlands (🖳 www.batnet.com/starbase/Cities.html) – general information about Dutch cities.

The City of Amsterdam (🖳 www.amsterdam.nl) – everything you need to know about Amsterdam, including what's on and where to go (in English and Dutch).

The Dutch Education System (🖳 www.minocw.nl/english/edusyst/index.htm) – contains an official, comprehensive description of the Dutch education system, including details of all types and levels of education.

Dutch Yellow Pages (🖳 www.goudengids.nl) – lists of companies providing services in Holland, including colleges, government, health care and travel (in English).

Housing Online (🖳 www.housingonline.nil) – housing and other information, including lists of available housing, activities for children, and recommended restaurants.

Ministry of Foreign Affairs (🖳 www.minbuza.nl/english/homepage.asp) – general information in English including 'The Netherlands in Depth' and 'Coming to the Netherlands'.

The Netherlands Board of Tourism (🖳 www.visitholland.com) – useful information for residetns as well as visitors.

Netherlands Foreign Investment Agency (🖳 www.nfia.com) – useful information for anyone planning to start a business or invest in Holland.

Netherlands Menu (🖳 www.nl-menu.nl/nlmenu.en/nlmenu.shtml) – directory of businesses and services in Holland, searchable by keyword, category and city.

Study In the Netherlands (🖳 www.nuffic.nl)

Luxembourg

Bonjour Luxembourg (🖳 www.luxembourg-city.lu) – the website of the Luxembourg City Tourist Office.

Lonely Planet (🖳 www.lonelyplanet.com/destinations/europe/luxembourg) – general information about Luxembourg.

Luxembourg Central (🖳 www.luxcentral.lu) – an idiosyncratic view of Luxembourg by Gary Little.

Luxembourg Government (🖳 www.gouvernement.lu) – the official website of the Luxembourg government (in French).

Luxembourg News (🖳 www.news.lu) – comprehensive news and what's on in Luxembourg.

Luxweb (🖳 www.luxweb.lu) – Luxembourg website directory.

The Miami University John E. Dolibois European Center (🖳 www.muohio.edu/Luxembourg/luxembourg/overview.htm) – general information about Luxembourg.

APPENDIX D: WEIGHTS & MEASURES

Holland, Belgium and Luxembourg use the metric system of measurement. Nationals of a few countries (including the Americans and British) who are more familiar with the imperial system of measurement will find the tables on the following pages useful. Some comparisons shown are only approximate, but are close enough for most everyday uses. In addition to the variety of measurement systems used, clothes sizes often vary considerably with the manufacturer (as we all know only too well). Try all clothes on before buying and don't be afraid to return something if, when you try it on at home, you decide it doesn't fit (most shops will exchange goods or give a refund).

Women's Clothes

Continental	34	36	38	40	42	44	46	48	50	52
UK	8	10	12	14	16	18	20	22	24	26
USA	6	8	10	12	14	16	18	20	22	24

Pullovers

	Women's						Men's					
Continental	40	42	44	46	48	50	44	46	48	50	52	54
UK	34	36	38	40	42	44	34	36	38	40	42	44
USA	34	36	38	40	42	44	sm	medium		large		xl

Note: sm = small, xl = extra large

Men's Shirts

Continental	36	37	38	39	40	41	42	43	44	46
UK/USA	14	14	15	15	16	16	17	17	18	-

Men's Underwear

Continental	5	6	7	8	9	10
UK	34	36	38	40	42	44
USA	small	medium		large	extra large	

Children's Clothes

Continental	92	104	116	128	140	152
UK	16/18	20/22	24/26	28/30	32/34	36/38
USA	2	4	6	8	10	12

Children's Shoes

Continental	18	19	20	21	22	23	24	25	26	27	28	29	30	31	32
UK/USA	2	3	4	4	5	6	7	7	8	9	10	11	11	12	13

Continental	33	34	35	36	37	38
UK/USA	1	2	2	3	4	5

Shoes (Women's and Men's)

Continental	35	35	36	37	37	38	39	39	40	40	41	42	42	43	44	44
UK	2	3	3	4	4	5	5	6	6	7	7	8	8	9	9	10
USA	4	4	5	5	6	6	7	7	8	8	9	9	10	10	11	11

Weight

Avoirdupois	Metric	Metric	Avoirdupois
1 oz	28.35 g	1 g	0.035 oz
1 pound*	454 g	100 g	3.5 oz
1 cwt	50.8 kg	250 g	9 oz
1 ton	1,016 kg	500 g	18 oz
1 tonne	2,205 pounds	1 kg	2.2 pounds

* A metric 'pound' is 500g, g = gramme, kg = kilogramme

Length

British/US	Metric	Metric	British/US
1 inch	2.54 cm	1 cm	0.39 inch
1 foot	30.48 cm	1 m	3 feet 3.25 inches
1 yard	91.44 cm	1 km	0.62 mile
1 mile	1.6 km	8 km	5 miles

Note: cm = centimetre, m = metre, km = kilometre

Capacity

Imperial	Metric	Metric	Imperial
1 pint (USA)	0.47 litre	1 litre	1.76 UK pints
1 pint (UK)	0.57 litre	1 litre	0.26 US gallons
1 gallon (USA)	3.78 litre	1 litre	0.22 UK gallon
1 gallon (UK)	4.54 litre	1 litre	35.21 fluid oz

Square Measure

British/US	Metric	Metric	British/US
1 square inch	0.45 sq. cm	1 sq. cm	0.15 sq. inches
1 square foot	0.09 sq. m	1 sq. m	10.76 sq. feet
1 square yard	0.84 sq. m	1 sq. m	1. 2 sq. yards
1 acre	0.4 hectares	1 hectare	2.47 acres
1 square mile	259 hectares	1 sq. km	0.39 sq. mile

Temperature

° Celsius	° Fahrenheit	
0	32	freezing point of water
5	41	
10	50	
15	59	
20	68	
25	77	
30	86	
35	95	
40	104	

Note: The boiling point of water is 100°C / 212°F.

Oven Temperature

Gas	Electric	
	°F	°C
-	225–250	110–120
1	275	140
2	300	150
3	325	160
4	350	180
5	375	190
6	400	200
7	425	220
8	450	230
9	475	240

For a quick conversion, the Celsius temperature is approximately half the Fahrenheit temperature.

Temperature Conversion

Celsius to Fahrenheit: multiply by 9, divide by 5 and add 32.
Fahrenheit to Celsius: subtract 32, multiply by 5 and divide by 9.

Body Temperature

Normal body temperature (if you're alive and well) is 98.4° Fahrenheit, which equals 37° Celsius.

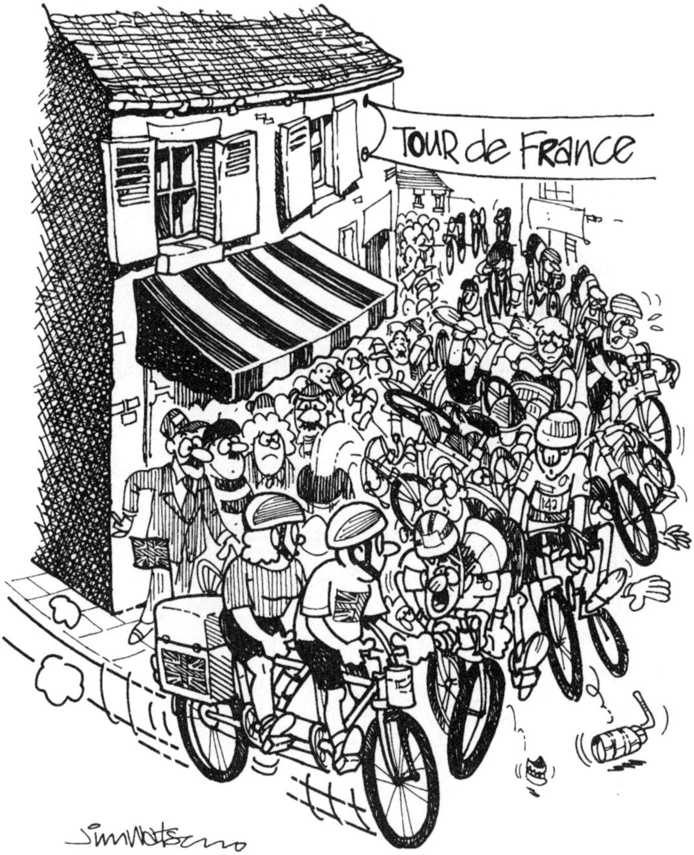
TOUR de FRANCE
142

APPENDIX E: MAPS

The map of the Benelux region opposite shows the provinces of Belgium and Holland (listed below).

Belgium

Antwerp

Brabant*

East Flanders

Hainaut

Liège

Limburg

Luxembourg

Namur

West Flanders

* Flemish Brabant and Walloon Brabant are often counted as separate provinces.

Holland

Drenthe

Flevoland

Friesland

Gelderland

Groninghen

Limburg

Noord-Brabant

Noord-Holland

Overijssel

Utrecht

Zeeland

Zuid-Holland

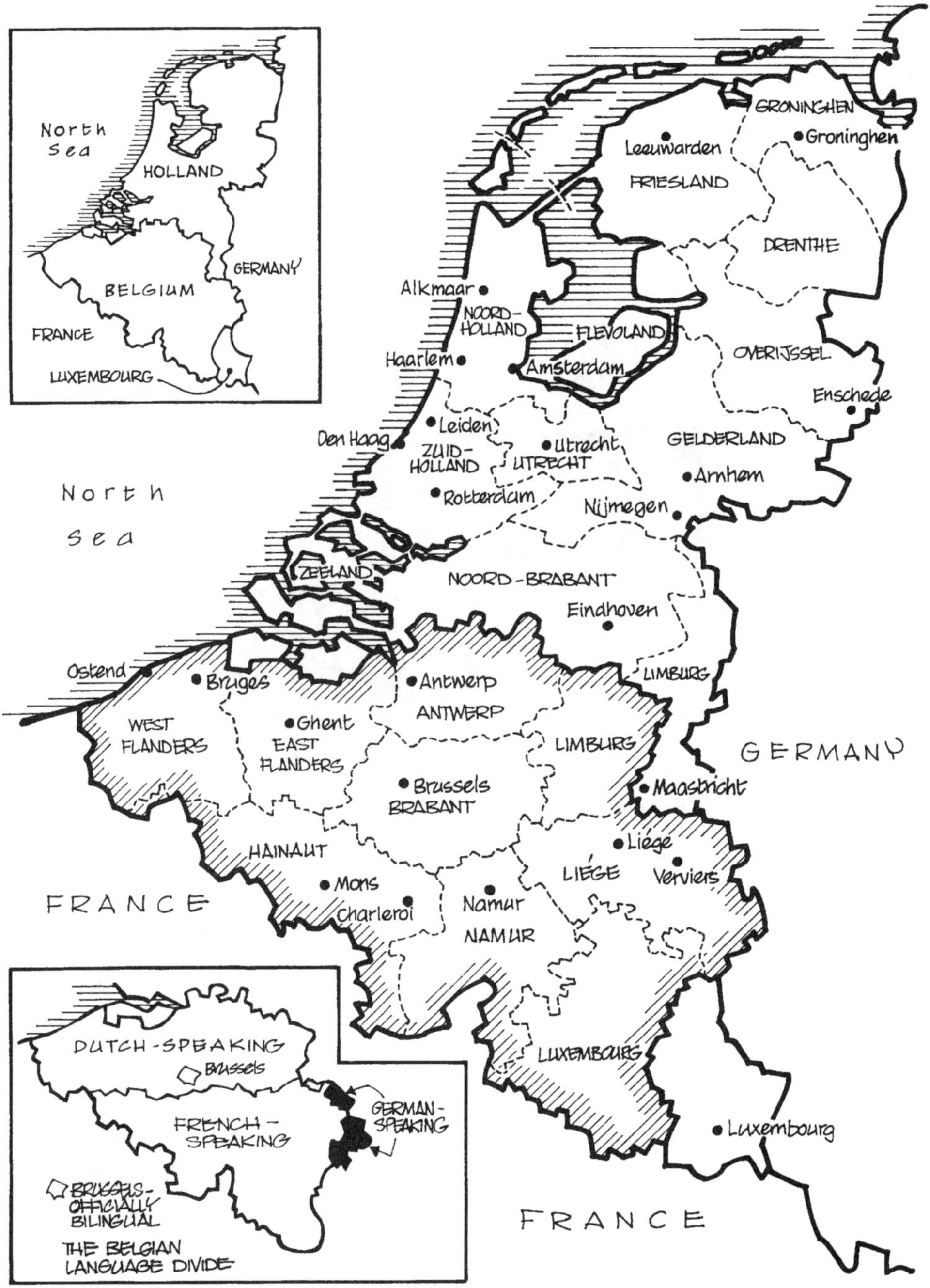
North Sea
HOLLAND
GERMANY
BELGIUM
FRANCE
LUXEMBOURG
GRONINGHEN
Groninghen
Leeuwarden
FRIESLAND
DRENTHE
Alkmaar
NOORD-HOLLAND
FLEVOLAND
OVERIJSSEL
Haarlem
Amsterdam
Enschede
Leiden
Den Haag
ZUID-HOLLAND
Utrecht
UTRECHT
GELDERLAND
Arnhem
North Sea
Rotterdam
Nijmegen
ZEELAND
NOORD-BRABANT
Eindhoven
LIMBURG
Ostend
Bruges
Antwerp
ANTWERP
WEST FLANDERS
Ghent
EAST FLANDERS
LIMBURG
GERMANY
Brussels
BRABANT
Maastricht
Liège
HAINAUT
LIÉGE
Verviers
Mons
FRANCE
Charleroi
Namur
NAMUR
LUXEMBOURG
Luxembourg
FRANCE
DUTCH-SPEAKING
Brussels
FRENCH-SPEAKING
GERMAN-SPEAKING
BRUSSELS-OFFICIALLY BILINGUAL
THE BELGIAN LANGUAGE DIVIDE

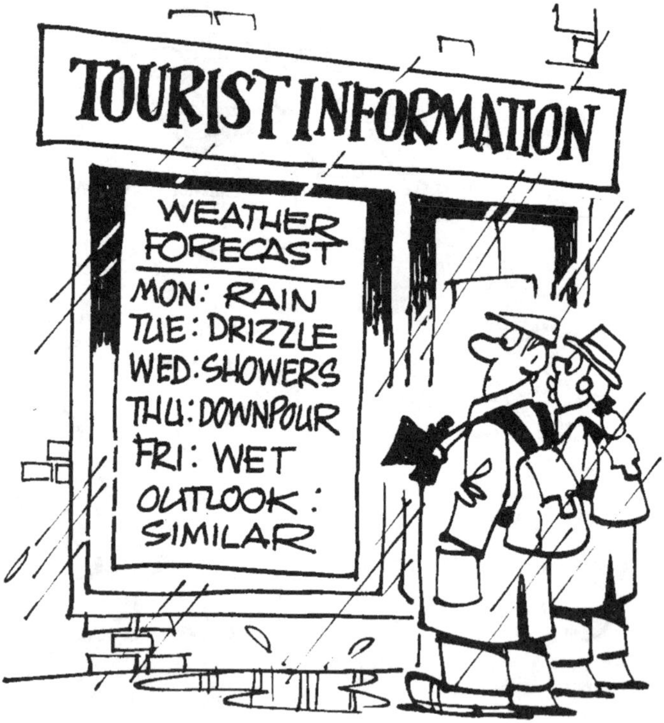
TOURIST INFORMATION
WEATHER FORECAST
MON: RAIN
TUE: DRIZZLE
WED: SHOWERS
THU: DOWNPOUR
FRI: WET
OUTLOOK: SIMILAR

INDEX

A

B

C

D

E

F

G

H

I

J

L

M

N

O

P

Q

R

S

T

U

V

W

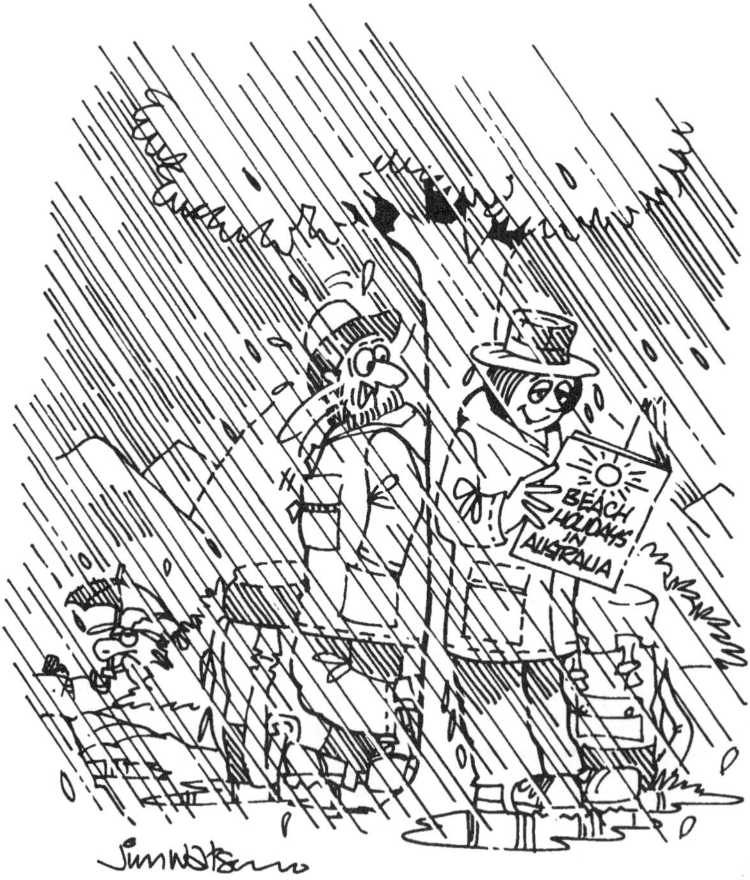
BEACH HOLIDAYS IN AUSTRALIA

BUYING A HOME ABROAD

Buying a Home Abroad is essential reading for anyone planning to purchase property in Ireland and is designed to guide you through the jungle and make it a pleasant and enjoyable experience. Most importantly, it is packed with vital information to help you avoid the sort of disasters that can turn your dream home into a nightmare! Topics covered include:

- Avoiding Problems
- Choosing the Region
- Finding the Right Home & Location
- Estate Agents
- Finance, Mortgages & Taxes
- Home Security
- Utilities, Heating & Air-conditioning
- Moving House & Settling In
- Renting & Letting
- Permits & Visas
- Travelling & Communications
- Health & Insurance
- Renting a Car & Driving
- Retirement & Starting & Business
- And Much, Much More!

Buying a Home Abroad is the most comprehensive and up-to-date source of information available about buying property abroad. Whether you want a detached house, townhouse or apartment, a holiday or a permanent home, this book will help make your dreams come true.

Buy this book and save yourself time, trouble and money!

Order your copies today by phone, fax, mail or e-mail from: Survival Books, PO Box 146, Wetherby, West Yorks. LS23 6XZ, United Kingdom (☎/▤ +44 (0)1937-843523, ✉ orders@ survivalbooks.net, 💻 www.survivalbooks.net).

ORDER FORM – ALIEN'S / BUYING A HOME SERIES

Qty.	Title	Price (incl. p&p)*			Total
		UK	Europe	World	
	The Alien's Guide to America	Autumn 2002			
	The Alien's Guide to Britain	£5.95	£6.95	£8.45	
	The Alien's Guide to France	£5.95	£6.95	£8.45	
	Buying a Home Abroad	£13.45	£14.95	£16.95	
	Buying a Home in Britain	£11.45	£12.95	£14.95	
	Buying a Home in Florida	£11.45	£12.95	£14.95	
	Buying a Home in France	£13.45	£14.95	£16.95	
	Buying a Home in Greece & Cyprus	£13.45	£14.95	£16.95	
	Buying a Home in Ireland	£11.45	£12.95	£14.95	
	Buying a Home in Italy	£11.45	£12.95	£14.95	
	Buying a Home in Portugal	£11.45	£12.95	£14.95	
	Buying a Home in South Africa	£13.45	£14.95	£16.95	
	Buying a Home in Spain	£11.45	£12.95	£14.95	
	Rioja and its Wines	£11.45	£12.95	£14.95	
	The Wines of Spain	£15.95	£18.45	£21.95	
				Total	

Order your copies today by phone, fax, mail or e-mail from: Survival Books, PO Box 146, Wetherby, West Yorks. LS23 6XZ, UUK (☎/▤ +44 (0)1937-843523, ✉ orders@survivalbooks.net, ▭ www.survivalbooks.net). If you aren't entirely satisfied, simply return them to us within 14 days for a full and unconditional refund.

Cheque enclosed/please charge my Delta/Mastercard/Switch/Visa* card

Card No. _ _ _ _   _ _ _ _   _ _ _ _   _ _ _ _

Expiry date_____   **Issue number (Switch only)** _____

Signature _____   **Tel. No.** _____

NAME _____

ADDRESS _____

_____

_____

* Delete as applicable (price includes postage – airmail for Europe/world).

LIVING AND WORKING IN GERMANY

Living and Working in Germany is essential reading for anyone planning to spend some time there including holiday-home owners, retirees, visitors, business people, migrants, students and even extraterrestrials! It's packed with over 350 pages of important and useful information designed to help you **avoid costly mistakes and save both time and money.** Topics covered include how to:

- find a job with a good salary & conditions
- obtain a residence permit
- avoid and overcome problems
- find your dream home
- get the best education for your family
- make the best use of public transport
- endure motoring in Germany
- obtain the best health treatment
- stretch your dollars further
- make the most of your leisure time
- enjoy the German sporting life
- find the best shopping bargains
- insure yourself against most eventualities
- use post office and telephone services
- do numerous other things not listed above

Living and Working in Germany is the most comprehensive and up-to-date source of practical information available about everyday life in Germany. It isn't, however, a boring text book, but an interesting and entertaining guide written in a highly readable style.

Buy this book and discover what it's *really* like to live and work in Germany.

Order your copies today by phone, fax, mail or e-mail from: Survival Books, PO Box 146, Wetherby, West Yorks. LS23 6XZ, United Kingdom (☎/🖷 +44 (0)1937-843523, ✉ orders@ survivalbooks.net, 🖳 www.survivalbooks.net).

ORDER FORM – LIVING & WORKING SERIES

Qty.	Title	Price (incl. p&p)*			Total
		UK	Europe	World	
	Living & Working Abroad	£14.95	£16.95	£20.45	
	Living & Working in America	£14.95	£16.95	£20.45	
	Living & Working in Australia	£14.95	£16.95	£20.45	
	Living & Working in Britain	£14.95	£16.95	£20.45	
	Living & Working in Canada	£14.95	£16.95	£20.45	
	Living & Working in France	£14.95	£16.95	£20.45	
	Living & Working in Germany	£14.95	£16.95	£20.45	
	Living & Working in Holland, Belgium & Luxembourg	£14.95	£16.95	£20.45	
	Living & Working in Ireland	£14.95	£16.95	£20.45	
	Living & Working in Italy	£14.95	£16.95	£20.45	
	Living & Working in London	£11.45	£12.95	£14.95	
	Living & Working in New Zealand	£14.95	£16.95	£20.45	
	Living & Working in Spain	£14.95	£16.95	£20.45	
	Living & Working in Switzerland	£14.95	£16.95	£20.45	
				Total	

Order your copies today by phone, fax, mail or e-mail from: Survival Books, PO Box 146, Wetherby, West Yorks. LS23 6XZ, UK (☎/▤ +44 (0)1937-843523, ✉ orders@survivalbooks.net, 💻 www.survivalbooks.net). If you aren't entirely satisfied, simply return them to us within 14 days for a full and unconditional refund.

Cheque enclosed/please charge my Delta/Mastercard/Switch/Visa* card

Card No. __ __ __ __   __ __ __ __   __ __ __ __   __ __ __ __

Expiry date _____   **Issue number (Switch only)** _____

Signature _____   **Tel. No.** _____

NAME _____

ADDRESS _____

_____

_____

* Delete as applicable (price includes postage – airmail for Europe/world).